Until 1992 Ian Dunlop was Canon and Chancellor of Salisbury Cathedral. He was educated at Winchester and New College, Oxford and then spent a year at Strasbourg University and a further year teaching at the Lycée Hoche at Versailles. It was his time spent there that inspired him to write his first book. He was ordained to a curacy at Hatfield in 1956, since when he has been Chaplain to Westminster School and Vicar of Bures in Suffolk. He is now retired and lives in Selkirk.

OTHER BOOKS BY IAN DUNLOP

Versailles
Palaces and Progresses of Elizabeth I
Châteaux of the Loire
Collins Companion Guide to the Country Round Paris
The Cathedrals' Crusade
Royal Palaces of France
Thinking it Out–Christianity in Thin Slices
Burgundy

MARIE-ANTOINETTE
A Portrait

Ian Dunlop

PHŒNIX

A PHOENIX PAPERBACK

First published in Great Britain by
Sinclair-Stevenson in 1993
This first paperback edition published in 1994 by
Phoenix, a division of Orion Books Ltd,
Orion House, 5 Upper St Martin's Lane, London WC2H 9EA

A CIP catalogue record for this book is available from the British Library.

ISBN 1 85799 214 8

Printed and bound in Great Britain by
Clays Ltd, St Ives plc.

To Deirdre
With All My Love

Contents

List of Illustrations

Acknowledgements

I would like to thank Princess Marie-Christine of Bourbon-Parma, the marquis de Breteuil, the baronne Elie de Rothschild, to whom I am also grateful for permission to quote the letter printed on p. 275, and the comtesse de Talhouët for their help and encouragement; the late Professor Hans Urbanski, Professor Richard Cobb, Madame Evelyne Lever, Monsieur Jean Chalon, Monsieur Jacques Charles-Gaffiot, Président de l'Association Louis XVI, Dr Ilsebill Barta-Fliedl for privileged access to the Hofburg, Mr Robert Tidmarsh for privileged access to Schönbrunn, Monsieur Jean-Pierre Babelon, Directeur du Musée de Versailles, Monsieur Jean-Marie Moulin, Conservateur en Chef du Château de Compiègne, Miss Rosalind Savill, Director of the Wallace Collection, Miss Undine Concannon, Archivist of Madame Tussaud's, and the Baronin Stella Musulin for her charming hospitality at Schloss Fridau.

Finally I would like to thank my sub-editor Emily Kerr for her careful help with the script and Gabriel Burchell and John Reid for helping me print out the text of this book on the wordprocessor.

Introduction

It was 10 May 1774; Louis XV was approaching the gates of death. A few days earlier he had been taken ill at Trianon with a particularly virulent form of smallpox. His doctor had insisted on his returning to Versailles. It was not seemly that a King of France should die at Trianon. The Dauphin, soon to be Louis XVI, had given orders that the moment the King was dead the Court was to retire to the Château de Choisy-le-Roi. The coaches and horses were in readiness in the vast courtyards of the Petite Écurie, across the Place d'Armes from the Château. It was arranged that a candle should be kept burning in the window of the King's bedroom. The moment of his death was to be marked by the extinction of the candle and the coaches were to enter the Cour Royale.

At a quarter past three in the afternoon the candle was put out. The Grand Chambellan, the duc de Bouillon, appeared in the anteroom, next to the King's bedroom, which was known, from its oval window, as the Oeil de Boeuf, and pronounced the historic formula: 'Messieurs, le Roi est mort. Vive le Roi!'

The new King was in his wife's rooms in the south wing of the Château, awaiting the inevitable news. Suddenly, writes Madame Campan, 'a terrible noise, exactly like a roll of thunder, was heard in the first room of the apartment; it was the crowd of courtiers who had deserted the apartment of the now dead King to come and salute the new power of Louis XVI. By this strange sound Marie-Antoinette and her husband recognised that their reign had begun. With a spontaneous movement which deeply touched those who witnessed it, they both fell on their knees and both, with tears in their eyes, cried: "God guide us and protect us; we are too young to reign."'

On 30 May, Maria Theresa wrote from Schönbrunn to her daughter: 'the prospect is great and beautiful . . . I flatter myself to see the reign of Louis-Auguste happy and glorious.' A few weeks later she returned to the theme:

> I cannot express my joy and consolation at all I hear of you; the whole universe is in ecstasy. There is good cause for it: a king of twenty and a queen of nineteen; all their actions full of humanity, generosity, prudence and the greatest judgement. Religion and morals, so necessary in order to draw down the blessing of God and keep a hold on the people, are not forgotten, in a word my heart is full of joy and I pray God that he may preserve you for the good of your people, for the universe, for your family and for your old mother to whom you give new life! How I love the French at this moment! What resources there are in a nation which feels so vividly! One needs only wish them more constancy and less frivolity; by correcting their morals that will change too.

The Empress had good reason for her optimism. The popularity of her daughter and her son-in-law was well established.

Nearly a year previously, on 8 June 1773, Marie-Antoinette, accompanied by the Dauphin, had made her first official visit to Paris. At eleven o'clock the cannon of the Bastille announced the arrival of the royal couple. At the Porte de la Conférence the ceremonial carriages and a truly royal escort were awaiting them. The baron de Frénilly, as a boy of seven, was taken to see them pass, and the event remained engraved upon his memory.

> The King had a countenance of little charm but of great nobility. The Queen had a radiance and a freshness about her and a face animated by an expression of goodness and gaiety. They were both dressed in white and occupied together one of those magnificent carriages, monuments of sculpture and of carving, which have since been imitated with a pettiness that is ridiculous. I was deeply impressed by the pomp – un-military,

> elegant and almost gallant – of their escort: the officers of the household, the personnel of the hunt and of the falconry; even the Cent Suisses in their old-fashioned ruffs and the *gardes du corps* in their very rich livery of red and blue heavily loaded with gold, were not in any way suggestive of soldiers.

The cavalcade jingled along the Quai des Tuileries, over the Pont Neuf and down the Quai des Orfèvres to Notre Dame, where a low mass was celebrated. Various civic receptions took place at the appropriate stations, ending with a harangue before the gates of the Collège Louis le Grand and a visit to the Church of Sainte-Geneviève. Finally they returned to the Tuileries for dinner.

The palace of the Tuileries, burnt down in 1871 by the *communards*, spanned the gap between the present Pavillon de Marsan and the Pavillon de Flore which mark the western extremities of the Louvre. It offered a frontage towards the gardens of 340 metres with fifty-one windows – or bays containing niches – on each floor.

Begun by Philibert de l'Orme for Catherine de Medici, it had grown slowly and only under Louis XIV was the vast façade completed.

The Jardins des Tuileries, laid out in 1664 by André Le Nôtre, were regarded as one of the greatest ornaments to Paris. In June 1782, the marquis de Bombelles wrote in his journal: 'Towards evening I revisited with pleasure the Jardin des Tuileries; this *chef d'oeuvre* of Le Nôtre offers beauties of a type so superior that one is never tired of admiring them.' Le Nôtre had left an area eighty-two metres deep between the west façade and the first of his plantations. The gardens therefore provided space for a vast concourse of people and the terraces of the Château provided an extended balcony on which the royal family could appear before the public.

Here, on this great occasion, Marie-Antoinette stood and overlooked the populace *en délire*. The duc de Brissac, who, as Governor of Paris, was at her side, made the gallant remark: 'Madame – no disrespect to the Dauphin – but they are 200 000 of your lovers.'

Deeply touched, Marie-Antoinette wrote to her mother:

> As for honours, we received all that it would be possible to imagine; but all that, although very good, was not what touched us most, but, rather, the tenderness and the eagerness of the poor people, who, in spite of the taxes which cripple them, were in transports of joy at seeing us. When we went for a walk at the Tuileries there was so great a crowd that we were three quarters of an hour without being able to move forwards or backwards . . . On our return from the walk we went up onto the open terrace and remained there for half an hour. I cannot tell you, my dear Mama, the transports of joy and affection which were shown to us at that moment. Before going back in we waved to the people, which caused great pleasure. How lucky we are in our estate to gain the love of the people at such an easy price! There is, however, nothing more precious. I felt it very strongly and will never forget it.

Everything that Marie-Antoinette did was reported to her mother by the Austrian Ambassador, the Comte Mercy d'Argenteau. Between the years 1770 and 1774 he is often lavish in his praise of the young Dauphine. 'There is not a day', he wrote, 'that she does not give proofs of good judgement, of a singularly perceptive mind – *justesse d'esprit* – and of a good, generous and sympathetic nature.' He even went so far as to say that 'Madame la Dauphine is so happily endowed that it is morally impossible that she should ever fall into errors of any consequence, either in the present or in the future.'

It was thus that Edmund Burke described her at the beginning of the Revolution:

> It is now sixteen years since I saw the Queen of France, then Dauphiness, at Versailles, and surely never lighted on this orb, which she hardly seemed to touch, a more delightful vision. I saw her just above the horizon, decorating and cheering the elevated sphere she just began to move in – glittering like the morning star, full of life and splendour and joy. Little did I dream that I should have lived to see disasters fallen upon her in a nation of gallant men, in a nation of men of honour and of cavaliers. I thought ten thousand swords must have leapt from their scabbards to avenge a look that threatened her with

> insult. But the age of chivalry is gone. That of the sophisters, economists and calculators has succeeded; and the glory of Europe is extinguished for ever.

* * *

Nineteen years later, on 16 October 1793, Marie-Antoinette was taken to the guillotine. Not, like her husband, in the privacy of a closed coach, but in an open tumbril, exposed to the execrations of the populace. 'The greatest joy of all the joys', wrote Hébert, 'experienced by the Père Duchesne [himself] came after seeing with his own eyes the head of the female VETO separated from her f . . . tart's neck.'

Apart from physical torture, Marie-Antoinette had suffered, during the months that preceded her execution, all that it is possible for human nature to suffer. Reading the accounts of her last days, one is left with a numb sense of incredulity – a reluctance to believe it possible that human beings could be so far from being human – capable of doing things, as the Duchess of Devonshire said, 'one would have hoped that the mind of man was incapable of'.

No contrast could have been more extreme than that between the delirious joy of the populace at her first reception in Paris and their equally delirious joy at her degradation and death. What had happened during those nineteen years? What was the cause of so great a decline and fall?

The decline, if not the fall, was not wholly unforeseen. Amid all the optimism and ecstasy over the new reign, one voice had sounded a more cautious note. It was that of the British Ambassador to Versailles, Lord Stormont. 'Whatever may be said,' he wrote, 'and I think with great truth, of the purity of the King's intentions, whatever dreams the levity of this country may form of halcyon days and a golden reign, every instrument of faction, every Court engine is constantly at work, and the whole is such a scene of jealousy, cabal and intrigue that no enemy may wish it more.' The mud-bespattered road to the guillotine began in the gilded salons of Versailles.

Du Côté de Versailles

In 1770 the Château de Versailles was, externally, much as Louis XIV had left it. It was beyond question the greatest palace in Europe. Not long after its completion it was painted by Jean-Baptiste Martin, one of those artists who had acquired an astonishing skill in imagining from the air that which could only be seen from the ground. Here it is – the perfect portrait of the palace; he shows to its full advantage the long, regular, ever widening procession of the forecourts, the complex many-faceted construction of the roof. His accuracy is scrupulous but his detail is never obtrusive.

When looking at the architecture of the entrance courts today, with their colourful mixture of brick and stone and blue slate, which Sir Christopher Wren said made it look like 'a rich livery', we need to remember that all the leaden ornaments to the roof and dormers were orginally gilded, and regilded every year. As Mademoiselle de Scudéry wrote in her *Promenade de Versailles*: 'As the sun was shining at its brightest at this moment, it seemed that it was only in order to show off the brilliance of all the gold with which the roof of this palace is ornamented.'

The entrance courts of Versailles, however, were the result of successive attempts to elevate the façades of a small *maison de plaisance* into something worthy of the greatest palace in Europe. It cannot be claimed that the result was entirely successful.

'When you arrive at Versailles,' wrote Voltaire, 'from the courtyard side you see a wretched, top-heavy building with a façade seven windows long, surrounded with everything which the imagination could conceive in the way of bad taste. When you see it from the garden side, you see an immense palace whose defects are more than compensated for by its beauties.'

Voltaire's 'immense palace' was a work of art not achieved at a single sitting. The vast central block represents the revision by Jules-Hardouin Mansart of an earlier building by Louis Le Vau.

In 1668 the old *maison de plaisance* had been enclosed by Le Vau on three sides by a building known as the 'Enveloppe' or 'Château Neuf', providing behind its classical façades two magnificent suites of state rooms, the Grand Appartement to the north and the Appartement de la Reine to the south.

Ten years later the Peace of Nijmegen marked the zenith of Louis' military success. It was no longer tolerable that he should not possess a palace more proportioned to his greatness and Mansart was commissioned to make Versailles a building that would lodge the Court and the Government in appropriate splendour. Two great wings, thrown out to north and south, left the stately block of the Château Neuf a mere projection on the garden front. The finished building had 2143 windows, 1252 fireplaces and 67 staircases; the length of the garden front was 670 metres.

Behind these dignified façades the royal apartments offered a suite of eighteen rooms, each more magnificent than the last, the Grand Appartement and the Appartement de la Reine now linked between their western extremities by the Grande Galerie. Madame de Sévigné was in ecstasies over it: 'this sort of royal beauty is unique in the world.' If, today, the marble panels, the painted ceilings of Le Brun, the richly gilded stucco decorations, seem heavily ornate, we must remember that they were meant to be seen by the flattering light of candles. 'Figurez-vous l'éclat de cent mille bougies,' said the abbé Bourdelot, 'dans cette grande suite d'appartements.'

Immediately to the south of the Château proper, and built in a simpler version of the style of the Cour Royale, was the huge annexe known as the Grand Commun. It provided sixty apartments for the higher functionaries of the Court. One of the most distinguished inhabitants of the Grand Commun in his day was the great garden designer André Le Nôtre. Next to Le Brun he made the greatest contribution to the creation of Versailles.

The gardens, circumscribed by the horizon, extended in every direction their network of radiating alleys, peopled with marble figures and opening, in accordance with some pre-ordained symmetry, into vast amphitheatres, where magnificent fountains rose from their gilded groups of statuary and tossed their waters into air. The windows of the Grande Galerie commanded the perspective of the gardens – 'the most beautiful outlook', admitted the eighteenth century architect Blondel, 'that it would be possible to imagine.'

All this was the creation of Louis XIV. It served as a model and a challenge to every prince in Europe who could afford to build and to many who could not.

Not only did the architecture of Versailles dictate the style of building to most of Europe, it set the tone for all the Courts throughout the Continent. 'A young man,' said Frederick II of Prussia, 'passed for an imbecile if he had not spent some time at the Court of Versailles.' Princes, making that indispensible accomplishment to their education, the *Kavalierstour*, prolonged their stay in France as far as their means permitted and formed their taste in the galleries of Versailles, Meudon and Saint-Cloud. They returned to their principalities and electorates convinced francophiles. Not only did French become the official language of their courts, but their music, their clothes and their food all had to be French if they were to be considered in good taste. Every Court had its French artists to adorn it and each prince sought relaxation in the arms of a French mistress. 'Who would have thought,' exclaimed Montesquieu, 'that the late King had established the greatness of France by building Versailles and Marly?'

In the eyes of the world, Versailles was the enchanted palace in which all the arts had contributed to its perfection: in the eyes of those responsible for its upkeep it was a fabric on the verge of ruin. In 1750, Le Normant de Tournehem, Madame de Pompadour's uncle, had drawn up a memorandum for the King on 'le dépérissement général des jardins'. Nothing had been done. Five years later the marquis de Marigny, Madame de Pompadour's brother, read another long letter to the King on the urgent need of restoration, 'in order to prevent the ruin of so important a house as Versailles, which had been, until the present day, the admiration of all Europe'.

The Seven Years' War interrupted the work of maintenance and in 1757 Lécuyer, the Contrôleur du Château, 'felt obliged to make new representations on the imminent ruin of this house if his Majesty does not have the goodness to accord him every year supplementary funds which shall be affected solely to this object. It is certain', he added, 'that the degradations will increase to a point at which it will cost enormous sums to do what could be done now at a far lower price.'

What had been for long apparent to Lécuyer was now becoming apparent to visitors also. In October 1760, General Fontenay, Ambassador from the Court of Dresden, wrote in his despatch: 'the Château de Versailles, from want of the most urgent repairs, is falling into ruin. It is propped up on all sides. Yesterday they walled up the passage which leads to Trianon [the way through to the gardens in the north-west angle of the Cour Royale] for fear that the vibration occasioned by the coaches might cause the vault which upholds the apartment of Madame Adelaïde to cave in.' Most of the domestic staff, he added, had three or four years' pay still owing to them. 'Voilá, Monseigneur, l'état de cette Cour autrefois si brillante.'

Seven years later Benjamin Franklin visited Versailles. 'The Range of Building', he wrote, 'is immense, the Garden Front most magnificent all of hewn Stone, the Number of Statues, Figures, Urns & in Marble and Bronze of exquisite Workmanship is beyond Conception. But the Waterworks are out of Repair, and so is great Part of the Front next the

Town, looking with its shabby half Brick Walls and broken Windows not much better than the Houses in Durham Yard.'

On 8 July 1765, Lécuyer again sent a report to Marigny. This time it was about the dangerous condition of the two porticos which marked the extremities of the entrance court, 'particularly the one on the side of the Chapel, where the ceiling and entablature are ready to fall at any moment, the woodwork being entirely rotten'. The suppression of the porticos, however, would greatly have weakened the architectural effect of the Cour Royale. Rather than waste money on costly repairs to a decaying fabric that was regarded by most critics as ugly and out of date, it was decided that it would be better to rebuild the entire entrance side of Versailles. The architect Ange-Jacques Gabriel was commissioned to draw up plans for what came to be known as the 'Grand Projet'.

Apart from one range of the north side of the Cour Royale, it was never built. The money was simply not available . For just as the structure of Versailles, still outwardly magnificent, was rapidly declining into ruin, so France itself, once the most powerful country in Europe, was no longer in a position to claim its former greatness.

On 20 March 1777, Frederick the Great wrote to his Ambassador at Versailles, the Baron von Goltz, on the inability of France to respond to the demands of the Court of Vienna: 'finally the total exhaustion of her finances would place insurmountable obstacles. This, above all, leaves France with, so to speak, only the title of a Power, without her being able to support the dignity thereof; and as long as she is unable to find the means to remedy this, not one of her Ministers, were he the greatest brain in Europe, could ever restore her to the position which she once occupied among the Christian Powers.'

The royal treasury was exhausted, chiefly by the Seven Years' War which had cost France much and gained her little. In 1769, Maynon d'Invau, Terray's predecessor as Contrôleur Général des Finances, addressed a confidential memorandum to Louis XV. 'Your Majesty's finances', he wrote, 'are in the most appalling disarray . . . Each year has accumulated a new debt on top of the debt of the previous years. The most urgent debts make a total today of nearly eighty million livres. To crown all, the entire revenues of one year are spent in advance . . . This situation is not just alarming; it cannot be maintained much longer and at any moment it could throw the kingdom into the greatest misfortune without there remaining any remedy available.'

The system of finance was both cumbersome and corrupt. Owing to the numerous exemptions taxes fell most heavily upon those who were least able to pay. Philibert Orry, Contrôleur Général des Finances in the early part of Louis XV's reign, admitted the iniquity of the system: 'all the subtlety and all the malice of the human mind were summoned up to make the apportionment unjust.' Against this arbitrary and biassed assessment for taxation the poor had only one defence – to remain too poor or at least to appear to remain too poor. 'The peasant', wrote Pierre Gaxotte, 'was afraid of spending any money; thus he began to neglect his cultivation, to neglect the upkeep of his house, to avoid making any profit, for the slightest profit would provide a certain warrant for an increase in his tax.' As the abbé de Véri put it in a report in 1778, the peasant would think: 'si je gagnais d'avantage, ce serait pour le collecteur' – 'if I were to earn more, it would be for the tax collector.'

There were some Frenchmen capable of seeing the defects of their country and their age. François de la Rochefoucauld, who made a tour of his native land in 1781, was a remarkable humanitarian. The state of the peasants in Brittany moved him to pity and compassion: 'They really are slaves,' he stated; 'their poverty is excessive. They eat a sort of porridge made of buckwheat; it is more like glue than food.'

To Nathaniel Wraxall, writing of the Loire Valley at the same time, it was the contrast between the loveliness of the land and the sordid conditions of the inhabitants which chiefly moved him. 'The extreme poverty and misery of the peasants in the midst of a delicious paradise – producing in abundance all the necessaries and elegancies of life – impresses me with pity, wonder and indignation. I see much magnificence, but still more distress; one princely château surrounded by a thousand wretched hamlets; the most studied and enervate luxury among the upper orders of society contrasted with the beggary and nakedness of the people.' There is no poverty so distressing as poverty in the midst of plenty.

In 1766 the English traveller Smollett was in Burgundy, and recorded that he 'saw a peasant ploughing with a jack-ass, a lean cow and a he-goat yoked together. The peasants in France', he observed, 'are so wretchedly poor, and so much oppressed by their landlords, that they cannot afford to enclose their grounds, or give proper respite to their lands by letting them lie fallow, or to stock their farms with a sufficient number of black cattle to produce the necessary manure, without which agriculture can never be carried to any degree of perfection. Husbandry will never be generally improved until the farmer is free and independent.' With no money available to improve his lands the peasant was incapable of increasing his crops. Bad harvests led inevitably to famine and famine led to demonstrations which could easily become riots.

In the middle of the century Jean-Baptiste de Machault d'Arnouville became Contrôleur Général des Finances. He introduced a new tax, known as the 'vingtième' because it was rated at five per cent, which was to fall on all alike in proportion to their wealth. It was immediately attacked by the privileged parties – the Parlements, the States Generals in the provinces and the clergy.

The clergy were exempt, as by divine right, from all taxation. They voted instead a *don gratuit* which was usually somewhere around three per cent of their enormous wealth. In 1749, when Machault was trying to impose his *vingtième*, they were his most tenacious opponents. Preferment in the Church was virtually reserved for members of the upper aristocracy and these ordained noblemen had all the arrogance of their caste. When the États de Languedoc were suppressed by Machault for resisting the *vingtième*, the Bishop of Castres said to the maréchal de Richelieu: 'this Contrôleur Général, who seems to have so little respect for us, would do well to remember that *my* ancestors have spent more in the service of the King with their blood than *his* have with their ink.'

The Church, in its deference to rank, had virtually capitulated to the law of primogeniture. When Louis XIV's brother, Philippe d'Orléans, died, Dangeau wrote: 'this Prince, a great rogue and a great libertine, died very expeditiously. Some were moralising about this matter and casting considerable doubts on his chances of salvation in the presence of the maréchal de Meilleraye. "I assure you", she said, most seriously, "that God would think twice before damning a person of that rank."'

If Dangeau is to be believed, members of the royal family did not receive communion with the same Hosts that were given to ordinary christians; they were given *hosties choisies*. 'Madame la Dauphine', he records, 'made her Easter communion at the parish church; a most extraordinary thing happened; there were two consecrations because they forgot, in the first place, to offer the *hostie choisie* for the communion of Madame la Dauphine.'

It must not be inferred from all this, however, that the divine spark was wholly absent from religion in France. In 1750, to mark the middle of the century, a jubilee was celebrated in which popular devotion knew no bounds: Notre-Dame was unable to contain its congregations, penitents queued in the rain to enter Sainte-Geneviève and Barbier observed that the jubilee was celebrated with more devotion than Easter. This popular outburst of religious enthusiasm coincided significantly with Machault's attempts to enforce the *vingtième* on the clergy. It coincided with the time when Louis XV had to decide whether to support Machault or not. He decided not to. On 23 December 1751 Louis issued an

Order in Council granting immunity from all taxation to the clergy. Le Roi très Chrétien was true to his coronation oath.

The clergy had won, but as is so often true, they lost more by their victory than they had gained. 'In putting their untenable pretensions to privilege under the protection of Heaven', writes Pierre Gaxotte, 'the Clergy were guilty of a grave error: they exposed religion itself to attacks which should only have been directed at the selfishness of its Ministers.' The persistence with which the clergy used the name of God to escape from a taxation which was manifestly equitable gave the Philosophes just the stick with which to beat them that they required.

For 1751 was also the date of the publication of the first part of the famous *Encyclopaedia.* These thirty-four volumes represent one of the great achievements of eighteenth century France. They offer a panorama of all human knowledge which brings before the public eye the power and progress of the human reason; 'an apotheosis', as Lanson described it, 'of civilisation and of the sciences, arts and industries which improve the intellectual and material condition of humanity . . . an irresistable machine set up against the spirit, the beliefs and the institutions of the past.'

All the great names of the Enlightenment – Voltaire, Rousseau, Diderot, d'Alembert, Condillac – were established by the second half of the eighteenth century. 'A new generation of thinkers,' writes Lanson, 'impatient, audacious, devoted to what they call the truth, ready to overturn anything which appears as an obstacle: art, eloquence, literature are for them no more than instruments of propaganda. They want to make *philosophy* the subject of every book, the preoccupation of every mind.' That, however, was only partially achieved.

By far the most influential of Rousseau's works, for example, was the *Nouvelle Héloïse*, which was a novel, chiefly about family and maternal love. Daniel Mornet, in his study of 500 private libraries of the time of Louis XV, found only one copy of Rousseau's *Contrat Social* but 165 copies of the

Nouvelle Héloïse. Buffon's *Histoire Naturelle* easily surpassed all Rousseau's writings with a score of 220.

Léon Cohen, in a complementary study of the sales registers of the three biggest booksellers in Paris, gives an interesting panorama of the readership of the time. Again, natural history came out top, but Racine and La Fontaine were still in constant demand; philosophy did not sell very well. He sums up his researches thus: 'It puts us on our guard against the natural tendency towards simplification. We are inclined to think sometimes that people at the end of the eighteenth century lived in a state of anticipation, already obsessed by the Revolution, that they pounced on the works of the philosophers as we would pounce on the daily papers in critical times; that they thought only of progress and reform. It was not so: life continued; France remained a Christian country and if one has any doubts one has only to enumerate the works of piety and edification which were stacked in the bookshops.' Religion might or might not have been at a low ebb; what is certainly true is that anti-clericalism was rife. 'The decline in religion', wrote d'Argenson in 1752, 'should not be attributed to English philosophers, who have only won about a hundred Philosophes in Paris, but to the hatred against the priests which reaches the utmost extremes.'

The *Encyclopaedia* was not directly anti-monarchical; it *was* anti-Christian. It did, however, by a sort of ricochet, rebound against a monarchy which based itself on the theory of divine right. On 21 December 1770, Louis XV wrote to the King of Spain: 'You are not unaware to what extent the spirit of independence and fanaticism has spread in my kingdom. Patience and mildness have been my guides up till the present, but now I have decided to make myself obeyed by all possible means. I am forced to this extremity by my Parlements forgetting themselves to the extent of trying to dispute my royal authority which I hold from God alone.'

'My authority which I hold from God alone' – that was no very secure position from which to confront an atheist. The great minds of the Enlightenment were attacking belief in

God on philosophical grounds, and thus, indirectly, undermining the monarchy. The Parlements were attacking the position of the King directly on legal and historical grounds and they made themselves powerful allies by a coalition with the aristocracy.

In former times the magistrates had been the enemies of the nobility, destroying their fortifications, abolishing their seigneurial rights and securing the triumph of the Justice du Roi. Now all that had been changed. The magistrates joined the ranks of the aristocracy. In 1732 the eldest son of the duc de Luynes married Marie Brulart, daughter of the Premier Président at Dijon; the duc de Lorges married a daughter of the Premier Président at Mesmes. The *noblesse d'épée* and the *noblesse de robe* were beginning to form a single class united in a common cause. It was nothing less than the destruction of the power of the monarchy and the reverting to the localised powers of the feudal age. Their opposition to the King was judged by Pierre Gaxotte as 'beyond any doubt the most important political event of the reign'.

As the magistrates stepped into the shoes of the old nobility so they purchased the *châteaux* and the *seigneuries* which went with them and they began to notice that a number of feudal rights had been allowed to fall into desuetude. The second part of the century saw a determined attempt to revive these feudal rights. Lawyers who were specialists in the subject, known as 'feudistes', were reinstating the aristocracy in their local pretensions. The comte Beugnot asserts that 'the agents of the duc de Nivernais were exercising, with an unbelievable harshness, feudal rights which were at best doubtful.'

The aristocracy of France had never been easy to control. Louis XIV had managed to do so and Versailles had played an important part in his achievement. It was, as Saint-Simon perceived, 'another stratagem of his policy'.

For the necessity of being constantly seen at Court achieved the domestication of the nobility. Under Richelieu their fortresses had been destroyed; under Louis XIV it became regarded as a punishment and a disgrace to be sent to live on their estates. This separation from their local position deprived them of their power. The King offered them their only chance of a livelihood – a position in the Household, a command in the army, a preferment in the Church. To obtain any such favour they had to be constantly seen at Versailles, for Louis kept a sharp eye out for absentees. 'He looked to right and to left at the *lever* and at the *coucher*, at his meals, when passing through the apartments and in the gardens of Versailles,' observed Saint-Simon; 'it went ill with a nobleman whose absence was noted; a certain disgrace for those who never came at all.'

In the course of the eighteenth century this centralising influence of Versailles became weaker and weaker. The abbé de Véri, whose journal is one of the most reliable sources for the period, gives a single but significant example, 'which did, perhaps on its own, alter the whole tone of the Court'. Under Louis XIV the ladies who had charges at Court were obliged to establish themselves and their families at Versailles: service was continuous. Under Louis XV the duc de Bourbon placed his mistress, Madame de Prie, in the Queen's household. In order that she should be free to accompany him to Chantilly he rearranged the system so that the ladies only served on a weekly basis. This, says Véri, enabled them to live in Paris so that they 'merely camped, as it were, at Versailles', which lost its position as a social centre and became, in his own words, 'le séjour de la tristesse et de l'ennui', 'the dwelling-place of melancholy and ennui'. It was, perhaps, not surprising that the Court should be boring if the King was bored with it himself, and that was exactly the case with Louis XV.

One of the most life-like descriptions of Louis comes from the pen of someone who was in a position to know him well and observe him accurately, his Intendant des Chasses at Versailles, Charles-Georges Leroy. 'A very remarkable air of grandeur was imprinted on his countenance and this was further enhanced by the manner in which he held his head. This manner was noble without being exaggerated, and, although this Prince was by nature shy, he had so mastered his outward appearance that his normal expression was one of firmness without the least touch of haughtiness. In private, and especially when he was conversing with someone whom he wished to treat well, his eye took on a singular expression of benevolence; he seemed to be inviting the affection of those to whom he was speaking.' Casanova made the same observation: 'never could the most skilful artist have managed to capture the expression of that magnificent head when the monarch turned his kindly regard upon someone.'

Leroy also gives us a character sketch of Louis: 'All that he needed to be a great King was more capacity for action and more confidence in himself.' This incapacity inclined him to an apathy in the conduct of affairs: 'his indolence,' continues Leroy, 'led him to yield easily to all that his ministers proposed, without taking the trouble to examine them, let alone to contradict them; his judgement was sound and the experience which he had of affairs often caused him to disapprove in secret of their conduct and their measures.'

The comte de Saint-Priest, who later became Ministre de la Maison du Roi, gives an example of this in his memoirs. In 1762, the year before the Peace of Paris put an end to the Seven Years' War, there were secret negotiations between France and England. Choiseul asked the King if he would rather conclude a peace or continue the campaign. 'Je vous laisse décider, Monsieur de Choiseul,' replied the King; 'ce sera comme vous voudrez.'

'Mais, Sire,' insisted Choiseul, 'comme vous voudrez vous-même.'

The King repeated 'comme vous voudrez' and never moved from that position.

'However strange this anecdote may seem,' wrote Saint-Priest, 'it is authentic; it shows a King who, in a matter of such gravity, would not even take the trouble to express his opinion.'

It was a downhill path. Louis soon reached the level of inertia – 'a complete inability to concentrate' – and this led inevitably to boredom and to the restlessness which is bred of boredom. As a result of this he was constantly on the move – from Versailles to Trianon, from Trianon to Marly, from Marly to La Muette, La Muette to Choisy-le-Roi, Choisy-le-Roi to Saint-Hubert. At all of these he was engaged in building and this provided him with the most satisfying of all distractions. Madame de Pompadour admitted that he was never so happy as when they were seated together at a table with Gabriel spreading his architecture designs before them.

Perhaps nothing speaks more clearly about the character of Louis XV than the alterations and redecorations which he made at Versailles. Whereas the taste of Louis XIV was for the grand, the imposing and the magnificent, the whole delight of his successor was for the exquisite, the intimate and the small. His *petits cabinets*, hidden in the topmost storey of the Cour de Marbre, were in direct, deliberate contrast with the heavy grandeur of the State Apartments.

The rooms were decorated with finely chiselled panels painted in a distemper known as Chipolin and finished with a *vernis Martin* which had the gloss and freshness of porcelain. Gilding was often replaced by soft colours. 'Les peintures couleur d'eau, petit vert, jonquille, gris de perle, bleu de Prusse font la gaieté des appartements.' The mouldings were gracefully turned, their arches breaking forth into delicate scrolls that curled in upon themselves and blossomed out into a spray of tiny flowers or became lost in a lace-like rosette at the foot of the panel. There was grace, lightness and refinement in every room, but none of the restlessness and fantasy of the more exuberant rococo.

In spite of his delight in the private and the intimate, Louis never failed in his public duty. He went to bed in the Chambre du Roi with all the protocol and all the solemnity of Louis XIV. 'I do not wish to undo', he said, 'anything that my forefathers have done.' But when the courtiers entitled to be present at the *coucher* had retired, he rose from the great bed and went and slept in a smaller bedroom in his private apartments.

The two bedrooms express the duality of Louis' character.

'To separate Louis de Bourbon from the King of France', wrote Madame Campan, 'was what this monarch found most piquant in his royal existence.'

This twofold existence made Louis a somewhat elusive figure to his contemporaries. 'Everything becomes more and more dependent on the character of the King,' wrote d'Argenson, 'and his character becomes ever more problematic.'

To those who saw him only in his official capacity, Louis could be stiff and awkward and had no conversation; ambassadors waited in vain for the few gracious words that might be expected to terminate an audience; the Queen took to communicating with him by letter rather than undergo the embarrassment of a conversation. Many anecdotes show him as insensible to the feelings of others, 'like a child who hurts you whilst playing'.

To those who saw him in his private life – and these were extremely few – Louis appeared in a different light. Most interesting in this respect are the memoirs of the duc de Croÿ and the duc de Luynes, both men of reliable character and belonging to the inner circles of the King and the Queen respectively, and those of Dufort de Cheverny, Introducteur des Ambassadeurs at Versailles.

'At supper in the *cabinets*', wrote the duc de Luynes, 'he is like an ordinary individual.' 'The dining-room was delightful,' writes the duc de Croÿ, 'the supper enjoyable and without restraint . . . the King was easy and gay, but always with a certain grandeur which one could not overlook.'

Louis' absolute need for private life offered to Madame de Pompadour the opportunity to use all her talents. They were the talents not of a courtier but of a rich bourgeoise. Dufort de Cheverny observantly distilled the truth when he wrote: 'she had the great art of being able to divert the most difficult man in the kingdom to amuse, whose natural taste was a love of privacy, but who felt that his position demanded the opposite, with the result that, as soon as he could extricate himself from public appearances, he would descend by a secret staircase to her rooms and lay aside his character of King.' These words – 'lay aside his character of King' – were to become increasingly significant.

It was for himself that Madame de Pompadour loved him. She had no love for the Court. 'Except for the happiness of being with the King,' she wrote to Mademoiselle de Lutzelbourg, 'the rest is one great fabrication of malice and platitudes, in fact of all the misery of which we poor human beings are capable.' Madame de Pompadour was unlike most royal mistresses in that she did not try to alienate the King from his family; indeed she did more than anyone to bring them together. 'Elle finit par gagner toute la famille royale,' wrote Pierre Gaxotte; 'she even became rather devout. She read books of piety, went to mass and sought out a confessor who was willing to pardon her former conduct and yet authorise her to remain with the King.'

The great historian Lavisse does not hesitate to name this period in Louis' reign 'l'Époque de Madame de Pompadour'. In spite of the many ominous cracks which were beginning to appear, the reign of Louis XV spanned one of the great periods in the history of France.

The country had the best internal communications in Europe. With the setting up of the Service des Ponts et Chaussées in 1760 the creation of roads and bridges became a major activity. By the end of the reign some 40 000 kilometres of road had been constructed, to a good standard. 'The roads are incredibly fine,' wrote the English traveller Joseph Jekyll in 1775; 'causeways as lofty as the Roman ones, nicely paved in the centre, of a vast breadth and straight as an arrow for leagues together and usually planted with trees on either side.' The Bishop of Langres, pronouncing the Oraison Funèbre of Louis XV, made a point of mentioning this great achievement: 'one can cross the kingdom today in less time than it used to take to traverse a single province.'

It was also a great age of urbanism. In Paris, writes Pierre Gaxotte, 'une nouvelle capitale sort de terre,' 'a new capital city springs up from the earth.' The faubourg Saint-Honoré, the faubourg Saint-Germain, the chaussée d'Antin, the Place Louis XV, presented their sober, dignified façades with a spaciousness of planning that gave plenty of light to the brilliantly decorated rooms behind them. In the provinces whole cities were transformed – Montpellier, Bordeaux, Nancy – with their Places Royales and their grand vistas.

The architecture of the mid eighteenth century was for the most part correctly classical. It was in the decorations and furnishings that the style Louis XV, or, indeed the style Pompadour, was at its most distinctive. An exhibition mounted in 1974 at the Hôtel de la Monnaie took for its title 'Un Moment de Perfection de l'Art Francais'. Nothing could bear more striking witness to the *douceur de vivre* of the French upper classes than the provision of an *objet d'art* to meet every little contingency of life – a *veilleuse* or nightlight of porcelaine de Sèvres, a *fontaine d'appartement* to provide the refreshment of running water indoors, or a beautiful little writing and reading desk charmingly named a *bonheur du jour*.

But it was not only the visual arts which flourished in the mid eighteenth century. The art of gastronomy also reached its moment of perfection. 'The long and peaceful reign of Louis XV', wrote Antonin Carême, 'saw the golden age of French cuisine.'

In 1764 Madame de Pompadour died and with her died the inspiration of an age. She left Louis with no-one able to coax him out of his boredom, no-one able to animate the ageing structures of Versailles. Louis was left to the resources of his own family.

On the ground floor of the palace, in the vast rooms which lie beneath the State Apartments, lived Mesdames, the four surviving daughters of Louis XV – Adelaïde, Victoire, Sophie and Louise. They had been brought up, for the sake of economy, at the Abbey of Fontevrault in Touraine.

By the time that the eldest of them was forty, they had become, according to the marquis de Ségur, 'very much old maids, hard, narrow-minded and mean'. Perhaps the best portraits of them come from the pen of Henriette Genêt, later to be Madame Campan, who was appointed their 'reader' in 1768. The youngest, Louise, was at least deeply religious and was soon to make an impressive gesture. The two middle ones were nonentities. Madame Victoire had been a lovely girl and still possessed, continues Ségur, 'sweet eyes and a charming smile'; poor Madame Sophie, on the other hand, was excessively plain – the Duchess of Northumberland had called her 'remarkably lean and horridly ugly'. Perhaps because of this she was so shy that it was possible, Madame Campan assures us, to see her every day for years and never hear her speak a word to anyone. 'She walked extremely fast and in order to recognise without having to face those who were ranged to either side, she had formed the habit of looking at them sideways, in the way that hares look.'

Sophie had one peculiarity: she was terrified of thunderstorms. Her reaction to this fear was to talk garrulously with anyone she came across; 'if she saw lightning', writes Madame Campan, 'she would hold their hand; for a thunderclap she would embrace them; but with the return of fair weather this Princess recovered her coldness, her silence, her detachment; she passed everyone by without paying attention to any until the next storm renewed her terror and her affability.' Both Sophie and Victoire tended to be dominated by their rather formidable elder sister Adelaïde, faithfully echoing anything she said and lamely following her lead.

Madame Adelaïde was energetic, ambitious and fairly intelligent. Handsome in her first youth, Ségur records, 'she had aged rapidly and was now a tall, commanding woman with a rather prominent nose and a very overbearing manner. Her voice was harsh and unmusical, her conversation abrupt and disjointed. She was absurdly proud of her royal rank, full of prejudices, imperious, ill tempered and strict regarding the most intricate demands of etiquette.'

She had been for some time her father's favourite and in 1752 he had installed her in an apartment adjoining his own on the first floor of the wing overlooking the Cour de Marbre. The Salon de Musique, with its beautiful gold and white panelling carved by Verberckt and its magnificent trophies of musical instruments, is one of the best surviving examples of the style Louis XV at Versailles. Adelaïde was a determined musician and could have played most of the instruments featured in the trophies. It was in this room in December 1764 that the young Mozart played the clavichord before the royal family.

In 1769 Adelaïde was relodged on the ground floor adjoining her sisters. Madame Campan tells of their daily visit from their father. Every morning Louis would go down to Adelaïde's rooms, often bringing coffee which he had made himself. Adelaïde pulled a bell rope which alerted her sister Victoire, who in turn rang to summon her next sister Sophie who passed the message on to the fourth sister, Louise. Poor little Louise was slightly deformed and very short in the leg. 'The apartments of Mesdames were enormous. Madame Louise lived in the remotest of them. In order to attend the daily reunion the poor Princess, running as fast as she could, crossed a great number of rooms and in spite of her efforts often had only time to kiss her father before he went off hunting.'

Madame Campan, who was privileged from the age of fifteen to see Mesdames at close range, draws a little thumbnail sketch of the Court in about 1767. 'The Jesuits had been abolished and piety was no longer to be found at Court save in the society of Mesdames. The duc de Choiseul ruled. The King thought only of the pleasures of the hunt.' But the apartments of Mesdames were not the centre of the life of Versailles. Theirs was a little world apart where the chief concerns were for gossip and the questions of etiquette.

'Etiquette', wrote Madame Campan, 'was still observed at Court in all the forms which it had received under Louis XIV; all that was lacking was dignity; as for gaiety, there was no longer any question of it. The meeting place where the wit and grace of the French was displayed was no longer Versailles. The seat of all intelligence and learning was in Paris.'

By the end of 1767 a great dullness seems to have settled over Versailles. The pleasantest moments for the Court were the yearly periods of absence – the Voyage de Fontainebleau, the Voyage de Compiègne, the more frequent Voyages de Choisy. It was at Choisy-le-Roi that Louis XV felt most at home. Those who had the privilege of following him there, and of wearing the blue uniform of those entitled to do so, saw him in his most informal mood; 'il est presque come un seigneur particulier', wrote the duc de Luynes, 'qui fait avec plaisir les honneurs de son Château.' It was at Choisy also that Luynes describes the King sitting on the river-bank and chatting with the boatmen and fishermen of the Seine. Choisy, however, was for the favoured few; Fontainebleau and Compiègne were for the whole Court.

It was during the Voyage de Compiègne in 1768 that there were rumours of a new mistress, brought at midnight from a private house and seen leaving the King's cabinets in the early morning. The duc de Choiseul, who came a week late to Compiègne that year, dismissed the affair as trivial and transient. He had met the woman and found her only 'médiocrement jolie'. The comte Mercy d'Argenteau, Ambassador from Vienna, however, was inclined to take a more detailed interest. He wrote to the Chancellor Kaunitz saying that the lady was now lodged in the Château, next to the old rooms of Madame de Pompadour; that she had attended mass in the private closet of the King. Soon it became clear that she was not just a mistress but a favourite. She appeared in the Château in a newly painted *chaise-à-porteurs* with the double coat of arms of a married woman. The arms of her husband were those of the comte Guillaume du Barry. He was the brother of the comte Jean du Barry, sometimes called the 'Roué'. Jean was not unknown to some of the courtiers and nor was his mistress Jeanne, a lady of somewhat easy virtue who had now suddenly become married to his brother.

Louis was soon captivated. Not only did the charms of his new mistress enslave his heart, he enjoyed the sense of power which the imposition of a *maitresse déclarée* upon the Court afforded. 'L'éclat qu'il mettait dans ses amours', wrote Mercy, 'était une preuve de son autorité.'

'This street walker', wrote Horace Walpole, 'has just received the homage of Europe. The holy Nuncio and every Ambassador but he of Spain have waited upon her and brought gold, incense and myrrh.'

Soon another name became attached to the affair – that of the maréchal de Richelieu, Premier Gentilhomme de la Chambre du Roi, a man as close to Louis as anyone. Such a position would have contented most courtiers, but Richelieu had political ambitions. He fancied himself as a statesman. Richelieu now began to appear as the rival to Choiseul, who dismissed the matter with disdain. 'Monsieur de Richelieu', he wrote, 'thought that I was jealous of him. I never accorded him such an honour.' Choiseul did not reckon on the combined power of Richelieu and Madame du Barry.

Behind Richelieu was his nephew the duc d'Aiguillon. There was already a party which supported the candidature of d'Aiguillon for the position occupied by Choiseul.

Since the duc de Choiseul had been responsible for the expulsion of the Jesuits, the anti-Choiseul party was known as 'le parti dévot'. There was, it need hardly be said, nothing particularly devout about the duc de Richelieu, the duc d'Aiguillon or Madame du Barry. 'Wise people who loved the King', wrote the duc de Croÿ, 'wept, prayed and kept silence.' But these were few in number; the large majority, whether clergy or laity, whether devout or not, genuflected before the altar of Madame du Barry.

'It was a strange and significant spectacle', writes Pierre de Nolhac, 'to watch these self-styled defenders of religion and virtue in so humiliating a position, reduced to reckoning on the moral weakness of their master in order to ensure their political victory.'

To this general rule there was one notable exception. 'In this universal abasement', Nolhac continues, 'there arose one protest, unique in its sincerity. It came from the very centre of the royal family; it was discreet, it was respectful both to the sovereign and to the father, but with a firm accent and an incomparable nobility. It was the act of Madame Louise.' She decided to leave the Court and enter the strict Carmelite house at Saint-Denis. 'She made a sacrifice', continues Nolhac, 'offering herself to God for the salvation of a father whom she loved. No-one suffered more than she did on behalf of this King who had degraded his crown as the eldest son of the Church, this hardened sinner to whom the priests were obliged to refuse the sacraments, this feeble spirit who was heading for eternal damnation. She had recourse to those mysterious laws which give to a life, voluntarily sacrificed, the right to ask for grace, such as the conversion of a loved one, of the divine compassion.'

Madame Louise had, in fact, been contemplating taking the veil for some time and hesitated only because she felt her health to be inadequate to withstand the rigours of the cloister. The immediate cause, however, of her self immolation was the King's infatuation for Madame du Barry.

As mistress of the King, Madame du Barry was a person with many natural enemies and it was only to be expected in the context of Versailles that she should be reviled. One of the best descriptions of her comes from the pen, not of a courtier, but of the Duchess of Northumberland: 'I own I expected her to be much handsomer . . . She is rather of a tall, middle size, full breasted, and is pretty but not to be called handsome & has a strong look of her former profession. Her complexion is fair and clear & her skin very smooth, but her Bloom is entirely gone off . . . Her eyes are of a lovely light blue & she has the most wanton look in them I ever saw; her mouth is pretty, her lips very red and her teeth fine, but she has a kind of artificial smirk which savours strongly of her old trade. Her chin is very pretty, her Voice loud, her Air very good & her manner obliging & civil but vulgar.'

The Duchess of Northumberland observed Madame du Barry from the lofty level of the English aristocracy, but she judged with a mind uncluttered by the prejudices peculiar to

Versailles. That Madame du Barry was possessed of more virtues that she was commonly credited with is abundantly clear, but her period of ascendency coincided with the King's period of decline. Her influence at least hastened that decline.

It was a decline first and foremost in popularity. Gone were the days when his mere presence could fill the streets of Paris or throng the gardens of the Tuileries with frantically cheering crowds. The Frenchman's love for the king was a very deeply implanted emotion. Even in 1789 a publication entitled *La Maison du Roi* could write of 'this fanaticism [*enthousiasme*] which the Frenchman has for his King, the effect of which all those who did not witness the return of Louis XV after his illness at Metz can only form a very imperfect idea'. Then he had been 'Louis le bien Aimé'. Now he did not even dare to show himself in Paris.

When, in September 1751 the Dauphine Marie-Josèphe brought her first son, the duc de Bourgogne, into the world the expressions of enthusiasm in Paris were 'très médiocres' and d'Argenson wrote: 'they complain about the lack of rejoicing on the part of the people of Paris at so important an event as the birth of a duc de Bourgogne. One would say that the people no longer love their kings whom they have loved for so long.'

On 25 December 1753, Lord Chesterfield wrote to his son from Paris: 'the King is despised, and I do not wonder at it; but he has brought it about to be hated at the same time, which seldom happens . . . he hesitates between the Church and the Parliament, like the ass in the fable that starved between two hampers of hay . . . The people are poor, consequently discontented; those who have religion are divided in their notions of it, which is saying that they hate one another. The clergy never do forgive; much less will they forgive the Parliament: the Parliament will never forgive them. In short the symptoms which I have ever met with in History previous to great Changes and Revolutions in Government, now exist and daily increase in France.'

Not only was the popularity of the King declining, his

health was causing concern to his physicians. In the event of his death the future of France would be in the hands of his eldest surviving grandson, Louis-Auguste, duc de Berry, since 1765 the Dauphin – 'a very feeble resource', according to his grandfather, 'against the republican rabble.'

In 1769 Louis-Auguste was fifteen and had reached puberty. It was urgently necessary that he should marry and beget a new heir. It was also necessary to cement the new foreign policy of an alliance between France and her traditional enemy Austria. This diplomatic *volte face* had been largely the work of the duc de Choiseul.

Etienne-François de Choiseul-Stainville, first duc de Choiseul, had been Ambassador to Rome and to Vienna. In September 1758 he was recalled by thc Cardinal de Bernis to help at the centre and in due course became the Premier Ministre. He was a somewhat debonair nobleman but with an immense capacity for work. The King, wrote Pierre de Nolhac, 'had gradually yielded all the reins into the capable and subtle hands of the duc de Choiseul; reassured in his royal conscience, satisfied in his private laziness, he left France to Monsieur de Choiseul in exchange for his leisure.'

In the attempt to consolidate the alliance with Austria, a royal marriage was one of the most obvious expedients. On the 24 May 1766 the Prince von Starhemberg, Austrian Ambassador to Versailles, was able to write to the Empress Maria Theresa: 'The King has made his intentions known in such a way that your Majesty may regard the project as decided and assured.' The Dauphin Louis-Auguste was to be betrothed to the Archduchess of Austria, Marie-Antoinette.

Du Côté de Schönbrunn

One of the great turning points of Austrian history was the year 1683. The Sultan Kara Mustapha laid siege to Vienna, but he was repulsed and the Turks driven by Prince Eugene further and further east, never to return. Vienna, however, had been badly battered.

The people who stand to gain most from the destruction of a city are architects. Their services are certain to be in high demand. The devastations of the Turks created almost unlimited opportunities for the architects of Austria. Out of the ruins of the Gothic town there arose a new baroque Vienna.

Among the many architects who profited from the situation, perhaps the greatest name is that of Johann Bernard Fischer von Erlach. In 1687 the Crown Prince Joseph, later to reign as Joseph I, was taking lessons in architecture from Fischer. It would be interesting to know what part, if any, Joseph himself played in the designing of his summer palace.

Among the many buildings destroyed by the Turks was a hunting lodge a few miles south-west of the capital. It had originally been called Katterburg, but this had been replaced by the more euphonious name, derived from its beautiful spring – Schönbrunn.

There were two designs produced and they have little in common with each other. The present palace of Schönbrunn occupies the low ground of its park, which rises to the south to a high horizon which was crowned in 1775 by the dramatic outline of the 'Gloriette'.

It was on this high ground that Fischer von Erlach, in his

first fantastic design, sited the palace. For a design it remained. It looks more like a fantasia upon a baroque theme than a serious proposition. In the way in which the architecture climbs the hillside, ramp upon ramp, terrace upon terrace, it seems, in some respects, to reflect the Château Neuf at Saint-Germain, but the whole lay-out has a baroque flavour about it which is, perhaps deliberately, un-French. The second design, both sober and practical, was that of a summer residence for the imperial family rather than an apotheosis of the Habsburg dynasty.

The main block of Schönbrunn, but not the wings, was completed by the death of Joseph I in 1711. He bequeathed it to his widow, Wilhelmine Amelie, who in turn left it to the Emperor Charles VI. He, however, showed little interest in Schönbrunn, devoting himself more to the extension and embellishment of the Hofburg, the imperial palace in Vienna. He even had dreams of an Austrian Escurial at Klosterneuburg. The Court of Vienna had more in common with the Court of Madrid than with that of Versailles. It was the Empress Maria Theresa who was to make Schönbrunn what it is today – partly a family home and partly a palace.

For the Habsburgs knew how to mix informality with protocol and to enjoy the privacy of family life uninhibited by the ceremonies of the Court. It was even stated by the Prussian envoy, Count Podewils, that all that the Empress Maria Theresa wanted to do was 'to live with the Emperor as though they were a bourgeois couple'. But although Schönbrunn may have been essentially a family house, it was a family house on a gargantuan scale. Ten of Maria Theresa's children lived to be adults; those who were unmarried were allocated five rooms each and those who were married ten rooms each whenever they came to Schönbrunn.

The pictures on the walls tell the same story. They are mostly family portraits. The little archdukes and archduchesses were painted again and again in a stiff and stylised manner which seldom appears to offer a convincing likeness. The huge canvasses of Martin van Meytens, containing hundreds of figures many of which may be presumed to be portraits, depict the ceremonial occasions of the Court and remind us that Schönbrunn was a palace as well as a family home.

In 1743 Maria Theresa began to make her alterations, using as her architect the young Nikolaus Pacassi. It does not appear that he was a very gifted architect, but it is more than likely that the Empress was the creative force. 'She enjoys building', wrote Podewils, 'without understanding anything about it, as is borne out by the house that she had built at Schönbrunn, to suit her own taste.' She often rejected the plans of her architects and her requirements for alterations, writes Georg Kugler, 'annoyed the builders and the results displeased those who were to live in the palace, above all her husband'.

The two great portraits of the Palace by Bellotto show a roofscape in which chimneys are conspicuous by their absence. It must be remembered that Schönbrunn was a summer palace and in common with many such buildings it had inadequate heating facilities. Many of the main reception rooms do have open fires or, more often, porcelain stoves which were serviced from a room behind so that no smoke or ash ever penetrated the state apartments; but in the lesser rooms there was often no heating. In the winter the Court moved back to the Hofburg in Vienna.

Unlike Schönbrunn, the vast complex of the Hofburg is not a single building following an architect's master plan, but rather a monument to the history of the Habsburgs which grew with almost every monarch from Ferdinand I, who died in 1564, to Franz-Joseph. This is partly due to the tradition that each succeeding sovereign did not inhabit the apartment of his or her predecessor. Frequently this offered the occasion for the addition of a new wing.

In 1660 Leopold I, who had come to the throne before the age of seventeen, began to build a large block of state apartments joining the Old Castle to another suite of rooms known as the Amalientrakt, built in the early seventeenth century by Rudolf II. This new block, the Leopoldinischentrakt, forms the south west range of the inner courtyard and overlooks the Heldenplatz on the other side.

Leopold's grand-daughter, Maria Theresa, took up her residence in the wing in the great suite of apartments facing the courtyard, which are now the rooms of the Austrian Federal President. She immediately enlarged the windows because of her passion for fresh air. The old fortifications of Vienna ran close to the Hofburg on the northern end of Leopold's wing, and Maria Theresa had a ramp for her coach built up to the top of the walls where a building known as 'Bellaria' gave access directly to her apartments on the second storey.

An outstanding feature of these rooms is the use of large ceramic stoves. These were loaded with logs from a corridor running behind the whole suite of apartments. It has been estimated that one and a half million cubic feet of wood was consumed in the Hofburg in the course of a winter. It sounds as if the palace was reasonably cosy.

Usually the Court moved from the Hofburg to Schönbrunn immediately after Easter: Easter is a moveable feast and April can be very cold. In 1752 Count Khevenhüller, the Court Chamberlain, noted in his diary: 'On 5 April everything was ready to make the move to Schönbrunn; but, as the weather has suddenly turned so much worse and it has even been snowing since last night, I was given this morning the order by the Empress to countermand the move until further orders, a fact about which those who do feel the cold, and especially the poor servants, were overjoyed.'

The reference to 'those who do feel the cold' was an oblique allusion to the fact that the Empress did not. Maria Theresa was a very remarkable person – one of the great figures of the eighteenth century. Any attempt to understand Marie-Antoinette must start with an attempt to understand her mother. Her story must be told.

On 13 May 1717 the Empress, Elizabeth-Christina, wife of Charles VI of Austria, was expecting her second baby. A year previously she had, after nine years of childlessness, fulfilled the prime function of a consort and produced an heir, Leopold. But it all ended in disaster. Lady Mary Wortley-Montagu, who was in Vienna at the time, recorded 'the tragical end of an only son, born after being so long desired and at length killed by want of good management'.

And now a new child was expected. It would be difficult to estimate the volume of mental suffering caused by the law of primogeniture. To the pangs of childbearing was added the desperate anxiety lest the child should be a girl. It was a girl. They christened her Maria Theresa.

In course of time it began to look more and more improbable that they would have another son and Charles negotiated with the ruling houses of Europe to have Maria Theresa recognised as his successor. The operation was known as the 'pragmatic sanction'. But Charles secretly went on hoping for a male heir. Maria Theresa was not given the education which might have equipped her for the task of ruling the Habsburg Empire.

The atmosphere in which she grew up was one of punctilious religious observance. The French Ambassador, the duc de Richelieu, was appalled by it. 'In Vienna, during all of Lent', he wrote to the Cardinal de Polignac, 'I have led an astonishingly pious existence, which has not left me a quarter of an hour of liberty. I admit frankly that if I had known in advance what sort of life an Ambassador might lead in Vienna, then nothing on earth would have persuaded me to come here.'

There is no record, however, how the little Archduchess Maria Theresa reacted to all this religious observance, but she enjoyed ceremony and the Church offered her plenty of it.

The life of a royal princess in the eighteenth century was not likely to be a happy one. Her marriage was an important card in the game of diplomacy. The inclinations of the heart were seldom if ever regarded. Maria Theresa had a childhood passion for Francis, the second son of Leopold, duc de Lorraine, but the chances of ultimate matrimony must have seemed slender indeed. At one time she was very nearly betrothed to Francis' elder brother Clement, but in June 1723 Clement died. Francis was now heir presumptive to the Dukedom of Lorraine and as such an eligible candidate for Maria Theresa's hand. Charles VI asked to see him and a memorandum was sent from Vienna on how the boy must behave in the presence of the Emperor.

Fortunately for all the first meeting took place at Schloss Trautmansdorf, a hunting lodge belonging to the Emperor. Francis was a high-spirited, good-looking youth of fourteen with all the charm of his age and a passionate love of hunting. He could not fail to appeal to such a mighty huntsman as Charles in whom he seems to have aroused the first stirrings of paternal affection. Charles had always wanted a son.

On 2 September he wrote to Duke Leopold: 'I can truthfully say that this young gentleman is quite remarkable for one so young in years; he is clever in everything he does, his manners are good, he is obedient. You can thank God for him, and it is obvious, dear Cousin, that he was brought up under your constant care and supervision. I can assure you that he is loved and admired by everyone here.'

Without any mention of formal betrothal, Francis became one of the family and was given the apartments in the Hofburg which had been those of the Dowager Empress Eleanore.

By the time Maria Theresa had reached her teens she was seriously in love with Francis. Sir Thomas Robinson, the British Ambassador, wrote: 'she sighs and pines all night for her Duke of Lorraine. If she sleeps it is only to dream of him, if she wakes it is but to talk of him to the lady-in-waiting.'

In 1730 Francis went to Versailles to pay his respects to Louis XV and in the following year he went to England to visit George II, who was delighted. 'Nothing could have given me greater pleasure', he wrote, 'than your sojourn in this country.' From London he went to the Hague and thence to Berlin. On 15 March 1732 Frederick II wrote to his sister: 'He is the most delightful Prince I have ever met.'

On 31 January 1736, 'wearing a magnificent suit of chestnut brown velvet ornamented with silver, the hems sewed with gold, the buttons made of diamonds', Francis formally asked for the hand of Maria Theresa.

Maria Theresa was now nineteen; 'her walk is graceful and majestic,' wrote Count Podewils, 'her figure is round and full, her hair is blond with a reddish tint, her deep blue eyes are very large and full of life and sweetness. Her white teeth show up charmingly when she laughs. Her manners are vivacious and pleasing; she is always gracious. Maria Theresa is a charming and most attractive woman.'

The first correspondence between the two lovers dates from their engagement. 'Most Serene Archduchess, my angel bride,' began Francis, 'nothing could be harder for me than to approach you by letter instead of throwing myself at your feet. Let my dearest bride be fully assured that in all the world there is no bridegroom more entirely devoted and respectful than my angel bride's most faithful servant, Francis.'

'Your dear letter made me very happy,' she replied. 'You will know that I feel the same about you . . . I assure you that all my life I shall remain your most faithful bride, Maria Theresa.' They were indeed a happy pair. Francis was consort to the most powerful heiress in Europe; Maria Theresa was able to marry the only man that she had ever loved.

In 1740, at the age of twenty-three, Maria Theresa succeeded to the Austrian throne. She found herself the ruler of a compendium of kingdoms, principalities and duchies which had in common neither race nor language, which shared no common frontier and acknowledged no common historical tradition. They shared only their allegiance to the house of Habsburg.

Maria Theresa had received no training in politics, economics or diplomacy, but she brought to the huge task of administering so dispersed and diverse an Empire a clear brain, a great heart and an astonishing capacity for work. Above all she was able to turn her femininity to good account. At her succession many of her subjects had doubted the possibility of a female ruler. Forty years later she was felt to be the mother of her peoples and occupied in their hearts a position not unlike that which Queen Victoria was to occupy in England.

Maria Theresa, according to the abbé de Véri, 'possessed to a superlative degree the art of honest charm. It was above all in the misfortunes of her coming to the throne that she developed this, and with a grace that was all her own. Her youth, her misfortunes and her beauty lent great strength to a happy talent.'

In 1741 Frederick II of Prussia annexed Silesia, one of her richest provinces. It was an easy victory. At the service of thanksgiving after the decisive battle of Mollwitz, Frederick chose as the lesson a passage from St Paul: 'Let a woman learn in quietness and all subjection. I permit not a woman to teach nor to have dominion over a man, but to be in quietness.' Five years later, when he was writing his *Histoire de mon Temps*, Frederick gave full recognition to her achievements.

> She introduced order and economy, unknown to her predecessors, into her country's finances; and her revenues far exceeded those possessed by her father even when he was master of Naples, Parma, Silesia and Serbia. She had learnt that it was necessary to introduce a better discipline into her army, she annually organised military camps in her provinces; she visited these camps herself so that she might animate the troops by her presence and bounty. She established a Military Academy in Vienna and collected the most skilful professors of all the sciences which tended to elucidate the art of war. By these institutions the army acquired, under her auspices, such a degree of perfection as it had never attained under her predecessors, and this woman accomplished designs worthy of a great man.

Her Hungarian subjects, according to Weber, honoured her with the title 'Femme-Grand-Homme'.

The ideal of the 'enlightened despot' was current in Europe at the time and this is what Maria Theresa succeeded in becoming. She may well have thought that her people would be happier as members of a great and efficiently run State, but the overmastering motive for her actions was the creation of such a State. Only a very formidable personality could have achieved that. A very formidable person she was to become.

On 25 June 1741 she was crowned in Hungary. For anti-feminist reasons she was obliged to take the title of 'King', and she acquitted herself extremely well. Sir Thomas Robinson describes the event: 'The Queen was all charm; she rode gallantly up the Royal Mount and defied the four corners of the world with the drawn sabre, in a manner to show that she had no occasion for that weapon to conquer all who saw her. The antiquated crown received new graces from her head and the old tattered robe of St Stephen became her as well as her own habit, if diamonds, pearls and all sorts of precious stones can be called clothes.'

Four years later her husband Francis was elected Holy Roman Emperor and crowned in Frankfurt. It was a hollow crown if ever there was one, but if it carried no power at least it carried the prestige of antiquity. Maria Theresa absolutely refused to be crowned with him. Aghast at her refusal, he wrote to her in his most illiterate French: 'ille me sauble que vous deverie ansi vous faire couronné care san cela fera ici un tres moves efet.' Maria Theresa never gave her reasons for refusing. Possibly she did not care to appear in the role of consort.

Her capacity for work was almost frightening. She was always up at four in the morning in summer and five in winter. She spent the whole morning reading dispatches and consulting with her ministers. She dined at one and had a brisk walk afterwards. She kept the windows of her apartments open in all weathers. The strict regime which she forced upon herself took no account of the fact that she was pregnant most of the time. She had sixteen children in all.

Her son, Joseph II, continued the tradition. Voltaire wrote, comparing him to the King of Prussia: 'with Frederick it was Sparta in the morning and Athens at night: with Joseph it was Sparta all the time. The King was a blend of Stoic and Epicurean, loving the arts, literature and conversation; the

Emperor, scorning delights, was at once the ruler and the slave of the State.'

Much the same was true of Maria Theresa. In her younger days she had enjoyed music and dancing. Molitaris, a visitor to Vienna, wrote: 'I can truthfully say that never in my entire life have I seen anything more beautiful, more moving and more perfect than her Royal Highness when she sang and danced.' Her father, Charles VI, had inherited an outstanding musical talent from his forebears and was a great lover of the theatre. He produced operas himself and conducted them. Vienna was already the musical centre of Europe and Maria Theresa saw to it that her children were taught to act, to dance, and to sing.

There was a private theatre in the Grosse Anticamera at Schönbrunn and the royal children often performed on the stage. The day after Crown Prince Joseph's marriage to Maria Josepha of Bavaria, 23 January 1765, there was a performance of *Il Parnasso Confuso*, written by Pietro Metastasio and set to music by Gluck. Count Khevenhüller wrote ecstatically in his diary: 'this spectacle was indeed, and *sans flatterie*, one of the most noteworthy ever mounted on a courtly stage, inasmuch as . . . the four Archduchesses Elizabeth, Amelia, Josepha and Charlotte excelled in it . . . and the Archduke Leopold performing on the harpsichord and directing the orchestra . . . all these noble persons distinguished themselves *ultra expectationem* and to the delight of all, singing with a natural beauty of voice and in exquisite style as well as acting and dancing.'

Maria Theresa's relationships with her children, however, were not unlike her relations with her subjects. She ruled them. She ruled them for their own good. 'Cruel only to be kind' was a maxim that would have appealed to her, and she would have claimed to be acting from the highest dictates of maternal affection when she ordered her son Joseph to be caned. When his tutors respectfully reminded her that corporal punishment was not in the Habsburg tradition, she answered: 'look at the Habsburg princes: their characters have shown that they have not been sufficiently chastised.'

Her daughters were brought up with equal strictness, but only given the slightest of educations. 'A wife', she taught, 'is subject to her husband in everything; she should have no interests or occupations except to please and obey him.' This was excepting always herself, as a ruling monarch. For other women it was not necessary to be properly educated. It was necessary that they should be disciplined.

'It is my wish', she wrote, 'that the children are to eat everything that is set before them without making any objections. They are not to make any remarks about preferring this or that, or to discuss their food. They are to eat fish every Friday and Saturday and on every fast day. Though Joanna has a revulsion against fish, no-one is to give way to her in this matter. All my children seem to have an aversion to fish, but they must all overcome this, there is to be no relenting in this matter.'

On another occasion she wrote to the Countess Lerchenfeld, governess to the Archduchess Josepha: 'I am more convinced than ever that my daughter is not ill, but that she has bad habits, and these must be uprooted immediately and thoroughly. I have been too gentle with her, I have spoken to her with too much friendship in order to encourage her. I cannot flatter myself that I can be successful with her until the source of her trouble, her violent temper and her selfishness, have been restrained.'

The same determination to eradicate vice was apparent in the Empress's attitude towards her subjects. She would not tolerate their bad behaviour. In 1753 she set up the Keuschheits-Kommission – the Chastity Commission. It was nothing less than a network of spies who had the right of entry into private houses in search of evidence of sexual misconduct.

According to Nathaniel Wraxall:

> It is hardly possible to conceive how minute and circumstantial a detail her enquiries embrace relative to the private conduct of her subjects of both sexes; their actions, amusements and pleasures, even the most concealed, are constantly

> reported to her. She employs emissaries and spies, who omit nothing from their information. I could relate from my own personal knowledge some curious and entertaining instances of her inspection into the conduct of the ladies of the Court; but the subject is too delicate for particular details . . . The presence of the Empress, and the terror inspired by her vigilance, as well as her resentment, operate in repressing all excesses. Superstition, confessors and penances add weight to temporal motives. But the principle of frailty nevertheless exists; even Vienna has its Messalinas, though certainly in smaller number and marked with fainter colours than elsewhere.

Casanova made the comment in his memoirs: 'There was plenty of money and plenty of luxury in Vienna, but the bigotry of the Empress made Cytherean pleasures extremely difficult, especially for strangers.'

Maria Theresa has left an unintentional portrait of herself in the voluminous correspondence which she entered into with her children. It stands out clear on every page. She was a person who would brook no opposition, for the simple reason that she took it for granted that she was always right. The complexities of human nature were beyond her understanding and the distinction between discipline and repression would have been too fine for her mental grasp. She does not seem to have envisaged the possibility of such a thing as counterproductivity. These failures in understanding mattered more in her relations with her children than in her dealings with her subjects.

After her daughters married and left the maternal home she kept in regular contact with them, advising, admonishing and rebuking them as if they were still in the nursery. In order to do this she had her informants in all the Courts to which they had gone. 'I have heard from Brandeis, from your ladies-in-waiting, and even from strangers', she wrote to the Archduchess Marie-Caroline after her marriage to Ferdinand, King of Naples, 'that you say your prayers carelessly, without veneration, attention or deeper feeling. Don't be surprised if the whole day is bad after such a beginning.

Recently you have acquired the habit of being rude to your ladies-in-waiting . . . You are bad-tempered while they are dressing you . . . You must make a special effort to improve in this respect.'

1763 was a bad year for Austria. The end of the Seven Years' War had left Prussia still in possession of Silesia. Maria Theresa had pawned the Crown Jewels and invited her nobles to send their silver to the Mint. The life of the Court had been subjected to severe economies; no more entertainments, no more balls, the card tables disappeared and dinner parties were drastically reduced. Two years later, Count Khevenhüller complained of the waning influence of the Court: 'This unfortunate spirit of innovation which showed itself soon after the death of Charles VI and increased from day to day, seems now to be in the ascendant. If it goes on like this there will soon be no more system and no more etiquette at Court.'

Count Khevenhüller was shocked by the neglect of etiquette. The fact was that Maria Theresa had no time to be ceremonious and Francis did not have the inclination. Even after he became Holy Roman Emperor he preferred to lead a private existence, hunting and playing cards with his personal friends. 'The Empress and my children', he said, 'constitute the Imperial family. I am only a private individual.'

Maria Theresa replaced the ceremonies of the Court with the ceremonies of the Church and substituted its fasts for the former feasts. Her son Joseph wrote to her, 'I offer, if it pleases you, to make a vow, like the nuns, not to leave your side. Your Majesty will be my Convent and her abode my Cloister.' The metaphor may have been better chosen than he realised.

In 1764 Joseph was made King of the Romans, heir to his father's title of Holy Roman Emperor. It was the occasion of his final capitulation to his mother. 'Order, forbid, correct me as of old,' he wrote in April of that year; 'I need your guidance, and what little good there may be in me I owe entirely to your care. Fashion me as you will.' His mother received his submission as something which was quite simply her due. She had made him 'co-regent' of Austria with her and together they had to restore the fortunes of the Habsburg inheritance. In this they were greatly assisted by their Chief Minister, the Count von Kaunitz.

Kaunitz was one of the strangest figures of the eighteenth century. As Frederick the Great admitted, 'His knowledge of political affairs was as profound as his personal tastes were frivolous.' A fastidious valetudinarian who could not believe he was not ill and could not bear the thought of death, he lived to well over eighty and was for forty years the indispensible adviser to Maria Theresa. He was to her what Lord Burghley had been to Queen Elizabeth. 'The favour of his sovereigns,' wrote the comte de Saint-Priest, 'by which he was maintained in place for forty years, could only have been earned by his talents; for his character was haughty, presumptuous and subject to a thousand little ridiculous fads. The alliance which he had had the adroitness to conclude with France in 1756 contributed greatly to his reputation. It was, in fact, of capital importance to the House of Austria to deprive the Princes of Germany of their principal and most consistent support, and it was no mean stroke of genius on the part of this minister.'

For it was to Kaunitz that the idea had first come, after the traumas of the Seven Years' War, that a new system of alliances in Europe was overdue. The rise of Prussia had upset the old balance of power. As for France, the traditional enemy of Austria, she was no longer the great power that she had been. She was beginning to realise that England – protestant, imperialist England – was her real and natural enemy and that Austria was no longer a threat to her interests in Europe. An alliance, therefore, between Austria and France seemed the obvious solution. It was, however, largely unpopular, especially in France, to whom Austria was the traditional enemy.

A first treaty was duly signed in July 1755. Since February of that year Maria Theresa was carrying her fifteenth child.

On 2 November that child was born. It was a girl and she was christened Maria Antonia – Marie-Antoinette. She was destined to become the living symbol of the French alliance – as her mother put it in a letter to Louis XV – 'the most tender pledge of the happy union between our states and dynasties'. She was to marry the Dauphin, Louis-Auguste.

The Archduchess

On 2 November 1755, Marie-Antoinette was born in the Hofburg in Vienna. A few days earlier Maria Theresa had given order to her Grande Maîtresse to seek out a wet nurse of respectable family and 'of pure principles and impeccable character'. Maria Constanza, the wife of Johann Georg Weber, Councillor to the Magistrature of Vienna, was chosen. For three months she had been suckling her own son Joseph, who thus became what the French call 'frère de lait' to Marie-Antoinette. In later life she always addressed him as 'frère'.

Joseph left to posterity his *Mémoires concernant Marie-Antoinette, Archiduchesse d'Autriche, Reine de France.* They were later edited and extended by the comte de Lally-Tollendal. Weber offers one continuous, uncritical panegyric. He presents, perforce, one side only of the picture. That does not necessarily mean that he presents it inaccurately. It means that it needs to be balanced by the other side of the picture. It is not everyone who is capable of inspiring such total devotion and there are enough instances of Marie-Antoinette being able to do so to show that this was a real and important side of her character.

Joseph Weber gives disappointingly few anecdotes of the childhood of the girl with whom he shared his nursery, but there is one picture, recounted to him by the Countess Brandeis, which is worth reproducing. 'The daughter of the Caesars was thus associated with me in the games of her childhood and the Empress took part in them; and since at that age nothing had yet made me aware of the infinite distance which separated me from the girl with whom I played, the august and good Maria Theresa was often afraid of hurting me by an unusual distribution of her caresses and took me upon one knee when she held her daughter upon the other, and honoured me with the same kisses which she lavished upon her.' In later life he treasured a little model theatre enframing the scene of the Last Supper, with moveable figures, which was among the many presents given to him by the Empress. He says nothing of the Emperor Francis, Marie-Antoinette's father.

The Emperor Francis was a somewhat unassuming and self-effacing consort, but he seems to have been a good father to his children and a devoted son of his Church. He left a memorandum to his children which Marie-Antoinette would have done well to have observed more closely. He foresaw with some accuracy the difficulties and temptations to which his daughters would be exposed. 'We are not on this earth for our own amusement,' he reminded them; 'God has not provided these amusements except for the refreshment of the mind.' They must be careful, very careful, of the company which they keep, for royal personages are usually 'surrounded by a crowd of people who seek only to flatter their taste and to entice them in that direction towards which they are already inclined'. Above all, he warned them 'never to be in a hurry to place your friendship or your confidence in someone of whom you are not absolutely sure.'

After these somewhat mundane admonishments, Francis took them into an exercise of spirituality which reveals the depth of his own devotion. 'I commend to you the practice of taking two days out of every year in which to prepare for death, as if you were certain that these two days would be the last in your life; by this means you will become accustomed to knowing what needs to be done in such a case, and when your last hour does come you will not be taken by surprise.'

It was Francis, however, who was to be taken by surprise. In July 1765 the elder members of the imperial family went to

Innsbruck to celebrate the marriage of the Archduke Leopold, Francis' second son, to the Infanta of Spain. On 4 July they set out at four in the morning from the Hofburg. Francis took a long farewell of his younger children and even recalled Marie-Antoinette for a second kiss. They were never to see each other again, for on 18 August he died suddenly in the arms of the Archduke Joseph from what appeared to be an apoplectic fit. Marie-Antoinette thus lost at the age of ten a wise and loving father who might, had he lived, have exercised an important influence on her.

It was a stunning blow to Maria Theresa. Apart from the intense pain of her bereavement she was, as a devout Catholic, in deep distress that her husband should have died without the last rites of the Church. When she returned to Vienna she wrote in her prayer book: 'My happy married life lasted 29 years, 6 months and 6 days; this is 335 months, 1540 weeks, 10 781 days and 258 744 hours.'

Meanwhile the negotiations for a royal wedding to seal the French alliance were proceeding slowly and rather uncertainly.

Towards the end of 1768 the duc de Choiseul was asked by Maria Theresa to appoint a French tutor and a French hairdresser for Marie-Antoinette. The hairdresser, named Larseneur, was recommended by Choiseul's sister, the duchesse de Gramont. The tutor, the abbé de Vermond, was recommended by Loménie de Brienne, Archbishop of Toulouse. Madame Campan said many harsh things about Vermond but she may well have been jealous of his position of confidence with the young Dauphine. According to the comte Mercy d'Argenteau, Maria Theresa's watch-dog at Versailles, the abbé de Vermond seems to have been the right man for this rather delicate assignment.

Shortly after the royal wedding, on 20 August 1770, Mercy wrote to the Empress: 'As for the abbé de Vermond, it would be difficult to give as much credit as it is his due for the care which he takes, for his honesty and his devotion . . . if he were to lose his position it would be an irreparable loss.' Four years later his opinion was still the same. On 7 June 1774, he wrote: 'Nobody knows the Queen better than the worthy and virtuous ecclesiastic who is her *lecteur*. This man, who is a unique example of probity, zeal and intelligence, lives only for the service and the glory of his august mistress.'

On 1 October 1776 Maria Theresa expressed her own satisfaction with Vermond: 'I am most touched by your service and your attachment,' she wrote, 'which is without equal. But I am also touched by the situation of my daughter who runs with great strides towards her destruction . . . in these circumstances she has need of you.'

Such was the man who came to Vienna to prepare the young Archduchess for the role that she had to play in France.

On 21 January 1769, Vermond wrote to Mercy of his first and favourable impressions: 'the charming character of Her Royal Highness makes the functions which I have to fulfil with her extremely agreeable.' He outlines the syllabus: 'I have included religion, the history of France, in which I lay stress on all that sets forth the character of our manners and customs; the knowledge of our great families and especially those who occupy places at Court; a smattering of French literature and in all these studies a particular attention to French language and spelling.'

He was quickly captivated by his royal pupil. 'I cannot praise enough the sweetness and kindness of her Royal Highness, but her vivaciousness and the ease with which she is distracted run counter, in spite of herself, to her desire to receive instruction. One can hardly date the beginning of her education at more than nine months ago, since she has been with Madame de Lerchenfeld. The Archduchess told me herself that the Grande Maîtresse, countess Brandeis, who was responsible for her upbringing, was very fond of her, spoilt her and did not trouble her with any sort of application.'

It was a warning note, but his overall impression was both favourable and optimistic. 'I am well convinced that both the Court and the country will be enchanted by our future

Dauphine; to a charming countenance she unites every grace of deportment and if, as one may expect, she grows a little, she will have all the attractiveness that could be desired in a great princess.'

In June that year there was a *fête* held at Schloss Laxenburg. He noted: 'her deportment and her bearing are assuming a tone of nobility and majesty astonishing at her age. If she grows a little more, the French will need no other token by which to recognise their sovereign.'

In October he was still multiplying his praises: 'those who have not seen her for six months are struck by her physiognomy which acquires new graces every day. It would be possible to find features of a more regular beauty: I doubt if it would be possible to find any more agreeable . . . whatever idea those who have seen her may be able to give to the French, they will be surprised by the note of goodness, affability and gaiety which is portrayed in her charming countenance.' By the spring of 1770 the little Archduchess was deemed ready to embark upon her great adventure.

Before her departure, Marie-Antoinette had, according to custom, to be married by proxy. The ceremony included as great a number of extravagant festivities as if the bridegroom had been present. It was preceded by a voluminous correspondence between Choiseul and the marquis de Durfort, the French Ambassador in Vienna, concerning precedence and protocol.

First, on Sunday 15 April, Durfort left Vienna only to return an hour later as if he had just arrived from France, in the quality of Ambassador *Extraordinaire* with a very considerable display of pomp. He brought with him two empty berlins, made in France to Choiseul's specification, one upholstered in crimson velvet on which were embroidered the Four Seasons, the other upholstered in blue and decorated with the Four Elements; these were to carry Marie-Antoinette to France.

The following day Durfort was received in audience by Marie Theresa and her son Joseph II, now associated with her on the throne. In the name of his Master, Durfort officially asked for the hand of the Archduchess in marriage. He brought with him a miniature of Louis-Auguste by the Swedish portraitist Hall, which Marie-Antoinette attached to her dress. Two days later, on Tuesday 17 April she renounced all claim to the throne of Austria. That evening there was a great banquet and *bal masqué* offered to some fifteen hundred guests at the Belvédère. As happened so often at Versailles a special wooden ballroom, magnificently decorated, had been constructed for the purpose. It was lit by 3500 candles.

The *Gazette de Vienne* for 25 April records, in a supplement, the safety precautions adopted for this occasion. 'Fire pumps were at hand and ready for use and eight hundred men had been stationed, both in the Grande Salle and in the apartments, who for the most part stood in the window embrasures ready for the slightest mishap, while others kept a watchful eye on the candles.

'The vigilance of the august Maria Theresa extended even further: nothing escaped her where the care for her subjects was concerned; doctors and surgeons were placed by her orders with a supply of medicines in different rooms in which beds were ready for any emergency.'

On Thursday 19, at six in the evening, the whole Court went to the church of the Augustins for the marriage by procuration. Marie-Antoinette's brother, the Archduke Ferdinand, stood proxy for the Dauphin. The papal Nuncio, Monseigneur Visconti, conducted the ceremony and blessed the rings.

Saturday, 21 April, was the day fixed for Marie-Antoinette's departure for France. It was not until 14 May that she arrived at Compiègne; the journey took her twenty-three days.

The departure of Marie-Antoinette from Vienna is described by Weber in all its heart-rending detail. 'The joy of seeing her Dauphine of France was altogether blotted out by the pain of no longer possessing her.' Marie-Antoinette was to be joined by Weber in France, but there were two *adieux* which she must have known were for life – one with her mother and one with Madame Weber. Her leave-taking of the latter is described by Joseph: 'My mother came into the room. I can still see Marie-Antoinette throwing herself upon her neck, holding her face between her two hands and saying "Dear nurse, I shall love you all my life. Do not forget me!" "Forget your Royal Highness!" cried my mother, falling, like myself at the feet of the Archduchess; "my whole life will be spent in adoration of you."'

Her farewell to her mother had to be in public. 'The whole Court was present,' continues Weber, 'the highest of the nobility and the Archdukes surrounded the Empress. The young Marie-Antoinette burst into tears and the spectators, touched by the sight, shared the cruel sufferings of mother and daughter. Maria Theresa went up to the wife of the Dauphin; she took her into her arms and hugged her; then she spoke these words which betokened at once her faith and her spirit: "Adieu, my dear daughter; a great distance is going to separate us – but be just, be humane and imbued with a sense of the duties of your rank and I shall be proud of the regrets which I shall always feel. You have the gift of pleasing others; use it for the happiness of your husband. Do so much good to the people of France that they will be able to say that I have sent them an angel."'

The moment of departure from the Hofburg was quickly over. 'We saw her', wrote Weber, 'sitting right back in her coach, her face bathed in tears, covering her eyes now with her handkerchief, now with her hands, putting her head out of the window again and again to see once more the palace of her fathers to which she would never return.'

The first night was spent at Melk, the great Benedictine monastery that dominates the Danube some fifty kilometres upstream from Vienna.

Melk, one of the most palatial of the monasteries of Austria, is both larger and more magnificent than Schönbrunn. Maria Theresa had expressed her appreciation of this with the words: 'I should regret it had I never been here.'

The entrance to Melk is from the west. Over its proud portico is written the text: '*Absit Gloriari nisi in Cruce*' – 'God forbid that I should boast save in the cross of our Lord Jesus Christ.' Through this portal Marie-Antoinette passed into the palatial suite of apartments reserved for the imperial family, and here, on the morning of 22 April, she said good-bye to her brother the Emperor Joseph II. On Saturday 26 and Sunday 27 she was the guest of the Elector Max Joseph of Bavaria at Nymphenburg.

In some ways Nymphenburg was a preparation for Versailles. 'Of all the Sovereigns in Europe next to the King of France,' asserted Pollnitz, 'the Elector of Bavaria has the finest Pleasure Houses. 'Tis certain that next to the gardens of Versailles there is none so magnificent as those of Nymphenburg, which is a place that Art and Nature seem to have joined their forces in order to render noble and magnificent.'

From Nymphenburg the Prince von Starhemberg, who continued to accompany the Dauphine, wrote to Versailles: 'Everyone seems charmed with the Princess whom I am bringing to you and I can only hope that she will enjoy as great a success as she has in all the places we have visited until now.'

Finally on 6 May Marie-Antoinette arrived at the Abbey of Schuttern near Kehl, just across the Rhine from Strasbourg.

The place selected for the ceremony of her reception into France was the Île des Épis, where a fairly large wooden pavilion of the purest French architecture was erected. It was over a hundred feet long and consisted of a central salon – the Salle de Remise. To one side was the Grand Cabinet Autrichien and the Antichambre Autrichienne; on the other side was the Grand Cabinet Français and the Antichambre Française. The Garde Meuble du Roi had furnished the rooms and hung the walls with Gobelin tapestries.

These tapestries, woven from Raphael's cartoons, were much admired by Goethe, who was at that time a medical student in Strasbourg, but of those in the Salle de Remise, he was sharply critical: their subject-matter deeply shocked him.

> It was none other than the history of Jason, Medea and Creusa; that is to say, the picture of the most disastrous of all marriages. To the left of the throne was seen the unfortunate bride, expiring in the agonies of the most cruel death. To the right was the distracted Jason, deploring the death of his children, who lay dead at his feet, whilst the Fury who had destroyed them fled through the air in her car drawn by dragons.
>
> I loudly called upon my companions to witness this flagrant attack on good sense and taste. 'What!', I exclaimed, 'will they actually set before the eyes of the young Queen, at the very first step she makes in her new dominions, the representation of the most horrible of marriages? . . . Had they nothing more appropriate than these frightful spectres to exhibit to their beautiful Queen on her first arrival?'

The baronne d'Oberkirch was equally horrified and the unfortunate allusion did not escape the eyes of Marie-Antoinette herself, who exclaimed, 'Ah! what an omen!'

In the Austrian part of the building Marie-Antoinette took off all her Austrian clothing, thus symbolically divesting herself of her Austrian past. She was then entirely reclothed to symbolise her new allegiance. Saying good-bye to her Austrian suite, she walked through into the Salle de Remise where her French attendants awaited her. The comte de Noailles, representing the King, introduced his wife, who was to be Marie-Antoinette's Dame d'Honneur and who was to play an important, if unfortunate part in the life of the young Dauphine.

'In doing justice to the virtues of the comtesse de Noailles,' writes Madame Campan, 'the people who were most sincerely attached to the Queen have always regarded it as one of her first misfortunes, perhaps as the greatest since her coming into the world, not to have found in the person whose natural function it was to be her counsellor a woman of enlightenment, a woman capable of making allowances and uniting a wise judgement with that charm which could engage the young to follow. The comtesse de Noailles had no outward attraction; her deportment was stiff, her look severe; she knew her etiquette backwards.'

The demands of etiquette, continues Madame Campan, 'were, it is true, tedious, but they had been worked out from the need to present to the people of France all that could command their respect, and above all to guarantee a young Princess, by means of an imposing *entourage*, against the lethal arrows of calumny. It would have been necessary to make the Dauphine appreciate the fact that in France her dignity depended to a great extent upon customs which were quite unnecessary in Vienna to maintain the respect and affection of the imperial family among the good and dutiful Austrians.'

Madame Campan is borne out by Jacob-Nicolas Moreau, who played a small part in the education of Louis-Auguste: 'When the comtesse de Noailles was nominated Dame d'Honneur,' he wrote, 'she repeated to me several times that the King had insisted that she should be a sort of governess to the Dauphine; she was nothing less than that. She had, no doubt, certain excellent qualities, but she never had that graciousness which might win the confidence of a young princess, nor the gift of being able to please without which, although one might occasionally instruct, one can never guide.'

From the Île des Épis, Marie-Antoinette made her entry into France. The architecture of Strasbourg, with its mixture of German and French traditions, was exactly suited to the occasion. The great Cathedral, built of a salmon pink sandstone typical of Alsace, with its single spire of the same open fretwork construction as that of Freiburg-im-Breisgau, was at first sight more German than French. And yet the Cathedral of Strasbourg, both in its structure and in its sculpture, owes much to Reims and to the great Gothic tradition of France.

Around the Cathedral the houses clustered in medieval fashion; with their high timbered façades and tall, many-dormered roofs, they were more suggestive of some Germanic town, but across the Place du Château, facing the south front of the Cathedral, the huge episcopal palace was purely and thoroughly French, like one of the grander *hôtels particu-*

liers of the Marais, in Paris. It was, according to the baronne d'Oberkirch, 'fit for a Sovereign'.

Here Marie-Antoinette was to be received into France and here she was to taste for the first time the thrill of a delirious reception.

A vast triumphal arch had been erected at the entrance to the Place Broglie. To make room for it they had been obliged to demolish one of the towers of the old medieval walls and to fill in part of the moat. Above the central archway were juxtaposed the arms of France and Austria joined by a blue and yellow ribbon bearing the inscription: 'Perpetua Imperiorum Concordia' – 'the perpetual concord between the two empires'.

The surroundings of the Château des Rohan had also received the most particular attention. 'In order to mask the irregularity of the houses opposite', runs a contemporary description, 'which form the quayside of the river Île, which passes beneath the terrace of the Episcopal Palace, they erected a superb decoration.' It was in fact a canvas screen, eighty feet high and fifty-five yards long, on which was painted 'an immense palace composed of three blocks united by a vast colonnade'. It was, perhaps, more of a portico than a palace, and between its Corinthian columns could be seen a garden *à la française* of which the perspective 'had been so well contrived that it produced a most grand effect'. After darkness had fallen, a sort of back-projection was achieved 'which, without fatiguing the eyes of the Princess, created a wonderful effect of brightness'. 'The whole town was illuminated,' writes Madame d'Oberkirch; 'the Cathedral, from the topmost cross to the foundations was like a single flame, all its ornaments standing out like constellations of stars.'

Not content with this, the magistrates had arranged that, while the Dauphine was at the theatre, the boatmen of the Île should fill the space between this backdrop and the Château with their boats, 'on which was represented a parterre with bosquets adorned with divers sorts of shrubs', which formed a floating garden beneath the windows of her apartment.

Such celebrations were the result of four months of hard thinking and hard working on the part of the Magistrates and their workmen to produce 'the means to manifest the general rejoicing, that was felt by all the inhabitants, that they should be the first subjects of His Majesty Louis le Bien Aimé to offer the homage of the French nation to this August Princess.' Anything that might offend her eye was kept out of sight. 'Before the Princess arrived', wrote Goethe, 'a proclamation had been published forbidding every person afflicted with any disgusting disorder to appear on her way. This', he added, 'excited several jests.'

Goethe was an eye-witness of the reception of Marie-Antoinette. 'I still remember well the beautiful and noble countenance, the gay yet majestic air, of the young Princess. We saw her very plainly through the glasses of her coach. She seemed to be conversing in a very affable manner with the ladies who accompanied her, and to be much amused with the sight of the crowd which thronged around her.'

'Oh! if I lived for a hundred years', exclaimed Madame d'Oberkirch, 'I would never forget that day – those celebrations; the shouts of joy coming from a people intoxicated with the pleasure of seeing their Sovereign.' It has to be admitted that the intoxication of the people was not solely due to their enthusiasm for the House of Bourbon: the fountains of the city were flowing with wine.

Madame d'Oberkirch, who was seventeen at the time, was a person inclined both by nature and upbringing to revere royalty, but her enthusiasm on this occasion is infectious. 'The entry of the Princess was magnificent. Three companies of young children were dressed in the uniforms of the Cent Suisses and lined Her Royal Highness' route. Eighteen shepherds and as many shepherdesses offered her baskets of flowers . . . Twenty-four young ladies, between fifteen and twenty, coming from the most distinguished families of the town, dressed superbly in the various germanic styles of Strasbourg, came and strewed flowers in the path of the Princess, who received them as Flora herself would have done.' The young Swiss Guards were allowed to assume the proper functions of that body and to mount guard in the Château des Rohan that night.

It was all, of course, enormously expensive and Strasbourg was in a very bad position financially. In June of the previous year the Remonstrance sent to the King had described it as 'un théâtre de banqueroutes'. The city was in debt to the extent of some 5 000 000 livres. That, however, was not allowed to diminish the splendour with which Strasbourg was to receive its future Queen.

From Strasbourg, Marie-Antoinette made her way westwards, driving through the beautiful country of northern Alsace. 'I was delighted to see the excellent cultivation of this most productive country,' wrote Goethe; 'everywhere verdant, everywhere promising abundant harvests; the villages and farms which adorn its best situations – in short, that immense and beautiful plain, prepared like a new paradise for man, strewed with pleasant habitations and bounded on all sides by richly wooded mountains. I blessed providence for having called me to the enjoyment of so charming a residence.'

The progress of Marie-Antoinette from Strasbourg to Compiègne, a distance of some 250 miles, was slow and cumbersome – slow because of the endless entertainments provided *en route*; cumbersome because of the prodigious number of the retinue by which she was accompanied.

Including the Guards, who numbered sixty-three in all, there were 180 persons in her suite. At the top of the list was her Chevalier d'Honneur, the comte de Saulx-Tavanes; the Dame d'Honneur, the comtesse de Noailles; the Dame d'Atours, the duchesse de Cossé; four *dames du palais*, the duchesse de Duras, the duchesse de Pecquigny, the comtesse de Mailly and the comtesse de Tonnerre; a Premier Écuyer, the comte de Tessé; a Premier Aumônier, the Bishop of Chartres. Under him was a chaplain, a registrar, a clerk of the chapel and a confessor. On the medical side were a *premier médecin*, a *premier chirurgien*, an *apothicaire* and one assistant. In charge of the kitchen was the Maître d'Hôtel du Roi, the marquis de Montdragon, and under him a *contrôleur d'office* and his clerk in charge of a staff of twenty-six. The list continues down the social scale to a crowd of porters, *garçons de chambre* and *gardiens de la porte*. They took most of their own furniture with them which required the use of eight transport waggons.

Before leaving Strasbourg Marie-Antoinette was provided with a beautiful map, specially drawn and embellished by Tonnet, showing the interesting details of the route to Versailles. It was very easily folded and unfolded and housed in a red morocco case enriched with gold tooling.

On 11 May the Dauphine arrived at Chalons-sur-Marne. The Intendant de la Province de Champagne, Rouillé d'Orfeuil, was responsible for all arrangements for her reception. His first concern was the condition of the roads. Over 2 000 livres were spent on repairs. At the entrance to the city a new and elegant gate, loyally named the 'Porte Dauphine' had been constructed and through its triumphal arch Marie-Antoinette entered Chalons.

Six young maidens had received a dowry, each of 200 livres, from the municipality, to enable them to marry. They received the Dauphine with bouquets of flowers and a recitation of verses:

> 'En ce jour glorieux, quel bonheur est le notre!
> Nous devons notre Hymen à la splendeur du votre . . .
> Nous donnerons des Sujets à la France
> Et vous lui donnerez des Rois.'

A Salle de Spectacle had been constructed adjoining Marie-Antoinette's apartment at the Hôtel de l'Intendance.

The first play, *The Hunting Party of Henri IV*, by Collet, was followed by another, *Lucille*, which ended with a ballet. Most of the actors and dancers were imported from Paris. Marie-Antoinette declared herself 'extrèmement satisfaite' with the performance. Back in her rooms she could watch from the windows a magnificent display of fireworks. A spectacular feature of this was the appearance of counterfeit horses with fireworks playing from their nostrils and spreading thence all over their bodies, impelling them 'avec une prodigieuse rapidité' along the alleys of the garden, and executing 'une infinité d'évolutions singulières'.

The glow of the fireworks lit up the faces of an enormous crowd of spectators, mostly seated on the reverse slopes of the town walls, which offered 'the image of the most beautiful amphitheatre'. Free food was distributed from the Dauphine's lodgings and all the city fountains flowed with wine.

'It is unique to the French nation', wrote Rouillé d'Orfeuil, 'to idolise to such an extent the blood of the princes by whom they are governed; it is unique to the Magistrates of France to devise the *fêtes* which are capable of responding to the sentiments of the nation.'

Meanwhile the preparations for the reception of Marie-Antoinette by the King and his Court were well advanced. On 13 May, at nightfall, the royal family arrived at Compiègne and the next day, at three in the afternoon, they set out to meet Marie-Antoinette. First were the coaches of the King and his attendants, then a long cavalcade of *gardes du corps*, *gendarmes*, *chevaux-légers* and the band of the *mousquetaires* with their drums, trumpets, timbals and hautboys.

Marie-Antoinette tells the story of her reception in a letter written to her mother the next evening at La Muette. She had travelled from Soissons along the right bank of the river Aisne. At Berneuil, on the fringe of the forest some fourteen kilometres from Compiègne, she was met by the duc de Choiseul, who had been sent to be the first to greet her. 'I saw, with pleasure,' she wrote, 'a man who is highly thought of by my dear mother and I treated him as a family friend.' While they were talking, two outriders galloped up to announce the arrival of the royal family. 'I saw a huge *cortège* arriving,' she continued; 'it was the King who had the goodness to come and surprise me. As soon as I saw him I threw myself at his feet in great confusion. He took me in his arms, kissing me again and again, and calling me his dear daughter with a kindness by which my dear mama would have been deeply touched.' The report in the *Mercure de France* completes the picture: 'the Dauphin kissed her tenderly to the applause of a great gathering of people.' At half past five they were back at the Château.

The Château de Compiègne was, at that time, a building very different from that which can be seen today – a mixture of ancient and fairly modern. Of the old Château Louis XIV had said: 'I am lodged at Versailles like a king, at Fontainebleau like a prince and at Compiègne like a peasant.' A gouache by that accurate depicter of architecture van Blarenberghe shows the north and east ranges of the entrance court as they looked in 1770. It is a simple, two-storey building with a mansart roof pierced with many dormers. Only the pavilion overlooking the Place d'Armes before the Château – one of the twin pavilions which exist today – is in the style of Gabriel's 'Grand Projet', which was designed and approved in 1752 but still far from being realised.

In spite of its unfinished condition, Compiègne was one of the favourite residences of both King and Court. Louis XV, like nearly all that race of Nimrods, was first and foremost a mighty hunter. 'Compiègne', wrote Dufort de Cheverny, 'was a delightful place for the satisfaction of this passion, with its immense forest, its alleys stretching out *à perte de vue*, rides which one could follow all day long without coming to an end.'

The duc de Croÿ observed in his memoirs on 15 July 1762: 'This Château, compact and commodious, with that great corridor at the top by means of which one can reach any part under cover, is most agreeable. The view onto the forest from the terrace, and a sort of free air which one breathes here more than usual, makes this the place where the court seems to have its greatest charm. Royal family and ministers are both more ready to talk and more accessible.'

Compiègne was to become the favourite royal house of Louis XVI, but at the time of Marie-Antoinette's arrival all that we know is that the rooms which she was to have occupied could not be ready in time because the workmen had not been paid. Marie-Antoinette made no comment on the place; all her attention was given to the kindness of the King. The King, writing on the evening of her arrival to Ferdinand of Parma, returned the compliment. 'The Dauphine has been here since four o'clock. I am very content with her and so is my grandson; he will be more so in a few days time.'

On 4 May, Maria Theresa had written her first letter since the departure of her daughter. It was nearly all about her duty to the King: 'love him, be subject to him, try to devine his thoughts . . . follow my advice and attach yourself to him alone and await his orders and directions.' Then she added, with apparent embarrassment: 'On the subject of the Dauphin I have nothing to say.'

Marie-Antoinette knew very little about the rather awkward-aged adolescent to whom she was betrothed. She was left to find out for herself.

Louis-Auguste

On Easter eve, 1761, the duc de Bourgogne, eldest son of the Dauphin Louis-Ferdinand and Marie-Josèphe de Saxe, died at the age of ten. The attention of the courtiers was immediately focused upon the figure of the next eldest son, Louis-Auguste, duc de Berry, who was now heir apparent to the throne. They saw a boy, rather tall for six and a half, with a round face, a pale complexion, blue eyes like his grandfather's – known to the Sèvres Porcelaine factory as 'bleu oeil de roi' – and fair hair. Already he showed signs of being somewhat bashful and reserved. His father had been so concerned about this that he called in a Jesuit, the père de Neuville, saying: 'I know no one better than you at discerning the man in the child.' Neuville reported that although Louis-Auguste showed less signs of vivacity than his younger brothers, 'as to solidity of judgement and the qualities of the heart, he gave promise of being in no way their inferior'.

In order that he might be able to be a companion to his elder brother during his last illness, Louis-Auguste had been transferred from female to male tutelage – *le passage aux hommes* – at the age of six, a year earlier than was customary.

Under his first governess, the comtesse de Marsan, a member of the great Rohan family, Louis-Auguste had learnt to read and write fluently, had become familiar with the main stories of the Bible and of Greek mythology and had made a start on Geography and Zoology. Now, under the supervision of the duc de La Vauguyon, he was to begin his real education.

Antoine-Paul-Jacques de Quelen, comte de La Vauguyon,

had the good fortune to be appointed *menin* – a Spanish term 'meninos' meaning a young nobleman attached to a royal prince – to the Dauphin Louis-Ferdinand, and was with him at Fontenoy where he particularly distinguished himself. In April 1758 the Dauphin appointed him Governor to his eldest son, the duc de Bourgogne, and in January the following year he was elevated to the rank of duc et pair.

He selected a team of assistants: the marquis de Sinety, sous-Gouverneur; Monsieur de Coëtsloquet, Bishop of Limoges, Précepteur; the abbé de Radonvilliers, sous-Précepteur. To these were added the père Berthier, the abbé Proyart and Jacob-Nicolas Moreau. They were mostly chosen on account of their antipathy towards the Philosophes. After the death of the duc de Bourgogne the same team continued with the education of Louis-Auguste and his younger brothers, the comtes de Provence and d'Artois.

Louis-Auguste's contemporaries were almost unanimous in the opinion that his education had been utterly inadequate and that the duc de La Vauguyon was entirely to blame. The truth is not quite so simple. In the first place La Vauguyon was not a free agent. His methods were largely dictated by the Dauphin.

Louis-Auguste's father, during his lifetime, had taken an active role in the education of his sons, causing them to be examined in his presence twice a week. He even went so far as to propose a syllabus. 'The objective proposed by Monseigneur le Dauphin', wrote Moreau, 'was to attach all the lessons of Morality, Politics and Law, which he considered necessary to the education of the young Princes, to the history of France.'

In principle the idea may have been a good one. It was to look at the successes and failures recorded in history and then to determine where the responsibility lay. 'War broke out at a time when the greatest need was for peace,' summarised the abbé Proyart; 'what occasioned this? the ambition of the Prince? the private interest of the minister? The result of this war was disastrous: was that to be attributed to the low morale of the troops, to the inexperience of the general or to some Court intrigue?'

'History is nothing but a succession of great moral lessons,' continued Moreau; 'and it is there, amidst the heaps of ruins, that one finds written on every monument those maxims which are already so deeply implanted in your heart: "be just in order to be free: be just in order to be powerful: be just in order to be happy." '

In April 1763 La Vauguyon had produced a document entitled: 'Première conversation avec Monseigneur le duc de Berry . . . et plan des instructions que je me propose de lui donner.' It was a long sermon delivered to a boy of eight and a half years old. He quotes Bossuet – not the most successful of royal tutors – as stating that 'you could comprise all the duties of a king in these four words: Piety, Goodness, Justice and Firmness.'

Throughout the 'conversation' the duc de Bourgogne was held up to his successor as the paragon of all the virtues. 'You must bring to life again for us', Louis-Auguste was told, 'those virtues which shone so brightly in the person of the late duc de Bourgogne, and in the persons of so many illustrious kings whose blood flows in your veins.'

It may be significant that Louis' elder brother had been the favourite of his parents; his next youngest brother, the comte de Provence was to succeed to this position; Louis-Auguste was always in second place. It is perhaps hardly surprising that he was lacking in self-confidence.

Louis' younger brothers, the comte de Provence and the comte d'Artois, shared his lessons and their relationship posed another problem of rank. It is not easy to combine being royal with being human; it is not easy to combine being heir to the throne with being an elder brother.

The abbé de Véri records an occasion when he was walking in the gardens of Versailles and was approached by one of Louis' *sous-précepteurs*, who confided, 'I am absolutely furious because of what I have just seen. The three boys were going out for a walk. One of the younger ones forgot his hat and was going back to fetch it. The Dauphin, who was nearer to the door, said: 'you go on; I'll fetch it.' Monsieur de La Vauguyon noticed that he was carrying his brother's hat. He made him go back into his apartment, and I have just heard with my own ears the great sermon given to this child, that he should never forget his dignity or his pre-eminence over his brothers.'

On 20 December 1765, Louis-Ferdinand died and Louis-Auguste took the title of Dauphin. His mother desired above all that his curriculum should be maintained unchanged. She adopted the most extravagant form of mourning. She cut her hair off and renounced the use of make up, saying, 'my soul shall be as free from sin as my face will henceforth be free of rouge.' After the official period of mourning was over, she continued to dress as a widow and the black hangings and yellow candles were not removed from her rooms, in which, wrote Général Fontenay to Xavier de Saxe, Marie-Josèphe's brother, the principal ornament was the model for her husband's mausoleum in Sens Cathedral. She even gave up the clavichord in the belief that to play it was in some way lacking in loyality to her husband's memory. 'Anything new', wrote her sister Christine to Xavier, 'causes her the most frightful revulsion.'

Marie-Josèphe was German and had much of the serious-mindedness of her race. Her attitude to her children showed more concern for their religious and intellectual attainment than for the development of their personalities. The confirmation of Louis-Auguste at the end of December 1766 brought him more to his mother's notice. In a letter to the Bishop of Amiens, written shortly after the ceremony, she noted with satisfaction that 'he appears to be imbued with everything concerning religion and has a horror of vice.' She began to see herself as a second Reine Blanche guiding the footsteps of a second Saint-Louis. But her interest appeared to be not so much in Louis-Auguste as a person as in him as a future king. His only role was to be the reincarnation of his father. 'Piety should always flow in your veins,' she wrote to him, 'with the blood of your pious father. You must make him live again in you by imitating him.' She was determined to ensure that all her late husband's orders concerning their sons' education should be scrupulously observed. 'The plan that I shall follow', she wrote, 'is that which this most judicious Prince drew up in his precious collections; I will borrow from them even his very words: everything that comes from him must be sacrosanct to us.'

Louis-Ferdinand had been in most things the opposite of his father – religious to the point of bigotry and moralistic to the point of puritanism. He never hunted and seldom even went out of doors. 'I could not myself live without that [hunting],' wrote Louis XV to the Infant of Parma in June 1770, 'and I believe that the lack of it contributed not a little to the death of my son.'

Louis-Auguste was to become a devotee of the chase like his grandfather; in September 1770 the comte d'Argental, Minister from Parma, noted that 'he causes much disquiet by reason of his inability to moderate his excessive passion for the chase.'

Early in 1767 Marie-Josèphe contracted tuberculosis. On 28 February Boue de Martange wrote to Xavier: 'I felt I was talking to death itself so greatly did I find her disfigured.' On 13 March Louis-Auguste noted in his journal: 'Mort de ma mère à huit heures du soir.' It was only then that the duc de La Vauguyon became a free agent as Governor of the heir to the throne and his two brothers.

Girault de Coursac has made a detailed study of the education of the young duc de Berry which reveals a somewhat different picture from that which has been most commonly accepted. It shows that Louis-Auguste was by no means unintelligent and that his education, far from being neglected, was careful and painstaking.

The abbé Proyart, at the time *censeur* at the Collège Louis-le-Grand, describes a visit which he made to Coëtsloquet before the death of Louis XV.

> I remember precisely the circumstances and the date on which the Dauphin's tutor, the Bishop of Limoges [Coëtsloquet], said, to me *à propos* this Prince: 'Monsieur le Dauphin, by the soundness of his mind, the goodness of his heart, by his application to all his duties, gives promise of being a just king, the affectionate father of his people and their example of good living.'
>
> I took the liberty of observing to the Prelate that the most widely spread opinion was not favourable to this Prince, and credited him with very little aptitude for languages and the sciences.
>
> 'Oh! that is wrong,' exclaimed Monseigneur de Coëtsloquet, 'if it is not just malicious. It is true that Monsieur le comte de Provence would translate his Livy more fluently on opening his book; but Monsieur le Dauphin also understands his latin authors and he appreciates their beauties and perhaps he could quote more significant passages than the greater part of our young men who have distinguished themselves at your university.

Quintin Craufurd, a wealthy Scotsman who lived in Paris and was a close observer of the Court, made the comment: 'It was very generally believed that the education of Louis XVI had been neglected, but that was a mistake; he received, on the contrary, a very good instruction. But the education of princes does not consist only in the precepts of their teachers; it is composed above all of what they see in those who surround them, of the examples that they are offered in the bosom of their families and of the position in which they find themselves during their first years.'

Louis' education was clearly not neglected. It may, nevertheless, have been misguided. The undoubted aim of La Vauguyon's system was to prepare the young prince for his glorious destiny as king. But when Louis succeeded to the throne his first reaction was an acute sense of his own incompetence to fulfil the role, and he blamed most of this on his tutors – 'they have taught me nothing.'

That his education was conducted on fundamentally wrong lines is suggested by Pierre Griffet in his *Mémoires pour servir à l'histoire de Louis Dauphin*.

> Princes receive, if I may say so, an education which is remote from life; during all their childhood they only see their governors and preceptors who never leave them and are, perhaps, very content that they should not talk to anyone else in the hope of continuing to govern them after their education has finished. The members of their Household who surround them, and who have the same interests and the same claims, do not suffer any others to approach them; all are perfectly agreed on this point and they work together to make the prince inaccessible. Children brought up in this way naturally become unsociable . . . of necessity they dread any kind of serious or solid conversation and shyness becomes so deeply rooted in their souls that it is impossible to cure them. Private individuals, on the other hand, are, for the most part, educated in colleges where they talk to everyone.

Shyness was certainly a quality very frequently found in princes of the House of Bourbon.

Above all it was the policy of isolation, of which Griffet complained, which deprived the young princes of the chance of fruitful intercourse with their fellows. Even a person directly concerned with the syllabus for the young princes could be kept at arm's length. Jacob-Nicolas Moreau, who has left copious memoirs of his times, complained: 'I have noticed for some time that Monsieur de La Vauguyon was always afraid of my getting near the young princes.'

Pierre Griffet was ably seconded in his views by Moreau. In his *Entretiens sur la condition et sur l'éducation des princes*, written in 1765, Moreau boldly asserted: 'as long as princes are brought up as princes they will always be badly brought up; everyone agreed but they all asserted that it was not possible to bring them up otherwise.' In the first part of his *Entretiens* he looks at the causes of 'the shy and indecisive character of those princes who are brought up as princes', and he indicates the faults in the education which they receive: 'I consider that I have proved it to be inherently bad, not in that it is capable of creating bad characters, but rather that it tends to produce men of no character at all.'

Moreau produced, as requested, three or four papers on

French law every two weeks and he naturally assumed that these were passed on to his royal pupils. It was from Louis-Auguste himself that he learnt that none of them had reached their destination. 'I was so persuaded that the Dauphin read me and was getting through his studies of common law from my papers that I was very surprised and hurt to learn that Monsieur de La Vauguyon wanted to appoint the abbé de La Ville *lecteur* to this Prince and to put him in a position to work with him. It seemed to me that if anyone should have the honour to do this work it should have been the one who provided the material. I said this to Monsieur de La Vauguyon; he gave me a very bad reception and even sought to humiliate me. I was extremely vexed, but I was not jealous: the abbé de La Ville was highly suitable.' Moreau's real fault in the eyes of La Vauguyon was that he was under the protection of the Noailles family. Again and again Moreau's memoirs give us an insight into the pettiness and constant jostling for position which invaded even the schoolroom at Versailles.

The method of teaching employed by Louis' tutors was a sort of moralistic catechism in which the pupil repeated in his own words the propositions of his tutor. Thus the abbé Berthier would lay down: 'the French, by nature meek, lovers of order and of their master, become uneasy and begin to grumble when the reins of government are not held in a firm and confident hand; then they cry, they complain and they grumble increasingly; one would say that discontentedness and uneasiness had become part of their essential character.' To this the young Louis responded in the margin: 'the French are uneasy and grumblers, the reins of government are never held as they would wish; they cry, they complain, they grumble increasingly; one would say that complaining and grumbling had become a part of their essential character.'

On another occasion Berthier held up Louis' father to his admiration: 'Monseigneur le Dauphin avait pris pour modèle de pieté Saint-Louis, et dans le grand art de règner, Charles V, le plus sage de nos rois.' Louis-Auguste obediently commented in the margin: 'je me propose pour modèle la dévotion de Saint-Louis et de Charles V.'

That is not education, it is indoctrination. It has been said that indoctrination tells you what to think: education teaches you how to think. According to this definition Louis-Auguste was scarcely educated at all.

It was Louis' marriage which had put an end to his formal education. La Vauguyon continued as Governor of the comte de Provence and the comte d'Artois. It was at this moment that the abbé Placide Soldini wrote a long and rather avuncular letter to Louis. Soldini was chaplain to the residents of the Grand Commun. He had been confessor to Marie-Josèphe who had placed her children under his spiritual care. He was one of the people closest to Louis.

'You are still too young', he wrote, 'not to accord to a constitution, which is not sufficiently formed, the sleep which is necessary to it. Go to bed, Monseigneur, as early as you possibly can.' He also gave advice on the matter of gastronomy: 'all these refinements of taste, which have no other function than to reawaken the appetite, do appalling damage to one's health. Avoid them as far as possible.'

Soldini had here a willing pupil. Louis-Auguste, although blessed with a hearty appetite, had a delicate digestion. As Mercy wrote on 15 August 1774: 'he no longer feels the stomach upsets to which he was once subject, and which at the least intemperance in his diet caused him fairly frequent indigestion.' It appears that these moments of intemperance were sometimes caused by the young man's attendance at the King's *soupers de chasse.* In June 1771 the two entries occur in his journal: 'Mercredi 19: S [souper]. Jeudi 20: j'ai eu une indigestion.'

As to his entertainments, Soldini reminded the young Prince that the Church still regarded the stage essentially as a possible source of concupiscence. Louis was given grudging permission 'to tolerate theatrical shows', but was to hold all actors as 'infamous'. He quoted the advice of the abbé Fleury to the young Louis XV: 'that you should never expose yourself to the spectacle or other such amusement without having well prepared your soul against the danger which it might encounter.' Louis did not take much notice of this particular advice. While he was still Dauphin he had theatrical pieces performed in his apartment and in later years when his wife formed a private theatrical company, he was a willing spectator. Curiously enough Soldini could see no objection to gambling – 'one of the honest and innocent amusements of the Court provided that it is done in moderation.'

During the whole of Louis' education he was never allowed to forget his royal rank. He was not allowed to forget his royal rank even when doing arithmetic. A typical mathematical problem was set in words such as these: 'the combined ages of three princes on 10 February 1766, is 30 years and 11 days. The second is 1 year, 2 months and 24 days younger than the eldest, the third is 1 year 10 months and 22 days younger than the eldest. Find the age of each prince on the said 10 February.' Ordinary pupils wrestled with problems about *men*; the royal pupil was confronted with problems about *princes*.

The duc de La Vauguyon would remind him repeatedly of his rank: 'you will sit one day in glory on the first and mightiest throne in the world,' or 'France and the whole of Europe has its eyes fixed on you.' 'Your happy natural dispositions give us hope that you will acquit yourself one day of the debt and that you will be a great Saint and a great King . . . I flatter myself that you are already resolved upon this, that your heart is aflame and that your soul is leaping up in rapture, if I dare thus to express myself, towards a goal so great, so noble and so worthy of a grandson of Saint-Louis.' To one so deeply unsure of himself this could have been a terrifying prospect.

Much may be inferred about the value of Louis' education from his own attitude towards it expressed after his premature accession to the throne. Lord Stormont tells us that one of his most typical expressions when he first came to the throne was: 'l'Univers va tomber sur moi.' The comtesse de Boigne affirms that: 'in private, the King used to complain bitterly of the way in which he had been brought up. He said that the only man that he had ever hated was the duc de La Vauguyon.'

Girault de Coursac has tried to rehabilitate the character of La Vauguyon and to blame Mercy for deliberately destroying it. But the great majority of his contemporaries were against the duc. 'I have never seen', wrote the abbé de Véri, 'a unanimity more pronounced than the general satisfaction caused by the death of the duc de La Vauguyon, so greatly does vice under the mask of hypocrisy inspire aversion.' Véri, tactfully, does not specify the vices, but he reproaches the Dauphin for maintaining La Vauguyon in office as Governor of the princes once these vices were known to him.

La Vauguyon died at the beginning of 1772. The duc de Croÿ noted that the Dauphin 'appeared but little affected by the death of his governor whom, it is believed, he no longer loved and to whom he no longer listened since he was married'. Louis XV, however, was more appreciative. On 10 February he wrote to the Infant of Parma: 'We have lost here the duc de La Vauguyon who was governor of my grandchildren; it is a loss for them of which I fear they are unaware.'

Rather surprisingly, Moreau was almost the only other contemporary voice to speak in his favour. 'I certainly did not lose a protector,' wrote Moreau, 'even less a friend; I would however dare to maintain that his memory has been too much sullied. His tomb was covered with execrations and curses from the whole Court. I have heard it said by those who knew him that he was amiable and gay in his youth; I have never seen him anything other than sad, with something false about him, and unhappy. Is it the Court which deforms characters?'

Even the marquis de Bombelles, one of the great memorialists of the period, who was well disposed towards La Vauguyon and reluctant to be hard on one who had obliged him, had to admit 'the harm which he did in neglecting those hopeful seedlings. I like to think that his intentions were consistently good, but it is claimed that no princes, with the exception of the King of Naples have ever been so badly brought up.'

When Louis and Marie-Antoinette began, at last, to have children the new duc de La Vauguyon offered his services in place of his father as Governor. Louis turned down the application. 'I am sorry to have to refuse you,' he said; 'but, you know, you and I had the worst possible of upbringings.'

Mercy claims that Marie-Antoinette always disliked the duc de La Vauguyon and resented the way in which he had brought up her husband. On 15 June, 1770 – a month after the wedding – Mercy wrote to the Empress: 'Her Royal Highness told me that she was pleased with the Dauphin, that she attributed his timidity and his coldness to the kind of education which he had received, and that apart from this he seemed to have a good disposition, that she was quite convinced that he held to the duc de La Vauguyon from fear, but in no way from confidence or affection.'

Another anecdote from Véri's *Journal* draws attention to Louis' fear of his seniors. Maurepas was gently chiding him for not taking up the abbé de Terray on a particular point. Louis' answer came straight from the heart. 'You are right, but I did not dare. It is only four months since I was still accustomed to feel afraid when I was speaking to a minister.'

The picture of Louis-Auguste which begins to emerge is of a young man of considerable intelligence, capable of sustained intellectual effort, deeply religious and of great personal probity, with a high sense of the duties of his position and the best possible of intentions. But there was one fatal flaw. In his pious determination to make Louis-Auguste a saint and a king, his Governor may well have overlooked the more fundamental need to make him a man. Earnest exhortation does not necessarily achieve its end. 'Learn then, Monseigneur,' wrote the père Berthier in his nineteenth *Entretien*, 'to understand men, and do not be content with judging by their external appearance!' It was not, however, made clear how such understanding was to be gained. The whole policy of isolation, complained of by Griffet, militated against it; the young Prince was never in a position to have experience of men. It was to be held up to gentle ridicule in 1762 by Michel Sedaine in his play *Le Roi et le Fermier.* A king, lost while hunting, is treated by a farmer, who is unaware of his identity, to a witty satire on the Court.

> "Who could have taught you so much?" asks the King.
> "In faith, I've got around a bit," says the farmer. "I have seen what it is not always in the power of a king to see."
> "What's that?"
> "Men."

Louis' father had made the same point in a conversation with the abbé Marbeuf. 'I consider you lucky,' said the abbé: 'you see a lot of men.' 'You are wrong,' replied the Dauphin; 'those who are men in your eyes are nothing more to us than figures in a tapestry.'

Malesherbes was later to recall a conversation in which Louis expanded on the subject of his education. '"I felt", he told me, "at the conclusion of my education, that I was still far from having completed it. I formed the plan of acquiring that instruction which I lacked. I wished to know the English, Italian and Spanish languages; I learnt them on my own. I brought myself to a good enough standard in Latin literature to be able to translate with ease the most difficult authors. Then, burying myself in the history of France, I strove to shed some light on the points which were obscure. I meditated on the legislation and the customs of the kingdom; I compared the course of different reigns and I analysed the causes of their prosperity or otherwise." This admission', concluded Malesherbes, 'gave me a very high opinion of his character and capacity.'

The comte de Saint-Priest who, as Ministre de la Maison du Roi had worked closely with Louis and had, no less than Malesherbes, every opportunity to assess the character of the King, sums up the argument. Louis, he said, 'was very well read in literature, the master of several languages, was knowledgeable on the subject of astronomy and above all geography and navigation, but these were of little use to him as ruler.' Saint-Priest agrees with almost all his contemporaries on the real point of weakness: 'the understanding of men, the primary skill required of kings, was unknown to him.'

This seems to be the one most important respect in which Louis' upbringing and education failed him: he always found difficulty in relating to people in general and to women in particular. In 1771, George III received a report from Mr Ainslie, a member of Lord Stormont's staff, on the Dauphin: 'The King, in speaking about a month ago in Madame du Barry's apartment, said: "the Dauphin is well made and perfectly well formed, yet had hitherto shown no desire for women, nay rather seems to loathe them."' It was not, perhaps, the most auspicious attribute in a young man about to be married.

The Wedding

On Tuesday, 15 May 1770, Marie-Antoinette left Compiègne for La Muette, a small *château* on the edge of the Bois de Boulogne belonging to the King. On the way they stopped at the Carmelite convent at Saint-Denis to meet the Venerable Madame Louise, one of Louis XV's daughters who had taken the veil.

The occasion was described by one of the nuns in a letter to the Mother Superior of the Carmelite house in the rue Saint-Jacques. It is one of the earliest descriptions of Marie-Antoinette seen through French eyes and from a source which was unlikely to be prejudiced. 'His Majesty arrived on the 15th at six in the evening. He requested that the nuns should be summoned, saying: "I want to show them Madame la Dauphine." She is, my dear Mother, the most perfect princess as to her face, her figure and her appearance, and, which is far more precious, she is said to be of the most delightful piety. Her countenance has an air at once of grandeur, modesty and sweetness. The King, Mesdames and above all the Dauphin appeared enchanted by her. They vie with one another to say how incomparable she is.'

At La Muette, Marie-Antoinette was given a magnificent parure of diamonds by the King. 'She eagerly took up a bracelet with a portrait of the King and put it on in place of her own with an infinite grace and sensibility,' wrote the marquise de Durfort to Mercy; 'she loses no occasion of seeking to please him.' In the same letter, dated 'à deux heures après minuit', she continued: 'I cannot wait to tell you of all the successes of our charming Dauphine; the whole royal family dote upon her; the King is enchanted by her and he did me the honour of saying to me that he found her better than her portraits; Monseigneur le Dauphin finds her charming.'

The wedding festivities of Louis and Marie-Antoinette are described by that prince of memorialists the duc de Croÿ, an indefatigable sight-seer with an observant eye, quick to detect the significant, and with a rare gift of describing a scene so that it comes to life before the reader's eye. Another account of the festivities comes from the pen of Papillon de la Ferté, who, as Intendant des Menus Plaisirs, was responsible for all the arrangements. It was a task which reduced him to the last stages of exhaustion. He got up every day at five in the morning, but found the days still too short for all that he had to do. Before the festivities had even started, he wrote, 'I began to feel acutely fatigued which necessitated my taking a bath every day.'

Wednesday 16 May was to be the great day. On the 15 Croÿ made his way to Versailles 'par un beau jour de cette fraiche verdure de mai'. The 16 dawned serene and beautiful – 'un temps superbe' – and he got up early to inspect the scene. The gardens were decorated with a series of trellis arches, each in the form of a Venetian window with fairy lamps in readiness for the nocturnal illumination, which ran right round the canal. In order to get the best view of the whole he mounted by way of the Petits Cabinets onto the roof of the palace – 'I believe that nothing in the world has ever equalled the beauty of that sight: it is from there that one ought to see Versailles.' At eleven o' clock he went to the King's rooms. The Cabinet du Conseil was nearly full: 'nothing could have exceeded the magnificence of the costumes.'

At about half past ten, Marie-Antoinette had arrived at Versailles. It was typical of the state of affairs in France that the Queen's Bedroom was not ready for her. The ceiling was in danger of collapsing.

This ceiling, like all others of the State Apartments, was coved and heavily ornate, with paintings by Boucher set in the richly gilded stucco surrounds. The Queen's Bedroom had been the first of the royal apartments to be redecorated in the style of Louis XV, and it remains one of the finest. Lécuyer estimated the sum of 50 000 livres for the reinstatement of the ceiling. The alternative idea was suggested of a flat, white ceiling centering upon a rose, 'qui couterait beaucoup moins et sera plus tôt fait'. Marie-Antoinette, impatient to occupy the room, favoured this solution. The comtesse de Noailles, impatient to restore the ancient rituals prescribed by etiquette, was also in favour. But Gabriel objected. His sense of artistic integrity forbade. The flat, white ceiling, in this noble suite of rooms, he explained to Marigny, 'would have looked horribly out of harmony'. He was well aware of the shortage of funds, from which he was the first to suffer, but he insisted. 'I could never propose, on any consideration, that one should do something badly which could be done well . . . I beseech you, Sir, to re-establish the ceiling as it was.'

It was, of course the King's decision. Gabriel obtained permission to redesign the ceiling on the former lines and incorporated in the angles of the cove the two-headed eagle of Austria – a symbol of the New Alliance of which Marie-Antoinette was the living pledge.

Since it had not been possible to complete the work on her bedroom, she was taken straight to rooms on the ground floor beneath the Queen's apartment to put on her wedding dress. There she found the *corbeil* – the traditional wedding present from the King.

Early in 1769 the duc d'Aumont, Premier Gentilhomme de la Chambre, had placed an order for a jewellery coffer – 'the most magnificent that has ever been made of its kind'. Its design was entrusted to François-Joseph Belanger, a versatile young architect who could turn his hand to stage scenery, to the lay-out of an 'English' garden or the designing of furniture, of which this cabinet was his first recorded work at Versailles. It was six feet long and three and a half feet high with a gilt bronze framework. Its three panels were covered in red velvet embroidered in gold and the large crown which surmounted it was likewise lined with crimson silk and studded with pearls and precious stones. Each of the drawers was lined with sky-blue silk and contained a cushion covered in the same, on which were laid the jewels which constituted the *corbeil*. For Marie-Antoinette herself there was a parure of diamonds centering upon a watch of blue enamel. In the other drawers were watches, snuff boxes and other small but costly gifts, already ticketed by Papillon de la Ferté, for her to offer to her suite.

The designing of the casket was not the only contribution to the festivities made by Belanger. His various activities reveal the minute care which was taken to ensure the success of the whole entertainment. He designed the invitation tickets; he designed the trellis decoration for the illumination of the gardens and canal; he produced sixteen colour wash drawings, small but very detailed from which the principal firework effects could be judged.

At one o'clock the Dauphine was conducted to the Cabinet du Conseil, where the royal family awaited her. The Dauphin offered her his hand, she saluted him and kissed the King's hand 'de très bonne grace et avec l'air d'aisance'. The procession then set off by way of the Galerie des Glaces and down the long string of linked rooms of the Grand Appartment, lined on both sides by some five thousand ladies of Paris in their most gorgeous finery, across the Salon d'Hercule and into the Chapel.

The Chapel at Versailles was the last important addition to be completed under Louis XIV and by far the most beautiful. The pure, pale, cream-coloured stone and the light flooding in from the tall windows between the fluted shafts of the Corinthian colonnade provide a refreshing contrast to all the rich colouring and lavish gilding of the Grand Appartement. Gilding is conspicuous by its absence in the lower parts of the Chapel and is used to focus attention on the altar and to conduct the eye thence, by way of the organ case, to the brilliant profusion of Coypel's painted ceiling, designed 'to bring all Paradise before your eye'.

Thus was the glory of God and the God-like status of the King at once expressed. In Gallican theology the King was the Lord's lieutenant in the land. The Chapel provided a worthy setting for the stately ceremonials of the Order of the Saint-Esprit and for such important functions as a royal wedding.

An observer, the Duchess of Northumberland, has left her comments on the scene: 'I was admirably placed for seeing the ceremony,' she wrote. She was also admirably placed to scrutinise the spectators and their clothes. 'I dare say the cheapest of their Gowns did not cost less than seven Guineas a yard.'

The royal family arrived shortly after one o'clock. 'The Dauphin disappointed me much,' wrote the Duchess; 'I expected to have found him horrid, but on the contrary, his figure pleased me very well. He is tall and slender with a Countenance *très interessant* & a look of good Sense. His complexion is rather pale & his Eyes are large. He has a great quantity of fair Hair which grows very well to his Face & his figure appeared very genteel, but I am told he is not so well in his own Clothes.' (He was wearing the costume, but not the robes, of the Order of the Saint-Esprit.)

'The Dauphine was very fine in Diamonds. She is very little and slender. I should not have taken her to be above twelve Years Old [she was fourteen and a half] . . . She really had quite a Load of Jewels. The Dauphin appear'd to have much more Timidity than his little Wife. He trembled excessively during the service & blush'd up to his Eyes when he gave the Ring. When Mass begun they presented him with a Book; he look'd quite relieved to have an Excuse for not looking about him.'

The duc de Croÿ was more impressed by the massed finery of the costumes and jewellery of the ladies of the Court, standing tier upon tier in the tribunes – 'so that all that one saw was a solid amphitheatre of fine clothes. Above all the sunlight brought out their brilliance.'

He was to revise his opinion on this when he saw the same

costume later that evening in the Grande Galerie in the flattering light of the candles. 'Everything had been lit up and the dresses showed up with a greater lustre by their light. It is astonishing how it shows them up and brings out all the gold and silver just as daylight tones them down.'

During the wedding, Papillon de la Ferté had to clear all the spectators out of the Grand Appartement and set gaming tables – lansquenet for the King, cavagnole and other games for the courtiers. A balustrade had to be erected to insulate the players from the 6000 spectators who were allowed to file past. The operation was made more difficult by the torrential rain which drove into the Château the hordes of onlookers who were gathered in the park for the firework display. 'This manoeuvre caused no hold up,' wrote Papillon, 'but caused me very great fatigue.' The firework display had to be postponed for three days. Finally, at ten o' clock they all proceeded to the new Salle des Spectacles for the banquet.

This Salle des Spectacles, or Opéra, was the last and loveliest of Louis XV's additions to Versailles. Before its creation it had been the custom to rig up a temporary ballroom in the Riding School of the Grande Écurie. But in 1767 the prospect of the marriages of Louis' four grand-children was already beginning to loom over the horizon and to disquieten the royal exchequer. To improvise four successive entertainment rooms and to have nothing to show for it in the end seemed uneconomical, and Papillon de la Ferté addressed a memorandum to the King urging the completion of the 'theatre of the reservoirs'. This was at the extremity of the north wing of the palace. It had been planned by Louis XIV but never built.

In March 1768, the King ordered a model from the Sieur Arnoult and promised to see about providing funds. This was certain to be the greatest difficulty, and Gabriel advised the selection of Parisian workshops, the contractors at Versailles being at that time 'weighed down by the misery and debts which they had incurred in the service of the King'.

It was no time to be indulging in costly new constructions.

On 28 December 1769, only four months before the wedding, Marigny wrote in despair to the King: 'all the contractors are deeply disheartened. I cannot conceal from your Majesty that the contractor for masonry on the Salle des Spectacles has withdrawn 200 of his workmen . . . the contractor for the panelling in the apartment of the Dauphin and Dauphine has announced that he will only begin the work when he has received his money.' But, as the duc de Croÿ observed, the more France seemed to be in decline, the greater the need to keep up appearances. The preparations for the *fête* went ahead without regard to cost. 'Vous m'avez donné carte blanche pour la Salle,' wrote Gabriel to Marigny, 'et vous avez été content.' If he had been subject to financial constraint, he added, he could not have achieved the same success.

It was even decided that the extravagance was in reality an economy and a good investment; an economy because it would put an end to the recurrent expense of temporary constructions, a good investment because 'in attracting foreigners to France by the *fêtes* and by causing the arts to flourish, it would be useful to commerce and would put new life into French manufactures'.

The new opera house was not, however, an extravagantly conceived design. For reasons of acoustics, the architecture is almost entirely of wood painted to resemble a marble known as Serancolin. The colour scheme is one of the most successful at Versailles. The marbling is achieved in a warm salmon pink against a dull grey-green known as 'vert-vert', both of an infinitely subtle variety of tone, and enriched with gilding. Contrasting with this is the cold, bright cobalt of the silken hangings and the more sombre blue of the patterned velvet upholstery.

The auditorium, in the shape of a truncated ellipse, is encircled by a colonnade which breaks into a graceful apse above the royal box. Each bay of the colonnade is backed by a mirror, and each mirror reflects – and thus completes – a half chandelier which hangs against its surface. The rest of the house is lit by fourteen great chandeliers suspended on blue silk cords. They are each of them five feet high and each contains ninety-six crystal pendants. These chandeliers, the duc de Croÿ recorded, were left illuminated throughout the performance, thus 'lighting up from below a superb ceiling, they produced the most admirable effect.'

Painted by du Rameau, and representing 'Apollo preparing crowns for those illustrious in the arts', the ceiling reflects the dominant colour scheme of pink and blue, which is continued in the smaller ceilings above each bay of the colonnade. By Gabriel's express instructions, du Rameau was charged 'to decide on all the tones and mixtures of colour that need to be observed in order to create an all-embracing harmony'.

The stage was fully equipped with the elaborate machinery required for theatrical productions in those days, but it could also be made to join up with the auditorium and thereby form a single unit. The scene could be set to reflect the amphitheatre, the floor of the pit jacked up level with the stage and the whole opera house transformed into one immense banqueting house or ballroom. These transformations required a task force of 300 soldiers who were encamped in the park. The soldiers also changed the scenery and acted as walkers-on for the operas.

'I saw this room', writes the author of a *Description of Versailles in 1837*, 'lit with a hundred thousand candles [the actual figure is just over 3000]; the mirrors, the chandeliers, the beautiful paintings and the gilding produced a wonderful effect.' This effect is skilfully captured in the watercolours of Moreau le Jeune. They show the table, set for twenty-two, in the centre of the Salle and the courtiers, crowded into the auditorium, as if they were spectators at a play.

The Duchess of Northumberland was there and the King had offered her one of his boxes. 'After this I need not say I had the best place in the Salle. I cannot pretend to describe the superb Building which, by an entire change of the Decorations is equally a Salle du Festin, a Théâtre and a Salle de Bal. I do apprehend that since the time of the Romans nothing of this kind has appear'd equal in Beauty, Size & Magnificence to this Salle . . . It has cost 200 000 Sterling; the Architect's name is Gabriel. I saw him there in Scarlet Velvet embroidered with Gold exulting (as well he might) at his own Success.'

The opera chosen for the occasion was *Perseus* by Quinault and Lully. It was a bad choice and in spite of the music being 'renforcée' and the scenes cut to make room for interludes of ballet, its failure could be inferred from 'the general expression of boredom on every face'. Papillon de la Ferté noted that 'Madame la Dauphine did not appear to fancy it. It is true that it is a very serious opera for someone who does not yet know the piece and who does not like music.' It might have been more true to say that Marie-Antoinette was bored by *Perseus* because she did like music. As Madame Vigée-Lebrun admitted: 'la musique de ce temps-là m'ennuyait horriblement.'

The Duchess of Northumberland fills in some of the details: 'the Music and the Singing were detestable. Mademoiselle d'Arnoult is a good Actress & a pretty Figure & her voice, if she did not scream so, would be very well. The Dancing is in great perfection, Mademoiselle Lany . . . fair surpassed the rest of the females, as Vestris did those of his sex.' Vestris was in some respects the Nijinsky of his age. It is recorded of him that he touched the ground 'solely out of consideration for his comrades, and not like Antaeus, to gather new strength for himself'. Madame Vigée-Lebrun gives a vivid description: 'tout à coup il s'élevait au ciel d'une manière si prodigieuse qu'on lui croyait des aisles.'

The soldiers had worked all night to transform the Salle du Festin back into an opera house. It went far better than Papillon de la Ferté had dared to hope, 'after such hurried preparations and with all the machines whose movement was so little known to the workmen'. As soon as the Court had left they all started dismantling the theatre and reinstating it as a ballroom. 'The next day was a day of rest for the Court,' sighed Papillon, 'but utterly exhausting for all of us.'

The firework display and illumination of the park, on Saturday 19, was the most magnificent ever seen at Versailles. Once again, the sketch by Moreau le Jeune provides a brilliant evocation of the scene; starting from the extremity of the canal, where the Temple du Soleil fixed the view, the lights ran round the entire perimeter, while gondolas, also brightly illuminated, provided an element of movement to the scene. There were some 200 000 people admitted that night to this unforgettable spectacle. In 1806, when the English traveller Nattes visited Versailles, his guide still remembered that wonderful evening: 'This immense park, illuminated through all its extent, was far more brilliant than when lighted by the sun in all his splendour. The waters in their varied falls reflected in a thousand ways the effects of the illumination; some, falling from a great height, seemed to shed torrents of light, while others, elevating their stream high into the air, appeared to descend in a shower of fire.' It was impossible for him to do justice to the scene; there were so many things which 'at the same moment dazzled the eye and astonished the mind'. In vain did he string together the details which he had noticed – 'all that you read of Fairyland would give but an imperfect idea of the reality.'

The Court saw the fireworks from the windows of the Grande Galerie; the King gave the signal for the display to begin by hurling a flaming lance from the central window. 'It was concluded', wrote Nattes, 'by a *giranda* of 20 000 rockets, which, by its prodigious detonations and the immense blaze of light, produced the effect of the terrific eruption of a volcano.' In spite of the huge crowd, no accidents occurred and everyone stayed as long as possible. Not so Papillon de la Ferté – 'pour moi, excédé de fatigue, je me suis retiré à deux heures.'

It is easy to forget that in the middle of all this extravagant entertainment a very young man and a very young woman had been joined together in Holy Matrimony. On the surface, the festivities of that week were a demonstration of the joy and enthusiasm with which France received its future Queen.

Beneath that surface, from the very start, the duc de Choiseul and the duc de La Vauguyon were engaged in an intrigue to get control of the young Dauphine in order to use her for their own ends. Choiseul was determined to retain his post and with it the Austrian alliance; La Vauguyon was equally determined to retain his influence over Louis-Auguste. Choiseul, together with the Bishop of Orléans, the comtesse de Noailles and the comte de Mercy, needed at all costs to maintain the abbé de Vermond in the position which he had occupied at Schönbrunn. The Prince von Starhemberg is our chief informant.

'As soon as we had arrived at Versailles,' he wrote, 'I advised the abbé to take possession of and to begin to exercise his function of *lecteur* to Madame la Dauphine which had just been conferred upon him by the King with 6000 livres of stipend and the promise of the first abbey to become vacant with a revenue of 12 000 livres, on the condition that he was to continue to instruct the Princess in the same way that he did in Vienna. As this arrangement had been proposed and obtained for him by the duc de Choiseul and the Bishop of Orléans without anyone knowing, I could easily foresee that he [the abbé] might suffer certain difficulties in its execution.'

Not only did Choiseul and his party need to maintain Vermond as the Dauphine's *lecteur*, they were determined that he should keep his appointment as her confessor. This was, of course, the key position. The confessor had access to the confidences of his penitent which gave him considerable power. It was therefore just as important for La Vauguyon, if he was to continue to wield his influence over the Dauphin, that the position of confessor should go to someone of his party. He could count on the support of the Archbishop of Paris, Christophe de Beaumont. Christophe de Beaumont, unlike some of his fellow bishops, was a man of great piety and integrity and he was closely linked with the Dauphin's confessor, the abbé Soldini.

Since the King was still officially supporting his minister Choiseul, the opposition was obliged to work on the

Dauphin himself. 'It did not take us long to realise', wrote Starhemberg, 'that Monseigneur le Dauphin had been prejudiced against him [Vermond] for on the third day [after the wedding], the Prince having come to the Dauphine's room when the abbé was there, but this latter having felt obliged to leave the room, Madame la Dauphine introduced him by name to Monseigneur le Dauphin, at which the abbé made a movement towards the door, but the Dauphin, without as much as looking at him and seeming not to have listened, shut the door in his face and left him outside.'

On another occasion, continues Starhemberg, La Vauguyon took it upon himself to lecture the abbé. He declared that his titles were merely honorific and that it was not in accordance with custom that he should go alone to the Princess' room and that as to his remaining her confessor, that position was of too great importance to be entrusted to one as inexperienced as himself. It was not for La Vauguyon to say so, but he was right. Vermond – and this says a lot about the eighteenth century clergy in France – was not competent to be a confessor. He did not really believe in the practice. On 21 January 1769, he had written to Mercy from Vienna: 'for the time that I am here I have yielded in my reluctance about confession to the views of H.M. the Empress. I can assure Your Excellency that my aversion of this function has been much diminished by the goodness and particular confidence which Her Royal Highness has shown to me. I began hearing her confession for the celebration of Christmas.' If Choiseul and Mercy were keen that Vermond should remain confessor to Marie-Antoinette it was not for purely religious reasons.

The post of confessor was given, in the end, to the abbé Maudoux. 'The choice of this confessor', wrote Mercy on 14 July, 'was of the greatest consequence and has ruled out several dangerous people whom it was proposed to establish with the Dauphine.' Louis had wanted his wife to have his own confessor, the abbé Soldini.

Of the intensity of the struggle to maintain Vermond as

lecteur Starhemberg leaves no doubt. 'Once the abbé had told me of all this,' he wrote, 'I deemed it necessary to take up my position, it being of the greatest importance to maintain this man with Madame la Dauphine, so that she should have someone confidential close to her person who could give every day, and so to speak every minute, such advice as, by all appearances, she will be in great need of, and in order that the duc de Choiseul and the comte de Mercy may be informed by him of everything that happens and can act in concert with us to use all the means necessary to sustain this Princess in the different attacks and persecutions to which, judging by all appearances, it is their purpose to subject her.'

In the same letter Starhemberg recounts how Choiseul had spoken to Louise XV 'avec la plus grande force et énergie' on the disastrous interventions of La Vauguyon. The King had listened attentively but made no reply. He spent the rest of the day, however, in a bad temper which was mostly with the Dauphin. 'Having gone during the afternoon to Madame la Dauphine's, where he did not find him, he sent for him and asked where he had come from and what he had been doing, to which the Dauphin having replied that he had been in his rooms, the King said to him curtly: "You would have done better to have been here."'

The roles of diplomat and spy were fairly easily reconciled and Mercy claimed to have built up a system of informants which provided him with the most intimate details of the Dauphine's life. 'I have made sure of three persons in the service of the Archduchess,' he reported on 16 November 1770; 'one of her women and two of her menservants, who give me full reports of what goes on. Then, from day to day, I am told of the conversations which she has with the abbé de Vermond, from whom she hides nothing. Beside this the marquise de Durfort passes on to me everything she says to her aunts.'

It was with her aunts, that is to say Louis' aunts – Mesdames – that Marie-Antoinette most naturally consorted. Mesdames were rigidly opposed to Madame du Barry on family and religious grounds. To begin with Maria Theresa approved of them. 'These princesses', she wrote in May 1770, 'are deeply virtuous and talented: that is fortunate for you; I hope that you merit their friendship.' A year later she was revising her opinion. In July 1771 she wrote: 'up till now you have been accused of being directed by Mesdames . . . and you should know that these princesses, full of real virtues and merits, have never succeeded in gaining the affection or esteem of either their father or of the public.'

Another person caught up in the intrigues was Moreau, for whom the comtesse de Noailles had procured the post of librarian to the Dauphine. He was given a frigid reception by Marie-Antoinette and Vermond, who wrongly supposed him to be a supporter of La Vauguyon.

'From the day after the marriage,' he writes, 'Monsieur le duc de La Vauguyon had tried by every imaginable means to bring about the dismissal of the abbé de Vermond. He never said a word to me about the project; I only knew of it from Madame la comtesse de Noailles. Madame la Dauphine was, and with good reason, offended and irritated by a manoeuvre so lacking in respect towards her and which had the intention of removing from her the only man with whom she could talk freely. I could never understand the ineptitude of the duc de La Vauguyon in this business. As to his motives, they were clear enough, but his intrigue failed and Madame la Dauphine never forgave him his dishonest procedures.'

In spite of being caught up immediately in the intrigues of the Court, Marie-Antoinette made a very good first impression. Starhemberg, in a letter to Maria Theresa dated 27 May 1770, emphasises her success with Louis XV. 'Her conduct towards the King surpasses all that I could have hoped for; she does neither too much nor too little, and she sets about it so well that there can be little doubt that, continuing the same, she will gain his entire affection and may perhaps arrive in the end at making herself the mistress of his will.'

There may have been an ominous significance in those last

words; Mercy and Starhemberg were hoping to be able to influence the King, and later his successor, through the person of Marie-Antoinette – and doubtless that influence would be used in the interests of Austria. Naturally the success of such a policy would depend on the quality of the relationship which the Dauphine could establish in the first place with Louis XV and in the longer run with her husband. But first and foremost, the influence of La Vauguyon must be destroyed and the position of Vermond firmly established.

For a bride and bridegroom as young as Marie-Antoinette, who was only fourteen and Louis-Auguste, who was sixteen, their married life could hardly have had a less auspicious start. But royal marriages were not concerned with the personal happiness of either party. They were concerned with the business of providing an heir to the throne.

Louis and Marie-Antoinette had little chance of establishing a relationship. They had neither of them had any say in their choice of partner; they had only met three days before their marriage and then only in accordance with the forms prescribed by protocol. They must have been physically exhausted. Marie-Antoinette managed to carry it off on every occasion and to charm and impress all who saw her. Not so the Dauphin: the Duchess of Northumberland recorded that after the wedding ceremony in the chapel 'the Dauphin as he passed looked quite fatigued, he seems very delicate and to have the appearance of a Boy who had outgrown his strength.' And yet the young couple were expected to consummate their marriage that night.

The Marriage

'I have not been surprised, after what the King himself said to me,' wrote Starhemberg on the attitude of the Dauphin to his young wife, 'that on the day of the marriage and the day after it, he had appeared to pay no very marked attention to her and that the two nights had passed without anything interesting happening. It is natural enough not to attribute the cause of this coldness to anything but embarrassment, shyness, and to a sort of imbecility which the whole appearance of this Prince suggests.'

In trying to assess the position from the point of view of Marie-Antoinette, Starhemberg sounded out the abbé de Vermond. 'She admitted to the abbé on the 20th of this month [that is to say four days after the wedding] that since the occasion of their meeting in the Forêt de Compiègne, Monsieur le Dauphin had not only not kissed her, but he had not even touched her hand. In spite of that she does not attribute this reserve to any indifference that he might have to her, and she even said to the abbé and to myself that she believes him to love her and that, for her part, she is disposed to love him, but that she would try and win his confidence, little by little, and she hoped to succeed in this.'

On 4 June, Louis XV, writing to the Infant of Parma, admitted freely: 'all is not yet completely accomplished; but that will come, I hope, soon. My grandson is not very given to caressing.' A week later, however, the King was a little more expansive, 'My grandson gets on very well with his wife, but not yet, I believe, as I would wish him to, for I have not yet spoken to him as there is no hurry.'

On 9 June Mercy remarked on an improvement in the relationship, claiming that the Dauphin had told Madame Adelaïde that he found his wife very amiable, that her face and her turn of mind pleased him and that he was very contented.

On 19 July the King invited La Martinière, his First Surgeon, to examine his grandson and to tell him if there were any physical obstacles to the consummation of his marriage. La Martinière gave the King his assurance that there were none. Mercy could report to the Empress that 'this Prince has no natural defect which would prevent the consummation of his marriage.'

On 23 July the King, writing from Compiègne to the Infant, refers to an indisposition from which the Dauphin had recently suffered: 'but thank God he is all right; he was purged yesterday, and he is simply longing for the day when he comes here together with his wife . . . he promises us that all will be achieved here; my desire for this is greater than my hope.'

It was a subject of intimate concern also between Maria Theresa and her daughter. On the 8 May 1771 – almost a year after their wedding – the Empress wrote: 'I cannot repeat often enough: no petulance about it; caresses, cajolings – but too much eagerness could spoil everything: tenderness and patience are the only means which you ought to use. Nothing has been lost; you are both of you so young . . . but it is natural for us aged parents to desire the fulfilment, being unable to flatter ourselves on having grandchildren.'

A month later she wrote from Laxenburg: 'do not be discouraged, keep up your charming gaiety more than ever and trust in God: all will be well.'

In August she returned to the theme. By now Marie-Antoinette's problem was shared by her new sister-in-law, the comtesse de Provence. That marriage also was so far unconsummated. 'The only thing which impedes our wishes', wrote Maria Theresa, 'is the extreme youth of these princes and a bit of shyness which is common to all those who have been brought up in innocence; it is disagreeable, but it bodes well for the future: once this charm is broken, all will go solidly well.'

It was a difficult situation for Marie-Antoinette and it was not made easier by the gossip – not always malicious – of Versailles. Earlier in 1771, on 27 March, Madame du Deffand had written to Horace Walpole: 'I nearly forgot to give you the most interesting news of all; it is that the Dauphine has been really Dauphine for the last four or five days. It is said that she could have been much earlier but that the Dauphin, in spite of his attachment to her, of which there can be no doubt . . . did not wish to become a husband. It needed the order of his confessor, and this order has had all the success that could be desired.' Moreau records the same event in a footnote to his journal for that day: 'Monseigneur le Dauphin has at last slept with Madame la Dauphine and, indeed, several times.' He also mentions the confessor. It would, of course, have been most improper for a confessor to have made any such revelation. Mercy, perhaps better informed, wrote on 16 April that since 22 March Louis had regularly passed the nights in his wife's room. He did not believe that anything had resulted from this: 'there is, however, a section of the public which believes the marriage to have been consummated.'

In September 1771 we have Marie-Antoinette's first reference to the subject: 'As for me, I live in hopes, and the tenderness which the Dauphin shows me more and more each day does not allow for any doubt, but I do wish it could all come to an end.'

In all her correspondence she seldom betrays any signs of impatience. The dominant note is that of hope. In December her sister Marie-Caroline, the Queen of Naples, became pregnant. There are no signs of envy, just a reaffirmation that the Dauphin 'is more loveable every day, all that my happiness needs is to be in the same condition as the Queen, and I do not believe there is any sense in the rumours which are being spread in this place about his impotence.'

One of the most painful occasions for Marie-Antoinette was on 6 August 1775, when the comtesse d'Artois gave birth to a son – the duc d'Angoulême – who was, of course, heir presumptive to the throne. Etiquette obliged the Dauphine to be present at the birth. When the comtesse was told that she had been delivered of a son she exclaimed: 'mon Dieu que je suis heureuse!' Those words must have pierced Marie-Antoinette to the heart, but Madame Campan insists that 'she showed every possible mark of tenderness to the young mother and would not leave her rooms until she had been put back in her bed.'

On her way back to her own apartments she had to endure the reproaches of the *poissardes* – the fishwives of Paris – who followed her all the way, telling her, 'avec les expressions les plus licencieuses' that it was her business, and not that of the comtesse d'Artois, to produce heirs to the throne.

'The Queen arrived at her apartment', wrote Madame Campan, 'in a high state of emotion, walking faster and faster; she shut herself in alone with myself to cry – not from jealousy of the happiness of her sister-in-law – of that she was incapable – but from the sheer agony of her position.'

During the next year the subject is more or less dropped, but in March 1773 Marie-Antoinette sent some important information to her mother. 'The King said to Lassone, my doctor, that he believed there was some awkwardness and ignorance between the Dauphin and myself . . . in the end he ordered him [Lassone] to give instruction to both of us. The Dauphin came into my cabinet, so that we should not be noticed in his rooms; he spoke without embarrassment and with much good sense. Lassone is quite contented and full of hope.'

A month later – in April 1773 – Marie-Antoinette again returns to the subject. 'The Dauphin has reacted very well to Lassone on the many occasions on which he has spoken with him. There is nothing wrong with him, he loves me and is full of willingness, but he has a listlessness and an idleness which never leave him except when he is hunting; I am, nevertheless, full of hope.'

In 1773, with the marriages of Louis' two brothers, there was an atmosphere of 'jeune Cour' about Versailles. The younger members of the royal family used to eat together when they were not obliged to eat in public. They also indulged in private, not to say secret, theatricals. Madame Campan's husband and father-in-law were also among the actors. The Dauphin, she records, was the only spectator: 'he laughed a lot at the figures of the persons as they came onto the stage, and it was from the time of these amusements that one first noticed him shake off that air of shyness of his youth and take pleasure in the society of the Dauphine.'

In July 1773, her hope seemed to have been fulfilled. On 17 July she wrote from Compiègne: 'I can now say to my dear mother and to her alone that since we have been here there has been a great improvement in my affairs and I believe that our marriage has been consummated, although there is no question of pregnancy; that is why the Dauphin does not want it known yet. How happy I would be if I had a child in May!'

In her next letter, of 13 August, she reports that the Dauphin had told their great news to the King – 'he kissed me most tenderly and called me his dearest daughter. It was thought best to make our secret known; everyone was delighted.'

These last two passages, although undoubtedly authentic, are not printed in Georges Girard's edition of the 'complete' correspondence between Maria Theresa and Marie-Antoinette. It is none the less true that on 30 August 1777 of that year Marie-Antoinette wrote to her mother: 'I am in the deepest possible state of happiness of all my life. It has now been more than eight days since my marriage has been perfectly consummated.'

There is a problem in reconciling this statement with those of 1773. It was not, however, until the following May – 1778 – that Marie-Antoinette could finally claim to be with child.

Whatever did happen in July 1773, it had an apparent effect upon Madame du Barry. While there was the possibility of repudiating the Austrian alliance and sending Marie-Antoinette back to Vienna, Madame du Barry could afford to be haughty. Now she had to try and ingratiate herself with the Dauphine. In January she arranged for the comte de Noailles to show Marie-Antoinette some diamond earrings valued at 700 000 livres. Madame du Barry was willing to persuade the King to buy them for the Dauphine. The Dauphine told the comte de Noailles that she had quite enough diamonds already.

The presence of Madame du Barry at Court had presented Marie-Antoinette with one of her first and most formidable difficulties. It was clearly the King's desire that the relationship between the Dauphine and Madame du Barry should not be one of mutual hostility. In all the vastness and protocol of Versailles it would have been possible for them to avoid speaking to one another. If they were to be brought into any relationship it would require a different context. It may have been for this reason that, in June 1770, Louis decreed a visit to Marly.

The Château de Marly occupied a site overlooking the valley of the Seine near Bougival. 'I must needs say,' wrote the English traveller Martin Lister, 'it is one of the pleasantest places I ever saw, or believe is in Europe: it is seated in the bosom or upper end of a valley in the midst of and surrounded by woody hills. The valley is closed at its upper end, and gently descends forward by degrees and opens wider and wider, and gives you a prospect of a vast plain country with the Seine running through it.' What he called a valley is in fact a large re-entrant of which the principal contour line takes the form of a capital U. At the focal point of the rounded end of the U was a substantial *château*, a building about three quarters the size of Chatsworth, the Pavillon du Roi. On the same contour line which forms the sides of the U were twelve separate pavilions, linked by a trellis pergola, for Louis' guests. The façades of both pavilions and *château* were painted in *trompe l'oeil* with pilasters resembling the red marble of Languedoc and bas reliefs brilliantly gilded against a ground of royal blue. The window frames and balustrades were also gilded. 'Everything here', wrote Madame Campan, 'seemed to have been created by the magic of a fairy's wand.'

The high, wooded hills gave a pleasing sense of privacy, and with it intimacy and exclusiveness, for although the gardens were open towards the north, their insulation from the world outside was secured by a clever use of ground levels. The lower gardens were considerably banked up and ended in a high terrace overlooking the Abreuvoir. The privacy and the exclusiveness were thus maintained. 'He who planted this garden', wrote Diderot, 'realised that it was necessary to keep it out of sight until the moment when one could see it in its entirety.' It was only to those privileged to enter the precincts that the whole glorious lay-out of Marly was revealed.

Louis XIV's intention in building Marly had been to recreate the charming *maison de plaisance* that Versailles had once been but could never be again; to have somewhere in which privileged house-parties could be offered brilliant entertainments and to which invitations could be greatly coveted. In due course the highest hopes of assiduous courtiers were to be summed up in the formula of application for an invitation: 'Sire – Marly?'

The significance of the choice of Marly on this occasion was that the royal family and Madame du Barry would be living together at close quarters in the atmosphere of intimacy and informality for which Marly had been designed. The attempt proved counter-productive. A nearer view of Madame du Barry only confirmed Marie-Antoinette in her dislike. 'The King has a thousand kindnesses for me,' she wrote to her mother, 'and I love him tenderly, but it is pitiable to see the weakness which he has for Madame du Barry, the stupidest and most impertinent creature that it would be possible to imagine. She played at our table every evening at Marly; on two occasions she sat next to me, but she did not speak to me and I did not exactly try to get into conversation with her.'

Marie-Antoinette herself was making great progress in her relation with both the King and the public. On her first arrival at Fontainebleau, in 1770, Marie-Antoinette had spent three hours being shown around by the marquis de Marigny. It was here that she first captivated the Court and, although she was not yet fifteen, she scored a number of triumphs against Madame du Barry and yet managed to endear herself to the King. In the Court theatre etiquette forbade applause, but when the duc d'Aumont inserted into a piece some verses which were highly complimentary to the Dauphine, she received ~~a~~ spontaneous ovation.

One of the most perceptive appreciations of Fontainebleau comes from Napoleon, who added it to his imperial residences in 1804. 'C'est la maison des siècles,' he wrote; 'the real home of our Kings.' Almost every sovereign from François I left his mark upon the palace. This meant continual alteration of the buildings and continual redecoration of the rooms. Inevitably the creation of something new entailed the destruction of something old; each gain involved a loss, but often the gains were great. By the time of Louis XVI Fontainebleau was a vast compendium – a medley of beautiful buildings in a number of different styles. 'It may not have been strictly speaking an architect's palace,' Napoleon reflected at St Helena, 'but it most certainly was a residence that was well thought out and perfectly suited to its use. There was not in Europe a palace more commodious or more happily situated for the sovereign.'

Of the three main courtyards, the Cour de l'Oval, following the irregular foundation of a feudal castle, retained most of the very simple architecture of Le Breton and was much as François I had left it. The rooms of the royal family were all in this part of the Château. The Galerie François I connected these with the two other courtyards: the Cour de la Fontaine, which opens southwards towards the lake, and the vast Cour du Cheval Blanc which was reached by Louis XIII's magnificent horseshoe staircase. Louis XV had upset the balance of this court by destroying the Galerie d'Ulysse and replacing it with a massive block, built inexpensively in red brick, in order to provide seventy-two new apartments. But whatever their respective merits, the successive styles of Fontainebleau proclaim that here is a house that has been loved and lived in, where the successive rulers have felt themselves more than anywhere else 'at home'.

It was, of course, the immense Forêt de Bière which attracted them to the place because of the superb hunting which it afforded. The romantic landscape greatly appealed to the comte d'Hézècques – 'this vast forest, in which one comes across the most beautiful trees, the most picturesque places, and a multitude of rocky outcrops which are all the more extraordinary for being situated in a land which is almost flat . . . An excursion into the forest at the end of the day at Fontainebleau offered an indefinable charm. These great trees, which had lent their shade to so many kings, shimmered in the wind and seemed to whisper their ancient memories. The rocks, in the gathering dusk, outlined their gigantic shapes against the sky; a stag, pursuing a hind, passes quick as a flash, his call, raucous and rather frightening, echoes through the forest.' The pure waters of the Spring of Bléaud – the Fontaine de Bléau, as it came to be spelt – determined the situation of the royal residence.

It was during this Voyage de Fontainebleau that an accident took place in the course of a hunt which was to enhance Marie-Antoinette's reputation for kindliness. The story is told by Joseph Weber: a wounded stag entered the village of Achères-la-Forêt and attacked a peasant who was digging his garden. Neighbours ran to fetch his wife who was labouring in the fields nearby. Her cries of despair, for her husband was badly hurt, were loud and long. 'It happened that Marie-Antoinette drove past at that moment in her barouche on her way to the *rendez-vous de chasse*. She stopped her vehicle and ran to the assistance of the unfortunate woman, who had in the meantime fainted. When she recovered consciousness she was in the arms of the Dauphine and the Dauphine was in tears. Marie-Antoinette emptied her purse into the poor woman's hands and was wondering what to do next when the Dauphin and the comte de Provence rode up and added their largesse to that of the Dauphine. Next to appear was the King. "How tragic," he exclaimed, "if this man were to die. How could we console the widow and the child?" "Oh, Papa," answered the Dauphine, "by relieving them of their misery; that would at least temper the cruelty of their lot."' The King promised a pension to the family and sent his surgeon daily to visit the wounded man, who survived to enjoy the benefits of the royal bounty.

During the Voyage de Choisy, in the summer of 1770, an incident occurred which brought to the surface the antipathy between Madame du Barry and Marie-Antoinette. One night, in the little theatre of the Château, the *dames du palais* were already installed on the front bench when Madame du Barry entered, accompanied as usual by the maréchale de Mirepoix and the comtesse de Valentinois. The ladies would not make room for the new arrivals and the comtesse de Gramont, one of Marie-Antoinette's household and sister to the duc de Choiseul, withstood the favourite to her face. Next day the comtesse de Gramont received a *lettre de cachet* ordering her to leave the Court and forbidding her to live even in Paris. All that Marie-Antoinette could do was to obtain a rather grudging permission for Madame de Gramont to go to Paris when she urgently required medical attention.

In September 1771 Maria Theresa was becoming anxious about her daughter's refusal to speak to Madame du Barry. The Empress, with her Chastity Commission in Vienna, can hardly have been supposed to approve of the favourite. But kings were kings and politics were politics. It was not for her to reproach Louis for his sexual misconduct. Nor was it for her daughter to. Mercy assured the Empress that Madame du Barry wanted one thing and one thing only: 'her whole desire is that Madame la Dauphine should speak to her once.'

Maria Theresa was beside herself with anger and anxiety. 'I can no longer keep silence,' she wrote, 'after my conversation with Mercy and all that he told you about what the King desires and what your duty imposes upon you and how you have dared to fail him! What good reason can you plead? None! You do not have to know or to see the du Barry as anything else than a woman admitted to the Court and to the society of the King. You are his first subject; you owe him obedience and submission; you owe your example to the Court and to the courtiers that whatever the King wishes shall be fulfilled. If one were demanding of you to demean yourself or to be familiar, neither I nor anyone else could possibly advise you to do so; but some trivial word, a certain regard, not for her, but for your grandfather, your master, your benefactor.' She wanted now to separate her daughter from the influence of Mesdames. 'You must cast off these other influences; it is for you to set the tone after the King and not to be led, like a child, when you wish to speak.'

The refusal of the Dauphine to address a single word to Madame du Barry was becoming a major issue at Court. Marie-Antoinette's position was not as secure as might have been thought. Through no fault of her own she had failed to fulfil her primary function as Dauphine – the production of an heir to the throne. Royal marriages had been declared null and void before now and princesses sent back to their countries of origin. 'My daughter must cultivate the King's good graces,' insisted Maria Theresa; 'she must be civil to the favourite on account of the benefit which may be gained for us and both Courts; the Alliance even may depend on her behaviour.' Europe waited with bated breath upon the outcome of the issue.

On 1 January 1772, Marie-Antoinette made up her mind. New Year's Day was the occasion of one of the big receptions of the Court. The favourite, introduced by the duchesse d'Aiguillon and the maréchale de Mirepoix, was, as usual, presented to the Dauphine. Having addressed a few words to the duchesse, Marie-Antoinette looked the comtesse in the eyes and said: 'Il y a du monde aujourd'hui à Versailles.' It was enough. The palace revolution was averted. The Chancelleries of Europe could relax. But Marie-Antoinette had seen the Court of France at its fatuous worst and her opinion of it was never to recover.

Madame du Barry attracted the bitter opposition of those who supported the duc de Choiseul. It was Choiseul who had brought about the Austrian alliance and the royal marriage; he had been the first to greet Marie-Antoinette on the edge of the Forêt de Compiègne. Marie-Antoinette was, naturally, on his side.

Before the year was out the duc de Choiseul had been deprived of his ministries and ordered to retire to his estates at Chanteloup, near Amboise. The 'parti dévot' had won. This left Marie-Antoinette in a very difficult position. 'This Princess,' wrote Madame Campan, 'young, open, light-hearted and inexperienced, found herself with no other guide than the abbé de Vermond in the midst of a Court ruled over by the enemy of the minister who had brought her there, surrounded by people who hated Austria and who detested the whole alliance with the imperial family.'

The abbé de Vermond was certainly to play an important and even formative role in the life of Marie-Antoinette. In the preamble to the *brevet*, dated 18 April 1770, by which Louis XV appointed the abbé de Vermond to continue in his post as *lecteur* to Marie-Antoinette at Versailles, his brief is described as 'to perfect Madame l'Archiduchesse Marie-Antoinette, future Dauphine, in the French language and in all other accomplishments in which a princess of her rank should be instructed.'

It was no easy task. It had been difficult enough in Vienna. Now with the vast new horizons of Versailles, the constant visits to Marly, Compiègne. Choisy-le-Roi or Fontainebleau, and the many calls upon the Dauphine's time required by etiquette, Vermond found it increasingly difficult to maintain the regularity of his study periods or to retain the attention of his easily distracted pupil. But by July he had established some measure of routine. On the 12 July Marie-Antoinette wrote to her mother saying that she saw the abbé every day from four until five o'clock.

In September Vermond drew up a long report on the proceedings for Mercy, who forwarded it to the Empress. 'The desire and indeed the necessity to talk about a thousand matters, the nature and the novelty of which made them of interest to the Dauphine, prevented her from paying any attention to my readings. As soon as it was possible for me to open a book I took up again *Les Synonymes Français*.' The title sounds desperately boring, but Grimm assures us that it was 'full of fine metaphysical discussions and that it enjoyed a great success'. Vermond claimed that this was the most urgent of all the young Princess' needs. 'Apart from the inexactitudes which were still present in the speech of the Dauphine, she was acquiring every day ideas which neither could nor should have been given her in Vienna. As a matter of fact I only read two or three pages each day; I was ready to accommodate her desire to talk about each topic; I took advantage of this to correct her ideas and to accustom her to the correct expression. It appears that the Dauphine's command of language was satisfactory, even in her private circle where she speaks with more vivacity and less attention. It happens that occasionally she makes use of a phrase which is not in the best French, but she always gives them an energy and a charm which is infinitely preferable to grammatical accuracy.'

To *Les Synonymes Français* succeeded readings from 'certain ancient booklets known by the name of *Bagatelles Morales*'. Once again the title seems unpromising, but Vermond claims that 'they reveal the manners, the customs and the absurdities of not a few Frenchmen, painted in colours which are as pleasing as they are interesting.' Vermond was certainly sugaring the philosophical pill to the utmost of his capacity.

Maria Theresa demanded a monthly report from her daughter on the progress which she had made with her readings; it caused some consternation. Vermond describes the scene himself. 'Madame la Dauphine said to me: "what shall I do? Mama asks me to give an account of my readings." "I am sure that you tell her only the truth, Madame," and I took the opportunity to point out to her how far she had fallen short.'

Vermond hoped that she would submit to this discipline which would have been in itself beneficial to her; 'but how could she write?' he asks; 'I can be of no help to her in this respect; I am almost never in Madame la Dauphine's room when she writes. She occasionally sends for me when she is finishing her letters, but she makes a point of detaining me only for a short time while her desk is open. She has said to me from time to time: "They would not fail to put it about that you dictate my letters" . . . Your Excellency knows this Court: what tales would not be told if I were found reading her papers? Madame la Dauphine therefore cannot write about her readings except when she is alone; she is quite competent to do so and my presence would be more useful in determining her than in assisting her.'

There is much in Vermond's report that shows the attractive side of Marie-Antoinette. 'She has so far not made any mistake of importance,' he continues. 'Your Excellency knows for himself how she listens and comes back to her little misapprehensions. Every day I admire her sweetness and, I am bold to say, her docility! She allows me certain respectful home truths in front of her Dame d'Honneur and the personnel of her bedroom, and stronger home truths, even stronger than in Vienna, when I am in her *cabinet*. I am well aware that I owe her confidence to the approbation of HM the Empress.'

It was, however, a discouraging task for the abbé. Marie-Antoinette's good resolutions were always for some future reform of her ways. Summer was too laden with outdoor pleasures; autumn was difficult with the Voyage de Fontainebleau; but in the winter she would resume her studies. In December, Mercy wrote to the Empress, the Dauphine had told Vermond that 'she wished during the winter to make up for time lost in the dissipations of summer and of the Voyages.' But in the new year the celebrations of the Carnaval postponed her readings until Lent.

With her husband's accession to the throne the reading hours became more and more scarce. In May Maria Theresa gave up trying. 'You have never had any love of reading nor any sort of application; that has often caused me concern. I was so pleased to see you devoting yourself to music. I have often pestered you to know about your readings for this reason. For the last year there had been no more question either of reading or of music and I hear of nothing but of horse racing and hunting, and always without the King and with a group of young people not of your choosing, which causes me deep anxiety since I love you so tenderly.'

In her reference to Marie-Antoinette 'devoting herself to music'. Maria Theresa introduces the one serious interest of her daughter: music. Almost unbelievably this was turned into a cause for complaint against her. 'Passionately fond of good music,' wrote the baron de Frénilly; (France is indebted to her for Gluck) 'she had accorded a pension to three charming musicians, Azevedo, Louet and Garat, and on account of this pension she was publicly declared to be the vampire of the State.' It is as the patron of Gluck that Marie-Antoinette played her most important role as a lover of music.

'Your Majesty, who is a protector of all the arts,' wrote Gluck in his dedication to the Queen of his opera *Iphigénie en Tauride*, 'knows how to accord to each the degree of esteem which they merit.' It was another way of saying that music has pride of place among the fine arts. If Marie-Antoinette put it at the top of her list it was probably because she was not noticeably interested in the others. She may have played a creative role in the designing of the gardens at Trianon, but evidence is lacking that she exhibited any particular enthusiasm for architecture or sculpture or painting. That she had a real appreciation of music is beyond doubt.

Gluck had played an important part in the life of the Viennese Court. He was Master of the Chapel and wrote the music for some of the *divertimenti*, such as *Il Parnasso Confuso* in which members of the imperial family took an active part.

The premiere of *Orpheus and Euridice* was given at the Hofburg. But Gluck's ambition looked towards Paris, and with the Archduchess Marie-Antoinette's marriage to the Dauphin he had hopes of a powerful patron. He chose for his début Racine's version of *Iphigénie en Aulide* in which he found 'all the energy necessary to inspire great music'.

Gluck's intention, as he states in his introduction to *Alceste*, was to reduce music (in opera) to its true function, that of enhancing the poetry in order to strengthen the expression of the feelings and the dramatic quality of the situations, without interrupting the action or slowing it down with superfluous ornament. Music should add to poetry what colour and chiaroscuro add to drawing. *Alceste*, he claimed, was 'a music that was severe, with no superfluous ornament, having no other adornment than its own beauty'.

The difficulty of presenting *Iphigénie* in Paris arose from its own excellence. The Director of Music at the Academy said that he would require, as a condition for accepting, six more of Gluck's operas, because 'a work like this is made to kill all the old French operas'.

The difficulties, however, were overcome and on 19 April 1774, *Iphigénie* was performed before a most appreciative audience, though there was some doubt whether the applause was entirely in response to the performance or to 'the desire of the public to please the Dauphine'. It was recorded in the *memoires secrètes* that 'she never ceased clapping her hands, which obliged Madame la comtesse de Provence, the princes and all those in the boxes, to follow suit.' Grimm claimed that the audience was 'deeply struck with the multitude of new beauties which sparkled in a music which was nevertheless passionate, emotive and dramatic'. Music, he states, was the one great interest of the time: 'in Paris one does not think or dream but of music. It is the subject of all our disputes, all our conversations, the soul of all our supper parties.'

The Coronation

With the accession of Louis XVI on 10 May 1774, the supporters of Choiseul were hoping for his return to power, and they looked to Marie-Antoinette as a means to this end. On 16 May the comte de Viri, Ambassador from Sardinia, wrote to the marquis d'Aigueblanche that Choiseul's party 'may well not have as much influence as had been expected through the favour of the Queen, for it appears that the King, whatever his affection for her, will not, perhaps, be disposed, in so far as she has managed to flatter herself, to allow her to interfere in any of the affairs of State.'

A day or two later he wrote to the King of Sardinia: 'the young Prince has made it known on several occasions to Monsieur de Maurepas that he was absolutely determined that women should have no influence, during his reign, in the affairs of State.' Choiseul, also, was personally disliked by the new King because of his erstwhile opposition to his father over the expulsion of the Jesuits. Although there were a number of changes in the ministries, no appointment was offered to Choiseul.

Two days after his accession, Louis wrote to his grandfather's former minister, the comte de Maurepas: 'Amidst the natural grief that overwhelms me, and which I share with the whole kingdom, I have great duties to fulfil. I am King; the word comprises many obligations. But alas! I am only twenty and have not the knowledge necessary . . . My certainty of your probity and of your profound knowledge of affairs impels me to ask you to help me with your counsels. Come then as soon as possible and you will give me great pleasure.'

Maurepas became Louis' confidential adviser with the unofficial title of 'Mentor'.

One of the most interesting sources of information about the King's relations with Maurepas was the abbé de Véri. He was unusually well-informed and his judgements were well balanced. His memoirs are among the most reliable sources for the early part of the new reign.

Joseph-Alphonse de Véri, like Turgot and Loménie de Brienne, had been trained for the clergy. In view of his noble birth and exceptional ability it was clear a prestigious bishopric and the fat revenues of a number of abbeys were within his easy reach. He chose, however, to become the *eminence grise* behind Maurepas. As the Prince de Montbarrey puts it: 'Maurepas does nothing without consulting his wife and Madame de Maurepas acts only in accordance with the advice of the abbé de Véri.'

Maurepas was installed at Versailles in the room above the King's Petits Appartements which had been those of Madame du Barry. Nothing could have symbolised more strikingly the change at Court brought about by the new reign than the designation of the apartment of a mistress as the apartment of a minister.

Lord Stormont noted, in a letter to Lord Rochford: 'His letter to Monsieur de Maurepas and the language which he has constantly held since his grandfather's death strongly indicate the same sentiments. He speaks of his inability, his inexperience and total ignorance in a manner which, in my opinion, does him honour, and gives room to hope that he will endeavour to learn, as the first step to knowledge is to feel the want of it.' His first actions in the face of his new responsibilities 'carry marks of good, plain, natural understanding'.

This was the opinion of Marie-Antoinette herself. In 1772 she wrote to her mother: 'He has a love of justice, order and truth, and, besides, a great deal of good sense and right feeling in his way of regarding affairs, but I dread his indolence and a sort of apathy, a want of nerve without which one cannot think or feel quickly enough to be truly efficient.'

Before the year was out Maurepas had persuaded the King to one of the most momentous reversals of policy, which would have had the approval of Choiseul; it was nothing less than to reinstate the Parlements.

Their dissolution, in the early days of 1771, just after the disgrace of Choiseul, had been the work of the Chancelier Maupeou. Each member of the Parlement had been sent a *lettre de cachet* condemning him to instant exile, in the middle of winter, to the often remote discomfort of his seigneurial *château*. In February an act had been passed abolishing the Parlement and replacing its functions with new courts. These measures were enforced by a *lit de justice* – a ceremonial whereby the King was entitled to override the rulings of the Parlement. Most of the Princes of the Blood – in particular the duc d'Orléans and the Prince de Conti – sided against the King and were sent into immediate exile.

Now, on 10 November 1774 the former counsellors were recalled and two days later, at a solemn *lit de justice*, restored to power. The abbé de Véri was pleasantly surprised by Louis' deportment on this occasion: 'we were astonished by the note of firmness and personal will with which the King pronounced his discourse.'

Lord Stormont made the same observation. 'The King spoke with great dignity and with as much readiness as if he had been accustomed to speak in public;' but, he added warily, 'whether this comes from a mind that feels its own strength or from one which wishes to conceal its weakness, a little time will tell.'

Marie-Antoinette was delighted. On 16 November she wrote to her mother: 'the great affair of the Parlements is finished at last; everyone says that the King played his part wonderfully . . . It all went off as he wanted it to, and the Princes of the Blood came to see us the next day . . . I am very happy that there is now no-one in exile or in trouble; furthermore it seems to me that if the King gives this task his backing, his authority will be greater and more solid than in the past.'

Not everyone shared her optimism. Lord Stormont, cautious and astute as ever, commented: 'the young King thinks that his authority is sufficiently assured by the dispositions which he has made. The chances are great that before the end of his reign he will be biting his nails because of them.'

That prophecy, however, was unknown to the chief actors in the drama. To them the prospect of a glorious reign was confirmed by Louis' display of kingly competence at the opening of the Parlement. All seemed to augur well for the ancient and profoundly religious ritual of the Coronation, known more properly in France as the *Sacre* – the anointing with holy oil which conferred the divine right upon the kings of France.

The year 1775 promised to be an important milestone in the country's history. But even the most exalted aspirations must sooner or later come down to earth. The political climate of the year 1774 had much about it that was good. But the harvest was bad.

The combination of a bad harvest and a severe winter was the formula for famine. If corn could be easily moved from one area to another the effects of the shortage could sometimes be offset. But if communications were cut by ice and snow the sufferings of the peasants were of necessity acute. The winter of 1775 was one of the coldest on record. Corn, flour and bread were therefore scarce and prices went up. The abbé Morellet, however, who was Lord Shelburne's informant, stated that the cost of bread 'is still less than what we suffered during the greater part of the abbé Terray's ministry'. It provided, nevertheless, the occasion for a number of riots behind which there may have been a centralised organisation. They were known as la Guerre des Farines.

In March uprisings were reported at Meaux, Lagny, Montlhéry and Pont-sur-Seine. In April more serious demonstrations took place at Dijon which erupted into a revolt on the 18th. Throughout April the movement spread at an alarming rate. On the 27th it reached Beaumont-sur-Oise and the next day Meru and Beauvais; on the 29th Pontoise, an important market for the supply of corn to Paris. On 1 May it broke out at Saint-Germain and Saint-Denis. On 2 May groups of malcontents began to converge upon Versailles.

Both Maurepas and Turgot were in Paris at the time and Louis was about to go hunting. He cancelled the hunt and dealt with the crisis himself. At eleven o' clock he wrote to Turgot: 'Versailles has been attacked and they are the same people as at Saint-Germain. I will confer with Monsieur le maréchal de Muy and Monsieur d'Affry [Colonel of the Swiss Guards] on the measures to take. You can count on my firmness.' To the surprise of some of his contemporaries Louis showed himself capable of vigorous and well thought-out action.

On 13 May Turgot wrote to Véri: 'the King is as firm as I am. But the danger is great because the disorder is spreading with incredible rapidity and because the atrocious measures of the instigators are followed up with very great intelligence. Firm determination is an absolute necessity.'

Véri answered Turgot from Toulouse. 'Hold fast to your measures and above all keep your Master to them, for the happiness of his life. A minister thrown out by factious agitations can still find repose on his estates. But a king who yields to them will raise up countless more and will find peace only in the tomb. Had you been wrong – and even very wrong indeed – in your measures for free trade in corn, a recourse to sedition should not be allowed to force the King to remedy an evil. He must subdue it first and then do the right thing from a position of strength. If the King is firm on this occasion, all will be well.'

To Véri, the uprisings looked like something orchestrated. 'They were heard to say "tomorrow – in two days' time – in three days' time we shall be in such and such a place" . . . this sustained and concerted action on the part of peasants in revolt is something unheard of.'

Unlike most rioters, they paid, for the most part, for the flour and bread which they pillaged, but they paid a price determined by themselves. They even claimed that it was a price set by the King. Some of them, when arrested, were found to have large sums of money on them. Specimens of bad bread, black and green with mould, were held up with cries of 'this is the bread we have to eat', but those who examined these loaves pronounced that they had been specially baked and artificially discoloured.

Véri's suspicions were shared by the Garde des Sceaux, Monsieur de Miromesnil. 'The progress of the brigands seems to have been concerted,' he told the Parlement; 'their arrivals are announced, the day, the hour and the places where they are to commit their acts of violence are all public knowledge. It seems that there was a plan drawn up to lay waste the countryside, to intercept navigation, to prevent transport of corn on the big roads in order to create famine in the great towns and especially in Paris.'

One of the actions which annoyed Louis most was that of his captain of the Guard who, when the insurgents reached Versailles, ordered a reduction of the price of bread to two sous a loaf; it was even said that the King had authorised this. He had not. 'It was there', wrote Véri, 'that the King showed the courage and the *sang froid* of which I have already spoken. He gave his orders calmly; he wrote to Monsieur Turgot in Paris and, when it was all over, he sent word to Monsieur de Maurepas in Paris to be calm and that order had been re-established.'

Order was, indeed, re-established, but the outstanding feature of the day was the inactivity of the police. 'What passes our comprehension', wrote Simeon Hardy, a Parisian bookseller, 'was the sight of the populace in a state of mutiny, absolutely its own master and able to execute any undertaking which it desired without opposition, although warning had been received the day before that it was going to happen.'

No letter from Marie-Antoinette has survived which gives

her own version of the events or her comments on them, but that she wrote such a letter may be inferred from her mother's reply, dated 2 June from Schönbrunn. 'I was enchanted by all that you told me of the bearing of the King and the orders he gave *vis-à-vis* the Parlement during this unfortunate uprising. Like you, I think that there is something beneath all this.'

Prince Xavier de Saxe, Louis' uncle, usually well informed, went further. 'It seems that the riots', he wrote, 'were occasioned not by misery and famine, for we have already seen the price of bread much higher than today without any murmuring, but by the fermentation of a few minds who were silently plotting a general revolution and of which one suspects the principal agents to be persons of the very highest distinction.' It has often been said that it was the Freemasons who were to blame.

Morellet was less inclined to accept that the risings had been orchestrated.

> Without believing that there was behind all this a first and single cause, a conspiracy begun and directed towards a single objective, one cannot close one's eyes to the fact that the first impulse once given was carefully maintained; and besides that, it was not put down with the rigour which would have been shown if the persons on whom such rigour depended had been favourable to the minister who was the most concerned with these troubles. Above all one was strangely surprised at the ease with which Paris was pillaged two days after Versailles had been. They had been warned the day before that on the following day there would be rioting in Paris, that the bakers would be pillaged; and in fact four or five hundred people, a small number of whom were armed with sticks, sacked all the bakers' shops in Paris from three in the morning to three in the afternoon, without opposition, without contradiction, and without our marvellous police of Paris, who are so praised up for their vigilance and their severity, doing anything to prevent it . . . Turgot went straight to the King, told him what had happened, and got the Lieutenant de Police (Le Noir) dismissed and the post given to a man you met at Montigny – a Monsieur Albert.

It was not a very satisfactory state of affairs.

For the moment, however, Louis had covered himself in glory. He had done what many people thought he was incapable of doing: he had acted like a king. It was with the sweet taste of success on his lips and with a deep sense of mission to right the wrongs of his people that he set out, in the brilliant early days of June, for the cathedral city of Reims, the royal sanctuary, to be crowned and anointed King of France.

The weather was fine and dry and everything possible had been done to improve the roads and embellish the wayside, so that from Compiègne to Reims 'it was like one garden'. Posting horses had been concentrated in vast numbers along the route, to the great inconvenience of travellers in other parts of the country. At Soissons alone there were six hundred available.

During the early days of the month colourful detachments of the Royal Household and the magnificent equipages of the aristocracy were to be seen converging on the coronation city. The approaches to the town had been adorned with a succession of truimphal arches: everything seemed to smile at the prospect of the happy event. But at Fismes, where the King traditionally spent the last night before his state entry into Reims, the duc de Croÿ had been appalled at the price of bread.

The contrast between the lavish extravagance of the Court and the poverty of the people might well have occasioned unfortunate demonstrations, but nothing was recorded save for one man standing at the roadside who greeted the King by pointing at his own, empty mouth.

On his arrival at Reims the duc de Croÿ lost no time in going to inspect the Cathedral – 'une des plus belles que j'ai vues et digne de l'honneur qu'elle a.' The duc de Duras and the staff of the Menus Plaisirs had been busy with the construction of the royal tribune, the boxes for the spectators and the decorations in general. 'I was astonished at the immensity of these works,' wrote Papillon de la Ferté; 'it is the most thorough undertaking ever completed by the Menus.'

The path which the King was to follow from the archiepiscopal palace (known from its T shape as the Palais du Tau) to the Cathedral was lined with tapestries and culminated in a colonnade before the west doors – 'un morceau superbe qui réussit à perfection', claimed de Croÿ, and which, he noted, 'although in a different style, went well with this beautiful, old portal.'

As for the choir itself, where the ceremony was to take place, the decor designed by Belanger had completely obscured its architecture. The King's throne was placed, beneath a gorgeous canopy, on the top of the choir screen. Level with this, and within the arches of the main arcade, had been contrived a series of 'boxes' with Corinthian columns and entablature, more like the Chapel – or, indeed, the Opera House – at Versailles. Croÿ did not approve of it: 'it looked too theatrical, too much like a *salle de spectacle* inserted into the most superb nave of the Gothic church.' The duc de Croÿ had the gift, rare among his contemporaries, of being able to appreciate the architecture of the thirteenth century and he found this gaudy finery like 'a little piece of gilded cardboard in a great and noble building'. But he was delighted by the tapestries.

He next went to the palace to inspect the regalia. The King was to offer a golden ciborium – 'un morceau superbe et d'un travail exquis' – to the Treasury of the Cathedral. Richest of all was the King's crown, encrusted with the most beautiful gems and estimated at a value of sixteen million livres. It weighed only two pounds and de Croÿ was able to lift it with one hand. The coronets to be worn – *les couronnes d'honneur* – were also on view, three with the strawberry leaves of a duke and nine with the raised pearls of a count.

In the French ceremony only twelve peers wore coronets; these were not put on at the moment of the King's crowning, as in England, but were worn throughout the ceremony. They were worn by the six Lay Peers, three maréchals de France, the Grand Maître, the Grand Chambellan and the Premier Gentilhomme de la Chambre du Roi. All except the

1. The Tuileries, garden front: engraving by Rigaud.

2. Versailles, the Cour de Marbre: painting by P. D. Martin.

3. Maria Theresa, Marie-Antoinette's mother: miniature attributed to Liotard.

4. The Hofburg; the Leopold wing containing Maria Theresa's apartments: drawing by Schutz.

5. Francis of Lorraine, Marie-Antoinette's father: painting by van Meytens.

6. Marie-Antoinette (right) dancing in *Il Trionfo d'Amore*, 1765: painting by van Meytens.

7. The Dauphin, Louis-Auguste: painting by van Loo.

8. Marie-Antoinette aged 14: bust attributed to Rosset.

9. Louis XV: pastel by La Tour.

10. The Château de Compiègne in 1770: painting by van Blarenberghe.

11. The Dauphine's charity: engraving by Moreau le Jeune.

first three Lay Peers wore the coronet of a count irrespective of their own rank or title.

The Twelve Peers of France, of whom six were lay and six ecclesiastical, were a body whose origins were supposed by romantic imagination to date back to Charlemagne; they were the dukes of Normandy, Burgundy and Aquitaine; the counts of Flanders, Champagne and Toulouse; the archbishop of Reims, the bishops of Langres and Laon, all of whom were also dukes, and the bishops of Beauvais, Noyon and Chalons, who were also counts. Their proper function was to act as a High Court to arbitrate in disputes between the King and his Tenants in Chief. They also had a ceremonial function at the coronation. They 'upheld' the crown while it was on the King's head.

From his inspection of the regalia, the duc de Croÿ returned to the Cathedral for a closer look at the arrangements in the Sanctuary. No individual places were reserved and he wisely resolved to be there in good time.

On Friday 9 June the King arrived at about five in the afternoon, escorted by a detachment of the Household Cavalry. De Croÿ was in ecstasies: 'the beauty of these coaches and horses, the noble noise of the fanfares and kettledrums and the great bell of the Cathedral, proclaimed the presence of the Master.' His coach – 'superbe, singulier et immense' – was drawn by eight horses whose tall, white plumes distinguished them from those of the outriders.

The King was received by the Archbishop and his suffragans at the west porch and was conducted into the cool emptiness of the Cathedral, where a few prayers were said. He then inspected the decorations and arrangements and complimented the duc de Duras on all that had been done. De Croÿ noted narrowly the King's deportment: 'he still looked as kind as ever, but bored by official occasions; what was lacking in all that was the air of grandeur which Louis XIV would have brought to it.'

Trinity Sunday, the day appointed for the coronation, dawned as fine and warm as ever. De Croÿ went to the

Cathedral at four o'clock in the morning and obtained the best seat, at the end of his bench.

At half past six the six Lay Peers of France, 'our six princes, representing the three ancient dukedoms and the three ancient counties of the kingdom, in all the magnificence of their majestic robes, with their coronets on their heads, made their entry.' The dukes were represented by the King's two brothers, the comte de Provence and the comte d'Artois, together with his second cousin the duc d'Orléans, and the counts by other Princes of the Blood – the duc de Chartres, the prince de Condé and the duc de Bourbon.

The comte de Provence, later to be Louis XVIII, but never to be crowned, conducted himself with considerable dignity, but the young Artois, *fait pour plaire aux dames* and later, as Charles X, to be the last King ever crowned at Reims, behaved with a careless irreverence which gave offence to many.

The six Lay Peers now joined the six Ecclesiastical Peers and formed a procession to go the King's bedroom in the palace to escort him to the Cathedral. The Bishops of Beauvais and Laon came first to the King's door. Twice they knocked and twice they received the answer: 'Le Roi dort.' The third time they were admitted. The other robed and coroneted personalities now took their places in the procession. The other officials, such as the maréchal de Contades, who carried the royal crown, were in Court dress – white silk stockings, trunk hose and a cloak reaching to the knees. They wore plumed hats upon their heads.

At half past seven this august procession entered the Cathedral. The duc de Croÿ was deeply impressed and made a note of all the details – the great ermine-lined mantles and the long cloth-of-gold surcoats created an effect 'which was all the more imposing for being never worn but on this day'. On reaching the altar, the procession was confronted by the no less imposing robes of the Archbishop and his clergy, 'which exhibited with the greatest possible brilliance the pomp of the Church'.

At last the King took his place under the great canopy in the centre of the crossing. 'Chacun est à sa place en silence.'

The service began with the singing of the *Veni Creator* by the King's musicians behind the altar. During their singing, the procession of the Sainte-Ampoule made its way up the nave and, passing beneath the royal tribune, entered the sanctuary. The Holy Oil had been brought from the Abbey of Saint-Rémi by the Prior, who rode upon a white horse. The Sainte-Ampoule having been placed with great reverence upon the altar, the Archbishop now donned his vestments for the mass and the service proper began.

First the King took his oath to preserve the Church in all its privileges, to protect his people and to maintain justice and mercy throughout the realm, ending with the words: 'I promise these things in the name of Jesus Christ to my Christian people subject to me.' The Bishops of Beauvais and Laon then asked the people if they accepted their King, to which they gave assent, noted the duc de Croÿ, 'by a respectful silence'. The King then took another oath in Latin. The duc noted that Louis pronounced this oath in a firm, clear voice, 'stressing the words with respect and attention as if he said after each word: "je m'engage à celà de bon coeur" ' – I promise this with a true heart.

The King now approached the altar. The Premier Gentilhomme divested him of his cloth-of-silver surcoat. His scarlet camisole was made to open at the chest, between the shoulders and at the crook of each arm – the points of the royal anatomy to which the holy oil had to be applied. The Grand Chambellan placed a pair of silk shoes, embroidered with fleurs de lys, upon the King's feet and the comte de Provence, representing the duc de Bourgogne, attached the spurs, which he then took off and returned to the altar. The Archbishop now took the sword of Charlemagne, which was named Joyeuse, from the altar, girded the King with it, ungirded him, drew the sword and gave it to the Connétable de France, who held it for the rest of the ceremony. As he gave it, the Archbishop said: 'take this sword given to you with the blessing of God, by which, in the strength of the Holy Spirit, you may be able to resist and repel all the enemies of the Holy Church and defend the kingdom committed to you.'

Now came the solemn moment after which the ceremony of the *Sacre* was named – the anointing with the Holy Oil. All good Frenchmen believed that this oil had been brought direct from Heaven by a dove for the baptism of Clovis. The Archbishop, using a little golden bodkin, took a drop from the Ampulla and mixed it with some oil on a golden paten, ready for the annointing of the King, who, as the rubric stated, 'alone among all the Kings of the earth is resplendent in this glorious privilege and is specially anointed with the Oil sent from Heaven'. This was the pledge of the divine right of the Kings of France.

The Archbishop now proceeded to anoint the King while the choir sang the anthem: 'Zadok the Priest and Nathan the Prophet anointed Solomon King in Jerusalem. And all the people rejoiced and said: "May the King live for ever."'

The duc de Croÿ noted the significance of these actions: 'thus the King receives the minor Orders of the Church, with the exception of the priesthood.' This was the significance of the robes with which the King was now vested by the Grand Chambellan – a blue dalmatic, such as a deacon wore, and over that the blue coronation robe, lined with ermine and covered with fleurs de lys. It was made to hang so that the King's right hand was free and draped over his left arm 'like a priest's chasuble'.

The ring was now placed upon his finger, the Sceptre in his right hand and the Hand of Justice in his left. The moment for the coronation had come. The Chancellor, mounting the steps, said in a loud voice: 'Monsieur, qui représentez le duc de Bourgogne, présentez-vous à cette acte.' One by one, as he named them, the Twelve Peers of France took their places on either side of the King. Taking the crown of Charlemagne from the altar, the Archbishop raised it over the head of the King and all the Peers reached out to 'uphold' it while the prayers were read. 'Dieu d'éternité, duc des vertus, vainqueur de tous ennemis, bénis cettuy ton serviteur à toy inclinant son chef' – 'God of Eternity, leader of all virtues and victor over all enemies, bless this thy servant who inclines his head to Thee.' Then the Archbishop placed the crown upon the King's head. 'This supreme moment', noted the duc de Croÿ, 'caused the greatest sensation possible.'

Louis was now conducted up the steps to the choir screen and ceremonially seated upon the royal throne. The Archbishop, followed by the other peers, now paid their homage; each, having made a profound bow, had the honour of kissing the King, saying at the same time: 'Vive le Roi éternellement.'

The completion of this ceremony was the signal for an outbreak of popular rejoicing. According to de Croÿ:

> the doors were thrown open, the people poured into the Church. Birds were released and all the trumpets announced in their blaring tones the presence of the Master – but what announced it even more were the hearts of the French. At this moment tears of joy ran down every cheek. The excitement was so great that an outburst of applause – something which has never happened before – accompanied the cries of 'Vive le Roi!' and everyone was beside himself with emotion. I know that I never have experienced such enthusiasm. I was quite astonished to find myself in tears and to see everyone else the same. The Queen was so overcome with joy that her tears fell in torrents and she was obliged to produce her handkerchief. This only served to augment the general emotion.

Marie-Antoinette was not herself crowned, but watched the whole ceremony seated in a superb tribune not unlike the royal box at the Opera. For such an occasion, of course, a very special dress had been created for her, and she was determined that it should arrive uncrumpled at Reims and demanded that it should be carried there on a stretcher. This method of transport, she told the duchesse de Cossé, the Dame d'Atours, would cost twelve louis. The duchesse de Cossé indignantly refused to authorise such expenditure, whereupon her dressmaker, Rose Bertin, went directly to the

Queen, who agreed that she should bring the dress herself to Reims, at a cost of some forty or fifty louis.

On 22 June Marie-Antoinette wrote an account of the ceremony to her mother:

> The coronation was perfect in all respects; it seems that everyone was contented with the King. He deserves that of all his subjects; both great and small, all took the greatest interest. The ceremony of the Church was interrupted at the moment of the crowning by acclamations which were most touching. I could not bear it any longer, the tears ran down my cheeks in spite of myself, and they were grateful to me. I did my best throughout the *voyage* to respond to the eagerness of the people, and although it was very hot and crowded I do not regret my fatigue, which has in no way affected my health. It is astonishing and very happy at the same time to be so well received after the revolts and the price of bread, which unfortunately continue . . . There is no doubt that, seeing people who, in their distress, treat us so well, we are more than ever obliged to work for their welfare.

And those words were written by the woman accused, on no reliable evidence, of having responded to the news of the shortage of bread: 'Why do they not eat cake?'

In all this enthusiasm and euphoria, however, there was one note of caution sounded. It came from the abbé de Véri. 'The acclamations of the people,' he wrote, 'which touched the heart of the King and even more so that of the Queen, whose tears and tenderness were noticed by all, are the normal accompaniment of pompous and exceptional ceremonies . . . but unfortunately they have the power to intoxicate and can give a false impression of the general opinion. Adulators may make much of them, but it is none the less true that the people of Paris and of the provinces on the whole were shocked at the expenditure occasioned by the coronation.'

The estimated cost of the coronation was 760 000 livres – 100 000 short of the cost of building the Petit Trianon. It was not suggested that so large a sum should not be spent; it was suggested that if the coronation took place at Notre-Dame de

Paris the money could be regarded as well invested. Such an occasion would have attracted numerous visitors, which would have been good for trade; it would have given to the people of Paris the sort of spectacle which they loved, which would have been good for the relationship between the King and his capital. But Louis was at heart a traditionalist. He did not wish to alter the time-honoured custom. The Kings of France were always crowned at Reims – except for Henri IV, who was crowned at Chartres.

There were also strong political undercurrents. Louis' two principal advisers, Maurepas and Turgot, were on the side of the Philosophes and against the Church. In March Turgot had addressed to Louis his *Mémoire au Roi sur la tolération religieuse.* 'You should examine the undertakings contained in the formula of the Coronation with regard to heretics ("to exterminate from all his States all heretics expressly condemned by the Church") and consider if they are in themselves just; and if they are unjust, it is your duty not to enact them . . . Now, the prince who orders his subject to profess a religion which he does not believe, or to renounce a religion which he does believe, commits a crime.' Louis was by nature tolerant, but once again his respect for tradition won. On 10 June he wrote to Turgot from Reims saying how much he appreciated the honesty and openness of his manner, but he concluded: 'I think it would be easier not to make any changes.' He did not wish to alter the sacred formulas.

For Louis himself this must have been one of the most memorable experiences in his life. 'The King appeared very sensible of this great moment,' wrote de Croÿ; 'and we saw at last, as one can only see on that occasion, our King decked out in all the radiance of royalty on the true throne – a sight which cannot be conveyed, so deep was the impression which it made.'

After the mass, the King exchanged the crown of Charlemagne for the lighter one already described, and the procession formed up to escort him back to the Palais du Tau for the banquet. 'The King, with this beautiful crown on his head, carrying the Sceptre and all the ornaments, surrounded by these twelve men in their coronets and all their rich majestic robes, made a truly impressive exit.'

Papillon de la Ferté congratulated himself on the success of the whole operation. 'In spite of the heat, the King stood up extremely well to this long ceremony, which was in fact, made shorter, thanks to the book containing the ceremonies and prayers which I had printed so that everyone knew what he had to do or say. I am very glad that I had this idea.'

When it was all over, Louis wrote to Maurepas: 'I am free of all my fatigues. This morning's procession was the last. I wish you could have been here to share my satisfaction . . . it is only right that I should work for the happiness of my people who contribute to my happiness. I am now going to attend to that. The need is urgent, but with courage and your advice I shall succeed.' Maurepas' reaction to this letter was to confide to the abbé de Véri: 'I am beginning to love him, as a father loves a willing child.' The Queen also assured Maurepas, Véri tells us, 'that after the coronation the King will occupy himself with his position as King and with public economy and order.' But Véri was sceptical: 'I believe in his good intentions,' he noted; 'but not so much in his ability to execute them.'

It had been on the advice of the abbé de Véri that Maurepas had proposed Turgot for the position of Contrôleur Général des Finances, vacated by the dismissal of the abbé de Terray, who was described by Moreau as 'un des plus mauvais prêtres'. Louis hesitated to appoint a Philosophe – one who sided openly with the encyclopedists – and objected to Maurepas, 'on dit qu'il ne va pas à la Messe' – to which Maurepas replied: 'Sire, l'abbé de Terray y va tous les jours.' It was a clever stroke: Louis, confronted by the honesty of Turgot and the hypocrisy of Terray, appointed Turgot. The clergy were outraged; Voltaire was delighted. On 3 August 1775 he wrote to the King of Prussia: 'We are losing Taste and gaining Thought. I do not know if our King will tread in your footsteps, but I do know that he is taking Philosophes for Ministers . . . Above all there is a Monsieur Turgot, who would be worthy to talk with your Majesty. The priests are in despair. Here is the beginning of a great revolution.'

The King

The first edict signed by Louis XVI had been the suppression of a tax known by the name of 'le don de joyeux avènement'. It was the sum of about 24 000 000 livres which he renounced for the benefit of his people. The preamble to the edict ended with the words: 'there are expenses which touch our person and the lustre of our Court. With regard to these we may follow more promptly the movements of the heart, and we are already considering the means of reducing these within more suitable limits; such sacrifices will cost us nothing if they can be effected to the relief of the people.'

Marie-Antoinette had been able to make a similar gesture. An ancient and onerous imposition, known as the 'droit de ceinture de la Reine', was wisely refused with the words: 'What need would I have of it? Girdles are no longer worn.' On 14 May 1770, four days after their accession, she wrote of Louis to her mother: 'what is certain is that he has a taste for economy and the greatest desire to make his people happy. In everything he has as much desire as need to learn, and I trust God will bless his good will.'

A few days later Papillon de la Ferté, Intendant des Menus Plaisirs, came to ask what were Louis' intentions for his personal pleasures. 'My *menus plaisirs*', answered the King, 'are to walk about in the park. I do not need you.'

Compared with his predecessor, Louis XVI must have seemed almost puritanical. Lord Stormont reported: 'he has more than once spoke with concern of the general licentiousness and dissoluteness that reigns here, and has had conversations on the subject with Monsieur de Maurepas and

Monsieur de Sartine. He asked the latter what people thought of him in Paris, what was the general expectation, and was much pleased with Monsieur de Sartine's answer, which was: "Sire, that the reign of your Majesty will be that of justice, probity and good morals."

'He consulted Monsieur de Maurepas upon the best manner of correcting the morals of his people and restoring them to a due sense of virtue and religion. Monsieur de Maurepas made him a very proper answer: "there is but one way, Sire, and it is one which your Majesty will certainly take, to show them a good example" . . . This prudent advice was the more seasonable as there is reason to suspect that their present Majesties are both desirous of introducing such regulations about kept mistresses etc, as the Empress Queen has attempted with little success and are still less calculated for this meridian than for that of Vienna.' If Louis was really contemplating the setting up of a Chastity Commission in Paris or at Versailles he can have had little understanding of the people that he ruled.

Louis found human beings difficult to understand because he found human relationships difficult. He tended to distance himself from those around him. 'It does not seem', wrote Véri, 'that the King has the slightest affection or preference for anyone. Women in general were not attractive to him and among those by whom he was surrounded, from the highest in rank to the lowest, one cannot detect that he has any predilection whatever.'

In spite of the insistence on his royal rank that ran through his whole education, Louis, when he came to the throne, showed few signs of natural dignity and little interest in proclaiming his pre-eminence. The abbé de Véri is again our informant. 'In one of the balls given in the great Salon d'Hercule,' he wrote in March 1775, 'there was such a considerable crowd that the King found it difficult to make an entry and would have had nowhere to sit had not a lady offered him half her tabouret. Those who were present were sufficiently aware of this embarrassing situation to be struck with it and to regard it as extraordinary.' Monsieur de Maurepas heard of it and felt obliged, in his capacity as 'Mentor', to remonstrate to the King about it.

'In your private life,' he said, 'the atmosphere of equality and ease is entirely appropriate and I would strongly advise you to maintain with your brothers and your family this level which your common upbringing provides you with. But in public you are their King as well as ours, and this dignity should not be forgotten when there are 800 onlookers. The foreign ministers who were present were scandalised by it; you came in without your Captain of the Guards and without being announced. Your armchair was not in place and you were jostled on your way in. We are not at all accustomed to see our King count for so little on a public occasion.' The King was so conscious of the justice of these reflections, observed Véri, that he blushed, hung his head and was silent.

Maurepas was undoubtedly right. The comte d'Hézècques made the same point about the decay of etiquette at Versailles: 'strip the Prince of the glory with which he is surrounded, and he will be no more in the eyes of the populace than an ordinary man.'

If, during his education, Louis had never been allowed to forget his royal rank, neither was he allowed to forget the rank of others. He was not infrequently made aware of the virtues and privileges of his aristocracy. Moreau had overrated their virtues in a passage on Charles VII. 'One can see in this reign how precious is that proud and brave *noblesse* which has no wish but to serve its King and which always regards itself as dishonoured by any disgrace to the throne.' Moreau is also guilty of overstating their privileges. 'Although you belong to the first family of the Universe,' he reminded Louis, 'and although your rank raises you far above the highest of the nobility, you must not imagine that all those beneath you are equal among themselves . . . Nothing offends more in France than to see men of low extraction raised by favour to dignities which belong by right to the high nobility; lowliness of birth is always a blemish in the mind of a Frenchman.'

One of Louis' difficulties was that he was not really a Frenchman. Royal blood is nearly always cosmopolitan. His mother was German, his father, through *his* mother, Marie-Leczinska, was half Slav. There was enough Spanish and Italian blood in the Bourbons to leave little room for anything distinctively French. As Michelet observed, Louis, born at Versailles, was 'tout allemand comme sa mère', whereas Marie-Antoinette, born in Vienna, was 'absolument française, pour mieux dire lorraine, comme son père'.

In a country noted for the ease of its conversation and the quickness of its wit, Louis' ponderous, rather teutonic character was at a disadvantage. It was observed that he was, on the whole, ill at ease with the French aristocracy and much more at home with men of humble rank. 'He was not fond of the Great,' wrote Soulavie, 'but he showed nothing but bonhomie when talking to peasants or artisans.' His 'heavy, lumbering gait' was compared with that of a farmer waddling behind his plough. He had, in fact, received instruction in how to follow the plough.

In September 1768, the *Mercure de France* published an account of two engravings illustrating the pastimes of the young Dauphin. 'Agriculture', it stated, 'has need of encouragement and could receive no greater encouragement than the example of a benevolent prince who pays honour to the work of the cultivator. This was the interesting spectacle which Monseigneur le Dauphin has just given us on 15 June last.' He chose for his outing a field under cultivation, examining the structure and the mechanism of a plough; then 'passing from the theory to the practice, he traced with as much strength and skill a furrow no less deep and as straight as those of the others.'

Louis had a craving for heavy physical labour which perplexed and worried his wife. 'Nothing the Dauphine can do', wrote Mercy to the Empress, 'can turn this young Prince from his extraordinary taste for everything in the way of building, masonry, carpentry and other things of this kind. He is always having something rearranged in his apartments and he works himself with the workmen, moving materials, beams and paving stones, giving himself up for hours at a time to this strenuous exercise, from which he sometimes returns more tired than a day-labourer who is obliged to do these tasks.' In her letter to Count Rosenberg of 17 April 1775, Marie-Antoinette complained: 'my tastes are not those of the King, which are only for hunting and mechanical works.'

For Louis also indulged in the rather improbable hobby of lock-making. It enabled him to combine his love for manual labour with his interest in mechanisms. A forge was established in the mansard roof above the Petits Cabinets. According to the comte d'Hézècques his work showed little evidence of real ability or of long apprenticeship, but it was not unknown for the King of France to be found on his knees before one of the doors of his palace, picking the lock.

The workshop window was provided with a hole through which a telescope could have been passed. 'One can sometimes see the King spend the whole morning in his cabinet,' wrote Véri, 'watching through his telescope those who were arriving at Versailles.'

Véri then gives a quick character sketch: 'a straightforward judgement, simple tastes, an honest heart, a true soul – *voilà son bon côté*. A tendency towards indecision, a weak will, a limited understanding in his way of seeing and of feeling things – *voilà le contraste*!' Véri returns again and again on this apparent inability to make decisions.

> It is perhaps to this multiplicity of opposing connections that the King owes in part his indecision. I can understand it very well in a young man [he was only twenty] whom everyone is priming with contradictory advice which each of them has supported with the respectable terms of religion, of virtue, of public good etc. What is to be feared for France is that this irresolution, mixed with a mistrustfulness, may not be part of the very character of the King and not just the product of the

circumstances in which he finds himself. That was the major defect of the King his grandfather. Those who knew the Dauphin his father often suspected him of the same.

In spite of these apparent ineptitudes, Louis began his reign amid acclamations of popularity which have seldom been surpassed. It was natural to the French to love their king. 'The lowest of chimney sweeps', wrote the Prussian Ambassador, von Vizine, 'is transported with joy at the sight of his sovereign.' No king had been more popular than Henri IV and on the morning of 20 July 1774, wrote the comtesse de Boufflers to Gustavus III of Sweden, the people of Paris found written beneath the statue of that monarch the word 'Resurrexit'. Even the Empress had allowed herself to be carried away. 'Everyone is in ecstasy,' she wrote; 'it promises the greatest of good fortune and you are bringing to life again a country that had its back to the wall.'

But there was a danger in this very enthusiasm – the higher the hopes the deeper the disappointment possible. Marie-Antoinette, writing in July 1774, made the observation: 'I am uneasy about this enthusiasm for the future on the part of the French. The late King left things in a very bad way; opinions are divided and it will be impossible to satisfy everybody in a country where their hastiness demands that everything be done in one minute.'

She was the first to admit her husband's virtues, but, as the comte d'Hézècques so clearly saw, 'Louis XVI was a good King, but unfortunately he lived at a time when his very virtues led inevitably to his ruin.' This is the true definition of tragedy. 'To a shy character, the result of a neglected education, this Prince joined such a kind-heartedness that, in an age of egotism, one never saw him in any circumstances, not even in the moment of danger, put his personal interest in the balance against that of his subjects.'

The abbé de Véri takes the argument one step further. 'It is very disturbing to feel that a king who was hard, even vicious and opinionated, would rule better than a king who was virtuous but weak. A king who was firm, virtuous and judicious would reach that point at which perfection is to be found. The annals of the nations do not record many.'

The comte de Tilly, who was a page at Versailles, makes an interesting reflection. The presence of the King in no way intimidated him; it disappointed him; Louis' countenance was 'simple et bonne' where he would have liked it distinguished and majestic. He looked at his page as a father might look at a son. Alexandre would rather have seen a look which said: 'if necessary, I know how to impose my will, how to command and how to punish.' Looking back when it was all over, Tilly could sigh: 'alas, we know only too well today how a just severity in a king is a cardinal virtue – a virtue which maintains power.'

On Louis' other virtues, however, the verdict of those who knew him is unanimous. But these virtues were often concealed by his shyness and by a sort of awkwardness which could be most unfortunate in a king.

The marquis de Séguret, who, as Premier Commis des Petits Appartements and Secretaire de la Cassette Privée du Roi, was in close and daily contact with the King, gives one of the most authoritative accounts; he comments on the embarrassment which a new face always caused Louis. 'The moment he saw one he blushed and his first reaction was to withdraw . . . this was nothing more than the result of the life of retirement which he led, of that lack of confidence in himself which he was never able to overcome, shyness, diffidence, even, if you like, weakness . . . which must have been deeply rooted in him because the influence of the Queen – that is to say of the finest, the most noble character that nature ever made – was unable to affect it.'

Chateaubriand gives a good example of this in his vivid description of his presentation at Versailles in the autumn of 1787.

> The fatal day arrived . . . all went well so long as I only had to cross the guard rooms. The paraphernalia of the military has always been pleasing to me and has never imposed upon me. But when I entered the Oeil de Boeuf and found myself in the

> middle of the Court, this is when my difficulties started. They looked at me; I heard them enquiring who I was. A mysterious destiny surrounded a *débutant*; he was spared that look of patronising disdain which, together with an extreme politeness, went to make up the inimitable manner of the *grand seigneur*. Who knows if this *débutant* might not become the favourite?
>
> When the King's *lever* was announced, those who had not been presented retired; I was conscious of a movement of vanity; it was not that I felt proud of remaining but I would have felt humiliated at having to go out. The door of the King's bedroom opened; I saw the King complete his toilette – that is to say receive his hat from the Premier Gentilhomme de Service. The King advanced on his way towards mass. I made my bow; the maréchal de Duras named me: 'Sire, le chevalier de Chateaubriand.' The King looked at me and appeared to want to say something to me. I would have been able to reply with a steady countenance; my shyness had disappeared . . . the King, more embarrassed than I was, finding nothing to say, passed on.

Madame de Boigne gives another account of Louis' awkwardness. 'With the best intention of being obliging to someone, he would advance towards him to the point of making him retreat until his back was against the wall; if nothing to say occurred to him – and this was often the case – he made a great guffaw, turned on his heel and walked away. The victim of this public exhibition was always the sufferer and, if he were not an *habitué* of the Court, departed in high dudgeon, convinced that the King had wished to offer him an insult.'

Other witnesses say the same thing. Miromesnil said to Véri:

> I have never known a man, whose inner self was more belied by his outward manner than the King . . . there could not exist the slightest suspicion of hypocrisy so far as the King is concerned, and yet the outward manner has no connection with the inward self. His nature is both good and compassionate, one can never mention some misfortune or suffering without noticing the look of sensitivity on his face; and yet his manner is brusque, his answers are often harsh and his air is

> anything but sensitive. He is firm and courageous in all the decisions that have to be taken in his study; his feelings of fear and misgiving have no place in his decision-making; and yet he cannot say 'no' to his wife, to his brothers, nor to those about him.

This contradiction seems to have gone right through his character. 'He has a great love for the State,' continues Miromesnil, 'and for the general welfare of the State . . . public affairs are close to his heart; and yet he is incapable of saying the right thing to a distinguished soldier, to a successful ambassador, to a provincial commander who had acquitted himself well in the assemblies or tribunals.'

This incapacity, however, was something superficial. Malesherbes, speaking to Bertrand de Moleville, said: 'you must have been astonished to notice how much he gains on acquaintance and how wrongly one judges him when one does not know him . . . Do you not think that if he had been brought up like all of us and helped to conquer that timidity and lack of self-confidence which are his two great faults, one could easily have made a great king of him? And even as he is, I am convinced that with good ministers his reign would have been one of the happiest and most glorious of the monarchy.'

This timidity and lack of self-confidence; this inability to say the right thing or to say 'no' was the more unfortunate because, as the abbé de Véri pointed out, there was 'an Augean stable, or rather a number of Augean stables, to be cleared out. First among them was the Maison du Roi. Its annual expenditure exceeded 30 000 000 livres. It included the households of the King's two brothers; those of his aunts and sisters, the buildings, the stables, the hunts, the kitchens and the crowd of superfluous *valets* who only served for a quarter of the year. In whatever direction retrenchment might be brought to bear, it would fall on the associates of the Master whose ears would be deafened by their cries.'

Among the multiple items of expenditure in the royal budget, a considerable sum was set aside for charity, especially around Versailles, but the charity extended upwards into the ranks of the aristocracy. The marquis de Séguret, who, as Secretaire de la Casette Privée du Roi knew more than most men of Louis' private spending, writes: 'The King received, on the first of every month, 136 000 francs . . . It was all in gold and done up in three bags of white leather.' There was a number of families which, although noble, did not have the means to educate their children properly or to support their sons in the army. 'Our kings', writes Séguret, 'have never refused to come to the assistance of this sector of the aristocracy in which they had an interest.' But the beneficiaries had to collect their subsidies in person. 'On the first day of each month there was a crowd of applicants just like that of the doors of a theatre on a first night.'

The King's charity overlapped his already considerable outlay on the Hunt. 'It was seldom', continues Séguret, 'that a hunt did not incur some damage to crops, that some accident did not take place, some fall, some wound . . . In these cases the King lost no time in making good the compensation. Any damages, assessed by the plaintiff himself, were paid then and there; any accidents were paid for according to the expense in which it might involve the victim, and the King's surgeon, who always followed the hunt, was charged to give all the attentions required at no cost.'

But apart from accidents and damage caused to crops, the Hunt nearly always made other demands on the King's charity. The chase often led him to remote villages and obscure hamlets. 'Then all these worthy people', writes Séguret, 'flocked around their good King, whom they loved so much but saw so seldom. The *curé* would present his respectful homage and never went away without receiving from the King some gifts for his poorest parishioners. It was unusual for the King not only to empty his own purse but those of his companions also.'

His companions no doubt thought it worthwhile. Not only did they enjoy the pleasure and privilege of following their King to hounds; they had a reasonable chance also of being invited to the *souper de chasse* that evening.

These suppers were described by the marquis de Séguret, who, as Premier Commis des Petits Appartements, was an eye-witness. 'Nothing could have been more agreeable than these intimate supper parties. Monsieur came regularly and was seated opposite his brother; he came from a double motive, the first of which was purely material – to satisfy his taste for gastronomy; the second was to display his wit and his knowledge, and he had plenty of these. He often monopolised the conversation and was in turn witty, informative and amusing: the latest anecdote, the fashionable play, all were the object of the most shrewd and the most pleasing observations.' The company was often no less brilliant – 'all of them men gifted with that French wit, with that Parisian urbanity, with that exquisite good breeding which is so seldom found elsewhere; once can imagine what these conversations were like.'

The comte d'Artois, who dined as late as five o'clock, only joined them for dessert. 'His presence', continues Séguret, 'always stimulated their gaiety. The King, as is well known, had a tender affection for this brother, whose frank, open and agreeable character compensated, so to speak, for his own sequestered and monotonous life. He treated him as his own son. It was easy to detect the difference between the positions of these two princes with regard to the King. Monsieur, when speaking of the King, never called him anything but "le roi", whereas the comte d'Artois always called him "mon frère", with that tone of friendship and familiarity which announces a mutual affection.'

As one would expect in France, the standard of cuisine was extremely high. 'It is true, one must admit,' wrote Séguret, 'that it would be difficult to take the art of gastronomy to greater lengths, and the delicious food of the petits appartements became proverbial.' But, almost unbelievably, the wine did not match the food. The King was served with a single bottle of champagne *nature*, chilled on ice, both in summer and in winter. He usually shared it with his two immediate companions whom he always designated before they took their seats, and these were privileged because, as Séguret affirms, 'on servait d'assez mauvais vin à la table du roi.' For the second course a single bottle of Clos-Vougeot was placed before Louis: 'he took one glass and passed the bottle to his neighbours.'

Much heart-burning was caused by the exclusiveness of these supper parties. Ladies were informed in advance of their invitation. The men were subjected to a more humiliating treatment. When there was a hunt, they were expected to apply for an invitation. When there was not, a special bench at the theatre was reserved for those who hoped to be invited. 'During the entertainment,' wrote the comtesse de Boigne, 'the King directed his large opera glasses on these benches and could be seen writing down a certain number of names.' The applicants then went to the anteroom of the *cabinets*, where an usher read out the names of those selected. 'The lucky chosen one made his reverence to the others and entered the holy of holies.' When the last name had been read, the usher banged the door shut 'avec une violence d'étiquette'.

Those not invited to the private supper parties had the right to eat at the King's expense at the *table d'honneur* in the Grand Commun, but to eat here was regarded as an indignity. 'One would have sooner eaten a chicken at the *rôtisserie*.' And yet these dinners were, by universal consent, regarded as the best at Versailles, both for good food, good wine and good company. 'Their society was most agreeable and enlightened; one met there artists, men of learning and men of letters; it was highly entertaining, but an *homme de Cour* could not make a practice of going there. My father frequently regretted it.'

When there was not a supper in the Petits Appartements the royal family usually ate together. After the heavy demands made on them by etiquette throughout the day 'they felt the need', wrote Séguret, 'to come together like a good bourgeois family, round the same table'. This family reunion was held *chez* Madame. They each had their own supper brought, but, as Marie-Antoinette seldom touched hers, for like Artois she also dined late in the afternoon, Louis did not bring his own. 'As soon as the King arrived, all took their places; the servants retired having already placed in reach of everyone what was needed for them to serve themselves . . . One cannot say exactly what took place or what was said at this august family reunion,' admitted Séguret; 'one may, however, conjecture, from the great outbursts of laughter which one often heard that these were not exactly mournful occasions.'

Such was the social life of the King. In his private life one of the most domestic of his tastes was a love of reading. There was no library worthy of the name in the King's Apartment and as soon as he came to the throne Louis determined to remedy this defect. He took a genuine interest in geography and history and many forms of science; he enjoyed the works of Molière and knew much of Racine by heart. He was, in fact, a great reader (he even bought a copy of the entire *Encyclopedia*), and it was only proper that he should collect his own books and that they should be suitably housed. He chose for the site of this library the central room in the former apartment of Madame Adelaïde, next after the Salon de Musique. These rooms form a continuation of the Petits Appartements du Roi on the north side of the Cour de Marbre.

On 10 June 1774, only one month after he succeeded to the throne, the work was commissioned. It was carried out that summer during the Voyage of Compiègne. Gabriel drew up the instructions. 'You will need to demolish immediately all the existing panelling and to trace out very carefully on the parquet the plan of the whole so as to establish the thickness of the woodwork, and to trace on the walls all the elevations.'

To the historian of art Louis XVI's library is significant as the last work at Versailles to be designed by Gabriel and the last to be carved by Antoine Rousseau; to the biographer it is evocative as the room in which Louis probably passed his happiest hours within the Château.

Gabriel and Rousseau had between them been largely

responsible for the development of the *style Louis XV* at Versailles. Now, in their old age, they were to create the style of his successor. It bears impressive testimony to their versatility that two of the chief exponents of the style of Louis XV should have created the noblest example of the style of Louis XVI.

It is a decor which manages to combine a sumptuosity suited to its situation with all the personal implications of the word a 'study'. As Evelyne Lever describes the room – 'elle invite à l'étude.' The decor owes much of its character to the gilded leather binding of the books.

Here, surrounded by emblems of his country's distinguished literary past, Louis loved to sit, either in a comfortable armchair by the fire or at a little desk drawn up in the window recess from which he could look down on the people who came and went about their business in the courtyards of the palace. Behind him, the vast mahogany table, made from a single section of a tree, was littered with books and papers.

This is how Arthur Young saw the room on 23 October 1787: 'In viewing the King's apartment, which he had not left a quarter of an hour, with those slight traits of disorder that showed he *lived* in it, it was amusing to see the background figures that were walking uncontrolled about the palace . . . men whose rags betrayed them to be in the last stages of poverty. One loves the master of the house who would not be hurt or offended at seeing his apartment thus occupied if he returned suddenly . . . this is certainly a feature of that *good temper* which appears to me so visible everywhere in France.'

Arthur Young was an enthusiastic admirer of 'that friend of mankind, Turgot'. As Contrôleur Général des Finances, Turgot's ministry did not last very long. He and Maurepas were not men capable of working together. 'At heart they were both good,' wrote Véri; 'what they lacked was just a little drop of oil.' Sénac de Meilhan, a son of the Court surgeon, suggests that Turgot 'did not know how to come to terms with human frailty . . . he behaved like a surgeon, accustomed to operate on dead bodies, not realising that he was operating on living beings.' Lord Stormont joins the chorus: 'he does not know how to soften or qualify a refusal; he is impatient of the slightest contradiction.' On all sides Turgot aroused opposition and hostility. The comte de Creutz, Ambassador from Gustavus III of Sweden, reported on 14 March 1776: 'Monsieur Turgot was the butt of the most formidable league composed of all the most distinguished people in the land.'

That Marie-Antoinette was among these there is no doubt; Turgot had affronted Madame de Polignac. But, as Véri records, Turgot was 'the target of all the Court, hated by the financiers, opposed by the parliamentary factions, deafened by the cry raised by the population of Paris, to all appearances abandoned by the most accredited among the ministers', and, needless to add, detested by the clergy. Turgot was supported only by the King. Véri records that a workman who helped Louis with his lathe had told him: 'Sire, I see here only yourself and Monsieur Turgot who are friends of the people.'

Véri regards Turgot as being partly responsible for his own downfall. 'The character of Monsieur Turgot seemed to me to play a greater part than anything else.' He puts the ultimate responsiblity, however, on Louis. 'The personal disposition of the King, which Monsieur de Maurepas seconded but did not instigate, was the true cause of this event.' Turgot's overall plan for regenerating France in one year was summed up by Louis in a marginal annotation: 'The system of Monsieur Turgot is a beautiful dream; it is the Utopia of an individual, projected by a man who has excellent intentions, but which would overturn the State.'

The extent of Marie-Antoinette's involvement in Turgot's dismissal is difficult to assess. Mercy, writing to Vienna on 16 May 1776, states that: 'The Contrôleur Général, learning that the Queen hates him, largely for this reason decided to resign; the Queen's plan was to demand that the King should dismiss Turgot and even send him to the Bastille.' Mercy is guilty of misrepresentation. Turgot did not resign; he was dismissed. On 12 May Louis sent Bertin to him to demand the remission of his portfolio and his resignation from office.

Maria Theresa, writing from Laxenburg on 30 May, was clearly more inclined to believe Marie-Antoinette's own account: 'I am very pleased that you had no part in the changing of the two ministers, [Turgot and Malesherbes] who have, none the less, a good reputation in the eyes of the populace and have only failed, in my opinion, by trying to do too much at once.' The abbé de Véri, always averse to the intervention of the Queen in politics, contented himself with the remark: 'Aussi la Reine n'a-t-elle agi que faiblement contre lui.' But, as Vincent Cronin sums up, 'a decision taken freely by Louis in the light of public opinion was attributed to the intrigues of a meddlesome wife.'

When Turgot knew that his hour had come he wrote three long and passionate letters to the King. 'You have no personal experience, but, to feel the reality of the dangers of your position, do you not have the experience, so very recent, of your ancestor? I have given you the picture of all the evils which were caused by the weakness of the late King. I set before you the progress of those intrigues which slowly undermined his authority. I dare to ask you to reread that letter and to ask yourself if you want to run the risk of the same dangers. I would even say of greater dangers.'

The situation, he said, had greatly worsened since 1770. 'People's minds are a thousand times more heated on all sorts of issues.' It was weakness that lay behind the cruelties of Charles IX; it was weakness that created the League against Henri III; it was weakness that had caused all the misfortunes of the previous reign. 'Do not ever forget, Sire,' concluded Turgot, 'that it was weakness which put the head of Charles I upon the block.'

The Queen

When Arthur Young had completed his inspection of the King's apartment at Versailles and made his comment on the *good temper* which he experienced on all sides, he met with a disappointment. 'I desired to see the Queen's apartment, but I could not. Is her Majesty in? No. Then why not see it as well as the King's? *Ma foi Monsieur c'est une autre chose*!'

Marie-Antoinette occupied the state rooms which form the first floor of the south range of the main block, overlooking the Parterre de l'Orangerie. This was the Appartement de la Reine, in which the State Bedroom had been redecorated in 1737 for Marie-Leczinska.

The life of Marie-Leczinska at Versailles had not been a particularly happy existence. Too ready to find pleasure in what she knew to be her duty, she had fallen passionately in love with her handsome young husband. But she was not made to inspire similar affections for very long in Louis' heart. Their relationship soon degenerated into indifference on his part and timidity on hers. Too nervous to say anything of importance to him, she took to communicating with her husband by letter.

Although ambitious courtiers could afford to ignore Marie-Leczinska completely, they respected her. In Europe's greatest school for scandal no breath of slander ever ruffled the serene calm of her existence. For although the French were not noticeably addicted to temperance or chastity in their private lives, these virtues were expected of their Queen. Caesar might indeed be permitted his indulgences; it was still required that Caesar's wife should be above suspicion.

Madame du Deffand, who was a niece of the duchesse de Luynes and knew the Queen well, described her in a letter to Horace Walpole. 'Her integrity and irreproachable conduct were combined with a rare discernment and great modesty, and her desire always to give pleasure made her company delightful.' But she was more than a virtuous woman: she was a Queen. 'This same Princess,' wrote Président Hénault, 'so good, so simple, so sweet and so affable, carries herself on state occasions with a dignity which commands respect. She keeps up in the Court that concept of grandeur which was always represented to us as that of Louis XIV.' It was only on her side of the palace that the true traditions of the French monarchy were maintained.

Here, in the former State Rooms of Marie-Leczinska, lived Marie-Antoinette and her ladies, their towering head-dresses and unwieldly trains imposing upon them a stately deportment and an odd, distinctive gait by which a lady of the Court could always be identified. 'It was a great art', wrote Madame de la Tour du Pin, 'to be able to walk in this vast apartment without treading on the train of the lady who preceded you. You had to avoid ever raising the foot, but to let it slide along the parquet flooring, always highly polished, until you reached the Salon d'Hercule.' The Salon d'Hercule, which connected the Grand Appartement with the Chapel, had a stone floor and ladies put their trains over their arms. Those who were to be presented at Court took special lessons in how to walk and the standard was extremely high. 'Les dames avaient en tout celà', admitted Hézècques, 'une adresse admirable.'

As for the Queen herself, she stood out in clear relief against the already brilliant background of the ladies of the Court 'as a great oak in a forest dominates the trees around it'.

'She had that which is more important on the throne than perfect beauty,' wrote the comte de Tilly; 'she had the figure of the Queen of France, even at those moments at which she was trying above all to appear a beautiful woman.' For Marie-Antoinette was not insensible to her personal charms.

'Always more the woman than the Queen,' wrote Besenval, 'she forgot that her fate was to live and die upon a throne; she desired to wield the sceptre which the gift of beauty accords to any lovely woman.' The comtesse de Boigne confirms the verdict of Besenval: 'the Queen liked to be surrounded by the most agreeable young men that the Court could offer; she was far more willing to accept the homage that was offered to her as a woman than that which was offered to her as a Queen.'

Tilly describes Marie-Antoinette with the exactness of a connoisseur. 'She had eyes which were not beautiful but which were expressive of every disposition: benevolence or aversion were displayed on her countenance in a manner which was entirely her own . . . Her skin was admirable; her neck and shoulders also; the bust a little too full and the figure a little lacking in elegance; I have never seen such beautiful arms and hands. She had two ways of walking: one firm and a little hurried, but always noble; the other less vigorous, more poised . . . but nevertheless not inspiring any lack of respect. No one ever made a curtsey with so much grace, saluting ten people with a single bow and turning her head and eyes at each one. In a word she was the sort of woman to whom one would instinctively have offered not a chair but a throne.'

But the most interesting portrait of the Queen comes from the most observant eye of the great portrait painter Madame Vigée-Lebrun:

> It was in the year 1779 that I first made a portrait of the Queen, at that time in the full radiance of her youth and beauty.
>
> Marie-Antoinette was large, admirably well made, well covered but not too much so. Her arms were superb, her hands *petite* and perfectly formed, her feet charming. No woman in France walked as well as she did, carrying her head high with a majesty which distinguished the sovereign in the midst of all her Court, without this majesty in any way detracting from all that her appearance had of sweetness and good will. In fact it is very difficult for anyone who has not set eyes on the Queen to get any idea of this reunion of so many graces and such nobility. Her features were not regular; she

> inherited from her family that long and narrow oval face which is peculiar to the Austrian nation. Her eyes were not large; their colour was almost blue; her expression was lively and sweet, her nose fine and pretty and her mouth not too large although her lips were thick. But what was most remarkable about her face was the radiance of her complexion. I have never seen one so brilliant, and brilliant is the word; for her skin was so transparent that there was no shadow upon it. For this reason I could not render the effect to my satisfaction. The colours were lacking with which to depict this freshness, these tones so exquisite which belonged only to this charming countenance and which I have found in no other woman.

When Marie-Antoinette became the Queen of France there was one man who viewed her accession with grave disquiet. A certain marquis de Pontécoulant had offended her when she was Dauphine and, in her youthful zest, she had vowed never to forget his offence. When he saw her mount the throne he concluded that all was lost and resigned from his position as Major in the Gardes du Corps, explaining to his commanding officer, the Prince de Beauveau, his motives for doing so. The Prince de Beauveau decided to take the matter to Marie-Antoinette who made the fine response: 'The Queen does not remember the quarrels of the Dauphine.'

They were noble words but they were not entirely true. Marie-Antoinette's first move was to procure the disgrace of the duc d'Aiguillon. He had been far too closely associated with Madame du Barry to be able to survive, but for the fact that Maurepas was his uncle. Marie-Antoinette acted in the matter with a moderation which did her no little credit.

On 7 June 1774, Mercy d'Argenteau wrote to the Empress: 'The Queen has forgotten everything that might have displeased her [when she was Dauphine], only the duc d'Aiguillon and his duchess are excepted from this rule of goodness.' But d'Aiguillon was at first permitted to retain his post as Captain of the light cavalry and to come again to Court – 'something rare,' noted the duc de Croÿ, 'and which reflected honour on Marie-Antoinette.'

Far from being grateful for this unwonted leniency,

d'Aiguillon remained in Paris, discontented and embittered, and made his house, writes the marquis de Ségur, 'the centre for the first attacks which assailed the reputation of the Queen. From here went out the cutting remarks, the scandalous stories, the libels, the verses, the songs – a whole arsenal of poisoned darts which, directed at the woman, pierced also the sovereign and began, little by little, to shake the foundations of the monarchy.'

It was in response to this that Marie-Antoinette insisted that d'Aiguillon should be dismissed from Court and not allowed to retire to his Château at Veretz near Tours, but was to be sent to his duchy of Aiguillon. Maurepas, who was capable of plain speaking with both the King and the Queen, had tried to reason with her. 'Madame,' he said, 'it seems to me that if the King is to do a wrong to anyone it should not originate in you.' 'You may be right,' answered the Queen, 'and I certainly do not intend to act like this again. But this I shall do.'

To her mother, Marie-Antoinette made light of the matter: 'we have already gained something from the notice which the King gave to Monsieur d'Aiguillon not to come to the coronation and to retire to Aiguillon: we have avoided the formula of exile, which is barbarous.'

To the Count Rosenberg, however, Marie-Antoinette wrote in significantly different terms. Rosenberg had accompanied her brother Maximilian, on his visit to France. He was an old friend of the family and Marie-Antoinette wrongly supposed that she could afford to be a little indiscreet and to say, for once, what she really thought.

'I must go back to the departure of Monsieur d'Aiguillon,' she wrote on 13 July 1775, 'in order that you may fully understand my behaviour. His departure was entirely of my contriving. The matter had come to a head: this dreadful man maintained a system of espionage and evil intentions. He had sought to defy me more than once over the affair of Monsieur de Guisnes; immediately after that judgement I demanded his removal of the King. It is true that I did not want a *lettre de cachet*, but nothing was lost thereby, for instead of staying in Touraine, as he desired, he was asked to continue his route as far as Aiguillon, which is in Gascony.'

The abbé de Véri remarked à propos the exile of d'Aiguillon,

> All that would be the merest trifle if the Queen's influence were confined to matters which had nothing to do with public order. But no-one can answer for this. The King fears her more than he loves her, for he can be seen to be in just as good spirits and even more at ease at those receptions at which she is not present.
>
> The influence of the Queen in great matters (if it became a reality) would not be to the advantage of the State. Her head, less good than her heart, is not fitted for it; she would be easily deceived and incapable of being a decision maker on all matters. Her husband would be the first to suffer from it. His reign would be disturbed by Court intrigues and even more by popular anger of which I can see the seeds becoming stronger every day. A slow and hidden fire will burst out one day through any aperture.

But there was a sequel to the d'Aiguillon affair which needs to be quoted. In July 1776 Madame de Chabrillan, the exiled duc's daughter, went to visit him and died at the Château d'Aiguillon. Marie-Antoinette wrote to her mother: 'it would have been inhuman to oblige him to stay in the place where his daughter had died. I asked the King to grant him liberty to go anywhere he pleased, excepting only the Court; the King granted it to me.'

Marie-Antoinette's first mistake as Queen was to involve herself in political appointments. The problem often arose from her attachment to the duc de Choiseul. To him she owed the Austrian Alliance which had placed her on the throne of France. But the return to power of the duc de Choiseul under Louis XVI was almost unthinkable. Marie-Antoinette, however, continued to agitate in favour of his party.

The retirement, in January 1775, of the duc de la Vrillière from his post of Secretary of State was the occasion of Marie-

Antoinette's first intervention. She wanted the post for Monsieur d'Ennery who was a member of Choiseul's party. Maurepas, Turgot and Véri wanted Monsieur de Malesherbes who was, however, extremely reluctant to take office.

One of the reasons why Malesherbes was reluctant to accept office was his fear of Marie-Antoinette: 'it was the complaisance with regard to all the wishes of the Queen in matters of government, which the public attributed to the King.' Louis, however, had not yielded to the Queen. His reported words were: 'Ce sont là vos désirs, Madame, je les connais; cela suffit. C'est à moi à faire la décision.'

On 17 June 1775 Véri wrote: 'it is essential that the choice of ministers and the direction of matters of importance are not left to the Queen. If she had any of the ability of her mother, Maria Theresa, Monsieur de Maurepas would have been the first to want her to fulfil the function of King in conjunction with her husband.'

On this matter of appointment – the choice between Ennery and Malesherbes – she made her position clear: 'I forewarn you', she told Maurepas, 'that I shall speak of it to the King this evening and that I will tell him again tomorrow what my wishes are. I repeat to you that I desire to be in accord with you. It is up to you. You know on what conditions.'

'This was the moment of combat,' wrote Véri, 'on the outcome of which would depend the stability of the present Ministry or the resignation of Maurepas . . . Our conversation was confined to the course to propose to the King in order to put an end to the influence of the Queen.' It was not Ennery but Malesherbes who was appointed.

This situation did not, however, lead to any lasting hostility between Maurepas and the Queen. 'The reconciliation', wrote Véri in 1775, 'took place in the month of September. The Queen and the ministers were, by arrangement, *tête à tête* when the King entered. "I recognised", she said, "that I was in the wrong over Monsieur de Maurepas and I now declare to you that I am very content with him."

The King, transported with joy, ran to embrace her while pressing with one of his hands those of Monsieur de Maurepas . . . all this produced a mixture of emotion and light-heartedness which brought about a concord which has not been broken to this day.'

In the letter to Count Rosenberg already referred to, Marie-Antoinette permitted herself an indiscreet remark about her husband, which was duly reported to her mother. 'Perhaps you have heard of the audience which I gave to the duc de Choiseul at Reims . . . You will readily believe that I did no such thing without mentioning the matter to the King, but you will never guess the adroitness with which I avoided seeming to ask his permission. I told him that I wished to see Monsieur de Choiseul but that the only difficulty was to choose which day.'

At this point Marie-Antoinette forgot all caution and made the famous remark: 'J'ai si bien fait que le pauvre homme m'a arrangé lui même l'heure la plus commode où je pouvais le voir.' The obvious note of contempt in the words 'the poor man' so shocked Rosenberg that he showed the letter to the Emperor Joseph. Joseph's immediate reaction was to write a letter to his sister in terms which showed only too clearly that he was his mother's son:

> My dear sister, in what do you think you are interfering? In ousting ministers, in having others sent to live on their estates, in giving some department to this man or to that man, in causing this person to win his case, in creating a new and expensive post at Court . . . even in using language hardly suited to your position? Have you once asked yourself by what right you interfere with matters of government and of the French Monarchy? What studies did you ever undertake? What knowledge have you acquired that you dare to imagine that your decisions or opinions are worth anything, above all in matters which demand the most extensive knowledge? You, an amiable young person whose only thoughts are on frivolity and fashion and your own daily amusement; you, who do not read or listen to reason for a quarter of an hour a month, who do not reflect or meditate at all, I am sure.

Would it be possible to write anything more imprudent,

> more unreasonable, more unseemly than what you indicate to the Count Rosenberg touching the manner in which you contrived a conversation at Reims with the duc de Choiseul? If such a letter were ever to go astray, if ever, as I hardly doubt, you let fall similar expressions and phrases to your intimate confidants . . . I promise you, by the attachment which I have pledged to you, that it would cause me infinite pain.

This letter was not sent. It shows, however, in its obvious sincerity, how Joseph felt about his sister's behaviour at Versailles. But he showed the Rosenberg letter to Maria Theresa who, with typical autocracy, suppressed her son's answer and sent her own:

'I cannot conceal from you that a letter written to Rosenberg has thrown me into the greatest consternation. What style! What levity! Where is that heart, so good, so generous of that Archduchess Marie-Antoinette? I can see in it only intrigue, base hatred, a spirit of persecution and ridicule; intrigue worthy of a Pompadour or a du Barry trying to play some role, but in no way worthy of a Queen, a great princess of the House of Lorraine and of Austria, full of goodness and decency.'

Then after castigating her daughter's 'ridiculous head-dresses' and her habit of going about without the King, she returns to the Rosenberg letter. 'What language! "The poor man"! Where is the respect and the gratitude for all his complaisances? I leave you to your own reflections and will say no more, though there is much more that could be said.' Too late in the day, having neglected her daughter's upbringing and education, Maria Theresa began to see the faults in her daughter's personality.

The abbé de Vermond has left a thumbnail sketch of her character: 'In spite of the extreme levity of the Queen, her taste for amusement and her very great antipathy to any sort of application, the time will come when she will tire of her present dissipations and very possibly her ambitions will be aroused at the same time. The sentiment which comes through most clearly in her is her desire – or rather her fixed determination – to be absolutely independent. She has made it sufficiently clear on all occasions that she will not be governed nor directed nor even guided by anyone at all.'

Unlike her brother Joseph, she reacted against her domineering mother. Although there was real affection between them, their correspondence shows that Maria Theresa was determined to control her daughter and that her daughter was determined not to be controlled.

Maria Theresa had not the slightest doubt that her constant rebukes were the direct expression of her love. 'With the old year,' she wrote on 31 December 1772, 'I come to the end of my preaching. You would do me a great wrong if you do not take them as the greatest marks of my tenderness and of the keen interest which I take in your future and your welfare, with which I am continually concerned.'

It was on receipt of this letter that Marie-Antoinette admitted to Mercy: 'I love the Empress, but I am afraid of her although she is so far off; even when I am writing to her I never feel at ease with her.' She therefore took little notice of the preaching.

'She is mistress of her own will,' wrote Vermond; 'she does not like to apply herself to anything, she cannot bear any restraints; she does not find much resource in the royal family; above all she is afraid of boredom.' It was this fear of boredom that led her into most of what her mother called 'dissipations'.

The French word *dissipation* is the word most frequently used by Maria Theresa. It does not have the same overtones of debauchery as 'dissipation' has in English. It means the dissolution of a cloud, the dispersing of care, the distraction of the mind from concentration; it means a refusal to think seriously, even a fear of thinking seriously. It is typical of the avoidance mechanism of a mind which dares not face its most prominent problem. For Marie-Antoinette that problem was almost certainly her unconsummated marriage.

Again and again those who were closest to her remarked on her high qualities of character and mind, and on this refusal to take things seriously which made them of no effect. In June 1774 Mercy wrote to the Emperor Joseph II: 'It would be necessary for the Queen to have the will to overcome the extreme repugnance which she has for any serious matter or reflexion; if this important point could be gained all the disadvantages which are to be feared would disappear. She is endowed with an excellent character, with a good sense of humour, with sagacity and discernment; but a little application is needed in the use of such great gifts; without that they remain unproductive and worthless.'

About this time Mercy wrote to Kaunitz: 'this young Princess, as the result of her vivacious and trivial nature, is embarrassed and at a loss at what to do by anything which demands any sustained reflexion, any connections of thought, any attention; the means whereby she frees herself from such embarrassment is to think no more of the matters which cause it.'

Mercy was constantly chiding his royal charge with her lack of concentration – but to no effect. 'She listens to my representations with goodness, but while admitting artlessly to her faults, she does nothing to correct them.'

Three year later, on 5 December 1777, Maria Theresa was beginning to lose patience and even to lose hope. 'There might arrive some serious set-back which would engage her in a change of conduct; but is it not to be feared that such a change would come too late to repair the damage which my daughter continues to cause by her irresponsible behaviour?' Her behaviour, it needs hardly be said, was eagerly observed by the whole of France.

In January 1775, her popularity in Paris was still at its height. She attended a performance of Gluck's *Iphigénie en Aulide*. There is an aria in this in which Achilles sings: 'chantons, célébrons notre Reine!' The singer, Henri l'Arrivée, seeing that Marie-Antoinette was in the royal box, made a gesture which unmistakably applied those words to her. Soon the whole house was on its feet, singing and applauding. The Queen was so moved that she was obliged to produce her handkerchief, a gesture which, says Madame Campan, 'merely added to the general euphoria'.

By the end of the year the situation had begun to change for the worse. In October the comte de Viri, Ambassador from Sardinia, wrote in his despatch: 'One notices with distress that the Queen always shows a greater inclination for the society of the younger set. Her conduct earns the general disapprobation of the Court and of all the Nation.' Viri had a particular interest in the affairs of France for his country had provided the wives of both the comte de Provence and the comte d'Artois. In August the comtesse d'Artois had given birth to the duc d'Angoulême, who, since Marie-Antoinette was still childless, was heir apparent to the throne. This inability to produce children was not only distressing to Louis and to Marie-Antoinette; it was a political issue of the first importance. Only too often in such a case the blame is put on the woman.

Rumours were circulating, continues Viri, 'now that the King is in a condition to cohabit with her, now that he is resolved to undergo the famous operation which has been talked about for so long.' The 'famous operation' which had so intrigued the Court, remains a mystery. It was never disclosed what the nature of the operation was nor is there any convincing evidence that it ever took place.

On 30 October Viri wrote again to d'Aigueblanche, 'One hears more talk than ever for the last two or three days of the determination which the King is supposed to have taken to have the famous operation which we are assured it is necessary for him to undergo if he is to cohabit with the Queen, and it is said that this will take place next week or at least after the return of the Court to Versailles, which will be 16 November. Cabals and intrigues play such a part in all that is put about today that I cannot say anything more to Your Excellency on this subject.'

A year later it was still a subject for diplomatic speculation. In December 1776 Frederick the Great wrote to his Ambassador at Versailles, the Baron von Goltz, mentioning a 'complete cooling off between the King and Queen. It even constitutes, as I have it on good authority, one of the objects of the Emperor's voyage. His Majesty intends to reform the conduct of his sister and to re-establish a good relationship between her and her husband.'

Goltz replied: 'The great obstacle to this perfect union is the incompatibility of the tastes and characters of the two spouses. The King is calm, rather passive, loving the solitude of his library, which he only leaves with reluctance except to go hunting. His wife is, as is usual at her age – which is nevertheless the King's – extremely vivacious, loving a quick succession of pleasures and their diversity. It seems to me that it will not be easy for the Emperor to remove the said obstacle.'

Goltz then returns to the matter of the operation and points out that a successful operation could be of advantage to the Queen unless it opened the door to other female relationships. He ends with the words: 'but I think that this change will be more a matter of time than brought about by the eloquence of the Emperor.'

On 4 April 1777 Goltz reports again: 'The lack of physical interest which Sa Majesté très Chrétien has so far taken in either his wife or in womankind in general is no doubt the result of a defect in some internal organ, very easy to correct by the admission of the doctors, but which the Prince has refused, either from fear of unfortunate consequences of the operation, or because his temperament does not excite him. As for his constitution, it is very strong . . . If this Prince were to develop a taste for women it might perhaps be a rather difficult question for the Ministers to decide – whether it would be advisable to give him a mistress.'

Five months later, after the visit of the Emperor Joseph to his sister, Goltz took up the same theme. On 9 September he wrote to Frederick: 'it is not impossible that the Queen might become pregnant. The little difficulty which made this impossible for the King has resolved itself without any operation. A pregnancy would without doubt increase the credit of the Queen.'

Meanwhile Viri had been noting a steady deterioration in

Marie-Antoinette's behaviour and in her reputation in Court and country. In November he claims that 'the conduct of the Queen continues to alienate her more and more from the opinion of the populace of Paris, where she is no longer received with the same applause; the too great complaisance of the King with regard to this matter gives rise to expressions of the most improper nature on the character and quality of mind of this Prince.'

In December, Viri is deploring the circulation of verses which censured the Queen 'dans les termes les plus indécents'. She appears, he writes, 'deeply affected on reading them, but in spite of this she does not alter her course . . . she gives access to a troop of young people who are known only for their lightness and absence of mind.'

Finally he introduces the note of real scandal, only to cover it with a polite veil of incredulity: 'it is claimed that the duc de Coigny is able to enter the apartment of this Princess at certain times, which gives occasion to a number of remarks which I would be inclined to regard as calumnies if the levity of the Queen's behaviour did not suffice to give them credit.' This was the sort of scandal that public opinion lusted for – the Queen of France involved in amorous intrigue!

The prince de Ligne comes to her rescue. 'Her so-called gallantry was never anything but a deep and perhaps distinguishing friendship for one or two persons and the general coquetry of a woman and a Queen who seeks to please everybody. Even in those earliest days, when her youth and inexperience might have encouraged some to be too much at their ease with her, there was not one of us, who had the happiness of daily contact with her, who would have dared to abuse it by even the most trifling impropriety; she made herself the Queen, without being aware of it, and we adored her, but did not dream of loving her.'

The prince de Ligne underlines the difference between the easy-going life of Schönbrunn and the stiff formalities of Versailles. 'Her father, Francis, received at his table the principal officers of the crown and allowed them the utmost liberty. Maria Theresa admitted to her intimacy most of the ladies of the Court and even stayed with some during the summer in their country houses. She might be seen walking up and down or knitting in the gardens, or reading in a grotto, without a single lady-in-waiting in attendance. It was thus that Marie-Antoinette, from her very childhood, had habits of innocent freedom and familiarity which, when she brought them to France, were judged severely.'

It was not long before the general disapproval of the company which the Queen kept became focused on particular friends who could be described as favourites. The first was the princesse de Lamballe.

Marie-Thérèse-Louise de Carignan was a princess of the House of Savoy. On 10 January 1767, the engagement was announced between her and Louis-Alexandre-Joseph-Stanislas, prince de Lamballe, only son of the duc de Penthièvre, who was the son of the comte de Toulouse, youngest son of Louis XIV and Madame de Montespan. He had been 'legitimatised'. The duc de Penthièvre was the owner of the Hôtel de Toulouse, one of the most beautiful of the private palaces of Paris, and now the Banque de France. He also owned the Châteaux of Rambouillet, Anet and Sceaux and the opulent estates belonging to each of them. Penthièvre was, next to the King, the richest man in France. His only son, the prince de Lamballe, was suffering from a painful and humiliating disease which resulted from his life of debauchery. It was the duc's pious hope that Marie-Thérèse-Louise might have a salutary influence upon his morals.

Her character was duly sketched by Mercy for the benefit of the Empress. 'She combines a great sweetness and a great charm with a thoroughly honest character – far removed from the love of intrigue and without any drawback. Although she comes from Piedmont, the princess is in no way in league with Madame [the comtesse de Provence] nor with Madame d'Artois.' She was highly strung and fainted on the slightest of pretexts.

A few days before the coronation, Louis agreed, without

the consent of his ministers, to her appointment as Chef du Conseil et Surintendante of the Queen's Household. It left much to be defined, however, as to the exact specification of the responsibilities and privileges of the position. The abbé de Vermond, with a view to appeasing the ministers, drew up a clear statement of these while at the same time suppressing certain abuses and certain expenses. This move, however, brought down the wrath of the duc de Penthièvre who refused to allow his daughter-in-law to accept a position 'stripped of any of its ancient prerogatives'. The post had to be revived as it had always been and with the huge salary of 50 000 ecus undiminished.

One of the reasons for so high a salary was the obligation incumbent upon the Surintendante to entertain the Queen. In January 1776 Louis de Bachaumont, author of the *Mémoires Secrets* records: 'the balls at Versailles will start up again on the 4th of this month; they will be hosted by Madame la princesse de Lamballe, which makes the etiquette less restricting. The Queen can dance and take supper with whomsoever she chooses.'

In her letter, already quoted, to Count Rosenberg of July 1775, Marie-Antoinette referred to the retirement of the comtesse de Noailles, now maréchale de Mouchy, from her Household: 'I asked the King to take advantage of the change-over and to appoint Madame de Lamballe as Surintendante. Imagine my delight; I will make my closest friend happy and that will give even more pleasure to me than to her. It is still a secret; I have not told the Empress yet.'

On 1 October, when the news was out, Véri made a more penetrating observation: 'the princesse de Lamballe has been appointed Surintendante de la Maison de la Reine, a position which was abolished some years ago. It was known that the Queen had desired the post for the princess. From the moment that Louis XVI was King and the retirement of the comtesse de Noailles has been effected, the people, who see the recreation of a purely ceremonial post, costly and embarrassing because of its prerogatives, take this as an ill omen for the future.'

Just at her moment of triumph, however, the princesse de Lamballe found herself confronted with a rival. Early in 1776 Mercy had informed the Empress of a certain cooling off in the relationship. 'If the princesse de Lamballe does not lay her plans better in the future,' he wrote, 'it is probable that the favour which she enjoys, and which appears to be somewhat diminished, could well fade out in the long run.' Meanwhile another star had risen above the horizons of Versailles – the comtesse Jules de Polignac. 'This year [1777],' noted the comte Valentin d'Esterhazy, 'the Queen appointed the comte Jules de Polignac as her Premier Écuyer and began, by this means, to make for herself the most implacable enemies.'

Yolande de Polastron, wife of the comte Jules de Polignac, was born in 1749 and was therefore six years older than Marie-Antoinette. Opinions about her differed. Mercy merely found her 'wanting in sense, judgement, or any quality worthy of the confidence of a great princess'. To the comte de Ségur she was the paragon of perfection. 'It would be impossible to find anyone who combined in their person a more charming countenance, a more sweet expression or more lovable qualities of heart and mind.' The comte de Tilly gives a fuller picture: 'When the comtesse Jules was first presented at Court, all eyes were upon her, not only because of the charm of her countenance, but even more by those touching little graces which make a deeper impression than beauty itself. Her very engaging attractions were all the more effective because they were the gift of nature. Nothing about her seemed to owe anything to art, nothing was artificial.'

'Her charming face', wrote the marquis de Bombelles in October 1782, 'attracted Her Majesty; she became the favourite and saw at that moment the whole of France at her feet. One might well think that so much good luck would excite much envy, and yet Madame de Polignac has no enemies. It is impossible to hate her. Her sweetness, her modesty, her honesty are innate qualities which never fail her.' A month later Bombelles returned to the theme: 'I say it again: there is no-one who would be able to be in favour with so much grace and such charming simplicity.' It is significant that the Polignacs were not only loved by their social equals. In April 1783 Bombelles notes that they were trying to sell the estate of Claye. The innkeeper of the Grand Cerf at Meaux told him that the local people very much hoped that the duc would not sell: 'They adore him there, and his wife also.'

For Yolande de Polignac, Marie-Antoinette conceived an extravagant affection. It was extravagant also in the financial sense of the word. 'This family,' wrote Mercy, 'without any deserts as regards the State, and from pure favouritism, had already secured for itself something like 500 000 livres of annual revenue.' The comte de La Marck tried to excuse the Queen, and explained:

> The pecuniary advantages that the favoured members of this society drew from their connection with the Court cannot be compared with the fortunes of old time favourites. In reality the comte and comtesse Jules de Polignac only received just what was necessary to keep up a household at Versailles, which became for a time that of the Queen and in which the King occasionally put in an appearance.
>
> The arrival of the comtesse Jules could not have happened at a more favourable moment; the tender affection which the Queen felt for the princesse de Lamballe, and which that princess returned with interest, was beginning to lose some of its warmth and intensity. The Queen's heart was, so to say, looking for the heart of a friend which had nothing in common with the glory of the throne; that is why, from the first moment, she felt for Madame de Polignac that sympathy which is, both in love and in friendship, the precursor of a lasting relationship.

In June 1780, when the comtesse Diane was expecting a child, the Court moved to La Muette so that the Queen could be closer to her friend, and the King actually paid her a visit. 'It is the only private house in Paris which he has entered since he became King,' wrote Mercy, 'and a distinction so outstanding has made even more of a sensation than all the more useful graces accorded to the favourite.' Louis also obligingly heaped titles and charges at Court on the comtesse and her friends. Not only was her husband created a duke, but when her daughter married the comte de Gramont he was created duc de Guiche; he was then promoted Capitaine des Gardes du Roi, a post already promised to the duc de Lorges. As Madame Campan observed: 'the number of discontented families in the Court increased.'

Of Madame de Polignac's character the comtesse de Boigne has much to say: 'She was dominated by her sister-in-law the comtesse Diane – ambitious, avid, dissolute and determine to secure every favour for herself and her family; tyrannised by her lover, the comte de Vaudreuil, as frivolous as he was immoral and who, by the intermediary of the Queen, proceeded to plunder the public treasury for his own benefit and for that of his companions in disorder.'

It appears that the real defect of Madame de Polignac was in the company which she kept. As the comte de La Marck wrote:

> Unfortunately for her and even more so for the Queen, the comtesse Jules de Polignac had an intimate friendship with the comte de Vaudreuil. This man combined a handsome face and an agreeable manner with a violent character, imperious and with the greatest possible avidity for the favours of the court and for the advantages which they procured. He wanted to interfere in everything, small or large, significant or insignificant, and his ascendancy over the comtesse de Polignac gave him many openings to gain his ends.
>
> The tender affection which the Queen had for the comtesse made it impossible for her to throw off the yoke of Monsieur de Vaudreuil. This latter arranged to his own liking the society of the comtesse Jules. The men whom one saw there most constantly were the baron de Besenval, the comte d'Adhémar, and one or two insignificant personages.
>
> The baron de Besenval was a man with a quick wit but very immoral and who enjoyed intrigue for the sake of intrigue even if it brought him nothing. . . . He was Swiss and, something which is not very common in this country, he was rich . . . He had no ambition to occupy any place of importance; he did not want to become a minister. But while not concerned to become one of the ministers, he wished to have a part in their making in order to exercise influence over them . . . As for the comte d'Adhémar he was, of all the Polignac

set, the one with most wit but no less ability than the baron de Besenval to attain his ends . . . he sang well, was an excellent comedian, wrote delightful verses. That was more than was needed for success in society.

Possessing no fortune of his own he married a rich widow, the comtesse de Valbelle, who was Dame du Palais to Marie-Antoinette, and who fell passionately in love with him. He, however, took no notice of her and profited both from her fortune and from her position as Dame du Palais.

> These three men, Vaudreuil, Besenval and d'Adhémar, dominated the Polignac society. Not one of them had any depth of judgement nor any high ideals . . . they wanted positions for themselves and for their friends and took no account of the talents which might have been necessary for their proper fulfilment, utterly devoid, all three of them, of that spirit of perspicacity which enables one to discern in the present those events which the future is preparing; sacrificing everything to their personal interests . . . Thus the Polignac set did much harm, I will not say only to the unfortunate Queen, but also to the true interests of the King, and consequently to the monarchy.

Perhaps the most innocuous of the coterie was the comte Valentin d'Esterhazy. His military record, according to his biographer Ernest Daudet, shows him as 'an officer full of courage and intelligence, with a good wit, well-read and diligent and very attached to the welfare of the service'. To this might be added that he was a model husband and a tender father.

Marie-Antoinette does not appear to have exercised much judgement in her selection of friends. The comte de La Marck made the interesting observation that 'among those admitted to her intimacy there were a number of foreigners, such as the Count Esterhazy, the Count Fersen, the Baron Stedingk . . . It was evident that she preferred the company of these. I allowed myself one day to to make the observation that this too noticeable preference accorded to foreigners could do her harm in the eyes of the French. "You are right," she replied sadly, "but these do not make any demands upon me."'

The name of the Swedish Count Axel Fersen ought to have been underlined. Already Fersen was in a class by himself. On 26 August he wrote to his father: 'last Tuesday I was at Versailles to be presented to the royal family. The Queen, who is charming, said when she saw me: "Ah! there is an old acquaintance!"'

In September he wrote again to his father: 'the Queen, who is the most beautiful and the most lovable princess that I know, was kind enough to seek information about me . . . her pregnancy progresses and is very noticeable.' In October he wrote again: 'everyone here gives me such a good reception and they all speak so much of you, my dear father, that this is a second fatherland. There is no-one, not even the Queen, who does not show me civility.' In November he writes: 'I often go and pay my court to her at her gaming table and she always says something to me. She has heard tell of my new uniform and she expressed a great desire to see it at the *lever*; I shall go on Tuesday, not to the *lever*, but to the Queen's rooms. She is the most agreeable princess that I know.'

Soon Fersen began to attract the notice of the French. 'Count Fersen,' noted the duc de Lévis, 'in high favour for some years at Court, was a *grand seigneur* of Sweden. He was of tall stature, his features regular without being expressive. His manners were simple and noble. His conversation lacked animation and he showed more judgement than wit . . . serious without being sad. His face and his whole appearance were perfectly fitted for the hero of some novel – but not a French novel.'

Georgiana, Duchess of Devonshire, who became a close friend of Marie-Antoinette (whom she calls 'Mrs B') wrote, on first seeing Fersen: 'He has delightful eyes, the finest countenance that can be and the most gentleman-like air. Thank God I an't in love with him.'

On 10 April 1779, Count Creutz, the Swedish Ambassador at Versailles, wrote to Gustavus III: 'I must confess to Your Majesty that the young Count Fersen is so high in the Queen's favour as to cause offence to a number of people; I admit that I cannot forbear from believing that she has a partiality for him; I have had indications too certain to be doubted. The behaviour of the young Count Fersen under these circumstances has been admirable, both by his modesty and by his reserve and above all by his decision to go to America; in thus distancing himself he has removed all the dangers of his position. It evidently needed a strength of mind beyond his age [he was twenty-four] to overcome this seduction. During these last days the Queen could not take her eyes off him and they filled with tears whenever she saw him.'

Fersen duly sailed for America where he became Aide de Camp to General Rochambeau. Creutz reported to his father that 'he was conducting himself with a wisdom and a discretion astonishing in a man of his age.' At about the same time Fersen wrote to his sister Sophie: 'I am wonderfully well here; I have plenty to do, the girls are pretty, kind and coquette; what more could I need?'

On 25 October 1786, Daniel Hailes, a member of the Duke of Dorset's staff at the British Embassy in France, reported to Lord Carmarthen on Marie-Antoinette's connection with the Polignac circle:

> Although a spirit of intrigue may be said to be woven into the characters of almost all Frenchmen, and particularly those brought up in a Court, the Duke and Duchess of Polignac can neither of them be supposed, from the narrowness of their capacities, to have laid, of themselves, any concerted plan whatever for the purpose of securing for themselves the duration of that favour which accidentally shone upon them. Monsieur de Vaudreuil and Monsieur d'Adhémar, both consummately ambitious and intriguing, and both attached, at first from motives of gallantry, to the Duchess, are those who have had the chief direction of her conduct. All their own little talents of society were successfully employed in a Court where pleasure was the principle concern. But in order that the source from which these streams of liberality were to flow might be well supplied, it was become an essential object with the party to have a Comptroller General at their disposal. Monsieur de Calonne, a man of wit and parts and infinite pliability, was fixed upon by Vaudreuil for the place.

> Monsieur de Vaudreuil has been justified in his choice, for no-one was ever truer to the trust reposed in him than the present minister of Finance; I mean to that of supplying with unbounded profusion everyone that could in any shape be considered to be of his party. No man was ever more systematical in his corruption . . . I know it has been said that the extent of the influence of the Queen's party goes no farther than to the disposal of certain places and pensions without interfering with the great line of public business, and particularly that of foreign affairs, but it ought surely to be observed that, when any set of them can command the person who holds the purse of the State, they must necessarily have the greatest influence in all internal, and a considerable indirect share in all foreign affairs.

The appointment of Calonne was made on 3 November, 1783. It was commented on by the Baron von Schönfeld, Minister from Dresden. 'The Queen's credit', he wrote, 'is the same as ever, although confined to the distribution of favours and outside the sphere of politics. One recent proof of the influence which this princess retains is the nomination of Monsieur de Calonne to the Contrôle Général, put forward chiefly by the people whom the Queen honours with her favour.'

Marie-Antoinette never really liked Calonne but she needed his financial support for the reconstruction of her *petits cabinets*. He is said to have reassured her with the words: 'si c'est possible, c'est fait; si ce n'est pas possible, cela se fera.'

The reconstruction of the *petits cabinets* dates from 1779. The first room to be altered was the Library, but this did not arise from any desire to read on the part of the Queen. 'Apart from a few novels,' wrote Besenval, 'she never opens a book.' Many of the books in the library were merely decorative, the Court bookbinder Martial having provided a selection of gilded leather backs to ornament the shelves.

The Méridienne, immediately behind the Queen's state bedroom, was a little octagonal room with a niche for a day bed. It was largely decorated with mirrors, for it was here that Marie-Antoinette tried her new and often preposterous coiffures, chose her jewels and the materials for her dresses and held her lengthy conferences with her dress-maker, Rose Bertin. An album was kept with samples of the materials of her costumes; this was brought to her every morning and she marked with a pin her choices for the day. The dresses were then brought up from the Garderobe.

The decoration of the Méridienne was designed by Mique and executed by the brothers Rousseau, sons of old Antoine Rousseau whose last work had been the King's library. It recalls their only work at Trianon, the little boudoir behind the Queen's bedroom. The delicate patterns carved on the panels have all the precision of the gilded bronze *appliqués* on the glasses and mirrors.

In 1783 the largest of the rooms, the Cabinet Interieur, was redecorated and became known as the Cabinet Doré. The decorations were in the very latest style and would almost pass for empire style. Eight large panels, which form the greater part of the decorative scheme, are richly embellished with gilt carvings among which figure the winged sphinxes, displayed eagles and smoking braziers of the new style. The Méridienne was one of the very last examples of the old style; the Cabinet Interieur was the first of the new. Here stood the Queen's harp and harpsichord, used when Marie-Antoinette sang with Grétry and Madame Vigée-Lebrun.

Madame Vigée-Lebrun herself said that Marie-Antoinette's voice was not 'd'une grande justesse'. There is no reason to suppose that she was a particularly accomplished musician in an age when such accomplishment was by no means rare among ladies of rank. It was as the patron of Gluck that she played the most important role as a lover of music.

Some of the most brilliant occasions of the Court were the *fêtes* offered to the Grand Duke Paul of Russia and his wife who arrived in France in May 1782. They travelled incognito as the comte and comtesse du Nord. The baronne d'Oberkirch was a personal friend of the Grand Duchess and has left a chronicle of their visit.

The official reception at Versailles was on 20 May. After

being presented to the King and Queen respectively, they dined with the royal family in the Grand Cabinet. Louis, more relaxed when seated at table, became more affable. At the formal presentation he had been stiff and ill at ease. 'Official occasions of etiquette', noted Madame d'Oberkirch, 'are tedious and tiresome for princes; I do not know how they can become accustomed to them.' But at dinner they could be more themselves. The comtesse de Provence – 'not pretty but with very beautiful eyes' – kept up a conversation 'sparkling with wit – *pétillant d'esprit* – and merry without malice, which is something precious, especially at Court'. As for the Grand Duchess, her conversation was simply brilliant: 'she exhibited a combination of wit and tact which is rare at her age.'

After dinner the Queen offered a concert in the Salon de la Paix and Madame d'Oberkirch was able to see Versailles in all its nocturnal glory. 'The Château was lit as for a *jour de grand appartement*; a thousand chandeliers hung from the ceilings, girandoles holding forty candles each stood on all the consoles . . . nothing could give an idea of this richness and splendour. The dresses were miraculous!' Above all shone the figure of Marie-Antoinette – 'la Reine, belle comme le jour, animait tout de son éclat.'

Although the baronne d'Oberkirch had not been presented, the Queen dispensed with the necessity and invited her to the concert, in the course of which she addressed her conversation to the baronne on five or six occasions. Madame d'Oberkirch, as her name implies, was Alsatian. 'You are from a country', said the Queen, 'which I found, as I passed through it, very beautiful and very faithful . . . I shall always remember that it was there that I first received the good-will of the French. It was there that I first realised what happiness it was to become their Queen.'

The Queen a Mother

'Madame ma chère mère,' wrote Marie-Antoinette from Versailles on 19 April 1778, 'my first impulse, which I regret not having followed a week ago, was to write my hopes to my dear mother. I was held back by the fear of causing too much grief if my great hopes had faded away; they are not yet entirely certain and I will not entirely trust them until the first days of the coming month: the time of my next cycle.' She had, in fact, all the normal symptoms of pregnancy.

It can be imagined with what excitement and hope this letter was read at Schönbrunn. 'May God be praised,' wrote the Empress on 2 May, 'and may my darling Antoinette be confirmed in this brilliant situation by giving heirs to the throne of France. No precaution could be *de trop*; I am delighted that you will make no late visits to Paris and that you have even given up billiards. I can see from that that you overlook nothing and are ready to sacrifice even the least dangerous of your amusements. But pray remember, my dear daughter, that the two months are not enough; it needs thirteen whole weeks, especially for a first pregnancy. Keep up, therefore, for these five weeks more, the same precautions.'

The Empress scarcely dared to believe the good news. To Mercy she wrote in a somewhat different vein: 'I admit to you that I am almost tempted to doubt it, right up to the moment that she brings into the world this child which she is supposed to be carrying; so reluctant to believe have I become on this matter, having seen my hopes so long frustrated.'

Hope, however, always overrode her more pessimistic

moods, but hope only bred renewed anxieties. 'You will follow blindly the advice of Lassone, who has justly merited my confidence. I hope that the choice of an *accoucheur* will be made by him: may it be a man of the highest skill and a Christian. I would not want your sister-in-law's.' Court intrigue had played a part in that appointment, and everyone was trying to introduce their own creatures. But soon anxiety gave place once more to excitement: 'If you could only see the joy that there is here over this great news. It cannot be greater in Paris.'

The pregnancy of the Queen had an interesting side-effect on the balance of power within the government. Austria and Germany were at war; Marie-Antoinette hoped that France would honour the Austrian alliance in supporting the Emperor. 'It is natural', wrote Louis to Maurepas, 'that the Queen should be afflicted by the plight in which she sees her brother and that she should make some effort to obtain help for him.' Maurepas suggested that the Queen might adopt the role of mediator: 'les reines ont souvent joué ce beau personnage.' Could she not persuade the Emperor to yield a part of the land which he had taken in Bavaria and to agree with the King of Prussia that he should keep the rest?

But Maurepas was troubled by what he saw as 'a second Ministry centred on the Queen'. The only real force to be feared was the influence of the Queen over the mind of her husband. It was exactly here that an interesting change could be observed. On 25 April 1778, Véri recorded that Mesdames had 'during the last month noted with astonishment that the tone of the King had become more firm and more decisive towards the Queen, instead of being timid and fearful as before.' Véri observed the coincidence between this firmer tone on the part of the King with the first evidence of pregnancy with the Queen. 'The King is so delighted about the pregnancy that he, for certain, has not the slightest notion of the popular suspicion that the child is not his.' Véri himself was not inclined to believe such rumours; he was tempted to see a connection between the new firmness and the prospect of fatherhood. 'Nature has placed a certain measure of shyness and shame in all husbands who cannot fulfil their conjugal duties. The King has passed many years in this uncertainty. The pregnancy has given him the contrary assurance, which he has only recently gained.'

On 16 May Marie-Antoinette wrote again from Versailles: 'I continue to be marvellously well . . . I met this morning with my *accoucheur* (it is Vermond, a brother of the abbé); it was I who felt more confidence in him than in the others . . . Lassone very much approves of him . . . I am most moved by the rejoicing which my dear mother tells me reigns in Vienna about my pregnancy . . . I forgot to tell my dear mother that at my second cycle I asked the King for 500 Louis, that is 12 000 francs, which I thought it fitting to send to Paris for the poor people who are kept in prison for debts owed to wet-nurses.'

On 29 May she wrote again. 'I continue to be wonderfully well and with not the least discommodity. We have been at Marly for the last ten days. It is such a charming place and I take advantage of it by going for walks, especially in the morning. This does me a lot of good without causing any fatigue.'

On 1 June her mother's letter crossed hers. 'May God keep you safe, and your dear child, and may He give you a son, or if not a daughter who resembles you in every way and will bring you the same consolation which you bring me.'

That summer, says Madame Campan, 'was extremely hot: July and August passed without the refreshment of a single thunderstorm.' The Queen, heavily pregnant by this time, was unable to sleep 'without having breathed the cool night air, walking with the princesses and her brothers-in-law on the terrace beneath her windows'. These promenades suggested a musical accompaniment and the musicians of the chapel were engaged to supply this. To provide illumination, the comte d'Artois kept all his windows open and all the candles burning in his apartments on the ground floor of the Aisle des Princes, which was at right angles to those of the Queen.

There are few more lovely sights than a great house or palace lit from within, each window offering a glimpse of gilded ornament and crystal chandelier, each casting its path of gentle, flattering light across the terrace. The combination of music and candlelight in the welcome cool of a summer evening lent enchantment to these nocturnal promenades. At first it provoked no comment, but the provision of a concert began to attract the populace of Versailles, who always had access to the gardens, and what started as a private distraction became a public occasion. Unfortunately the King, who liked to go to bed early, was very rarely present.

'Nothing', wrote Madame Campan, 'could have been more innocent than these promenades, of which first Paris, then France and even Europe was soon occupied in a manner extremely offensive to the character of Marie-Antoinette.' It is true that one or two people who would not normally have had access to the Queen took advantage of these occasions to do so. It was immediately seized upon by the enemies of the Queen. 'The most scandalous accounts were circulated and printed in the lampoons of the time; nothing was further from the truth than these calumnious rumours.'

There is a very disappointing lacuna in the correspondence between Marie-Antoinette and her mother between 25 November 1778 and 1 April 1779. It leaves unrecorded their reactions to the actual birth of the first child. It is described in detail by Madame Campan. 'At last, on 11 December 1778, the Queen felt the first pangs.' Marie-Thérèse-Charlotte, or Madame fille du Roi, came into the world just before mid-day on 19 December.

In the great bedroom a special bed was prepared near the fire and huge screens of tapestry had been erected to keep off the multitude of onlookers. According to Madame Campan's description:

> The etiquette which permitted entry to everyone who presented themselves without distinction was observed with such exaggeration that at the moment when the *accoucheur* Vermond proclaimed with a loud voice: 'the Queen is about to

> give birth!' the crowd of curious spectators was so numerous and so tumultuous that it was thought to endanger the life of the Queen . . . It was no longer possible to move in the room, which was filled with a crowd so mixed that one could fancy oneself in a public place. The princesse de Lamballe fainted and had to be carried out.
>
> Immediately after giving birth, Marie-Antoinette also fainted. Vermond shouted out, 'Air! hot water! I must let her blood from her foot.' The windows had been sealed up for the winter; the King opened them with a force that only his love for the Queen could have given him. The basin of hot water did not arrive in time and Vermond was obliged to let the Queen's blood without it. It was an anxious moment, but all ended well – 'la Reine revient des portes de la mort.'
>
> The rejoicings which succeeded to this moment of alarm were as extreme as they were sincere. People were kissing each other, they were crying with joy; the comte d'Esterhazy and the prince de Poix, who were the first whom I told, covered me with their tears and their kisses in the middle of the Cabinet des Nobles.

Marie-Antoinette's reactions to this public delivery are not recorded, but perhaps her attitude towards royal motherhood can be sensed in her words when she first saw her infant daughter: 'poor little thing, you are not what was wanted, but you will be no less dear to me. A son would have belonged more particularly to the State. You will be mine; you will have all my care, you will share all my happiness and you will sweeten my sufferings.'

Although her tardy motherhood brought Marie-Antoinette to a more responsible outlook on life, it did little towards reconciling her to her obligation to live in public and the advent of a family merely furnished her with another pretext to live her own private existence at Trianon and in her Petits Cabinets. Her life began to run on more domestic lines. There was no longer either the same need or the same opportunity for the hectic hedonism which had so concerned her mother, for her interest now extended to the nursery. But, as the grounds for reproach became less, so the need for calumny became greater. As a barren wife, her enemies had not needed to take her too seriously; as a mother, and therefore potentially a mother to the heir to the throne, she became a more formidable obstacle to their plans.

On 16 February 1779 Marie-Antoinette made her first entry into Paris since the birth of her daughter. Her reception was less than enthusiastic. 'I should not conceal from your Majesty', wrote Mercy to the Empress, 'that the demonstrations of the public did not exactly correspond with what they had promised themselves . . . In certain quarters of the town there reigned a great silence.'

Véri, writing on the same subject, recalled a preacher who had warned Louis XV from the pulpit: 'Your people have no right to murmur if they are discontented, but they have the right to be silent, and their silence is a lesson to kings.' Véri goes on to record that 15 000 livres were thrown to the populace to stimulate their acclamations, but what little response it evoked did not ring true. 'When a crowd is moved by its heart,' he observed, 'it expresses itself in a far more noisy manner.'

In April 1781 Marie-Antoinette was again with child and on 22 October she gave birth to a son.

One of the most evocative accounts of this great event comes from the pen of a Swedish officer, the Count Curt von Stedingk. It was written to King Gustavus III in the full flood of his excitement:

> The Queen has been brought to bed of a dauphin, today at twenty-five past one in the afternoon. Yesterday she was wonderfully well; she played cards as usual on Sunday evening and was chatting a lot to her circle of friends. At nine o'clock this morning, after a very peaceful night, she took a bath and stayed in it for over an hour; she felt a few twinges, but very slight . . . Madame de Polignac was alerted at half past eleven. The King was at that moment about to go off hunting with Monsieur and the comte d'Artois. The coaches had already come up and many of the personnel of the hunt had started off. The King went to the Queen's room; he found her in pain, although she did not want to admit it. His Majesty immediately countermanded the hunt. The coaches went back. That

> was the signal for everyone to rush to the Queen's apartment; the ladies for the greater part in the most complete *négligé*, the men just as they were.
>
> I went to the duchesse de Polignac's rooms; she had gone to the Queen's but I found there the duchesse de Guiche, Madame de Polastron, the young comtesse de Grammont, Madame des Deux-Ponts and Monsieur de Chalons. After an agonising quarter of an hour, one of the Queen's ladies, with her hair all dishevelled, and absolutely beside herself, burst into the room and cried, 'a dauphin!! but you must not mention it yet.'
>
> Our joy was too great to be contained. We rushed out of the room, which opens into the Salle des Gardes de la Reine. The first person whom I encountered was Madame who was going at full gallop to the Queen's apartment. I cried out, 'a dauphin! Madame! What luck!'

It was not, of course, good news for Madame; it put her husband at one remove from heir presumptive to the throne.

Meanwhile, in the Chambre de la Reine, all was silence. Although everything had, in fact, gone extremely well – 'one has hardly ever seen an easier childbirth' – there was still a moment of anxiety, in view of what had happened at her first delivery: 'at first they had not dared to tell her that it was a dauphin,' continues Stedingk, 'for fear of causing too strong an emotion.' To Marie-Antoinette this silence meant only one thing: she had produced another daughter. '"You can see how reasonable I am," she said; "I have not asked you anything." The King, seeing her distress, felt it was time to relieve her of it. He said to her, with tears in his eyes, "Monsieur le Dauphin demande d'entrer." They brought her the child, and those who witnessed this scene say that they have never seen anything more moving. She said to Madame de Guémené, who took the child, "take him. He belongs to the State, but I take back my daughter."'

Beyond the double doors, the Antichambre de la Reine was the scene of an outburst of emotion. 'The joy could not have been greater,' continues Stedingk.

> They were laughing, they were crying; men and women who hardly knew each other fell upon each other's necks. Those who were the least attached to the Queen were carried away by the general rejoicing. Half an hour later the doors of the Queen's bedroom opened and the announcement was made: "Monsieur le Dauphin!" Madame de Guémené stood, radiant with joy, holding the Prince in her arms, and solemnly processed with him to her own apartment. The acclamations, the applause which penetrated the Queen's bedroom, certainly penetrated her heart. Everyone was trying to touch the child. When he reached his apartment, one of the Archbishops wanted him to be decorated with the *cordon bleu* but the King said that he must be made a Christian first. The baptism took place at three that afternoon. The great number of esteemed persons, the good order which reigned, but above all the feeling of emotion and the joy of all who were present, made this ceremony both beautiful and august.

'Nothing could equal the joy which we feel,' wrote Madame de Bombelles; 'what I found most profoundly touching is the pleasure which the King took in the baptism; he never ceased looking at his son and smiling at him. The cries of those who were outside the chapel at the moment when the child was brought in, the joy which could be read on every face affected me so deeply that I could not withold my tears.'

The marquis de Bombelles was some distance from Versailles, for the news only reached him on 28 October: 'Sunk in the least cheerful of reveries, since I was not expecting a letter from my wife, I opened somewhat listlessly a packet from the Court; the letter fell from my hands when I read that on the twenty-second, at half past one, the Queen was delivered of a dauphin. I ran like a madman to announce this happy news to all my household and in the first emotion of so natural a joy I wrote to my wife: "Ah! mon Amie!" I started: "we are all raving, we are all beside ourselves with delight! A dauphin? A dauphin! Is it possible? Yes, it is indeed true. What are they saying? What are they doing at Versailles?"'

In Vienna, Marie-Antoinette's brother, the Emperor Joseph II, wrote to his Ambassador Mercy: 'it is really in a transport of joy that I send you this courier at once and add two letters for the King and Queen which convey only the first promptings of the heart and the compliment which I pay them on this event. I did not think I was capable of feeling the joy of a young man . . . that this sister, who is the woman I love best in the world, should be the happiest, is very gratifying.'

In October 1782, a scandal in the great family of Rohan was the talk of the palace and the talk of the town. 'There is no talk but of the bankruptcy of the prince de Guémené,' wrote the marquis de Bombelles, 'and unfortunately no other name can be given to the total cessation of payment of the annuities which an infinite number of people received from him.' Bombelles put some of the blame on the prince's *homme d'affaires*, Monsieur Marchand, who kept his master in the dark and encouraged investors to place their money with him. The extent of the debt was in the region of 22 000 000 to 28 000 000 livres. Thousands of people were ruined: 'le cri d'indignation est général.' The anger of the populace was the greater because just at that time a man had been hanged for fraudulent bankruptcy. Guémené took the normal course for one of his distinction: he applied for royal letters of protection known as an 'Arrêt de Surcéance'. 'If high position', wrote Bombelles, 'is a safeguard against punishment, it is none the less true that Monsieur de Guémené was a fraudulent bankrupt . . . It is no use pleading that Monsieur de Guémené is the man with the most limited intelligence in the kingdom. One only needs instinct to be aware that in taking one's neighbour's money, because he feels it is safe in your hands, one plays him a dirty trick if one deceives him.' Bombelles then made his most penetrating accusation: 'most of our great lords believe they can do anything they like.'

The impact of this scandal on the life of Marie-Antoinette arose from the fact that the princesse de Guémené was the governess of her children, a position from which she now felt herself obliged to resign. For a moment it looked as if the position of governess might remain vacant. On 10 October Bombelles recorded that 'the Queen had her daughter in her apartment for some of the morning without the presence of any *sous-gouvernantes*. This caused quite a stir at Court because it had never happened before.' Those who were concerned with the education of the royal children felt threatened, for, 'if Her Majesty decided to bring up Madame fille du Roi herself that would cause a great simplification in the customary forms and would render obsolete a number of charges.'

Marie-Antoinette, however, did not take over the upbringing of her children; she confided them to the duchesse de Polignac. She was of course assisted by a number of other ladies, of whom, perhaps, the vicomtesse d'Aumâle had the most direct influence on the child's upbringing. Neither Marie-Antoinette nor the duchesse de Polignac was prepared to allow her responsibilities to interfere with her pleasures. 'On 3 March 1783,' writes Bombelles, 'the Dauphin was officially weaned. Neither the Queen nor the duchesse was present – they had gone to Paris.' Louis went to the Dauphin's rooms and 'made known in a loud voice his dissatisfaction and made no secret of the fact that she had gone without his permission'.

In the following month an incident occurred which cast some doubt on the quality of the upbringing which the royal children were receiving. Once again, Bombelles is our informant:

> On 12 April the Queen was out riding and had a fall, the results of which might have been serious. Madame fille du Roi and the abbé de Vermond were present at her return. Vermond made some allusion to the danger which the Queen had run and to the concern which her daughter – then aged only four and a half – must have felt. The little girl deeply shocked him by saying: 'It's all the same to me'.
>
> 'Madame', answered Vermond, 'does not know what it is to break one's head. The Queen would have died.'
> 'It would be all the same to me.'
> 'Madame certainly does not know what death is.'
> 'No, Monsieur l'abbé, I am not ignorant. We don't see people when they are dead. I wouldn't see the Queen any more and that would please me because I could do what I like.'

> The Queen felt quite ill and ordered her daughter to be taken back and put in disgrace.

The duchesse de Polignac put the blame on Madame d'Aumâle whose only correction of the little Princess was to threaten to tell her mother, which thus made her a bogy to her daughter.

Marie-Thérèse persisted in expressing her dislike for her mother, whom she accused of lack of attentiveness. 'For example, when she takes me to her aunts she walks in front of me, *dare-dare*, and never even looks to see if I am following, whereas my daddy takes me by the hand and pays attention to me.' Bombelles found the promise of character in this four year old girl disturbing.

On 27 March 1785, another son, Louis-Charles, duc de Normandie was born. It looked as if the succession to the throne was reasonably well assured. Marie-Antoinette had one more child, Sophie, who died before she was a year old.

The Court of Louis XVI

'One might compare the Château de Versailles', wrote the comte d'Hézècques, 'to a vast labyrinth . . . It needed a long familiarity to be able to find one's way about.' Much the same could be said of the institution which it was built to house. Moreau, in a moment of exasperation, used the same word: 'qui donc croire dans cette labyrinthe de la Cour?' It is a question with which many a subsequent historian has also been faced. The problems of precedence and the intricacies of etiquette presented another labyrinth which was, if anything, more difficult to master.

There are endless anecdotes which reveal the apparently childish fatuities of etiquette and precedence. The marquis de Bombelles describes a typical example. It was the custom for the Pope to bless and to present swaddling clothes to a new-born dauphin. The Dauphin was born on 22 October 1781; the swaddling clothes arrived on 7 January 1783. They were presented by the Prince Doria-Pamphili, Archbishop of Seleucia, who was the new Papal Nuncio. 'The King was in the bedroom in which the *lever* takes place. When the arrival of the Prince-Archbishop was announced. His Majesty went and sat on an armchair behind the balustrade of the bed . . . having on his right and on his left his two brothers, standing. The Nuncio made three reverences. The King stood up and put his hat on; the Nuncio put on his hat and pronounced his harangue. The King replied with few words, but very well.'

All, however, was not well from the point of view of etiquette. 'During this audience the dukes absented themselves, even the duc d'Ayen and the maréchal de Duras, who by their charges at Court – the one First Gentleman of the Bedchamber and the other Captain of the Guard – were under the obligation to be present; this was because the princes of the House of Lorraine and the princes of the House of Rohan had the right to be covered in the presence of the King, a right which dukes did not have on such occasions; these latter avoid having to witness the exercise of a right which wounds their prerogatives.'

The Rohan, in particular, lost no opportunity of establishing and publicising their claim to be *princes étrangers*, that is to say descended from a ruling sovereign – in their case of Brittany – and thus to form a separate caste between the royal family and the high nobility. The high nobility lost no opportunity to disregard this claim. The sort of occasion on which this rivalry could break out was a Court ball, where ladies were called to dance in order of precedence. At the festivities in celebration of the wedding of the Dauphin precedence had been given to the House of Lorraine in view of their relationship with Marie-Antoinette, but in 1777, when her brother, the Emperor Joseph, visited France, the Rohan clan persuaded the King to call Mademoiselle de Rohan, daughter of the prince de Rohan-Rochefort, to dance the minuet immediately after the royal family. Her partner, however, the marquis de Lusignan, refused to take the floor, saying, according to Théodore de Lameth: 'I am the most unhappy of men to be obliged to disobey your Majesty, but the nobility will never concur in the placing of whoever it might be between itself and the royal family.'

The problems of etiquette were, in fact, more often than not problems of precedence. Foreign princes, with the exception of *les Grands d'Espagne*, were not accorded any precedence in the Court of France. They therefore travelled 'incognito'. When, in February 1775, Marie-Antoinette's brother, the Archduke Maximilian, came to visit her, he was officially the 'comte de Burgau' and as such had no precedence at Versailles. 'There was not the slightest doubt', wrote the comte de La Marck, 'that it was the Archduke, travelling under an incognito title, who should have paid the first visit to the princes of the House of Orléans, the House of Condé, the House of Conti and the House of Penthièvre.' He did not do so and his failure to do so was construed as a claim that they should have paid the first visit and called upon him and that he had taken umbrage.

'I saw at close quarters', continued La Marck, 'all that was connected with this affair and while I affirm that the French princes were entirely within their rights, I can also affirm, from the Queen's side, that she had no intention to wound anyone.'

To compensate for the deliberate absence of the Princes of the Blood from Versailles, La Marck and a few other noblemen improvised a *fête* for the young Archduke in the riding school of the Grande Écurie. This *fête* added to the discontent of the princes and it was from this moment, states La Marck, that Marie-Antoinette's coldness towards the duc de Chartres can be dated. 'The coldness was reciprocated and from this time on one was continually seeing him seize with alacrity every opportunity to censure the activities of the Queen and to pour ridicule on her and on the members of the Polignac coterie.'

The duc de Chartres was the son and heir of the duc d'Orléans, first Prince of the Blood. The family was descended from Philippe, the brother of Louis XIV, and his second wife, Lizelotte von der Pfalz. Their son had been Regent during the minority of Louis XV. He died in 1723 and was succeeded by Louis 'le Pieux'. His son, Louis-Philippe 'le Gros', held the title until his death in 1785, when it passed to his son Louis-Philippe-Joseph; until his father's death in 1785 he was known as duc de Chartres.

In 1769 the duc de Chartres married Marie-Amélie de Bourbon-Penthièvre. There had been the most blatant bargaining for her hand in marriage.

Her brother, the prince de Lamballe, was heir to an annual income of some 3 000 000 livres. He was desperately ill and in the event of his death Marie-Amélie would inherit her father's fortune; in the meantime, however, she only carried a dowry of 50 000 livres and the duc d'Orléans would not accept the marriage of his son with the daughter of a bastard race. The prospect of 3 000 000 livres a year, however, overcame his scruples. The duc de Choiseul, a great friend of Penthièvre, succeeded, not without difficulty, in obtaining the King's consent.

At this critical moment there was a marked improvement in the condition of the prince de Lamballe. It was reported to the duc d'Orléans that his life was no longer in danger. The negotiations were immediately broken off, to the great mortification of Penthièvre and the disgust of Choiseul. Whereupon the prince de Condé – perhaps better informed as to the real state of Lamballe's health – began to negotiate on behalf of his son, the duc de Bourbon. He might have succeeded had not Marie-Amélie formed a passionate attachment to the duc de Chartres whom she had never even met.

It was perhaps fortunate for her that her brother's health took a turn for the worse which this time proved fatal. On his death the duc d'Orléans shamelessly renewed the negotiations for his son's marriage. On 4 April 1769, the wedding took place in the Chapel at Versailles. The Duchess of Northumberland, who was in Paris at the time, was 'not able to see the Show, being very ill', but she quickly informed herself of the details. 'There was a vast deal of finery at the Wedding, especially among the English. Lord Edward Bentinck had one Suit which cost 250L . . . and the finest Chariot, Running Footmen, Liverys etc and surpassed those of everybody there.' She noted also that the bride 'brought an immense fortune' to her husband.

The Château de Saint-Cloud had been, since 1658, the main seat of the House of Orléans. Set in a garden of cascades and fountains and perched on the high ground across the river Seine from the Bois de Boulogne, Saint-Cloud enjoyed the combined advantages of a house in the country with proximity to Paris. The great bird's-eye-view by Allegrain, in the collections of Versailles, leaves little or nothing to be desired as a portrait of the palace and its gardens.

The Château occupied three sides of a quadrangle open towards the river. The block on the left as one entered the Cour d'Honneur was the oldest part. In 1677 it was answered across the courtyard by a similar block containing the celebrated Galerie d'Apollon, painted by Mignard. In August the same year the duc d'Orléans entered into an agreement with Jean Girard 'for the construction of the great building which H.R.H. desired to have in his Château of Saint-Cloud between the existing wings'. The text on an engraving by Mariette states that Girard was the architect of this new block and Jules Hardouin-Mansart of the two wings.

But it was the gardens for which Saint-Cloud was chiefly famous. The central feature was the Grande Cascade which received its final form from Le Pautre in 1667. Even Bernini, usually so rude about anything French, could not refrain from exclaiming 'É bella! É bella!' when the waters were turned on for him.

Beyond the cascade and closely embowered by the trees of a *salle de verdure* was a *pièce d'eau* known from its central fountain as the Grand Jet. Thanks to reservoirs high up on the plateau of the park, the column of water could reach a height of forty-two metres. The English traveller Martin Lister, who visited Saint-Cloud in 1698, described how it 'threw up a spout of water ninety feet high, and did discharge itself with that force that it made a mist and a coolness in the air a great compass round about, and gave now and then cracks like the going off of a pistol'.

As at Versailles, the gardens of Saint-Cloud were normally open to the public. In August 1782 the marquis de Bombelles described the scene.

> The need to amuse oneself on Sunday takes the citizen of Paris out of town; he needs an outing; it is the reward for his week's work. Saint-Cloud is the destination of his choice. The Suisse in charge of the lower gardens provides food and his fish stews are highly esteemed for the way in which he seasons them and

for the freshness of the fish which he catches beneath his windows.

After mass in the parish church, father, mother and children establish themselves in the gardens of Saint-Cloud. They spend the whole day there and only return at nightfall. It is also the *rendez-vous* for less estimable persons. Second class courtesans come on pleasure outings and one is annoyed to have to admit that their finery and sometimes their faces are an ornament to these, the most magnificent and the most attractive of old gardens. It is said that the duc de Chartres intends to cut down the majestic alleys and to plant an English garden. That would be one more vexation that he has caused the public, of which he has already fallen foul by his destruction of the Palais Royal.

The Palais Royal was originally Richelieu's chief residence in Paris and was known as the 'Palais Cardinal'. A few years before he died, Richelieu made it over to Louis XIII whose widow Anne d'Autriche lived in it for some years, renaming it the Palais Royal. From the beginning the vast ensemble incorporated a theatre and a long, rather dull French garden.

The property passed to Anne's second son, Philippe duc d'Orléans on the occasion of his marriage with Henriette d'Angleterre, the sister of Charles II. Certain enlargements and reconstructions were carried out under the supervision of Mansart. In the eighteenth century, Constant d'Ivry rebuilt the façades of the two main courtyards much as we see them today.

In 1780 the duc d'Orléans made the whole property over to his son, the duc de Chartres, who immediately embarked on the vast project which enclosed the gardens with the elegant buildings designed by the architect Victor Louis. A colonnade running right round the gardens provided a covered way off which boutiques, cafés and other places of entertainment, not all of the most respectable nature, were built to increase the income of the duc de Chartres.

Next in rank after the duc d'Orléans was the prince de Condé. The family was descended from Henri de Bourbon, brother to the King of Navarre and uncle to Henri IV. By far their most distinguished member was Louis II, known as le Grand Condé, who, at the age of twenty-two, had ushered in the reign of Louis XIV with the brilliant victory of Rocroi. In the reign of Louis XVI there were three generations living: Louis-Joseph, prince de Condé; his son Louis-Henri-Joseph, duc de Bourbon; and his grandson Louis-Antoine-Henri, duc d'Enghien. Their family seat was the Château de Chantilly.

On 10 June 1782 the prince de Condé gave a magnificent reception here for the 'comte and comtesse du Nord' – in reality the Archduke and Archduchess Paul of Russia. 'Today the whole of France went to Chantilly,' wrote the marquis de Bombelles; 'it was very difficult to find horses in Paris.' He and his wife arrived at half past twelve and were conducted to their lodgings in the Maison de Sylvie at the end of the lake. 'We sat down to dinner at half past two,' continues Bombelles; 'after dinner we all mounted into barouches smartly harnessed and in sufficient numbers to accommodate more than 180 persons. Monsieur le prince de Condé led the way. First he made the whole procession pass through the middle of the stables, one of the most beautiful buildings known of this sort.' A huge vaulted tunnel passes from end to end of the building, opening out in the centre into a vast rotunda containing a cascade whose waters, 'limpiae et bonne', maintained the freshness of the building and satisfied the thirst of the horses. There was room in the stalls for 240 horses – 'les mieux logés de l'Univers'. The Count Valentin d'Esterhazy, writing in August 1785, said: 'we were to have supper in the stables. They say that it is a spectacle that is unique to have supper with 240 horses without there being the slightest odour of manure.'

The Château de Chantilly was one of the most remarkable show places in France. The gardens, laid out by Le Nôtre for the Grand Condé, with their Gargantuan flights of steps and their glittering expanses of water, afforded a seemingly endless succession of bosquets and pavilions, like the background of a series of paintings by Watteau or Fragonard.

The baronne d'Oberkirch also describes the reception of

the comte du Nord. 'Chantilly est le plus beau lieu du monde . . . les eaux, les bois, les jardins sont délicieux.' The famous 'hospitalité des Condé' provided everything for the ease and enjoyment of their guests: 'la liberté la plus entière règnait dans cette maison.' When the day was done, Madame d'Oberkirch retired to bed. 'I went to sleep to the sound of distant music and the fanfares which still re-echoed in the forest. These few days at Chantilly were truly enchanting. It was all gaiety and lust for living such as one seldom encounters at Court. I learnt later how much the Queen regretted not having come to this *fête*, but the King would not have allowed it. The throne of France is surrounded by a rampart of etiquette which is not easily breached. Some say that it is a necessity; that is possible, but it is very restricting.'

By the end of her visit the comtesse du Nord was utterly exhausted. All the Court functions had been too much for her. 'She told me', relates the baronne, 'that she would rather be a peasant in Normandy and live with the Grande Duke in a cottage.'

Madame d'Oberkirch was one of a large number of memorialists who have painted their pictures of the Court of France. Outstanding among them are two ladies, the marquise de la Tour du Pin and the comtesse de Boigne. They are both severe in their criticisms of the age.

'The licentious reign of Louis XV', wrote Madame de la Tour du Pin, 'had corrupted high society. The nobility of the Court set the example of all the vices. Gaming, debauchery, immorality and irreligion were flaunted openly.' Brought up in the household of her great-uncle the Archbishop of Narbonne, 'in which all the rules of religion were daily violated', her formative years had exposed her to 'everything that could have corrupted my mind, perverted my heart, depraved and destroyed all idea of morality and religion'.

Hypocrisy in religion is always more easy to suspect than to prove. The outward forms of Christianity were always respected at Versailles. The King and Queen went to mass every day, and where the King and Queen went, assiduous courtiers went too. Madame de la Tour du Pin tells how the ladies who followed the Queen to the Chapel were met at the doorway of the Salon d'Hercule by their lacqueys armed with huge red velvet sacks, fringed and tasselled with gold. As soon as the royal family had entered, the ladies dived into the galleries to the left and right of the royal closet and scrambled for the seats nearest to the King. Their lacqueys then arranged the velvet sacks about their knees and tucked their trains in beneath the pews. By the time they had opened their missals the Celebrant had usually reached the Gospel.

Such behaviour did not pass unrebuked. The Cardinal de Luynes – a man of genuine if simple piety and with an endearing absence of mind – directed his sermons with unerring aim at the vices of the Court, no other vices being known to him. 'How is it that luxury follows you to the very steps of the altar?' he asked; 'how is it that these cushions and sacks of velvet covered with fringes and tassels precede your arrival at the Temple of the Lord?' Unfortunately, having composed this tirade for the Court, he read it, in a moment of total abstraction, to an entirely bucolic congregation. 'Quittez, quittez ces habitudes somptueuses,' he urged the bewildered peasants, who were as innocent of the irreverence imputed as they were ignorant of the articles mentioned. The story got round, Madame Campan informs us, and so amused the Court that titled ladies would get up early to witness these strange miscarriages of zeal.

It is doubtful whether the Chapel at Versailles offered to Madame de la Tour du Pin a more authentic vision of Christianity than that of her uncle's Château de Hautefontaine. This Château, situated between Compiègne and Soissons, was common to both memorialists, for Madame de Boigne was also related to the Archbishop. Her mother, the marquise d'Osmond, found the tone of the household most distasteful. One day an old Vicar General, seeing her obvious embarrassment, tried to comfort her. 'If you wish to be happy here,' he advised, 'try to conceal your affection for your husband; conjugal love is the only one which is not tolerated.' Because Hautefontaine was the home of an Archbishop, the company attended mass on Sunday. 'No-one brought a prayer book,' observed Madame de Boigne; 'there were always books of a frivolous if not scandalous nature, and they were left in the pews for any floor-polisher to consult.'

Such a generation naturally had little respect for the stately tradition which was their heritage – 'happy to scoff at the outmoded ways, the feudal pride and grave etiquette of our fathers,' wrote the comte de Ségur, 'anything that was long-established seemed to us tiresome and ridiculous.' The works of Lully were 'brought up to date', those of Molière condemned as 'in exceedingly bad taste'. Beaumarchais was the height of fashion. The baron de Frénilly describes the impact of *The Marriage of Figaro*. It had just taken the Comédie Française by storm 'in spite of the police, in spite of the archbishop of Paris, in spite of the King. Everyone proclaimed the work scandalous, dangerous and revolutionary. That was good form. Everyone rushed to see it; that was also good form. I can remember a session of the Académie Française when Monsieur Bailly made an elegant diatribe against this piece; all applauded, but all looked at their watches: it was time to go to the theatre.'

Despite this new atmosphere, life at Versailles seems to have continued very much the same. Chateaubriand, after his presentation to Court in 1787, made the significant observation: 'Louis XIV était toujours là.' In the state bedroom, now hung with purple and gold brocade and lit by porcelain chandeliers, the ceremony of the *coucher* continued in all its formality. 'At eleven o' clock,' wrote the comte d'Hézècques, 'the service and the Court arrived. Everything was prepared; a magnificent gown of gold brocade and lace; on an armchair of red morocco, the nightdress of white silk embroidered at Lyons; a shirt wrapped in a piece of taffeta; on the balustrade a folded cushion of cloth of gold on which were laid the nightcap and the handkerchiefs. By their side the slippers, of the same stuff as the gown, were placed near the Pages of the Bedroom, who leant against the balustrade.'

These boys, usually in their early 'teens, played an important part in the life of the Court. On the occasions when the Queen gave a ball, continues Hézècques, 'the pages waited on the ladies to show them to their places, to offer them refreshments, to conduct them to supper or to their coaches. Perfectly at home in the *grand monde*, they performed their functions with the free and easy manner of their age and the politeness of their rank. Foreigners were always impressed by the sight of these little gilded youths, most of whom still wore upon their cheeks the bloom of childhood, bustling about, running, calling out, hustling the personnel of the buffet and escorting the ladies without appearing in the least disconcerted by all this grandeur, nor troubled by the weight of their superb apparel.'

The comte Hilarion de Beaufort, who was page to the comte de Provence, described the function of the pages at his *lever*. They stood by a marble-topped commode: 'I knew every vein in it,' he wrote, 'for I had much idle leisure in which to study it.' They waited while the Usher threw open the doors to the *Grande Service* with a courteous: 'pray enter, Gentlemen'; they waited while the marquis d'Avaray helped his Royal Highness on with his shirt – sometimes affording the pages a glimpse of his Royal Highness' posterior, 'plump and white'; they waited while his Royal Highness donned his Court coat of embroidered satin; they waited while the barber enveloped his Royal Highness in a huge wrapper of muslin and lace to protect his clothing while his hair was powdered and curled; they waited while his face was gently wiped with a soft cloth in case any specks of powder had trespassed upon it. 'Now came the great task for which the two pages had been waiting. Just imagine: it was no less than to step forward and each remove one slipper from the Prince's feet. We carried them back with as much respect and solemnity as possible to the commode by which we had been standing.'

Young Hilarion had joined Monsieur's household in January 1776. He describes how his headmaster, the Governor of the Pages, conducted him to the palace for his presentation: 'proud as a young peacock in my embroidered coats, I was convinced that I was already a personage at Court.' His disillusionment was immediate: Monsieur received him in silence, 'scarcely deigning an indifferent glance at my small person, he gave me only the courtesy of a barely perceptible nod.'

In contrast to his brother, Louis XVI took a delight in his pages and not infrequently joined in their youthful escapades. Between the Queen's apartment and the King's was a passage which the King often used. It was lined with upholstered benches on which a number of the palace servants slept, providing an irresistible temptation to bored but spirited young noblemen – their open mouths inviting a syringe full of water or their closed lips the delicate application of a moustache by means of a burnt cork. In this they received the encouragement of their sovereign and when the victim awoke, blinking and spluttering, 'the King, laughing heartily, would flee from the scene of battle with as much speed as his young army.' Naturally this sort of behaviour endeared him to the young. 'These childish pranks I have just described', concludes Hilarion, 'have, for me at least, the consoling merit of adding yet another tribute to the memory of the finest man the world has ever seen.'

The King was still addressed, and then only by his intimate friends, in the third person; 'le Roi a-t-il fait une chasse heureuse?' – 'Did the King enjoy the hunt?' It was still the height of honour to hold the candle for him at the *coucher*. The little sartorial distinctions which had intrigued the Court in the early days of Versailles continued to enjoy their vogue. Those invited to Trianon wore a scarlet coat embroidered with silver; for Compiègne the uniform was green; for Choisy, blue. It was more distinguished to be invited to hunt a stag than a roebuck, and the braiding on the uniform made it clear what sort of animal one was entitled to pursue. A *débutant* was only permitted to follow the first run of the day.

Among the crowds, however, which jostled in the anteroom and thronged the galleries of Versailles, were many characters who formed a striking contrast with the finery of the courtiers. One of these was the capitaine Laroche, Concierge of the Ménagerie. Vulgarly bespangled with jewels and gold braid, he made his punctual attendance at the *coucher* almost unbearable by reason of his extremely unhygienic habits: 'jamais sanglier dans son bouge', admitted Hézècques, 'ne laissa échapper d'odeurs plus fétides.'

Another grisly character who rubbed shoulders with the élite was the doorkeeper of the main anteroom, which adjoined the King's bedroom. It was known from its oval window as the Salon de l'Oeil de Boeuf. 'This fat Swiss', relates Hézècques, 'vegetated behind an enormous stove in the Oeil de Boeuf, where he ate and digested his food beneath the noses of dukes and princes. At night he unrolled his little bed in the Grande Galerie and could claim to be the most sumptuously lodged man in France.'

Perhaps the most extraordinary of these intruders were the *poissardes* or *dames de la Halle* who constituted one of the most eccentric of all the trades of Paris. 'These gross fishwives,' according to Larousse, 'some of whom are quite rich despite their old and sticky clothing and their filthy language . . . displaying their heavy gold bijouterie, their lace, their silks of colours as loud as their voices – these gross fishwives enjoyed, under the *ancien régime*, privileges which they managed to perpetuate. On the occasion of a royal wedding, the birth of a royal child, on New Year's Day or on the celebration of some victory, they had the right to go and congratulate the King at Versailles.' They were given afterwards, noted Mercier in his *Tableau de Paris*, 'a dinner in the Grand Commun; one of the Premiers Officiers de la Bouche did the honours.'

Amid the many contrasts of his Court, Louis was ill at ease. He belonged, at heart, to a France that was fast disappearing. 'Louis XVI', wrote the prince de Montbarrey, 'would have liked to have retained the ancient forms; but he did not have the strength to command their continuance, and his complaisant weakness allowed the change to take place against his will.' The public could still watch him eat at the *grand couvert* 'avec une bonne humeur qu'il faisait bon de voir'. They were still admitted to watch the gaming, but the former occasions became more rare and the latter more short. 'The Queen's private society reduced to nothing the official ceremonies of the Court, except for Sundays and major feasts, which were reserved as the occasions demanded by etiquette, and consequently occasions of boredom.'

Those who looked for entertainment and the *douceur de vivre* looked towards Paris and not towards Versailles. It was in Paris that one found what was the latest and most daring of theatrical productions.

The theatre was often the topic of conversation at the *toilette* of the Queen. 'She wanted to know everything', Madame Campan tells us, 'about any production at which she had not been present. The question, "were there many people there?" never failed to come up. I have known many an affable duke reply, with a bow: "il n'y avait pas un chat." That did not mean, as one might suppose, that the place was empty; it was even possible that it was full, but in these circumstances it meant that it was only financiers, good citizens and provincials who filled it. The nobility, I should say the high nobility, only knew their equals. To be one of them one had to have been presented at Court.'

But even this qualification was not enough; the ladies of the Court, 'then as always wondrous fond of place', created at the centre of their charmed circle a further nuance of distinction, an inner ring within the inner ring. 'There was even among this class', continues Madame Campan, 'a privileged élite; it was known as *les gens titrés*, and those who lived at Versailles and who had daily access to the King and Queen were not without a certain contempt for those who paid their court only once a week. In that case a lady *presentée et titrée* and bearing the most illustrious of names could be disdainfully classified as what was known as *les dames du dimanche* [Sunday ladies].'

To have been presented provided the *entrée* into the

charmed circle: to be about to be presented constituted an ordeal which most girls of noble lineage had to face at the age of seventeen. The rite of initiation is described by one of the most readable of the memorialists of the reign, the marquise de la Tour du Pin, at that time comtesse de Gouvernet. She was presented immediately after mass on Sunday 27 May 1787.

Her aunt, the princesse d'Hénin, had taken her, two days previously, to a dancing master, a Monsieur Huart, for an instruction which lasted three or four hours on two successive days. 'It would be impossible to imagine anything more ridiculous', she wrote, 'than this rehearsal for my presentation. Monsieur Huart, a fat man with his hair done beautifully and powdered white, in a baggy petticoat, stood at the far end of the Salon, representing the Queen. He dictated to me what I had to do, now personifying the lady who was to present me, now returning to the Queen's position to represent the moment when, taking off my glove and bowing down to kiss the hem of her skirt, she made the gesture to prevent me. Nothing was forgotten in this rehearsal, nothing neglected.'

On the day itself, however, she had reason to be grateful to her instructor. 'Thanks to the good lessons of Monsieur Huart I acquitted myself very well with my three curtsies. I removed and replaced my glove without too much awkwardness. I then went on to receive the accolade of the King, the princes his brothers, and of Monsieur le duc de Penthièvre, of Messieurs les princes de Condé, de Bourbon et d'Enghien. By a good luck for which I have thanked Heaven a thousand times, Monsieur le duc d'Orléans was not at Versailles on the day of my presentation and I thus avoided being embarrassed by this monster.'

Another account of the complexities of presentation comes from the baronne d'Oberkirch. 'My proofs were made out and examined by the court genealogist, and I was told that the King and the royal family had fixed my presentation for Sunday 13 June.' Her dress, made by Bauland because

Mademoiselle Rose Bertin kept her waiting too long, was of gold brocade with sprigs of flowers '*admirablement beau* – it won me a thousand compliments; there were no less than twenty-three yards in it; it was enormously heavy.'

The decision as to who should be presented rested in the last resort with the King. Chérin, the genealogist, merely verified the proofs. They had to date from before 1399; that is to say before the practice of *annoblissement* was known. Somewhat paradoxically, to have been ennobled, since it implied that one was previously not noble, was to be excluded from the high nobility. 'To have no known origins', explains Madame d'Oberkirch, 'is the first condition of all nobility, it is what is known as *remonter à la nuit du temps*. Such families were called *chevaleresque*. Anyone who had been *noblesse de robe* could have no place in the high nobility, however ancient his title. Etiquette excluded him from eating with a Prince of the Blood and his wife could never be presented.'

To have convinced Chérin, however, of the authenticity of one's antiquity entitled one to ride in the coaches of the King. *Les honneurs de la Cour* allowed one to be admitted to the balls given by the Queen and, for men, to hunt with the King. *Les honneurs de la Cour*, however, were not to be confounded with *les honneurs du Louvre*, which were reserved for duchesses, wives of marshals, ambassadors or knights of the Saint-Esprit; these had the privilege of being allowed to enter the courtyard of any royal palace in a coach and four and enjoyed the *droit du tabouret* which entitled them to sit on an upholstered stool in the presence of the King or Queen. When they were presented to the King he greeted them with a kiss, something, says Madame d'Oberkirch 'which embarrasses His Majesty Louis XVI'. Later, after describing her own presentation, she states that 'the King seldom speaks to those presented; we are assured that he has a very great shyness with women.'

The King's incapacity and the Queen's unwillingness to maintain the traditions of the Court led to a considerable falling off of attendance. On 13 August 1782, the marquis de Bombelles reflected: 'in the days of Louis XV and the late Queen one could pay one's court almost every day; but at present one can only succeed in doing so on Sundays, at the high feasts and sometimes on Tuesday, the day appointed for Ambassadors to come to Versailles. If one could then follow in the wake of the Corps Diplomatique, it is possible to attract the attention of our princes and princesses: that is what is called "paying one's court". Sometimes they speak a word to you: that is what is called "being well treated"; and when they neither speak to you or look at you, that is what is called "wasting your time". That is what happens most often at Versailles.'

One could only count on being well treated by the King's sister, Madame Elizabeth. 'The desire to be obliging', continues Bombelles, 'is painted on her countenance and her excessive shyness does not prevent her from saying something polite to all those who have the honour of making their court to her.'

On 6 June 1783, after a performance of *Zémir et Azore*, Madame d'Oberkirch found herself at a supper party near enough to Madame Elizabeth to observe her closely: 'she was in all the radiance of her youth and beauty,' wrote the baronne, 'but refused all offers for her hand in order to remain with her own family. "I could only marry the son of a King," she said, "and the son of a King must reign over the States of his father. I would cease to be French and I do not want that. It is better to stay here, close to my brother's throne, than to sit on any other."'

Among her many admirers was the comte d'Hézècques. 'Madame Elizabeth', he wrote, 'was, without question, one of those rare persons whom one only meets at long intervals along the journey of life. Without forgetting her rank, she afforded, beneath the sumptuous decor of the palace of our kings, the example of the most solid piety. She lived in the middle of her family, adored by all and admired by the common people.'

Madame Elizabeth lived in close friendship with her ladies-in-waiting, among whom the marquise de Bombelles was perhaps the closest. Her letters and her husband's memoirs are full of anecdotes which reveal Madame Elizabeth's tender solicitude for those who served her. She was not free, according to Bombelles, from the shyness which was common to all her family. 'Her timidity', he wrote, 'prevented her from giving full play to her wit. The King, who loves her and reveres her conduct, has only a very feeble notion of the graces which adorn the mind of his sister, and the Queen, with whom Madame Elizabeth is rather more at ease, is still far from realising how agreeable it would be for her to take into her friendship a sister-in-law so perfectly lovable.'

The Court of France was a kaleidoscopic mixture of grandeur and vulgarity, of stuffy etiquette and simple family relationships. It could still lay on a reception of the utmost magnificence when occasion demanded. In 1782, during the visit of the Archduke Paul of Russia and his wife, the 'comte and comtesse du Nord', there was a full dress ball, a *bal paré*, at Versailles. 'The whole Court was dressed in its greatest finery,' wrote Madame d'Oberkirch; 'the comte and comtesse du Nord were, as usual, particularly remarked upon. The costume worn by the princess was magnificent; she wore the famous parure of chalcedony, the most beautiful to be found in Europe.

'The Queen danced with the Grand Duke; it would be impossible to display more grace and more nobility than our august sovereign.'

The ball took place in the great Salle de Spectacle which had been built for Marie-Antoinette's wedding festivities. Bombelles was in ecstacies. 'This room, one of the most beautiful examples of its sort, in which the ornaments are still in their first brilliance, was illuminated by more than four thousand candles. The clusters of light had been disposed with a perfect taste. The best dressed women in Paris thronged the boxes and balconies . . . the magnificence and elegance with which the Queen was dressed made it unnecessary for strangers to ask for her to be pointed out to them. I have never in all my life seen such a superb spectacle as the assembly of nearly two thousand richly dressed people in a veritable palace of the Sun.' As the duc de Croÿ wrote: 'The finest assembly in the finest place that one could ever see.'

It was not, however, at Versailles that the most important item on the programme of entertainment was to take place. No royal visit would have been complete without a reception at the Petit Trianon.

It was on 23 May 1782 that Madame d'Oberkirch paid her first visit to Trianon. It inspired her to one of her more lyrical passages. 'Mon Dieu, la charmante promenade!' she exclaimed; 'how delicious were these groves perfumed with lilac and peopled with nightingales; butterflies spread their golden wings to the spring sunshine. Never in my life have I passed a more enchanting time than those three hours spent in visiting this retreat.' It is not possible to understand Marie-Antoinette or even to picture her properly, without paying a visit, at least in the imagination, to the Petit Trianon.

The Petit Trianon

One of the first acts of Louis on ascending the throne had been to give the Petit Trianon to Marie-Antoinette. 'Vous aimez les fleurs,' he said; 'j'ai un bouquet à vous offrir.' She was delighted to have a place of her own. The staff were put into her own livery – scarlet and silver – and the orders were signed in her own name.

At first the public was pleased to hear of Louis' gift; it was a refreshing novelty to have a king whose only mistress was his wife. It seemed innocent enough. The Empress Maria Theresa wrote to her daughter: 'the generosity of the King over Trianon, which I am told is the most adorable of houses, gives me great pleasure.' But her second thoughts were more penetrating: 'may this charming first gift of the King not be the occasion of incurring too great an expense, let alone of *dissipations*.' There was not much scope in the actual building for expensive alterations, for it was already perfect. The little boudoir behind the Queen's bedroom, made in 1787, was the only decoration which she added. It was in the gardens that she was to incur an expenditure which was to realise her mother's deepest fears.

Louis XV had developed a serious interest in botany and in 1750 had appointed Claude Richard, described by Linnaeus as 'the ablest gardener in Europe', as Jardinier-Fleuriste. He was joined later by Bernard Jussieu, 'the Newton of Botany'. Jussieu was a character calculated to please Louis, for he was utterly indifferent to any consideration of interest which might have accrued from his royal connection. Not the least attraction of the new horticultural gardens was the simple, straightforward manner in which the King could talk to his gardeners, who felt in their turn that they could treat him as a man rather than a king.

It was not long before the idea occurred to Madame de Pompadour of building an exquisite little house to go with the gardens. The earliest designs are dated 1761, but the Seven Years' War had still two years to run. On 10 February 1763, however, the Treaty of Paris put an end to the war and on 24 February the duc de Praslin, Ministre des Affaires Étrangères, was ordered to pay 700 000 livres from his war budget towards the building of the new house. The total spent on the house and chapel was 861 456 livres. By July of the following year 120 masons and 75 stone-carvers were at work on the site.

The important carvings were done by Honoré Guibert. He worked mostly in the 'Greek' style and his partnership with Gabriel was probably fruitful to both of them. Together they produced a building which, by the simplicity of its conception, the purity of its line and the delicacy of its ornament, is at once the first and finest example of the classical revival, later to be labelled 'Louis XVI'.

Simplicity is the keynote of the Petit Trianon, but simplicity is nearly always deceptive. It cannot be achieved without a perfect command of technique. In designing his façades, Gabriel appreciated nicely the variety of texture possible in the fine, honey-coloured stone of Saint-Leu d'Esserent. A rusticated lower storey, fluted pilasters and a delicately chiselled entablature set off the contrasting smoothness of the undecorated wall spaces.

A skilful use, also, has been made of a drop in the ground level to obtain two façades of two storeys and two of three. The north and west fronts have their basements masked by a terrace or *perron*, whereby the reception rooms can be approached directly from the gardens. The more imposing height of the entrance front is balanced by the low buildings of the forecourt.

The interior reflects in its decoration the original purpose of the building and is inspired by the vegetable kingdom. The beautiful lilies in their circular wreaths which adorn the panels of the Salon de Musique, the swagged drops over the mirrors and the bunches of roses in the Cabinet du Roi – later to be the Queen's bedroom – are carved with a delicacy and a precision which had to pass the scrutiny of a botanist king. In the festoons of fruit which appropriately ornament the dining-room, the strawberry is given a prominent place. The cultivation of strawberries was one of Louis XV's particular interests.

The term *maison de plaisance* is significant. Not only was the Petit Trianon to be strictly private, but the privacy of its inmates was to be insulated as far as possible from the irksome presence of servants. There was already at Choisy-le-Roi a *table volante* which went down through the dining-room floor into the kitchen to be reloaded with the next course and to re-emerge into the dining-room. A similar table was designed by Loriot for Trianon and exhibited in the Louvre in 1769. There is some doubt, however, as to whether it was actually installed. In 1782 Madame d'Oberkirch noted that the *table volante* at Choisy was out of use and rusty.

The Petit Trianon is not as small as its name implies. It has a surprising number of rooms upstairs. It should be considered as a small, compact and remarkably exquisite stately home. The main reception rooms are on the first floor. Everything is designed to minister to the refined hedonism of a polite society; nothing anywhere sounds the note of royalty. The often oppressive grandeur of Versailles has been completely left behind.

The pale green of the first anteroom, at the head of the stairs, is cool and refreshing; the ornament, in white, is just enough to preserve the decor from dullness. The dining-room is a more formal apartment with an elaborate cornice. This room has been very well restored. The walls have recovered their delicate colouring of *vert d'eau*, with the carving of Guibert in crisp relief against it. The frames of the mirrors and pictures have been reconstructed from designs found pencilled on the plaster.

The Salon de Musique is a very fine room, but we might be in the Château du Marais or Montgeoffroy or one of the beautiful eighteenth century *salons* of Le Lude. The tall, rectilinear panels are offset by richly carved roundels at their base, and make this a graceful and elegant ensemble.

To pass from here to the boudoir is to pass from the stately to the exquisite. The oak panels are carved with a minute precision which will stand the closest scrutiny and which gives an overall texture to the room, like a covering of lace upon a satin counterpane. It was in this room that the *glaces volantes* were installed. When evening came and the windows needed to be obscured, instead of closing the shutters, a mirror could be raised by means of a counterpoise, to fill the window recess. Mique used to call this room 'le cabinet des glaces mouvantes'. Queen Victoria made a similar use of mirrors in her drawing-room at Osborne.

Next to the boudoir, the Queen's bedroom was hung with muslin on which, wrote the comte d'Hézècques, 'the embroidery and the vivacity of the colours would have defied the most experienced paintbrush'. He also describes the somewhat bizarre portraits in the bedroom of Marie-Antoinette's brothers and sisters. Here she could feel in the bosom of her own family, but whatever the pleasure that these memories could have evoked in her heart, 'the pictures must have inspired reflexions of a more serious nature, for these princes and princesses were represented as monks and nuns digging their own graves.' The furnishings of these rooms, he continues, 'was more distinguished for its elegance than its magnificence'.

The rooms on the first floor must rank among the greatest achievements of French interior decoration, but the windows still looked out, to north and west, on the serried rows of frames and glass-houses of the botanic garden. In 1775 the Scottish gardener Thomas Blaikie, who worked in France for a number of clients, made a visit to Versailles. At Trianon he met Claude Richard 'who showed us very civilly the garden which formerly was one of the first Botanic gardens in

Europe; there are still a great many rare and curious plants but, as this belongs to the Queen who is not fond of plants, they are turning it all into a sort of English garden – what a pity such a valuable collection should be destroyed! This seems much to affect old Mr Richard.'

At Versailles itself, Blaikie arrived to find 'the gardens of which there is so much talk all in disorder as the old one which was done by the famous Le Nôtre is destroyed and they are to replant it nearly on the old plan.'

The practical reason for the felling of all the trees was that the bosquets contained a lot of dead wood. It was decided that it would be best to cut them all down and start afresh. On 15 December 1774 the comte d'Angiviller put the timber up for auction. In the eyes of many, however, the plantations of Le Nôtre were ripe for replacement as being old fashioned and in bad taste.

During the last years of Louis XV the criticisms of the gardens of Versailles mounted in a steady crescendo. The vicomte d'Hermenonville, himself the author of one of the most famous landscape gardens in France, was one of the severest critics. 'Le Nôtre', he claimed, 'massacred nature; he invented the art of surrounding himself, at great expense, with a belt of boredom.' Nature, however, survived the massacre. During the last hundred years she had been steadily enriching the work of Le Nôtre in her own inimitable manner, giving a grandeur and a nobility to the plantations which were not of man's making. The gardens had become, in the words of the poet Delille, 'chefs d'oeuvre d'un grand Roi, de Le Nôtre *et des ans*'.

One of the few remaining admirers of Le Nôtre was the duc de Croÿ. On 15 May 1770, on the eve of the royal wedding, he took a walk right round the gardens to inspect the preparations for the fireworks. It was a glorious day – 'le plus beau jour du printemps' – and the woods were resplendent in the fresh and varied greens of early spring. 'I could not cease to marvel at the height of the trees,' wrote the duc, 'which are too often ignored. These are the tallest oaks I have ever seen, equal in their height and in the straightness of their shafts to the tallest pine trees. Their shade, and the number of birds which they shelter, deserve more praise than they receive, but at that time the English taste for artificially natural prairies meant that one made a point of finding fault with these superb gardens which, although perhaps a little monotonous, are the richest in the world.'

It was at their moment of mature perfection that the trees of Versailles were destined to disappear. The felling of a noble wood is a profoundly moving spectacle and the destruction of Le Nôtre's trees made a deep impression upon the duc de Croÿ. Few people have ever appreciated the gardens of Versailles more wholeheartedly than he did. He knew exactly when and where to enjoy them best; he was prepared to walk to the far end of the great Pièce d'Eau des Suisses, for the sake of the wonderful view; he was prepared to get up early to see the sun rise upon this princely scene. Now that the trees had gone he could hardly bear to revisit Versailles. 'I did not dare look that way in the gallery,' he admitted; 'they had been so beautiful when last I saw them, and my heart bled for them.' What was most satisfactory to him, however, was that it had been decided that the replantations were to follow the broad outlines traced by Le Nôtre.

In the latest fashion for garden lay-out such expressions as *beau désordre*, *heureuse négligence*, and *piquante bizarrerie* were beginning to creep into the vocabulary of gardening, and the new, easy landscapes of England were contrasted favourably with the boring symmetry of the French school. But for Versailles Blondel had proclaimed the old lay-out to be 'better suited to set forth the magnificence of a great prince than to offer to the mind a peaceful walk and a retirement conducive to philosophy'. As Delille so aptly put it, 'kings are condemned to magnificence.' It was possible, however, that Queens were not.

Only in one corner of the gardens was the new taste for informality to be indulged and that was in the creation of the Bosquet de la Reine or Bosquet de Vénus. This was where

Louis XIV had created his labyrinth, but this was now swept away and replaced by a *jardin anglais*. 'His Majesty', wrote the comte d'Angiviller, in September 1782, 'preferred a private garden, planted with trees and flowering shrubs, mostly exotic species. This was executed some three or four years ago and is beginning to produce a most agreeable effect.' It was not, however, here at Versailles that the *jardin anglais* was to show its real charms, but at Trianon.

The term 'English Garden', however, was ambiguous. There were two adjectives for it in French: one is *pittoresque* and the other *paysagé*. The first consists more in identifying and enhancing the natural beauties of the land – as a delicate touch of make-up might bring out the natural beauties of a face. The second is an attempt to create a fictitious landscape by introducing hills, rocky outcrops, ravines, cascades, lakes, islands and any other features which fancy might suggest.

Carmontelle, in his preface to the *Jardin de Monceau*, puts the case for the latter: 'If you want to turn a picturesque garden into a landscape of illusions, why deny yourself? It is only illusions that can amuse. Let us transport into our gardens the transformation scenes of our operas.' Carmontelle was the creator of the gardens of Monceau – some of which have survived as the Parc Monceau at the end of the avenue Hoche. They were ridiculed by Thomas Blaikie, who worked here for the duc d'Orléans. 'The garden', he wrote, 'is a confusion of ruins, temples etc crowded one upon another; in one place you see a gothic ruin, just by that a Grecian and next a Chinese temple or pavilion which makes a most singular contrast in so small a compass.'

The new gardens at Trianon were usually described as *pittoresque* but there was much about the design which belonged to the *jardin paysagé*.

On 2 July 1774, Mercy reported to the Empress that the Queen was now wholly occupied with the designing of a *jardin à l'anglaise*. A visit to the comte de Caraman, whose garden in Paris was regarded as one of the most successful in the new fashion, provided Marie-Antoinette with the adviser that she was looking for; Caraman was duly appointed Directeur des Jardins de la Reine.

On 31 July the King gave orders that 'everything that the Queen should desire was to be carried out with all the care and all the diligence possible.' His commands were obeyed and two years later, in September 1776, Mercy was beginning to change the tune of his letters to Vienna. 'At first the public took a favourable view of the King's giving Trianon to the Queen,' he wrote; 'they are now beginning to be uneasy and alarmed at the expenses which Her Majesty incurs there.'

In the same year the duc de Croÿ made his first visit since the days of Louis XV. 'I thought I must be mad or dreaming,' he exclaimed; 'never have two hectares of land so completely changed their forn nor cost so much money.'

The ground to the north-east had been cast into a miniature range of hills and a lake had been dug, fed by a cascade which gushed from the mouth of a mysterious grotto. Next to the grotto stood the little Belvédère, designed by Mique and remarkable for the exquisite ornament of the carvings without and the delicacy of the painted arabesques within. The frieze was moulded in lead, fixed onto the entablature and painted to resemble stone.

East of the lake, through green meadows and loosely planted groves, meandered a river, now forming a little backwater towards the Château, now dividing its stream to leave an island, planted with lilac and laburnum. On the island were the twelve stately columns of Mique's Temple de l'Amour, carrying their stone cupola over Bouchardon's figure of 'Love carving his bow from the club of Hercules', 'une magnifique statue,' wrote d'Hézècques, 'représentant ce Dieu dans toute la beauté de l'adolescence.'

The planning and designing of the gardens of the Petit Trianon were carried out with great care and precision. Two painters, Frenet and Châtelet, provided artist's impressions of the proposed landscape. These were then translated into three dimensions. Models of the more architectural features, such as the Temple de l'Amour or the Belvédère, were made by

Deschamps, using wood for the columns and wax for the capitals and other sculptured ornaments. No details were omitted; even miniature farm instruments were inserted into the scene.

This manner of proceeding gave Marie-Antoinette a certain creative role, in that every model had to pass her inspection. It is recorded that the project for the *rocher* was rejected as many as fourteen times before it was finally approved.

The process took up most of the year 1781. The Belvédère was being built at the same time. Fontanieu, Intendant du Garde Meuble, wrote to Mique saying that he had been ordered to see to the furnishing of the 'petit pavillon du rocher de Trianon' and suggested an early meeting to discuss the subject, adding: 'you know our mistress: she likes to have her pleasures promptly.'

There was a rich variety of trees, many of them species acclimatised in the gardens of Trianon. 'The glory of *la petite* Trianon,' wrote Arthur Young, 'is the exotic trees and shrubs. The world has been successfully rifled to decorate it. Here are curious and beautiful ones to please the eye of ignorance and to exercise the memory of science. Of the buildings, the Temple de l'Amour is truly elegant.' The duc de Croÿ was also superlative in his praise of the temple: 'le superbe palais de l'Amour . . . de la plus riche architecture Grècque'. He was, however, critical of the mixture of Greek and Chinese taste in the whole design, but, like Arthur Young, he was chiefly enthusiastic about the trees. 'What is really superb', he wrote, 'is that Monsieur Richard, making full use of his taste and talents, placed here great and rare trees of every sort; as I was at that time reading with enthusiasm the notebook of the admirable Monsieur Besson on the Alps . . . Monsieur Richard showed to me these trees and shrubs in their natural state, in the same order as in the Alps, right up the tree-line.'

The trees formed the background to this artificial paradise. Only the trickle of water and the song of the nightingales could be heard. 'One could fancy oneself', wrote the prince de Ligne, 'three hundred miles from Court.' The truth of that statement is the measure of Marie-Antoinette's success. It was exactly what she wanted to feel.

Marie-Antoinette protected her privacy by a series of *consignes* or regulations, the first of which were drawn up in 1776 by Bonnefoy du Plan who held the important post of Concierge. The first clause sets the tone; 'il est défendu par ordre de Votre Majesté que son Château et jardins soient publics.' The Queen pencilled her *oui* in the margin. There followed a list of those persons who were to be admitted and the conditions stipulated. The *consigne* ends on a milder note: 'during the absence of Your Majesty, does she order Bonnefoy to permit entry into the Château and gardens to honest people who are known to him under the conduct of a Suisse?' To this Marie-Antoinette appended a gracious *oui* in the margin.

But Trianon was at that time still only a place where Marie-Antoinette might pass part of the day. It was not until 1779 that she first spent a night there. She was convalescing from scarlet fever and stayed there from 12 April until 21 April. From this time onwards she often slept here and the Petit Trianon became once more the *maison de plaisance* which had been the original intention. A new set of orders, drawn up in June 1780 and signed 'Marie-Antoinette', were designed to safeguard the privacy of her dwelling.

These measures were certainly necessary. In the same month Mercy reported that Bonnefoy was unable to exclude the gate-crashers. 'You had the proof last Tuesday,' wrote Bonnefoy to Mique, asking him to double the locks; 'there were perhaps six hundred people, whereas the Queen's list did not reach two hundred.'

In the following month Mercy noted: 'the Queen is more and more occupied with her *maison de plaisance* and she goes there almost every day, either in the morning or in the afternoon. Her Majesty is only accompanied by two or three persons.' But by now she had a new interest.

In 1778 Mique had been commissioned to design a private

theatre for Trianon. *Comédie intime* was becoming fashionable; it had been introduced to Versailles by the duchesse de Villequier and in due course the duchesse de Villequier invited the Queen. It was not long before Mercy had the delicate task of breaking the news to Vienna that Marie-Antoinette had started an amateur company of her own.

The Queen's instruction to Mique was that the stage should correspond exactly with those of Fontainebleau and Choisy-le-Roi, so that the scenery made for one could be used in both the others. Mique produced a design which is in some ways a miniature of the Opera at Versailles. The arrangement of the vault, with its ring of *occuli* windows and its ceiling, painted by Lagrène, follows the prototype almost exactly. The colour scheme also, based on the same bright cobalt, owes much to that of Gabriel.

A private theatre meant an amateur theatrical company. It was largely composed of members of the comtesse Jules de Polignac's circle.

It was when visiting Madame de Polignac that Marie-Antoinette made the significant remark: 'je ne suis plus la Reine: je suis moi' – 'I am no longer the Queen: I am myself.' However much one may sympathise with Marie-Antoinette's need to enjoy the warmth of real human friendship in a relationship which enabled her to be herself and to disregard the barriers of rank, the fact is that her action was seen by her enemies as a virtual abdication – 'Je ne suis plus la Reine.'

In the early summer of 1787 three gentlemen of Lorraine named Cognel, Thiry and Jacquinot spent several weeks in Paris and on Sunday 3 June they made an excursion to the Petit Trianon. François Cognel describes their visit.

'The Queen comes here often to lay aside the weight of grandeur; she loves to be alone here for hours on end or to indulge in games which are not at all those of her rank . . . There are certain alterations being made in the Queen's bedroom and boudoir although both have been newly redecorated, but it seems that the Queen is not too certain as to what is really to her taste.'

Just as the three Lorrains were about to leave the gardens the arrival of the Queen was announced and their guide put them hastily into the dairy. The Queen came straight towards the dairy and they could observe her closely. 'She was wearing a simple linen dress with a fichu and a lace cap; in these modest clothes she appeared if anything more majestic than in the grand costume in which we had seen her at Versailles. Her way of walking is unique to her. One cannot discern her paces; she glides with an incomparable grace and holds her head even more proudly when, as we saw her then, she believes herself to be alone.' As Marie-Antoinette passed by the dairy they all felt the urge to genuflect.

Not everyone found the Queen more majestic in a simple linen dress. The portrait of her by Madame Vigée-Lebrun in a muslin gown and straw hat, exhibited in the Salon in 1783, was badly received.

The private theatre accentuated this separation between Marie-Antoinette and the Queen. She seems to have delighted in playing the part of a village maiden or *soubrette* that was as far removed as possible from her royal rank. In August 1780 Mercy was invited to a performance of *Le Devin du Village* and *Rose et Colas* – no doubt in order that his reports to Vienna could show the innocence of it all. At first he demurred, suggesting that his inclusion would cause even greater discontent among those excluded, but Marie-Antoinette merely replied that no-one would see him. He would be conducted to the theatre by a man who would ensure that he met no-one at all and he would have a box with a gilded grid in front of it.

Le Devin du Village had a cast of only three – Colette, played by the Queen, Colin, played by the comte d'Artois, and the Devin, played by Vaudreuil. 'The Queen has a very agreeable voice,' wrote Mercy, 'and sings well in tune; her style of acting is noble and full of grace. In sum, this entertainment was as well produced as is possible for a *spectacle de société*.' Madame Campan agreed with Mercy: 'the role of Colette was really played very well by the Queen.'

The only spectators were the King, the comte and comtesse de Provence, the comtesse d'Artois and Madame Elizabeth. The gallery was filled with minor domestics. There were no courtiers. Mercy observed that the King watched 'with an attention and a pleasure which was plainly expressed in his countenance'.

All the theatrical arrangements were in the hands of Monsieur Campan, but the duc de Fronsac, Premier Gentilhomme, considered that such affairs fell by right within his competence. 'You cannot be First Gentleman when we are actors,' the Queen wrote to him; 'besides, I have already let you know my wishes with regard to Trianon; I have no Court there; I live as a private individual.'

This attempt to live as a private individual was innocent and understandable enough, but it was extremely ill-advised. The Court was offended and the public scandalised.

Mercy, writing to Vienna, gave a good appreciation of the situation. 'Those who approach sovereigns have always some ambitious plans in their minds . . . and the smaller the number of persons who obtain exclusive access, the more insistent are their intrigues, the more difficult to clear up and, in consequence by far the most dangerous. A great Court ought to be accessible to a great number of people.' He was undoubtedly right. 'Versailles,' wrote the duc de Levis, 'that theatre of Louis XIV's magnificence, was no more than a little provincial town to which one only went with reluctance and from which one made one's escape as quickly as possible.'

There is also another side to this. It is necessary to many people's vanity to be always 'in the know'. This necessity and this vanity tend to be increased when the person is a courtier and the subject of the knowledge is the royal family. When such people have no access to knowledge they invent and when they invent they exaggerate. The little snowball of gossip becomes the great avalanche of calumny. Calumny, as Dr Johnson defined it, is a profession which requires neither labour nor courage.

One example will suffice. There was a performance in the

theatre at Trianon of Marmontel's play *Le Dormeur Eveillé*. The scenery represented the Palace of the Sun, of which the most conspicuous features were twisted columns of gold studded with diamonds. Needless to say, neither the gold nor the diamonds were real, but in 1789, when the Deputies from the States General came to inspect Trianon, they came with minds already deeply prejudiced. 'The extreme simplicity of this *maison de plaisance*', wrote Madame Campan, 'did not correspond with their preconceptions. Some insisted on being shown into the smallest of *cabinets*, saying that richly furnished rooms were being concealed from them. Finally they indicated one which, by their account, was supposed to have been studded all over with diamonds and twisted columns with rubies and sapphires.'

Madame Campan insists on the lack of extravagance at Trianon. The furniture was still in 1789 what it had been in Louis XV's reign and 'had become very dowdy'. Even Marie-Antoinette's own bed – 'a bed which had seen better days' – was that slept in by Madame du Barry. 'The reproach of prodigality, widely made against the Queen, is the most inconceivable of popular errors which were established . . . about her character.'

The performance of *Le Dormeur Eveillé* was part of Marie-Antoinette's entertainment of Gustavus III of Sweden in June 1784. The royal family each had a copy of the play specially bound in red morocco tooled in silver – the Queen's livery – with her own armorial bearings. Another copy, bound in green and gold with the royal arms of Sweden was offered to her guest.

Besides the theatre, Gustavus was treated to an illumination of the gardens. The buildings were lit by the glow of an encircling fire, hidden from the eyes by means of a ditch. Hundreds of thousands of candles in little pots, some fitted with coloured transparencies, cast pools of light round every clump of trees and 'brought out the different colours in the most charming and agreeable manner'.

The scene is described by the baron de Frénilly: 'The whole

park was illuminated from an invisible source by fairy lights concealed behind trees, behind clumps, behind little screens painted like bushes which could be moved, which from the terrace round the house and from certain viewpoints contrived with great art, revealed the park and its ornaments lit as if by a beautiful sunset.'

A series of watercolours by the chevalier de Lespinasse has captured the appearance of the gardens by this floodlighting. Above the waters of the lake the Belvédère shone with a lustre that might have been its own, the great light of the dry faggots picking out some of the trees with a pale luminosity and casting others into a dark, unnatural relief, whitening the surface of the rocks and accentuating the cavernous recesses of the grotto. On the other side of the Château, the Temple de l'Amour was aglow, shining 'with a brightness that made it the most brilliant point in the whole garden'. 6400 faggots were employed for the illumination of the temple alone.

'C'était un enchantement parfait,' wrote Gustavus to his brother; 'the Queen had allowed any honest persons, who were not invited to the supper, to walk in the gardens, but they were required to be dressed in white, which truly created the spectacle of the Elysian Fields. The Queen would not sit at table but did the honours as might have done the mistress of the most respectable of houses.'

Gustavus and Marie-Antoinette had already exchanged plans of Trianon and Drottningholm and the King of Sweden was most interested in the creations of the Queen of France.

In the same year the English Garden was considerably extended by the laying out, after designs by Mique, of the Hameau. Round the borders of a small lake were disposed a dozen rustic houses such as might have formed a tiny village, or the background of a painting by Greuze – a farm with a monumental gateway, several thatched cottages and a mill worked by a rivulet fed from the lake. The trees were so arranged as to permit a view of the church of Saint-Antoine, thus giving, as it were, a background of reality to this artificial scene. The artificiality was taken to the lengths of representing the crumbling masonry and leprous plaster of a hovel in need of repair.

It was this that earned the Hameau its most severe censure from the marquis de Bombelles. On 12 December 1783 he was passing along the road from Versailles to Marly and turned aside to see the newly constructed village. 'With great expense,' he observed, 'they have applied themselves to the task of making the Hameau de la Reine look genuinely poor. Perhaps with only a little outlay Her Majesty might have managed to remove, within a radius of twenty or thirty leagues, the signs of misery which mark our real hamlets and to improve the dwellings, the refuges of so many good citizens, instead of representing them in their hideous dilapidation . . . To imitate, in places destined for one's amusement, something which reminds you in the most sterile manner of the ill-fortune of your subjects or fellow citizens, is to make sport with it and to become callous about their condition.' The eye of sentimentality sees only the picturesqueness where the eye of humanitarianism sees only the squalor.

Gouverneur Morris, a distinguished American visitor, made a similar observation; 'Royalty has here endeavoured at great expense to conceal itself from its own eye. But the attempt is vain. A dairy furnished with the porcelaine of Sèvres is a semblance too splendid for rural life.'

Each cottage had its garden planted with trim rows of cabbages, cauliflowers and haricot beans; strawberries, raspberries and gooseberries were also cultivated; pear trees, plum trees and cherry trees, numbering in all exactly a thousand, afforded the beauty of their blossom in spring and the abundance of their fruit in summer. Vegetables and fruit were taken to the Petit Trianon from these gardens and milk and butter from the dairy.

For the Hameau was a working village. Cows grazed upon the pastures, poultry strutted in the farmyard; women brought their washing to the *lavanderie* and gathered the fruit in autumn; peasants cultivated the land and dug their gardens, the miller ground his corn, fishermen plied their nets in the lake, which had been stocked with 2349 carp and twenty-six pike. These fish were constantly fed and the bread thrown to them accounted for at least 950 livres a year.

During the summer of that year, says the comte de Vaublanc, 'the Queen held a ball in the gardens of Trianon every Sunday. Anyone properly dressed was admitted and especially nurses with children. She danced a quadrille to show that she took part in the pleasure to which she invited the others. She summoned the nurses, had the children presented to her, talked with their parents and heaped kindnesses upon them. Usually most of the royal family were there but I observed to a friend that a very small number of members of high society were present at these reunions.'

Some of the upper aristocracy of England were among those invited to Trianon, in particular the Duke of Dorset, who was British Ambassador, and the Duchess of Devonshire. In their correspondence to each other they called Marie-Antoinette 'Mrs B.'. On 6 April 1786, Dorset wrote to Georgiana: 'we all dined with Mrs B. *dans le hameau dans le jardin de Trianon*. We were thirty in all; the chief amusement after dinner consisted in throwing each other's hats into the *pièce d'eau*, and Lord George was the only one who could punt a boat, so that he was deputed to fish them out again.'

The later years of Louis XVI's reign saw a renewed interest in country life. 'The present fashion in France for passing some time in the country', noted Arthur Young, 'is new. Everybody that has country seats is at them, and those who have none visit those who have; this remarkable revolution in manners is one of the best customs they have taken from England; and its introduction was affected the easier, being assisted by the magic of Rousseau's writings.'

The Queen was no exception to this new fashion for country house life, but with her it had to be a game of make-believe. When she entered the salon at Trianon the ladies did not rise from the piano or their embroidery frames and the gentlemen did not interrupt their tric-trac. The formality of the Court gave way to the ease and freedom of the country house.

Louis was delighted with this experience of family life. He was frequently at Trianon, often spending the whole day there, where he could sit and read in the garden in a tent 'of twill lined with blue taffeta and provided with Venetian blinds'. Marie-Antoinette, pregnant for the third time, was probably closer to him now than she had ever been. She gave up gambling for high stakes and took to loto which was Louis' favourite game.

It may have been this enrichment of her family life which enabled Marie-Antoinette to detach herself, in 1785, from the Polignac clique. The duchesse de Fitzjames, says the *correspondance secrète*, 'enjoys more and more the favour of the Queen and arouses even some jealousy among the friends of the duchesse de Polignac'. This emancipation even led to a revival of the life of the Court at Versailles. In May 1785, 343 gentlemen and 241 ladies were presented. The Queen's ballroom began to regain its popularity.

It was just at this time that Marie-Antoinette was described in the most complimentary terms by one of her most impartial admirers. Eric Magnus, Baron Staël-Holstein, had succeeded Count Creutz as Swedish Ambassador at Versailles in 1783. Even before this promotion he was received well by both Louis and Marie-Antoinette, so much so that Creutz complained to Gustavus III that, 'as the King himself admits, Monsieur de Staël had private audiences with the Queen which, as Ambassador, I am not myself able to obtain.'

The Baron was thus particularly well placed to observe Marie-Antoinette. On 19 February 1785 he wrote to Gustavus: 'the more I have the honour of seeing the Queen, the more strongly I am in the opinion which I have always held of her character. She likes the truth and one can speak it to her provided that she is convinced of the probity and disinterestedness of the speaker. In handling any matter with nobility and candour one is certain to please her, even if one is of a different opinion from her own. Once she has distinguished flattery or falsehood, she abhors them, but, as with all the princes in the world, she cannot always guard against the adroitness employed by courtiers to obtain their ends.'

The year 1785 had dawned serene and beautiful. The war in America was over and the treaty signed to the satisfaction of France. The comte Beugnot, then a young lawyer practising in Champagne, could write a lyrical passage in his memoirs. 'The shame of the treaty of Paris was effaced, the present seemed assured, the future appeared with the most rosy tints. Abundance reigned in our ports and in our markets. There was an influx to Paris of visitors from all the capitals of Europe, and, as if the gifts of God had crowned those of the politicians, harvests of every kind during the years 1784 and 1785 were admirable. Liberty had come and established itself in the middle of France without having been invited . . . an air of contentment animated our meetings, our theatrical performances, our family gatherings. It seemed that, in this beautiful land of France, we were savouring the sweet taste of public felicity.'

He spoke too soon. The sky may have seemed cloudless enough to the young Beugnot, but in the very town where he lived, Bar-sur-Aube, a plot was hatching which was to break like a thunderclap over Versailles and of which he was to be one of the closest witnesses and one of the most detailed recorders.

On 9 August 1785, Marie-Antoinette was back at Trianon. She had decided, somewhat unwisely, to reopen the theatre with a performance of *The Barber of Seville* and was rehearsing the part of Rosine. It was the last performance that she was ever to give here. A few days earlier, Madame Campan had been approached by the jeweller Boehmer to obtain for him an interview with the Queen. He said that the Queen had agreed, through the intermediary of the Cardinal de Rohan, to buy a diamond necklace valued at 1 600 000 livres. He wanted his first instalment. Suddenly Marie-Antoinette found herself confronted with the whole monstrous conspiracy known as the 'Affaire du Collier'.

The Diamond Necklace

Marie-Antoinette knew all about the necklace. It had been lovingly collected over a number of years by the jewellers Boehmer and Bassange. It contained in all 647 diamonds giving a total of 2 842 carats. A band of seventeen equally sized stones encircled the throat; from this depended one central festoon set between the smaller ones each enclosing a pendant. Below this a long double chain of brilliants hung in the form of a capital M to which were attached two rather heavy tassels. The marquis de Bombelles, who was shown the necklace by Boehmer in February 1783, described it as 'one of the most beautiful things of its sort possible because of the size, the clearness, the equality and the sparkle of the stones'.

Boehmer had made several attempts to persuade the Queen to buy it – or to persuade the King to buy it for her. She had made as many refusals, asserting that she had all the diamonds that she wanted; that the recent purchase of Rambouillet and Saint-Cloud by the King would make any further extravagance unwise and that the money would be better spent on a battleship. But still Boehmer persisted. Finally, according to Madame Campan, 'he threw himself on his knees, burst into tears, joined his hands and cried: "Madame, I am ruined, dishonoured if you do not buy my necklace!" He even threatened to commit suicide by jumping into the river.' The Queen lectured him on his folly, suggested that he divided up the necklace and sold it piecemeal and dismissed him from her presence.

There, so far as she was concerned, the matter ended. But on 1 August Madame Campan left Versailles for a short sojourn in her country house at Crespy. Two days later Boehmer arrived, very troubled that he had had no reply from the Queen to a letter. He claimed that she owed him money. Madame Campan retorted that all his bills had been paid and asked for what object the Queen could possibly owe him so exhorbitant a sum. 'For my necklace,' replied Boehmer, and went on to say that the Queen had expressed a desire to possess the necklace and had purchased it by the intermediary of the Cardinal de Rohan. Nothing could have sounded more impossible to anyone who knew the Queen.

Louis-René-Edouard de Rohan was the fourth member of his family in succession to be Archbishop of Strasbourg. According to the baronne d'Oberkirch he had come to regard the revenues of the Church as his own by hereditary right. 'He received us in his episcopal palace, which is worthy of a sovereign. He ran his household on ruinous lines . . . He had no less than fourteen *maîtres d'hôtel* and twenty-five *valets de chambre*. It was three in the afternoon, the eve of the octave of All Saints, and the Cardinal was just coming out of his chapel in a soutane of purple silk and a rochet of English lace beyond price. He had an alb, for great occasions when he officiated at Versailles, in needlepoint of such richness that one scarcely dared to touch it. His coat of arms and his motto were placed above each of the large flowers.'

Not only did he have the palace in Strasbourg and another in Paris, he built and appointed at Saverne 'one of the most charming residences in the world'. The garden front is 180 yards long and offers a straight row of thirty-five windows to each storey, proportioned to a colossal order of Corinthian pilasters. 'Having encumbered the land with his palaces and his subjects with his debts,' wrote Bombelles, 'he was a man of the most outstanding mediocrity whose outlook was that of a child spoilt by fortune and the adulation of fools.' Madame d'Oberkirch is a little more indulgent: 'He is a handsome prelate,' she admits, 'very far from being devout, very much a womaniser; witty, amiable, but of a credulity for which he was to pay dearly.'

He had been appointed Ambassador to Vienna by Louis XV. The baron de Breteuil had already been nominated to the post and, as the abbé Georgel, the French plenipotentiary at Vienna, said, 'His coaches had arrived and his *hôtel* was furnished.' This was the beginning of a bitter rivalry between Rohan and Breteuil which was to have the most unfortunate consequences. Maria Theresa, moreover, was deeply shocked by Rohan's behaviour. His impiety, his immorality and his fantastic extravagance ill became his position in the Church. She referred to him as 'ce vilain évèque' – 'this wicked bishop'.

On the death of Louis XV, Rohan returned to Versailles. He was not reappointed to the Embassy in Vienna: the post went once again to Breteuil. This was a great set-back to Rohan's ambitions. In order to restore his position, Louis-René de Rohan lost no opportunity of adding jewels to his crown. The most important ecclesiastic position in France, that of Grand Aumônier, had been virtually promised to him in advance on the death of the Cardinal de La Roche-Aymon. When Louis XVI showed a reluctance to honour the promise, Madame de Marsan put pressure on him which amounted almost to blackmail and when, on 17 October 1777, La Roche-Aymon finally died, Louis was obliged to confer the *grande aumônerie* on Rohan. Marie-Antoinette had to accept the inevitable. She wrote to her mother: 'we are just reaching the moment when the Cardinal de La Roche-Aymon will die and the prince Louis will have his place. I cannot conceal from my dear mother that this pains me very much and that the King also is not pleased.'

All that the King could do was to decline to recommend Rohan to the Pope for a Cardinal's hat. Rohan successfully obtained this through the patronage of the King of Poland. The prestigious position of Proviseur of the Sorbonne became vacant and Rohan managed to get a majority of votes against the royal candidate. It seemed that he was going from strength to strength. He reckoned, however, without the force of counterproductivity. In the last resort everything at

Versailles depended on the good will of the King and this often had to presuppose the good will of the Queen. Every new success in Rohan's climb was in fact a new nail in the coffin of his ambition to be Chief Minister. He realised it too late.

This Prince Bishop who had disgraced her Church, this ambassador who had scandalised her mother, this shameless womaniser who had outraged her own modesty – he was the last person in the world to whom Marie-Antoinette would have entrusted any commission whatever. 'It is necessary to take note once more', wrote the baron de Besenval, 'of the deep hatred which the Queen felt for the Cardinal, and which he had so justly merited by filling his despatches from his Embassy in Vienna with uncomplimentary remarks about her. He had even gone so far as to say, in those letters, that her coquetry gave hopes to a lover that he might be successful in his advances to her.'

Madame Campan informed Boehmer that the Queen had not spoken to the Cardinal since his recall, and advised him to go to Versailles and see the baron de Breteuil who was the minister in charge of the Maison du Roi, but she warned Boehmer that since he had purchased the charge of Court Jeweller and had taken his oath of fidelity, 'it was unpardonable to have acted without the clear orders of the King, the Queen or the minister.' To this Boehmer made the astonishing reply that he had indeed been given direct orders from the Queen and had also received a number of letters signed by her which he had been obliged to show to bankers in order to extend his credit.

A note found later in the papers of the Cardinal confirmed the date of this interview with Madame Campan. 'Today, 3 August, Boehmer went to the country house of Madame Campan who told him that the Queen had never received the necklace and that he had been tricked.'

For the events which followed the memoirs of the maréchal de Castries give what is probably the most authentic account. 'It seems that it was on 2 August that the Queen first suspected that someone had bought diamonds in her name. She had charged someone [presumably Madame Campan] to gather information on this affair. However, it is said that Boehmer returned a second time to the Queen and gave her a memorandum which, in her distraction, she destroyed. On the more positive information that she was given about the acquisition of a diamond necklace, she charged the baron de Breteuil, Ministre de la Maison du Roi, to see Boehmer and to order him to give an account of what had happened. It was not until Friday 11 August that Breteuil forwarded to the Queen the memorandum of Boehmer and it was on that day that she first spoke of the matter to the King.'

The memorandum of Boehmer and Bassange was in fact dated 12 August. In it they stated that on 24 January the Cardinal had called at their establishment: that he had seen the necklace and had said that he was interested in buying it; that he was purchasing it on behalf of an unnamed third party; that he might not be permitted to reveal the name of that party; that two days later they had been summoned to the Palais-Cardinal and that it was agreed that the price would be 1 600 000 livres, the first instalment of 400 000 to be paid in six months' time and further instalments of the same sum at six-month intervals. On 29 January the contract was signed.

'On 1 February,' continues their memorandum, 'we received a letter from the Prince . . . conceived in these terms: "I should like Monsieur Boehmer and his associate to come to me this morning and to bring with them the object under discussion." We went at once to the Palais-Cardinal, carrying the great necklace with us in its case.

'It was in the course of this interview that the Prince informed us that it was Her Majesty the Queen who was the purchaser of the necklace and showed us, in evidence, the contract with the marginal notation "approved" alongside every clause and paragraph and, at the bottom, the signature "Marie-Antoinette de France".' It is perhaps surprising that both the Grand Aumônier and the Court Jeweller should have been unaware of the fact that the Queen never added 'de France' to her signature.

The contents of Boehmer's memorandum was all that was known to Marie-Antoinette when she took the matter to her husband. Between them the decision was finally reached to confront the Cardinal with the facts as revealed. The day chosen was 15 August, the Feast of the Assumption.

On 15 August, therefore, Louis and Marie-Antoinette were in the Cabinet Intérieur, which had been Louis XV's study; with them were the baron de Breteuil and Miromesnil, Garde des Sceaux. The Cardinal de Rohan was sent for. As soon as he arrived Louis confronted him with Boehmer's statement, asked him to read it and to explain it. 'The Queen stood with downcast eyes,' writes the maréchal de Castries, 'without saying a word. When he had read it the Cardinal stated that everything contained in the memorandum was correct and that, since the Queen was present, he could see very well that he had been deceived; to this memorandum was attached a letter from the Cardinal which certified as authentic the signature of the Queen which committed the jeweller to hand over the necklace. Seeing the Cardinal's confusion he [Louis] said to him, "pull yourself together; go into my *cabinet* alone and set down in writing whatever you can say in your justification."'

The Cardinal passed into the Arrière-Cabinet. During his absence the King proposed that he should be arrested. Miromesnil was shocked at the idea of arresting him in his pontifical robes. He was the first of many. When Rohan returned he had not written much, but it was now for the first time that he named a certain Madame La Motte as his deceiver. Breteuil was given the order to arrest him. The Cardinal said to the King: 'I beseech your Majesty, out of consideration for my family, not to create a scandal.' 'I cannot,' said Louis, 'either as a king or as a husband.' The Queen finally spoke and asked him how he could have thought that she would have chosen him to entrust with such a commission. On 22 August she wrote to her brother, the

Emperor Joseph, 'I was present at the meeting and was really touched by the reasonableness and the firmness which the King displayed . . . When the Cardinal made a plea not to be arrested the King replied that he could not spare him without failing in his duty both as sovereign and as husband.'

'It is said', continues Castries, 'that the Cardinal, still engrossed in his imaginings, made certain signs to her to remind her of what formed the basis of his opinion and that these signs were all that was needed to make her lose her patience. She confided, a few days later, to one of her *dames du palais* [presumably Madame Campan] that she felt at this moment feelings of fear, surprise and anger which nearly made her ill.'

The Cardinal was ordered to leave. He passed through the series of Petits Appartements du Roi, into the Cabinet du Conseil and finally into the Grande Galerie. Here, according to Castries, Breteuil gave the order of arrest to one of the guards: 'Je vous ordonne, Monsieur, de la part du Roi, d'arrêter Monsieur le Cardinal et d'en répondre.'

It would hardly have been possible at Versailles to create a greater stir. The Cardinal de Rohan, the Grand Aumônier du Roi, arrested before the eyes of all the Court in his pontifical robes on his way to say mass in the Chapel! 'One can understand', wrote Mercy to the Emperor, 'the utter stupefaction provoked by so unexpected an event.' A few days later Daniel Hailes, who was on the staff of the British Ambassador, the Duke of Dorset, reported on the affair to Lord Carmarthen: 'The universally credited account is, that that the Cardinal has forged an order from the Queen to the Jeweller of the Crown to deliver to him diamonds to the amount of 1 600 000 livres, and which diamonds he actually received. What makes this event more extraordinary is that the Cardinal is known to be a man of extremely good parts and is in the enjoyment of the greatest honour and revenues to which any subject in the Church can aspire.'

The Cardinal certainly behaved, at the moment of his arrest, with a dignity worthy of his position. He also had the presence of mind to ask for, and was granted, permission to write a note which he gave to one of his attendants. It was addressed to his Vicar-General, the abbé Georgel, whom he ordered to burn all the correspondence in the little red portfolio relating to the affair. The abbé Georgel was Rohan's right hand man and he has left voluminous memoirs. It was largely owing to Georgel's unflagging zeal that the evidence was amassed which finally secured the Cardinal's acquittal. In collecting this evidence he uncovered the story of one of the most fantastic hoaxes in history.

In the same letter in which Marie-Antoinette had told her brother of the interview leading to the arrest, she put the case as she saw it. 'The Cardinal admits to having purchased, in my name and through the use of a signature which he believed to be mine, a diamond necklace valued at 1 600 000 livres. He claims that he has been tricked by a Madame Valois de La Motte. This common adventuress has no standing at Court and has never had access to my company.'

The self styled 'comtesse' de La Motte is best known to history through the memoirs of Jacques-Claude Beugnot, who later was to receive the title of count from Napoleon. Their connection was simple: they both lived at Bar-sur-Aube in Champagne.

Jeanne de Saint-Rémi de Valois had started life in the village of Fontête where Beugnot's father had regularly given alms for her support. She lived with a brother and a sister in a condition not far removed from nakedness and starvation. 'One thing only', wrote Beugnot, 'had been preserved in the last debris of the family – its geneaology.' This might have remained of no account had not the *curé* of Fontête managed to interest the marquise de Boulainvilliers in these orphans. The genealogy was submitted to the highest authority in such matters. Chérin – 'minutieux dans ses examens et inflexible dans ses jugements' – pronounced that the children were indeed descendants of the baron de Saint-Rémi who was indeed an illegitimate son of Henri II. The surname Valois was permitted.

This recognition of their family status resulted in Jeanne and her sister being sent to the convent of Longchamp. It was their 'escape' from here which brought them to Bar-sur-Aube. In the year 1780, Jeanne de Saint-Rémi de Valois married Marc-Antoine-Nicolas La Motte, an officer in the corps de la Gendarmerie, a man as impecunious as he was undistinguished.

It was in the same year, 'by malevolent coincidence', says Georgel, 'that there arrived in Strasbourg Joseph Balsamo, "comte" de Cagliostro, who was to exert a strange and nefarious influence upon the Cardinal de Rohan, seducing him into the treacherous by-paths of the occult and the supernatural. I do not know what monster of evil, what arch-enemy of mankind, vomited up on these shores this scintillating new genius of charlatanry, this new apostle of the "Universal Religion" who wielded despotic power over his proselytes, subjugating them utterly to his will.'

Whatever the truth was about Cagliostro, it is certain that he behaved with the most carefully calculated discretion. 'The newcomer's assiduities to the poor, his disdain for the rich, enhanced his reputation as a superior being and aroused universal excitement and fanaticism.' In spite of his disdain for the rich, Cagliostro managed to include some of the great names of France among his conquests. 'It got abroad', wrote the comte Beugnot, 'that Monsieur le duc de Chartres, at whose court it had been decided not to believe in God, was fully disposed to believe in Cagliostro, so deep is the truth that there is in our human frailty a source always open to credulity, and that, if this source is not absorbed by religion and its mysteries, it will find a random outlet in objects which are either ridiculous or dangerous.'

Among those who flocked to see Cagliostro was one who was already connected with Madame La Motte – the marquise de Boulainvilliers. Another was soon to follow – the Cardinal de Rohan. He had to pretend to suffer from asthma in order even to be admitted into the great man's presence. But the ruse sufficed. 'This first encounter', continues

Georgel, 'served only to intensify the Cardinal's desire for a closer acquaintance. In this he finally succeeded, or rather, it was the wily charlatan who gradually insinuated himself into the confidence of the Cardinal, into control over his mind and will – and all so smoothly, so imperceptibly, that the Cardinal credited himself with having effected the intimacy.'

Another witness of Rohan's relationship with Cagliostro was the baronne d'Oberkirch. She gives a detailed account of their meeting at the Château de Saverne. She was deeply impressed by Cagliostro and deeply afraid: 'He at once attracted and repelled you: he frightened you and at the same time inspired you with insurmountable curiosity . . . he was possessed of a demonic power; he enthralled the mind and paralysed the will.' As for Rohan she was filled with pity and contempt. 'If I had not heard it with my own ears, I would not have believed it possible that a Prince of the Roman Catholic Church, a Rohan, a man of intellect and honour in many fields, could have allowed himself to be utterly dominated by a mountebank.' Frénilly agreed that the Cardinal 'believed in everything and everyone except, perhaps, in God'.

In September 1783 Madame La Motte came into contact with Rohan. As he stated in evidence for his trial, his coach happened to meet that of Madame de Boulainvilliers on the road from Strasbourg to Saverne. 'I went to greet the marquise,' he stated, 'who introduced me to a young lady seated beside her, whose name she said was a famous one – Valois!'

Beugnot is not liberal with his dates, but it must have been after this that he records the sudden appearance of Madame La Motte at his apartments in Paris. She had just received notice of an audience granted her by the Cardinal de Rohan. She came back later 'radiant with hope'. The great man had promised to espouse her cause.

At a dinner which Beugnot gave her in Paris she talked of one possibility of approaching the Queen. 'That was the first time,' noted Beugnot, 'that she pronounced in my presence the name of the sovereign.' Her next move was to Versailles. Beugnot describes her as 'dying of hunger and considering that all means were permissible against a social order that had deprived her of everything'.

At Versailles Madame La Motte tried the attention-getting ruse of pretending to faint in front of a member of the royal family. A slight movement of compassion from the comtesse de Provence brought a small pecuniary reward, but that was all. Madame La Motte could not penetrate the exclusiveness which is necessary to a royal family. Since she had not been able to obtain the confidence of the Queen, there was nothing left for it than to pretend that she had.

It was perfectly easy for Madame La Motte to penetrate Versailles. Two years later Arthur Young wrote, 'the whole palace, except the chapel, seems to be open to all the world; we pushed through an amazing crowd of all sorts of people . . . many of them not very well dressed, whence it appears that no questions are asked.' After the Affaire du Collier was over, on 22 August 1785, Marie-Antoinette wrote to her sister Marie-Christine: 'I have never seen this La Motte woman . . . it is said that she has been encountered on two or three occasions on my little staircase in the Cour des Princes; it was evidently a trick planned to deceive her dupes and to make them believe that she had been received in my cabinets.' A manuscript in the municipal library of Dijon also records that 'the woman [La Motte] appeared frequently at Court, that is to say in the antechambers of the Queen and the other princesses to ask for assistance'. The abbé de Véri, writing on 12 May 1786, says the same: 'knocking at all the doors, she found her way into the Queen's rooms, into those of the princesses of the royal family . . . A suppliant before all those who were great, proclaiming in front of these others her favour with them and above all with the Queen.' At the same time she was becoming familiar with the topography of Versailles and its gardens and with the movements and habits of Marie-Antoinette.

It was while she was thus engaged that Madame La Motte

learnt that the Cardinal de Rohan was desperately anxious to find his way into the Queen's favour. He had to confess to Madame La Motte that he was unable to help her into the Queen's good graces admitting, according to Georgel, 'the profound distress which he felt at having incurred the hatred of the sovereign'. It was, he said, a continual source of bitterness to his heart which poisoned his happiest moments. 'Such a confidence', observes Georgel, 'became the infernal spark which caused the most disastrous conflagration.' For once Madame La Motte knew of the Cardinal's passionate desire to be reconciled with the Queen she began to pretend that she was now on good terms with Marie-Antoinette and might be able to help him. A series of letters forged by Madame La Motte's secretary, Rétaux de Villette, prepared the way.

Some time after the first mention of the Queen, Beugnot began to notice that the relationship between Madame La Motte and the Cardinal was becoming intimate: 'a burning ambition was combined with a tender affection. Each of these two sentiments enflamed each other and thus the unhappy man was given over to a sort of frenzy. . . I had the opportunity to read some of the letters which he wrote to Madame La Motte; they were red hot; the impact, or rather the momentum of these two passions was frightening. It was lucky for the memory of the Prince that these letters were burnt, but it is a loss to the history of the human heart; they would have shed light in one more corner of the cavern.'

It so happened that on 12 August 1784 Beugnot called at the La Mottes' house in Paris. He had called for no particular reason and found only a Mademoiselle Colson at home. They passed the time together and at midnight Beugnot was preparing to leave when it occurred to him that if he waited for the return of the La Mottes he could go home in their carriage. Shortly afterwards they arrived, accompanied by Rétaux de Villette and a woman whom Beugnot had not met. 'The face of this woman', he noted, 'caused me at first sight the sort of perplexity which one feels when confronted by a face which one is certain one has seen somewhere before.' As he said good-bye to her it came to him: what at first troubled his memory was 'her perfect resemblance to the Queen'.

During the summer of 1784, Madame La Motte had sensed the need to give the Cardinal more striking proof than the forged letters of her ability to affect his reconciliation with the Queen. If only he could be led to believe that he had actually met her!

The only way was, of course, by impersonation. The evidence for this dramatic episode comes from the woman who, without knowing it, played the part of Marie-Antoinette in the scene best known to history as the Bosquet de la Reine. Her name was Marie-Nicole le Guay d'Oliva. She was a prostitute. 'One afternoon in July,' she stated in her deposition for the trial, 'I was seated at a small *café* under the arcades [of the Palais Royal] when I saw a tall young man walking alone, passing back and forth before my table . . . he looked and stared at me fixedly.'

The man was La Motte. What caused him to be so keenly observant was that the woman bore a striking resemblance to Marie-Antoinette. A few days later he followed her home and told her that 'a personage of the highest rank in the Kingdom' had need of her and the next day he produced his wife as that personage. She succeeded in convincing Mademoiselle d'Oliva that the person who had need of her was none other than the Queen.

In order to make use of Mademoiselle d'Oliva's resemblance to Marie-Antoinette a *rendez-vous* had to be arranged of a sufficiently convincing nature. Under what possible circumstances could the Cardinal be brought into the presence of Mademoiselle d'Oliva without risk of his discovering or even suspecting the impersonation?

It was here that Madame La Motte's knowledge of the ways of the Court and the habits of the Queen could be put to good effect. For some years Marie-Antoinette had made a habit of walking on summer evenings in the gardens of Versailles. It had started in 1778 during her first pregnancy.

Not only did these nocturnal excursions do harm to the already tarnished reputation of the Queen; they may well, suggests Madame Campan, have provided an element of verisimilitude to Madame La Motte's little plan.

In order to lure the gullible Cardinal into her clutches, Madame La Motte had to convince him that he had really come face to face with Marie-Antoinette. These much publicised walks in the garden made such an idea plausible. Clearly, however, the meeting could not take place in sight of the palace or its parterres. Madame La Motte must have known the gardens of Versailles well; out of all the possible trysting places she decided on the Bosquet de la Reine.

The site was well chosen. Its name was interchangeable with 'Bosquet de Vénus'; it had all the right overtones. It was situated beneath the high wall of the Orangerie to the west of the Hundred Steps which descend from the parterres adjacent to the palace to the level of the road to Saint-Cyr, which was conveniently close. The Bosquet de la Reine was out of sight, easily accessible and offered an easy line of retreat.

Madame d'Oliva, in her deposition for the trial, recounted the story of what happened. On 11 August without being told what it was all about, she accompanied the La Mottes to Versailles. The following day she was given her first indication as to her task. 'Tonight,' said Madame La Motte, 'I will take you into the park of the palace, and you will hand this letter to a very great nobleman who will meet you there.' At midnight they made their way to the Bosquet de la Reine. According to d'Oliva:

> The night was the darkest, without one beam of moonlight, so that I could distinguish nothing beyond the persons and objects familiar to me . . . Then Madame La Motte gave me a rose, with these instructions: 'you are to hand this flower to the great lord who will join you here, but you are to speak only these words, no more: *You know what this means.* Now, remember that the Queen is close by watching and listening.'
>
> These words of the comtesse La Motte so overwhelmed me that I felt myself shaking from head to foot. Madame La Motte then led me to an arbour and left me with instructions to stay

> just where I was. Faithful to her instructions I did not stir from the spot where she had stationed me. Then the great unknown lord appeared and came towards me, bowing, while Madame La Motte stood off to the side as if to observe the scene. I did not know who the great nobleman was . . . It is impossible for me to describe the state I was in. I was so nervous and excited, so confused by the strange scene itself as well as by the thought that the Queen was witness to it, as my seducers had convinced me, I was trembling so much that I still do not know how I managed to get through even half the orders that were given me.
>
> Somehow I presented the rose to the great unknown lord and spoke the words I had been told to speak . . . As for the letter, it remained in my pocket completely forgotten. At this moment Madame La Motte ran towards us, speaking in low but urgent tones: 'Hurry! hurry! leave quickly now!' At least that is all I remember hearing.

The unknown lord disappeared into the darkness and the rest of the party returned to their coach. Back at the La Mottes' residence in Paris the poor woman at last relaxed. 'We all had supper together; the repast was gay.' This was the occasion at which Beugnot had first seen Mademoiselle d'Oliva and noted her resemblance to the Queen.

Rohan gave his own account of the incident in an interview with the maréchal de Castries and Vergennes after he had been taken to the Bastille. 'At the time expected I saw a woman approaching with a black veil, holding a fan in her hand with which she held up her veil, which was lowered; I believed, by the light of the stars, that I could recognise the Queen distinctly; I said to her that I was happy to find in her kindness a proof that she had set aside her prejudice against me; she replied with a few words and just as I was about to explain myself, someone came up and told her that Monsieur and the comte d'Artois were only a few paces away; she left precipitately and I saw her no more.'

The success of the impersonation by Mademoiselle d'Oliva in the Bosquet de la Reine greatly encouraged Madame La Motte and greatly increased her daring. 'Her deeply criminal mind', wrote Georgel, 'conceived a manoeuvre the audacity and the danger of which would have deterred the most cunning and the most determined of brigands.

'Madame La Motte had had occasion to see the famous necklace and Boehmer had not concealed from her that such a jewel was a dead loss on the market and that it was a great embarrassment to him . . . He added that he would offer a handsome reward to anyone who procured him an outlet.'

This was the sort of prize commensurate with Madame La Motte's ambitions. By late November 1785, the plan was fully formulated in her mind. All that she had to do was, in Georgel's words, 'to persuade the Cardinal that the Queen ardently desired the necklace; that, wishing to buy it without the King's knowledge and to pay for it in instalments out of her savings, she desired to give the Grand Aumônier a particular mark of her good will in charging him to make this purchase in her name.'

The Cardinal, summoned from Saverne, 'wished that he had wings'. He arrived at his house in Paris 'most unexpectedly on a fine, cold day in January'. No sooner had he heard of the Queen's desire than he accepted the conditions. On 1 February Boehmer and Bassange brought the necklace round to him. It was only then, as we have already seen, that Rohan told them that he was purchasing the necklace on behalf of the Queen. 'We expressed great joy and satisfaction at this information,' the jewellers admitted, 'and the Prince told us that it was to be delivered to Her Majesty the same day.'

The story of the delivery of the necklace is recounted by the abbé Georgel, in one of his most flowery passages. Madame La Motte, 'intoxicated with the joy of seeing the prodigious success of her inconceivable intrigue, had set the scene at her apartment at Versailles on which was to be played the handing over of the necklace to the man who would arrive, saying that he had been charged by the Queen to be its bearer. It really was a stage and a performance.'

It was 1 February, the day of the Investitures of the Cordon Bleu. The Cardinal arrived at dusk, his valet carrying the jewel case. At the door of the La Motte residence the valet was dismissed and the Cardinal entered alone, 'to offer upon the altar the sacrifice of his good faith. It was a room with an alcove and with a little cabinet behind a glazed door. The skilful stage manager placed her spectator in the cabinet; a dim light pervaded the apartment; a door opens; a voice cries, "De la part de la Reine!" Madame La Motte advances respectfully, takes the case and passes it to the so-called messenger: thus was accomplished the handing over of the necklace. The Prince, silent and hidden witness, believed that he recognised the messenger; Madame La Motte told him that it was the *valet de chambre de confiance de la Reine* at Trianon.'

The *valet de chambre* was in fact Rétaux de Villette, the man who later confessed to having forged the letters and signatures of the Queen. On a previous occasion Madame La Motte had arranged for Rohan to see Villette returning to Trianon after taking his leave of her. 'Thus did this far-sighted magician place from time to time the *pierres d'attente* on which she was going to construct her edifice of magic.' The necklace was taken to London by Monsieur La Motte and sold. An affidavit signed by William Grey, jeweller of New Bond Street and dated 20 May 1785, puts it beyond any reasonable doubt.

In August 1784, Beugnot was surprised and intrigued to see the La Mottes establish themselves in one of the biggest houses in Bar-sur-Aube and to furnish it with the utmost splendour – waggons arrived daily from Paris loaded with expensive furniture, porcelain and silver. Madame La Motte had the imprudence to appear in a diamond parure worth at least 200 000 francs and their carriages, specially ordered from England, 'announced that the expense was the last thing that had been considered. We all agreed in thinking that Monsieur le Cardinal de Rohan had borne the cost of all this brilliant extravagance and we marvelled at the good use to which he put the funds of the Grande Aumônerie.'

Although the absurd pretension of the La Mottes made them the laughing stock of the provincial aristocracy which centred on the Château de Brienne, Madame La Motte managed to be received by the duc de Penthiévre at Châteauvillain. 'She dined at his table,' records Beugnot, 'and received a welcome which astounded those who made up his court. The Prince conducted her as far as the door of the second salon which opens into the staircase, an honour which he did not accord to duchesses and which he reserved for Princes of the Blood, so deeply were the lessons of Madame de Maintenon on the honour to be shown to illegitimates impressed upon his mind.'

On 17 August while Madame La Motte was at Châteauvillain, Beugnot went to spend a few days at the Abbaye de Clairvaux. It was the Feast of St Bernard. The Abbaye de Clairvaux, as it was in 1785, would not have been recognised by its founder, but they celebrated his name by inviting the abbé de Maury to pronounce his panegyric.

The Abbot, Dom Rocourt, lived the life of a nobleman. 'He was polished in his manner towards the men, gallant towards the ladies – and he was an ass. He had at his disposition three or four thousand livres of income, beautiful coaches and never travelled without four horses and preceded by an outrider. He had himself addressed as 'Monseigneur' by his monks and by those of his court, as also by any of the large number of those who had need of him. He ruled as a despot over I don't know how many convents, both of monks and nuns, which appertained to his abbey.'

Madame La Motte stopped at Clairvaux on her way back from Châteauvillain. She was received obsequiously by Dom Rocourt. 'He knew for certain', recounts Beugnot, 'of the intimate relationship which existed between Madame La Motte and the Cardinal de Rohan and he treated her like a princess of the Church.'

Just as the company was sitting down to dinner the wheels of a coach were heard on the gravel and the abbé de Maury arrived from Paris to deliver his panegyric. The Abbot asked him if there was any news. 'What do you mean by news?' exclaimed Maury; 'what world are you living in? There is a piece of news which no-one can understand, which astonishes and confounds the whole of Paris. The Cardinal de Rohan, Grand Aumônier de France, was arrested on Tuesday, the Feast of the Assumption, in his pontifical robes, as he came out of the Cabinet du Roi!'

'Does anyone know the motive for so outrageous an arrest?'

'No, nothing precise. There is talk of a diamond necklace which he is supposed to have bought for the Queen and did not buy. It is impossible to imagine how one could, for such a trifle, have arrested the Grand Aumônier de France in his pontifical robes – you understand – *in his pontifical robes* and as he left the Cabinet du Roi!'

'As soon as the news reached my ears,' continues Beugnot, 'I turned my eyes towards Madame La Motte who had let drop her napkin and whose face, pale and motionless, was turned downwards towards her plate. After the first moment she made a great effort and rushed out of the dining-room.' Beugnot followed her home. He pressed her urgently to leave at once for England, but to no avail. She would not admit any complicity, putting all the blame on Cagliostro, but at least, out of consideration for the Cardinal, he persuaded her to burn his love letters. It was this which gave Beugnot the opportunity to read some of them. At three in the morning he left her. At four she was arrested and taken to the Bastille. The Cardinal was already there.

When Rohan came for trial before the Parlement de Paris, the first issue was simple: was he guilty of obtaining diamonds under false pretences or had he been duped? It was not, in the eyes of contemporaries, an easy question to answer. It was put in epigrammatic form by Frederick the Great: 'the Cardinal de Rohan will be obliged to call upon all the resources of his not inconsiderable intellect to convince his judges that he is a fool.'

Such, however, is the force of counterproductivity that a man's worst enemies may prove his greatest friends. On 1 December 1785, Daniel Hailes wrote to Lord Carmarthen: 'Madame La Motte had just published a memorial in answer to the charges brought against her by the Cardinal de Rohan, but there is so little appearance of probability in her allegations, and the memorial itself is so ill drawn up, that the friends of the Cardinal have rather reason to be satisfied with it than otherwise.' Madame La Motte's memoirs, also, have 'so little appearance of probability' that they may be discounted as an historical source.

On 16 May 1786, Castries noted: 'a memorandum has appeared by Target [the lawyer defending Rohan] on behalf of the Cardinal de Rohan which gives convincing support to the claim that he has been deceived. Villette, who did the forgery, has admitted to it, and the rest is perfectly clear, Mademoiselle d'Oliva, who played the part of the Queen, being in agreement. Since the Cardinal did not tell Boehmer and Bassange that the necklace was for the Queen until after it was in his possession – and consequently that a lie could not have been useful to him – and since he urged them on that same day to go and thank the Queen – with all these facts established, it can be convincingly proved that he is a fool, that his mind is as debased as are his tastes and that he deserved to be the victim of companions so unsuitable to him.'

Beugnot was a lawyer and the interest which he took in the trial of Rohan was professional. He sums up thus: 'the big issue which dominated this sad affair was this: that Monsieur and Madame La Motte had had the audacity to pretend, one night, that in one of the *bosquets* of Versailles, the Queen of France, the wife of the King, had made a *rendez-vous* with the Cardinal de Rohan, spoken to him, handed him a rose and permitted him to throw himself at her feet; and that, on his side, a cardinal, a high officer of the crown, had dared to believe that such a *rendez-vous* had been granted to him by the Queen of France, the wife of the King; that he went to it, received a rose and threw himself at her feet.' The real crime was that of *lèse-majesté*.

The offence of the Cardinal de Rohan was that he had believed it possible; the tragedy of Marie-Antoinette was that it had been possible to believe. No doubt the rumours about her were grossly exaggerated; no doubt the accusations against her were mostly untrue; but there was just enough in her behaviour to enable the mud of calumny to stick. Once the mud sticks it becomes possible to destroy the victim's character completely.

Besenval dismisses the idea that the Queen could have been in any way involved. 'This incident astonished everyone and was the subject of every conversation. Many people wished to implicate the Queen, such was the relentlessness of the public against her on every occasion. But how could anyone presume that she could have wished to procure clandestinely a necklace which could have no value for her if she could not wear it?'

Contemporary opinion was divided on the matter of the Queen's involvement. Historians have shown themselves the same. Louis Hastier, in a book with the rather presumptuous title of *La Vérite sur l'Affaire du Collier*, draws attention to a letter from Marie-Antoinette to Mercy dated 19 May 1786. She writes: 'I will say nothing about the great affair; the baron [de Breteuil] will tell you my thoughts, above all not to talk about the *rendezvous* and the terrace, and he will explain my reasons.'

Hastier regards this as virtual proof that Marie-Antoinette was present, as an amused spectator no doubt, at the scene in the *bosquet*. Maurice Garçon, in his preface to the second edition of this book, does not accept this interpretation in view of the overwhelming fact that the final charge brought against Madame La Motte dwells at some length on this episode. Beugnot makes it the centre-piece of the case. Whatever motive Marie-Antoinette may have had for wanting silence on the subject, it was most certainly not hushed up.

On 11 June 1786, Mercy wrote to Kaunitz a full account of the trial. The Procureur Général, Joly de Fleury, had drawn up the Instruction. The Cardinal was to be obliged to admit that he had acquired the necklace 'malignantly'; that he knew the Queen's signature to be false and therefore had deceived the jewellers; that he must seek Their Majesties' pardon for having 'dared to act without the respect due to their most high and sacred persons'; it was required that he should be exiled from the Court, should resign his office of Grand Aumônier. Right up to the last 'it was considered certain that the judgement would be given along exactly these lines.'

It was not, however to be so. The maréchal de Castries gives a concise account: '31 May 1786 – the Cardinal de Rohan is judged at last: twenty-six voices acquit him of all charges, twenty-three varying in their judgement . . . Madame La Motte to be whipped and branded [and, he might have added, imprisoned for life]; Villette banished, Cagliostro cleared and the case against Mademoiselle d'Oliva dismissed – *hors de.Cour.*' William Eden, later Lord Auckland, who was an astute observer of affairs in France at the time, wrote to William Pitt: 'When d'Oliva was told that she was judged *hors de Cour* she thought it a prohibition against going to Versailles and promised heartily to obey it.' The baron de Besenval, who seems to have been present, evokes the emotions generated by this sentence: 'The Palais de Justice was full to overflowing and the joy was universal when it was known that the Cardinal was declared innocent. The judges were applauded and received such a welcome that they could hardly pass through the crowd, so great was the hatred for the opposite side, so deeply unfavourably disposed were the people against the Queen and against the Court.'

The maréchal de Castries sums up: 'In arranging the solution to this astonishing trial, the Procureur Général gave on the day before conclusions so strangely drawn up, so obviously dictated by and for the Court, that the Parlement, driven to the opposite extreme, did not pronounce a single word against the Cardinal on his foolish conduct, on his culpable credulity, in the indecence in fact of all that he had suspected and admitted possible with regard to the Queen. The King, as the result, dealt with him according to his deserts, but dealt with him too rigorously in exiling him to his Abbey of La Chaise Dieu, in requiring him to resign from his charge [of Grand Aumônier] and in refusing him permission to take the waters in a place which his health demanded.'

Besenval took up this theme: 'the prejudice against the Court was so strong that there were cries of tyranny when it was learnt that he was losing his charge and was exiled. In general a crowd is always beside itself, but a French crowd is always more so than any other.'

William Eden, reflecting on the events at a later date, says: 'many of the details of that trial furnished matter of just indignation against one of the first persons of the hierarchy, Sa Sainteté le Cardinal Rohan, whose vices, follies and ridiculous ambition had made him the dupe of the La Mottes and Cagliostros. It was attempted to involve the Queen of France in the odious parts of the transaction in which her person and her handwriting had been counterfeited. It is, however, certain that though she probably had seen the necklace, and may have wished to possess it, she was utterly incapable of any act or thought tending to fraud.'

One would need to have a very poor opinion of Marie-Antoinette to believe that she could have stooped so low as to participate in such a swindle. Her undoubted fault was that she had so poor an opinion of the Cardinal as to believe that he could have stooped so low. He may have been stupid; he may have been gullible; he may have been infatuated by ambition or rendered imbecile by the hypnotic powers of Cagliostro, but he was a Rohan. Family pride, if no higher consideration, would have made him incapable of dishonesty or theft.

The verdict of the Parlement was given at nine in the evening of 31 May 1786. The highest court of justice in the land declared the Cardinal innocent on all the counts: 'We cannot find the Cardinal de Rohan guilty of "criminal presumption" in accepting the idea that the Queen of France appointed a midnight *rendez-vous* with him in the dark *bosquets* of the gardens of Versailles.' That in itself would have been bad enough for Marie-Antoinette. But the Parlement went further and dealt her a deliberate smack in the face: 'With Her Most Christian Majesty's reputation for frivolity and indiscretion, with her succession of male and female "favourites" of dubious repute, we find it entirely plausible that the Cardinal de Rohan did so presume.'

It was a blow from which Marie-Antoinette was never to recover. As the comte Beugnot wrote in his *post mortem* on the affair: 'the Revolution was already present in the minds of those who could contemplate such an insult to the King in the person of his wife.'

The Sunset of the *Ancien Régime*

If a revolution was already present in the mind of the Parlement, Marie-Antoinette seems to have been unaware of the fact. 'At this period,' (July 1786) wrote William Eden in his memoirs, 'the Queen appeared to possess all the happiness and cheerfulness of private life, together with all the splendour and magnificence of royalty and to have no foresight of the calamities which were coming towards her.'

The King was in a state of even greater euphoria. At the end of June he had made an official visit to Cherbourg, where the harbour was being reinforced by the construction of an enormous jetty. On Tuesday 20 June Louis spent the night at Rambouillet, and on the 21 he set off for Caen accompanied by the duc de Coigny, the duc de Villequier and the prince de Poix. It was the same day on which Madame La Motte was whipped and branded in the courtyard of the Palais de Justice.

Marie-Antoinette did not accompany Louis; she was pregnant at the time – Madame Sophie was born on 29 July and died eleven months later.

Calonne, who was Contrôleur Général des Finances at the time, prepared a detailed report for Louis on every place through which he was to pass, which enabled him to talk intelligently with all the people whom he met. The mayor of Harfleur, Letellier, described the King's progress. On the first day at the village of Saint-Croix-Grand'Tonne, about half way between Caen and Bayeux, Louis began to feel 'le plus piquant appetit' and stopped at the inn for refreshment. The consternation caused by the unexpected arrival of the King in such a place can well be imagined. 'The good people of the house', continues Letellier, 'wanted to hide themselves, so great was their confusion and embarrassment'; Louis quickly put them at their ease. '"Have you any fresh eggs?" he asked. "Yes, still warm." "And butter?" "Straight from the churn." "Splendid!"' The King took his seat at the travellers' table and insisted on sampling their household bread which he ate with considerable relish. 'The rumour passed from mouth to mouth in the village; by degrees the peasants began to congregate; the King could see in their eyes how much they loved him and at his desire they were enabled to drink – and copiously – to his health.'

On his return to Versailles the comtesse de Sabran wrote: 'he is enchanted by his excursion and everybody is enchanted by him.' He had spent sixteen hours in Cherbourg and watched the positioning of one of the great cones for the jetty. 'It is reported', continues the countess, 'that the royal barge went aground on approaching the shore and that all the sailors and numbers of other people present threw themselves into the sea and took the boat on their shoulders so that the King was carried ashore in triumph with cries of "Vive le Roi!" and expressions of the greatest affection. The King, they relate, was moved even to tears, as were all the spectators not excepting some English who were present out of curiosity.'

The next day Madame de Sabran was still full of the news. 'There is no talk but of the King's visit . . . of everything that he said and everything that he did; of how good, how human, how affable he was towards his poor people; of the interest which he took in all the constructions at Cherbourg and in all the manoeuvres; of how well informed he was, which he showed to good advantage: in a word – it was perfect.'

It was certainly a new and wonderful experience for Louis. It was the first time he had ever seen the sea, but it was the demonstrations of popular affection which moved him most. 'The love of my people has touched the deepest springs of my heart,' he wrote to Marie-Antoinette: 'jugez si je ne suis pas le plus heureux roi du monde.'

Naturally he was intent on repeating the experience. As his journey neared its end he said: 'I see that we are approaching Versailles, but I will leave it more often now and I will go further than Fontainebleau.' Fontainebleau, however, was the destination of his next visit.

The Queen, according to the comte d'Hézècques, often used to go to Fontainebleau by river; 'she embarked at Choisy-le-Roi and went up the Seine as far as Melun in a magnificent yacht, which afforded her and her suite the commodities of a large house – salons, kitchens and a great number of trees in pots which formed a sort of parterre.'

Throughout the reign, the Voyage de Fontainebleau, usually lasting for several weeks in the early autumn, continued to offer a welcome break from the monotony of Versailles. 'It is well known', wrote the comtesse de Boigne, 'that the Court of France is never seen in greater magnificence than at Fontainebleau.' The King was at his most affable, the Court theatre was at its most brilliant; first nights of the latest plays were produced here with a great wealth of costumes and scenic effects.

It was, of course, exceedingly expensive. A troop of comedians would be paid 650 livres for the performance and ten livres a day for each member of the cast. Then there was all the 'petit monde obligatoire à cette occurrence' – the tailors, embroiderers, sempstresses, wig-makers, laundresses, the designers, painters, makers and movers of scenery, and on top of that the enormous cost of transporting these, together with their baggage, from Paris. In 1783 the figure for theatrical entertainments at Fontainebleau amounted to 468 204 livres. In 1785 it had reached 600 000.

Besides the expense of the theatre, there was the prodigious cost of transporting the tapestries. In 1786 Thiérry de la Ville d'Avray was in charge of the Garde Meuble du Roi. He stated that no less than 411 tapestries, including a set woven from the paintings in Mignard's gallery at Saint-Cloud, had been taken to Fontainebleau from Paris and taken back. He added that it was all 'one vast theatre of corrupt dealings'.

Finally there was the cost of the actual transport of the King and his Court. Mercy said that the endless cavalcade 'resembled that of an army on the march'. On 16 November the British Ambassador, the Duke of Dorset, reported: 'their Majesties, the Dauphin and the rest of the royal family, are removed from Fontainebleau to Versailles. The expense attending these journeys of the Court is incredible. Your lordship may have a faint idea of it from the number of Post Horses that have been employed these last three days. The Duke of Polignac told me that he had given orders for 2115 horses for this service on the roads. Besides this an adequate proportion of horses are ordered for the removal of the heavy baggage.' Calonne, he mentions, had been obliged to borrow to meet this heavy expense.

The ever rising cost of the Voyage de Fontainebleau perplexed contemporaries because the courtiers were lodged at their own expense. The comtesse de Boigne provides the details in a passage which deserves to be quoted in full.

'Those who were invited were only accorded the four walls of an apartment; one had to procure one's own furniture and one's own linen and live as best one could. In point of fact, since all the ministers and all who had "charges" at Court kept tables for those who attended them, one had no difficulty in obtaining invitations to dinner and supper. But no-one concerned themselves about you except for providing the lodging. When the Château was full – and a very large part of it was in such poor repair that it was uninhabitable – the guests . . . were distributed about the town. Their names were written in chalk – *marqués à la craie* – on the doors as in a posting house.'

The marquis de Bombelles gives his own account of the Voyage de Fontainebleau in 1783. On 8 October they left Versailles before eight in the morning. 'Bombon,' (his little son) 'sa mère et moi avons voyagé dans une diligence,' he wrote; 'the high road was as full of traffic today as the rue Saint-Honoré. One has to see for oneself the number of carriages of all sorts to believe how many were there.' His post horses were not yet tired and took them 'with a delightful speed', so that they arrived at Fontainebleau by half past one.

Monsieur de la Suze, Grand Maréchal du Logis, had accorded them, a hundred yards from the Cour du Cheval Blanc where the Ministers were lodged, the whole of the Hôtel de la Feuillade. 'As I had provided for in advance, we found dinner ready and everything arranged as if we had been there for several days. My angel, Bombon and I went round the Château after dinner to see who was lodging where and to amuse ourselves by observing the commotion caused by the continual arrival of people with their furniture and their baggage.'

To this must be added an official document, dated 1786 – 'Observations placed before the eyes of his Majesty by the grand maréchal du Logis on the increase which is occurring in the expense of hiring lodgings for the service of the Court at Fontainebleau.' There were, he states, 176 lodgings in the Château itself. There followed a list of those entitled to such a lodging, which amounted to 245. Thus seventy-three people who were entitled to lodgings in the Château had to be *logés à la craie*. To compensate them it was necessary to obtain larger and grander apartments. In 1783 the cost of these lodgings had been 35 280 livres. In 1785 it was 41 610. 'The grand maréchal views the rapid progress of these expenses with regret for the present and alarm for the future.'

There was to be no future. The year 1786 saw the last Voyage de Fontainebleau. Faced with the figures, Louis decided to discontinue the visits. It must have been a painful decision for him, for he loved the place, and above all the hunting which it afforded, and he was in the middle of creating his own Petits Appartements there. It may have been painful also for Marie-Antoinette, for she had just had two of her rooms, the Salon de Jeu and the Boudoir, beautifully redecorated and magnificent new hangings ordered for her bedroom.

The Salon de Jeu was in the very latest style known as

'Pompeian', which was chiefly the work of the brothers Rousseau, who painted the doors and panels. The overdoors, by that great master of *trompe l'oeil*, P. J. Sauvage, and the ceilings by Barthélemy complete the decor. The room was provided with no less than thirteen different gaming tables – each game in those days requiring a different sort of table.

The Boudoir de Marie-Antoinette was the most perfect piece of interior decoration in the whole palace. Designed by Mique, it was executed by the same team that created the Salon de Jeu – Jean-Simon Barthélemy for the ceiling and the brothers Rousseau for the paintings – but here the overdoors are not in *trompe l'oeil* but are achieved in three dimensions by the sculptor P. L. Roland. The overall colour scheme is of silver and gold. Almost all the surfaces are covered with decoration, but with so light and delicate a touch that it is never ornate.

It was during the last Voyage de Fontainebleau, on 25 October, that Mr Hailes, a member of the British Embassy staff, wrote to Lord Carmarthen on the financial condition in France: 'at the moment that this country is in the profoundest state of tranquillity that it can at any period expect to enjoy, it is obliged every year to have recourse to new loans. I know that the pretext for borrowing is the paying off of the debt contracted during the war, but the Government borrows this year near two hundred millions of livres, and the amount of the reimbursement is no more than seventy-five.' He adds the further details: 'as if the derangement of the finances were not yet great enough, and as if Cherbourg were not sufficient to swallow up all the unemployed treasure of France, immense works are carrying on or intended to be carried on, in all the Royal Houses. The additions to Saint-Cloud are estimated at eleven millions; fifteen hundred workmen have been employed for some months at Fontainebleau, Compiègne, Rambouillet, and other places have been improved in the greatest style of magnificence, and it is said that Versailles is very shortly to undergo a thorough repair, the expense of which can hardly be calculated.'

The purchase of Saint-Cloud in October 1784 was connected in the first place with the project for the virtual reconstruction of Versailles. This would have necessitated the absence of the Court for about ten years. A complete *déménagement* to the Tuileries would have spelt ruin to the tradesmen at Versailles, so the plan was that the Government departments and some of the offices of the Court, such as the Grande Écurie, should remain at Versailles, while the Court itself removed to Saint-Cloud, a distance of ten kilometres.

The extravagant projects for a new Versailles *au goût du jour* submitted by Mique, Paris and other architects came to nothing. Louis could not possibly have afforded it, but Marie-Antoinette persuaded him to go ahead with the purchase of Saint-Cloud to provide her with a residence which combined the attractions of a country seat with an easy proximity to Paris. The King agreed to pay the duc d'Orléans six million livres – twice the sum which Augeard thought it was worth – on condition that he paid off his debts.

'The Queen, or rather the King, has just bought Saint-Cloud,' wrote the marquise de Bombelles on 16 October 1784; 'the Queen is absolutely delighted by it.' One of her first acts was to put the Suisses into her own livery and to put up the regulations signed, 'de par la Reine'. This, observed Madame Campan, 'produced a profound and very vexatious impression, not only on the people, but among those of a higher class.' 'Do you want the Emperor to have a property in France?' asked Calonne, 'should the Queen die with no surviving children.' In the Parlement, d'Esprémenil declared that 'it is equally impolitic and immoral to see palaces belonging to a Queen of France.'

The Château de Saint-Cloud was still, at that time, much as it had been left by Philippe d'Orléans at the end of the seventeenth century. It was not suited to the needs of Marie-Antoinette. Mique was given the task of enlarging the central block by extending it some ten feet into the parterre of the Orangerie and of remodelling the private apartments on the south side of the entrance court. This wing, known as the

Aisle du Fer-à-Cheval, contained large state rooms with ceilings painted by Coypel, Pierre and Nocret; it was now divided up into smaller rooms – those of Marie-Antoinette overlooking the Cour d'Honneur and those of Louis facing south onto the gardens.

In the centre of the King's suite was his bedroom. In the middle of the south wall there was a chimney piece surmounted by a mirror. In the external façade this space was occupied by a large window beneath the apex of the pediment, above which was a chimney. The apparent contradiction of having a window behind the mirror over a fireplace is resolved by the inventory, drawn up in 1792 when Saint-Cloud became the property of the nation. It specifies that in this room the most ingenious device had been contrived. Over the fireplace there was indeed a mirror, but one which could be made to disappear suddenly by the touching of a spring, revealing behind it a window through which one could command a magnificent view over the Bassin du Fer-à-Cheval and right down the Allée de la Balustrade towards Sèvres. The device could not have failed to intrigue so mechanically minded a man as Louis.

As at Trianon, Marie-Antoinette's way of life at Saint-Cloud betrayed the belief that a Queen could live and behave as an ordinary individual. The gardens were usually open to the public and a ballroom was established in the park. Marie-Antoinette enjoyed attending these public entertainments, but her appearance at them provoked a widespread disapproval which was expressed by the comte de Vaublanc: 'I have seen these balls on many occasions,' he wrote, 'and I share the fears of many on the danger of behaving in so familiar a manner.' 'She used to station herself', wrote Soulavie, 'for the tournaments and other sports of the watermen, like an ordinary spectator among the townspeople. It did not make her any more popular. Only Monsieur Le Noir knows what it costs the police to subsidise the banal cry of "Vive la Reine!" The populace went in shoals to the *fêtes* at Saint-Cloud, but the words on their lips were already the significant ones: "we'll go and see the fountains and the *Austrian woman*."'

L'Autrichienne – there was no title that was to do more harm to Marie-Antoinette. In due course it was to identify her with the enemies of France. A further cause of her unpopularity was her extravagance in building. Trianon had provided the first ground for widespread discontent: Saint-Cloud was to furnish the second.

Another continual source of expenditure was Compiègne, which, as Louis told the comte d'Angiviller, was his favourite of all the royal houses. It was under scaffolding for most of his reign.

In September 1782, a year after the birth of the first Dauphin, Marie-Antoinette inspected the new right wing of the Cour d'Honneur. She was very satisfied with the distribution of the rooms and asked if the apartment could not become her own. Le Dreux, Gabriel's successor, replied that these rooms had received as yet no special destination and that her apartment there could be arranged 'avec grandeur, dignité et commodité'; it could in fact be as grand and as commodious as that of the King.

'I am very pleased about that,' said the Queen, 'because the children are coming and that is the proper place for them.' The rooms opened onto the southern extremity of the terrace and could be kept private for the Queen and her children.

Of all her rooms the Salon des Jeux is the only one to retain today its original appearance. It is a lovely room, cool and spacious. It must always be remembered that Compiègne was designed as a summer palace. The original hangings in the Queen's bedroom were of sky blue embroidered with silver. In a *mémoir* of 24 September 1784, Thiérry de la Ville d'Avray had especially recommended silver 'in order to unite in this royal house both magnificence and freshness'.

Not surprisingly, the expenditure on the royal houses was an issue of some importance to the Notables. On 21 April 1787, the comte de Brienne informs us, 'the King gives evidence of excellent intentions as regards economy; he has said that if he had known the state of affairs he would never have bought Rambouillet; he has decided to demolish Choisy and La Muette and has already given orders for the removal of the furniture.'

Both buildings must have enshrined happy memories for Louis and for Marie-Antoinette. It had been to Choisy-le-Roi that the young Court had gone after the death of Louis XV, and a week later they had moved to La Muette.

Situated in the Bois de Boulogne near the Porte de Passy, and close enough to the Château de Madrid to share a governor, La Muette was architecturally disappointing. It was a building of roughly the same proportions and dispositions as Cheverny in the Loire valley, but with the capacious out-buildings needed for any residence of the Court.

'Toute la Cour de La Muette est joyeuse,' wrote Baudeau on 26 May; 'one can watch the Queen, the princes and princesses frolicking on the big balcony in front of a crowd which lays continual siege to the gates. Yesterday there were about two hundred coaches, coming in or going out; the acclamations are unbelievable.'

On Tuesday 31 May, Baudeau was again at La Muette. 'The royal family continues to live almost as *bourgeois* at La Muette where they appear to take pleasure in seeing the great concourse of people, to whom they also give much pleasure. The King goes out on foot nearly every day with very few attendants and no muskets or halberds. The people overwhelm him with blessings and cries of "Long live the King!"'

Compared with La Muette, Choisy-le-Roi was large and architecturally distinguished. It was about the size of Dampierre in the Vallée de Chevreuse, but an Englishman might have been reminded of Petworth. It had been built by Jacques Gabriel for Mademoiselle de Montpensier – 'la Grande Mademoiselle' – in about 1680. It belonged subsequently to the Grand Dauphin and the princesse Conti. In 1739 it was bought by Louis XV and became one of his favourite residences.

Choisy was less often used by Louis XVI, but the Scottish gardener Thomas Blaikie found him there in 1785. The easiest approach from Paris to Choisy was by the Coche d'Eau from the Porte Saint-Paul. It offered an imposing view of the Bastille on the left, followed by the more civilised ensemble of the Château de Bercy. Choisy was on the right hand side, going upstream, and its gardens came right down to the river:

> We went first and called on Mr Brown [the head gardener] who seems an exceeding good hearty man; here we were well received; he conducted us to the palace to see the King at Breakfast who was to go a-hunting; this breakfast might pass for a dinner as it seemed not of tea or coffee but of good solid meat; the King was dressed almost like a country farmer – a good, rough, stout man about twenty-five; the Queen which is a very handsome beautiful woman sat opposite with Madame Elizabeth by her, which is young and handsome; the whole company seemed exceeding free and gay, with an open cheerfulness which is not common to be seen amongst the higher Ranks in England; the King and his suite left the table and got upon horseback without much ceremony, leaving the rest at table.

For Marie-Antoinette Choisy was her nursery for roses. 'It was a soil so favourable to flowers', wrote Lafont d'Aussonne, 'that every kind of flower, in that place, appeared to be of a superior and privileged sort. Louis XV raised there the most admirable hyacinths in the Universe. Marie-Antoinette had cultivated there the most beautiful roses of Europe and of Asia. Against a long wall, nine feet high and adorned with a pretty white trellis, the gardeners had attached, arranged in tiers and by shades of colour, all the rose trees which the Princess preferred. And as soon as the time of flowering came to sound the hour of her triumph, Versailles came running to Choisy. The Queen, from early morning and throughout the day and evening, went with her ladies to see the espalier so favoured by Flora.'

Versailles, Trianon, Marly, Saint-Cloud, Fontainebleau, Compiègne, the Louvre and Tuileries, Vincennes, Rambouillet, Saint-Germain, Saint-Hubert, La Muette, Choisy-le-Roi, Blois and Chambord – not to mention the Dauphin's establishment at Meudon or that of Mesdames at Bellevue nor those of the comte de Provence and the comte d'Artois – entailed an enormous expenditure, and it was a form of expenditure that was very visible to the public eye.

On 23 November 1786, after the return from Fontainebleau, the Baron Staël-Holstein wrote:

> The Contrôleur Général is busy making a new adjustment of the finances. His work has no other aim than to invent some means of being able to meet the immense expenditure with which the State is burdened by the outrageous squandering and the lack of order in the administration of this country. It is very distressing to observe that they are only looking for means the effect of which would be merely momentary, and that instead of remedying the wrong by an administration that was wise, noble and enlightened, they only think of the people in order to dream up means of increasing the pressure on them, as if the greatness of the State could maintain itself for long when its citizens are groaning under the burden of taxation.

In August 1786 Calonne presented the King with a 'plan for improving the finances'. The deficit was well over the 100 000 000 livres mark and it was becoming increasingly difficult to obtain loans. Calonne's proposals, contained in this document, are reminiscent of those of Turgot and it was certain that the Parlement, which had shown its hostility to the Court over the affair of the diamond necklace, would do all in its power to oppose the reforms.

To counter this opposition, Calonne suggested to Louis the summoning of an Assemblée de Notables. Such an assembly had not been called upon since the days of Richelieu. At the end of December 1786, Louis finally made up his mind, but it was not until February 1788 that the Notables could be assembled. According to the ancient formula the members were to be 'men of substance, worthy of the confidence of the public . . . attached to the service of the King . . . zealous for good and remote from any intrigue.' They were chosen by

Louis on the advice of Calonne, but there was a large element of *ex officio* members in which selection was not possible.

In his opening address, Calonne admitted to a deficit of 112 000 000 livres. Somewhat tactlessly he put the blame entirely on his predecessors and in particular on Necker. This at once aroused a storm of opposition and the clergy, as always, flatly refused to renounce their privileges. What had been intended as a consultation became a confrontation and the only way in which Louis could extricate himself was by agreeing to call the States General. This august assembly had not been called since 1614.

During the meeting of the Notables the expenditure on Compiègne was specifically condemned as excessive. Louis and Marie-Antoinette were never to live in the rooms that had been so carefully created for them. Le Dreux, no doubt anxious to see his palace put to its proper use, suggested that the States General might be held here or at Soissons. In either event the Court could have been established at Compiègne. It seems that the idea bore belated fruit in Louis' mind, for on 6 December 1790 there was recorded a delivery of furniture to Compiègne 'pour les États Généraux'. It may have been one of the greatest mistakes made by the King to summon the meeting to Versailles which was in reach of agitators from Paris.

On 8 August 1788, Louis agreed to summon the States General. In September the Parlement was recalled. On 5 October the abbé de Véri noted in his journal: 'the current of opinions tends in the direction of some sort of revolution; it is a torrent which is steadily increasing and is beginning to burst the embankments.'

On the same day Véri records a conversation between Louis XVI and Malesherbes:

> 'You are a great reader, Sire, and you are more knowledgeable than you are thought to be. But reading counts for nothing if it is not accompanied by reflection. I have recently reread in David Hume's *History of England* his passage on Charles I. Read it again and reflect upon it. Your positions have much in

> common. That Prince was mild, virtuous, devoted to the law, never insensitive, never taking the initiative, just and beneficent; he died, however, on the scaffold. He came on the scene at the moment at which the dispute was arising about the prerogative of the crown as against those of the nation . . . You are in the same position. The question has arisen between the previous practices of authority and the complaints of the citizens. Happily there is no element of religious quarrel in it.'
>
> 'Ah! yes, very happily,' said the King, taking him by the arm; 'there will not be the same atrocities.'
>
> 'And besides,' replied Malesherbes, 'our gentler manners will set your mind at rest about the excesses of those days. But they will strip you by degrees of many of your prerogatives. It is for you in your council to make a definite plan as to the concessions which you are prepared to make for the general good and as to those on which you should never yield. Only your own resoluteness can be decisive in the success of such a plan. Without that nothing can be foreseen with any certainty. I would answer for it that it would not go as far as the fate of Charles I, but I would not answer for it that there would be no other excesses.'

On 19 November Louis held a *séance royale* in which he obliged the Parlement to accept the policy of further loans proposed by Loménie de Brienne. At the end of the meeting the duc d'Orléans stood up and publicly accused Louis of acting illegally. Louis' answer was: 'c'est légal parce que je le veux.' Philippe d'Orléans was exiled to his Château de Villers-Cotterets. He now began to appear as one of the centres of opposition to Louis and Marie-Antoinette, and the *cafés* of the Palais Royal were hotbeds of discontent. Philippe had replaced the Christian religion in his life with the rather vague but now fashionable Freemasonry. He was Grand Master of all the *loges* in France. In 1786 one *loge* had gone so far as to adopt the slogan: 'Liberty, Equality or Death.' Brissot said of Philippe d'Orléans that 'he liked conspiracies which only lasted twenty-four hours. Beyond that limit he was afraid.'

5 May 1789 was fixed for the opening of the States General. 'The greatest day in the history of France', wrote the Baron

Staël-Holstein, 'was Tuesday. Nothing could have been more imposing to the eye or to the mind than the majestic array of a powerful nation, summoned by its king to collaborate with him in the regeneration of their country.' The marquis de Ferrières, however, noted that 'a general atmosphere of anxiety seemed to trouble men's minds; there was a vague desire for change . . . It was in the *cafés* of the Palais Royal that this new development of the national character revealed its true nature.'

The comte d'Hézècques described the opening, but seen with the perspective of history. '4 May arrived at last, the day which was to have seen the dawn of the fortunes of France and which augured only the sunset of its ancient monarchy.'

It was a brilliantly fine day after the recent rain and the solemn procession of all the Deputies left the parish church of Notre-Dame and crossed the Place d'Armes in front of the twin blocks of the royal stables. In one of the windows of the Petite Écurie, observed Hézècques, 'on a balcony, almost breathing his last, the heir apparent to the throne was lying on a heap of cushions. That was the symbol also of the monarchy which had, as he had, one foot already in the grave.'

The procession passed along the rue de Satory and finally arrived at the Cathedral of Saint-Louis. The Blessed Sacrament was carried beneath a sumptuous canopy born by four noblemen, the four tassels held by the King's two brothers, the comte de Provence and the comte d'Artois, and the latter's two sons, the duc d'Angoulême and the duc de Berry. Madame de Laage de Volude was in raptures: 'nos petits princes étaient charmants avec l'habit de chevalier français.' The younger, the duc de Berry, was only eleven but had just received his first communion.

Another observer was the marquis de Bombelles. 'Never have I witnessed a spectacle more imposing', he wrote, 'than this procession seen from the top of the steps to the portico of Saint-Louis. The square, lined by the two regiments of French and Swiss Guards, offered a space large enough to afford the spectacle of all the Deputies walking two by two and in good order – the Blessed Sacrament following and the King accompanied by all his family, coming immediately after. To see thus the head of an illustrious nation coming with its representatives to implore the divine bounty, was something as imposing as it was superb.' The sun of the *ancien régime* was never more brilliant than at the moment of its setting.

Already, however, there were discordant notes to be detected. Bombelles records that 'to the astonishment of everyone, Monsieur le duc d'Orléans walked in the procession in his place as the Deputy for Crépy,' and not, therefore, as first Prince of the Blood, and that the cries of 'Vive le Roi!' were loud and persistent, but that the cries of 'Vive la Reine!' were conspicuous by their scarcity.

Marie-Antoinette appeared in the full splendour of court dress – 'a single head-band of diamonds and her beautiful *aigrette*; a violet dress over a white skirt spangled with silver.' It was the last occasion on which she was to wear it. As a foretaste of the disasters which were soon to overtake her, she was insulted by the crowd. According to Madame Campan, she was greeted with shouts of 'Vive le duc d'Orléans!' in so hostile a manner that she nearly fainted.

The following day the three Estates met in solemn assembly in the great hall constructed by the Menus Plaisirs. When all were seated, wrote the comte d'Hézècques, 'the King rose to his feet. He invited the Queen with a gesture to be seated, which she declined with a profound curtsey. A religious silence reigned throughout the hall. Louis XVI, whose bearing was noble and majestic especially when he did not have to walk, magnificently dressed and sparkling with jewels, dominated from the altitude of his throne this celebrated session; and, as if all the pomp of this world did not suffice to inspire respect, the heavens appeared to want to contribute to it. At the moment when the King began his speech a ray of sunlight pierced through the taffeta curtains which covered the sky-light of the vault and shed its lustre upon the royal countenance.' Louis finished his discourse amid the most lively applause.

Barentin, the Garde des Sceaux, then mounted the tribune to receive the orders of the sovereign. 'The King sat down and the whole assembly followed his example, and the noblemen, in accordance with their ancient privilege, put on their hats. The combined effect of all these white plumes offered a unique spectacle.' The Garde des Sceaux having expounded the King's intentions, Monsieur Necker, 'motivated as always', continues d'Hézècques, 'by the spirit of pride, took from his pocket an enormous note book and, on this day consecrated to pomp and ceremony, did not blush to occupy the Assembly for an hour and a half about himself, about the way in which he had managed affairs and about his plans; since nature had not endowed him with a pure and sonorous voice, he passed his script to a doctor Broussonnet who, for a whole hour, importuned the assembly with a reading better suited to a *lit de justice* than to so solemn a day.'

All, however, was not well. 'The hypocritical meekness of the clergy,' wrote Staël-Holstein, 'the opinionated stubbornness of the nobility, the blind anger of the Tiers État, afford a sorry spectacle. Never has a country been placed between so much evil and so much good. On the one side famine, bankruptcy, despotism and civil war; on the other peace, liberty and power; and yet the choice is in doubt, or rather they want the good without consenting to the means. The whole entourage of the Queen and King [was this order of precedence deliberate?] is on the side of the nobility and the clergy.' Such was the real background to the States General. Outwardly, however, it began with due decorum.

Marie-Antoinette was placed conspicuously on the royal dais. 'How beautiful was the Queen on that great day!' exclaimed the marquise de Laage de Volude; 'the sadness of her countenance only enhanced a deportment so dignified and noble.' Behind this sadness lay both the insults of the previous day and the imminent death of her elder son.

More than a year before, on 22 February 1788, Marie-Antoinette had written to her brother the Emperor: 'My son is causing me great anxiety. His figure is deformed both by one hip being higher than the other and by the back in which the vertebrae are out of line and projecting. For some time now he has had a constant fever and he is very thin and feeble.' At the beginning of March he was sent to live at the Château de Meudon.

Perched on the high plateau between Sèvres and Val-Fleury and overlooking the wide meanders of the Seine near Billancourt, Meudon was renowned for the purity of its air and for the magnificence of its prospect. It had been, since 1695, the official seat of the Dauphin. According to the *Mercure Galant* it could claim to enjoy 'the most beautiful view in Europe' and to possess 'the most beautiful gardens in the world'. The latter could well be regarded as the masterpiece of Le Nôtre.

A rather grand renaissance château, started in 1520, dominated one of the most obvious perspectives. A grotto, added by Primaticcio in about 1555, commanded another axis more or less at right angles to this. The property was purchased by Louvois in 1679 and it was he who called in Le Nôtre to perfect the gardens. At the death of Louvois Meudon was added to the crown estates and became the residence of the Grand Dauphin. The old renaissance Château was not found adequate to his requirements and in 1705 he commissioned J.-H. Mansart to replace the grotto with a further block of apartments which amounted to a second Château. The Château Vieux and the Château Neuf each commanded its own perspective of the gardens.

With the death of the Grand Dauphin in 1711 the domain of Meudon went into a gentle decline from which it was never to recover. In June 1770 the Contrôleur, Le Dreux, warned Louis XV that the gardens were becoming a wilderness. It was just this that made them attractive to Madame Roland. 'We often used to go to Meudon,' she wrote: 'it was my favourite excursion; I preferred its tangled woods, its solitary lakes and tall, majestic groves to the well-trodden paths, the trim uniformity of the Bois de Boulogne, the decorations of Bellevue or the well-groomed alleys of Saint-Cloud.'

It was here, at the beginning of March 1788, that the little

Dauphin was sent to live in the hopes that the purer air might restore his failing health. The young Prince spent the summer at Meudon with his governor, the duc d'Harcourt, and returned at the end of October to Versailles for the winter not noticeably any the better. Louis was an affectionate father. His journal records no less than forty visits to Meudon during this period.

On 17 February in the following year the duc d'Harcourt wrote to the comte d'Angiviller asking for the *bassins* nearest to the Vieux Château to be repaired, 'because the exhalation from these basins, which no longer hold water, could be prejudicial to the health of the Prince.' Occasionally his frail little form, dressed in a sailor suit crossed by the ribbon of the Saint-Esprit, could be seen on the terrace before the Château. 'The young Prince', wrote Madame Campan, 'had fallen, in a few months, from flourishing health to a rickety condition which caused a curvature of the spine and an attenuation of the features, and which made his legs so feeble that he had to be supported like a decrepit old man to enable him to walk.' 'His body was just one sore,' wrote the marquise de La Rochejaquelein; 'he suffered with great resignation. One day he desired to be carried out into the gardens. The duchesse d'Harcourt was about to ring. "Do not ring," said the Prince, and named the valet de chambre who was on duty that day, complaining that he always hurt him. Madame d'Harcourt replied: "he does what he can to ease you; perhaps he is not so successful as the others, but he is equally zealous; if you were to decline his services you would plunge him into despair." At this the Dauphin cried: "ring at once then; I would rather suffer a little than cause any pain to this worthy man." ' Such was the character of Marie-Antoinette's elder son. The marquise need hardly have added: 'he was adored by all his servants.'

Attempts were made to ease his life in these painful conditions. On 13 May the Garde Meuble installed a *fauteuil méchanique* – that is so say a lift – in his apartment, upholstered in 'apple-green Italian velvet and green *toile dauphine*'.

On 8 April 1789, the princesse de Lamballe and her lady-in-waiting, the marquise de Laage de Volude, paid a visit to Meudon. 'We went this afternoon', wrote the marquise to her mother, 'to see the little Dauphin. It is really heart-rending . . . he had the fancy to go to bed on his billiard table; mattresses were laid for him. The princess and I exchanged glances; the same thought had occurred to us both – that it looked like his bed for lying in state. Madame de Lamballe asked him what he was reading. "A very interesting period in our history," he answered; "the reign of Charles VII; there were many heroes then." I took the liberty of asking Monseigneur if he read it right through or just the most striking passages. "Right through, Madame," he said; "I don't know enough to be able to select, and it all interests me." Those were his actual words. He turned towards me his beautiful eyes, the eyes of a dying child.'

In her letter of 17 May, Madame de Laage returns to the theme. 'The poor child is so ill! The things that the poor little one says are incredible; they pierce his mother's heart; his tenderness towards her knows no bounds. The other day he begged her to have her dinner in his room; alas, she swallowed more tears than bread.'

On 4 June the young Prince died. 'Monsieur le Dauphin lay in state in his coffin,' continued the marquise; 'I went to Meudon with the princess to offer holy water. The whole place was silver and white and in the room where he lay the light was so brilliant that I have never seen anything like it. His crown, his sword, the insignia of his Orders were placed on the little coffin, which was covered with cloth of silver; on either side were two rows of monks who never ceased their prayers by day or by night.'

On the same day, Bailly, the leader of the Tiers État, came to offer the King their condolences for the death of his son, but, according to Boullé, demanding at the same time that the King should receive a deputation from the Tiers État on the current situation. Bailly insisted 'with so imperious a tone' that Louis finally agreed to this violation of his private grief, but he asked in his outrage: 'are there no fathers in the assembly of the Tiers État?'

The Tiers État was steadily emerging as the dominant force in a movement which was gradually revealing itself as a revolution. A fortnight later it was to proclaim itself 'the National Assembly'.

Marie-Antoinette's grief over the death of her son may well have diverted her attention from the storm clouds which were gathering. In the National Assembly two men, both of noble birth but apparently on opposite sides, were forming a personal alliance which could have been of critical importance to her. One was the comte de La Marck and the other the comte de Mirabeau.

Auguste-Marie-Raymond, prince d'Aremberg and comte de La Marck, was the younger son of one the oldest families of Belgium, at that time a part of the Austrian Empire. In France he held the position of Grand d'Espagne, but he commanded the regiment which bore his own name in the service of France and sat as one of the nobility in the States General. He was an ardent royalist and more disposed to see the virtues of the *ancien régime* than its failings. He was in some way a strange bed-fellow for Mirabeau.

Honoré-Gabriel Riquetti, comte (and later marquis) de Mirabeau, well known from the portrait by Boze, is described by La Marck – 'his stature was tall, squarely set, thick. His head, already well beyond ordinary proportions, was made to seem even larger by an enormous head of hair, curled and powdered. He wore a town suit of which the buttons, of coloured stones, were of a disproportionate size; the buckles of his shoes also were very large. His whole appearance was remarkable for its exaggeration of the current fashion, which was hardly in keeping with the good taste of courtiers. His features were rendered ugly by the marks of smallpox. His eyelids were heavy, but his eyes flashed fire.'

La Marck, however, in spite of this rather patrician reaction, came to be the friend and confidant of Mirabeau who was to die in his arms. It was Sénac de Meilhan who first introduced them to each other. 'After dinner', records La Marck, 'Monsieur de Meilhan brought the conversation round to politics and administration, and everything that might have struck one at first as ridiculous about Mirabeau disappeared at once. One was impressed only by the wide range and perspicacity of his views, and he carried everyone away by the brilliance and energy with which he expressed them.'

In the early days of the States General, in May 1789, Mirabeau and La Marck found themselves together again and arranged to dine that afternoon *tête-à-tête*. Mirabeau opened with the challenge: 'You must be very ill-contented with me, are you not?' 'With you and with many other people,' came the reply. 'In that case,' continued Mirabeau, 'you ought to begin by being so with the inmates of the Château. The vessel of the State is being beaten by the most violent tempest and there is no-one at the helm.'

Revolution

'In the spring of 1789,' wrote the marquise de La Tour du Pin, 'after a winter which had been cruel for the poor, and before the opening of the States General, we had never seemed more intent on our own amusement without troubling ourselves about the misery of the people.'

This *insouciance* was widespread. Among the rich and noble the pursuit of pleasure was as devoid of responsibility as of any sense of values. 'As for us, the gilded youth of France,' wrote the comte de Ségur, 'we walked upon a carpet of flowers which covered an abyss.' It is a theme to which he constantly returned. 'Never was such a terrible awakening preceded by such sweet sleep and such delightful dreams.'

Observers from the embassies of Europe were more often aware of the real situation. The Baron Staël-Holstein, as Necker's son-in-law, was close enough to the events to be well informed and yet remote enough from the issues to judge them with reasonable impartiality. On 9 July 1789, he wrote:

> It really is a bizarre spectactle to witness the inconsistence in the behaviour of the King of France in a situation as critical as that in which he finds himself. Guided now by Monsieur Necker, now by the intrigue of which the Queen and the comte d'Artois are the leaders . . . proceeding without any coherent plan, he may very well expose himself to the dangers of each of the opposing parties. Monsieur Necker continually tells him and sets before him the need to adopt a uniform system, to employ every possible means of fending off this Revolution which is brewing; that he should make common cause with the nobility, with the clergy, with the Parlements,

> who appear openly to declare their wish that there had been no States General; that he should take a ministry whose ideas conform with his own and follow consistently this path; that if, on the contrary, he is, with reason, afraid of the terrible misfortunes that this would entail, he should frankly favour the cause of the people and, not being able to avoid the revolution, to put himself at the head of it in order to guide it.

To those within the precincts of the palace, however, nothing seemed really amiss. On 13 July Madame de La Tour du Pin dispatched her English groom to Paris to make a few minor purchases. 'I mention this little circumstance', she wrote, 'as proof that we had not the smallest notion of what was to happen in Paris the next day. There was merely talk of a few minor incidents outside the shops of certain bakers who were accused of adulterating their flour. The little army which was drawn up on the plains of Grenelle and the Champ de Mars reassured the Court, and although there were daily desertions, no-one was worried.' On 13 July Gouverneur Morris noted: 'the fashion at Court is to believe the disturbances in Paris are very trifling.'

Although the governor of the Bastille, the marquis de Launay, had been preparing for an attack since 7 July, the capture of the Bastille seems to have taken everyone by surprise.

Some two years earlier it had been described by François Cognel, a citizen of Nancy, who has left his record of a visit to Paris and Versailles. 'We went to the Bastille,' he wrote; 'this building, raised and maintained by that despotism in which the liberty of citizens is finally lost, fills one with terror; the sombre grey of its stone walls, the mysterious gloom of its towers, the isolation in which it is left by the broad moat which surrounds it, make its aspect menacing and one cannot but groan at the thought that in the centre of the capital of France there should stand an edifice designed for the arbitrary shutting away of citizens from their society.'

Jacques Godechot, in his study of the taking of the Bastille, could only find evidence of the existence of seven prisoners in

July 1789: four accused of forgery who were really rather out of place here, one who was mad, one left over from the previous reign accused of complicity in the *attentat* of Damiens, and finally the comte de Solanges, suspected of murder, who had been imprisoned at the request of his own family. Compared with other prisons at that date – including those in England – the Bastille was relatively comfortable. One of the conditions, however, for release was an undertaking not to reveal anything about the prison and its inmates, so that the truth, should anyone have been interested in ascertaining it, would have been difficult to discover. Lurid imagination filled the gap.

One of the most authentic accounts of the taking of the Bastille comes from Louis Deflue, Lieutenant in the Grenadiers. On 7 July he was sent by the baron de Besenval with a sergeant and thirty-two fusiliers to reinforce the garrison. On the following day Monsieur de Launay took him all over the fortress and made various dispositions for its defence, but he complained often 'of the weakness of the garrison and of how impossible he would find it to save the place in case of an attack'.

On 12 July they were aware that the attack was imminent: on 14 July it began. One of the problems confronting the defenders was that once a drawbridge was raised it became impossible to fire on those on the other side of it. Two apertures were therefore made through the planks of the bridge, large enough to admit the mouth of a cannon. First de Launay tried a subterfuge. He wrote a letter to his attackers pointing out that he had 20 000 pounds of gunpowder in his arsenal and threatening that, if they did not capitulate, he would blow up the fortress, the garrison and the whole surrounding quartier Saint-Antoine. Louis Deflue was ordered to pass this letter through one of the holes made for the cannons. A plank was pushed out from the opposite side and an officer of the Queen's regiment, 'le brave Maillard', teetered out along it and grasped the letter. But it was of no avail. 'I went back to the Gouverneur,' continues Deflue, 'and made my report to him . . . I rejoined my troop, which I had drawn up to the left of the gatehouse, and I awaited the moment for the Gouverneur to blow up the fortress, but I was utterly astonished to see four of the Invalides approach the drawbridges, open and let them down, at which the mob rushed in, disarmed and seized us, giving us each a guard, entered the rooms, ransacked the whole, seized the armoury and threw the archives out of the window.'

Only one of the defenders had been killed and three or four wounded. It was claimed that the casualties on the side of the attackers amounted to 160, 'but this number', Deflue assures us, 'seems to be much exaggerated'. More important is his evidence on a matter that was so commonly believed that even the British Ambassador, the Duke of Dorset, in common with most foreign diplomats, accepted it as truth. 'As for the story that was invented and generally believed that Monsieur de Launay lowered the drawbridges and then raised them again after allowing some of the rioters to enter in order to shoot them down – as to this story, I say, I declare that it is false and fabricated; it is all the more improbable because it is utterly impossible to raise a drawbridge in the face of a multitude intent on crossing it and of which one half is on top and the other half inside.'

Whatever may have been the real significance of this obsolescent prison, it had become the outward symbol of tyranny and arbitrary rule. The psychological value of its capture would be difficult to over-estimate. 'Bliss was it in that dawn to be alive,' wrote Wordsworth; 'but to be young was very heaven.'

The first reactions to the fall of the Bastille were for the most part ecstatic. Edward Rigby, an English doctor then in Paris, saw a crowd approaching down the rue Saint-Honoré; they carried a banner 'on which was inscribed "La Bastille est prise et les portes sont ouvertes!" A sudden burst of the most frantic joy instantaneously took place; every possible mode in which the most rapturous feelings of joy could be expressed, was everywhere exhibited. Shouts and shrieks, leaping and embracing, laughter and tears, every sound and every gesture . . . manifested, among the promiscuous crowd, such an instantaneous and unanimous emotion of extreme gladness as I should suppose was never before experienced by human beings.'

The crowd passed on in the direction of the Palais Royal, but it was soon replaced by another. 'The impression by it on the people', noted Rigby, 'was of a very different kind. A deep and hollow murmur at once pervaded them, their countenances expressing amazement mingled with alarm. We could not at first explain these circumstances, but as we pressed more to the centre of the crowd we suddenly partook of the general sensation, for we then, and not till then, perceived two bloody heads raised on pikes of the marquis de Launay, Governor of the Bastille, and of Monsieur Flesselles, Prévôt des Marchands . . . It was a chilling and a horrid sight! An idea of ferocity and savageness was impressed on the spectators, and instantly checked those emotions of joy which had before prevailed.'

The impact of 14 July on the Court is recorded by the marquise de La Rochejaquelein. 'On 13 July the regiments of Bouillon and of Nassau arrived at Versailles; they were lodged in the Orangerie. The next day, the 14, we went out at about six in the evening to look at the regiments. A crowd of courtiers, as brilliant as it was numerous, was walking about on the parterre above the Orangerie; the officers had assembled the band and the soldiers were doing German dances. Happiness was on every face.

'Never will I forget the sudden change. First we heard a whispering about our ears. Then Monsieur de Bonssol, an officer of the Garde du Corps, came up to us and said: "go back indoors – go back indoors; there has been an uprising of the people of Paris. They have taken the Bastille; it is said that they are marching on Versailles." In an instant the terrace was deserted; we returned to our apartments.'

The news of the fall of the Bastille was received with horror by the rich and the respectable. Down in the Loire Valley, at the Château de Cheverny, Jean Dufort was writing his own chronicle of the events. 'On 26 July we were quietly at dinner when the letters and papers reached us from Paris; we learnt of the deaths of Foulon, Bertier and Flesselles . . . my wife felt quite ill and dinner was disrupted. The private letters contained the most appalling details.' In the case of Bertier there were acts of cannibalism recorded. Gouverneur Morris was deeply shocked: Bertier, he said, was 'put to death and cut to pieces, the populace carrying about the mangled remains with savage joy. Gracious God! what a people!'

The activists of the French Revolution can certainly be accused of the most hideous atrocities, but they had no monopoly. At the time of the fall of the Bastille Gracchus Babeuf wrote of 'the justice of the people' to his wife. 'How could it be anything other than cruel?' he asked. 'Executions in all their forms, quartering, torture, breaking on the wheel, the burnings, the floggings, the hanging, the executioners abounding on all sides have corrupted our morals. Our masters, instead of civilising us, have made us barbarians because they were barbarians themselves.'

The atrocities following the fall of the Bastille provoked the first wave of emigration. Madame de La Rochejaquelein describes it. 'The night before the King went to Paris' – that is to say the night of 16 July – 'we spent the evening with Monsieur le duc de Serent. He was to leave France that night taking with him the two princes, sons of the comte d'Artois whose governor he was. He kept his departure secret from us, but he and the rest of his family had tears in their eyes when they took their leave of us.

'We did not go to bed that night. Our windows overlooked the rue des Reservoirs; all night long we heard the sound of coaches and horses.' The emigration had begun. The comte d'Artois, the prince de Condé and their families left France. The Polignac family followed them. 'Nothing could have been more moving', wrote Madame Campan, 'than the parting of the Queen and her friend; the extremity of misfortune had eclipsed the memory of political opinions which had come between them. At the moment of their departure the Queen sent a last letter – "Adieu le plus tendre des amis! Que ce mot est affreux, mais il est nécessaire. Adieu."'

Many of those who did not leave France left Versailles. The Rochejaquelein family sought sanctuary with the duc de Luynes at Dampierre. On the 17 July the King, accompanied by the maréchal de Beauveau, the duc de Villeroy and the duc de Villequier, went to Paris. 'Marie-Antoinette held back her tears,' wrote Madame Campan, 'and shut herself up in her *cabinets* with all her family. She sent for various members of the Court: their rooms were found padlocked. The terror had driven them out. Le silence de la mort regnait dans tout le Palais.' Marie-Antoinette could not believe that the King would be allowed to return to Versailles. He did, however, come back unharmed. He had sported the tricolor cockade; he had walked, said Bailly, 'with the confidence of a good king in the midst of a good people'; cries of 'Vive notre père!' were mingled with those of 'Vive le Roi!' 'His return to Versailles', observed Madame Campan, 'filled his family with an inexpressible joy ... it was then that he repeated several times: "happily no blood was shed. I swear that there will never be a drop of French blood shed by my order." A maxim full of humanity,' commented Madame Campan, 'but too loftily proclaimed in these times of faction.' A lot of blood can be spilt by the refusal to shed a single drop.

When the King returned to Versailles, writes Madame de La Rochejaquelein, 'we all came back and we took up again exactly the same way of life as before without worrying about the future, which was nevertheless menacing. For the most part we deluded ourselves completely about the state of affairs; my mother was one of the small number of people who foresaw great calamities.'

They were not long in coming. 28 July, wrote Madame de La Tour du Pin, 'was one of the days of the Revolution when the most extraordinary thing happened which has been the least well explained, because, in order to understand it, it would be necessary to imagine that an immense network extended over the whole of France so that at the same moment and as the result of the same action, trouble and terror were spread throughout every commune in the country.' This simultaneous outbreak of national hysteria is known as 'La Grande Peur'.

Madame de La Tour du Pin experienced it at Forges les Eaux, a spa in Normandy, between Rouen and Amiens. She was standing at her window when a large crowd of people erupted into the main square 'showing signs of desperate fear'. The women were weeping and lamenting, the men swearing and threatening in their fury, others raising their hands to heaven and crying, 'We are lost!'

At the centre of the mob was a man in rather shabby clothes and with no hat, his horse soaked in sweat and with cuts on its rump that were still bleeding. He was exciting the crowd with a vivid account of an Austrian army pillaging, raping and burning in the village of Gaillefontaine, only two leagues distant. It would be difficult to over-emphasise the improbability of such an event.

At this moment Madame de La Tour du Pin was joined by her husband. When he arrived he found her holding the local *curé* by the collar of his soutane and trying to prevent him from causing further hysteria by ringing the tocsin. Then they both rode off to Gaillefontaine. The people here were armed and in a similar state of over-excitement, believing that Forges was being ravaged by the Austrians. There was, it need hardly be said, not a grain of truth in the inflammatory accounts which were being spread, not just in Normandy, but all over France.

Down in the Loire Valley, Dufort de Cheverny records a similar wave of madness sweeping the country south of Blois, but here the imaginary invaders were not the Austrians but the English. The people were in the thrall of panic. Somebody had grievously and maliciously misled them. That the Grande Peur was orchestrated is beyond reasonable doubt.

It is difficult to guess at what point Louis and Marie-Antoinette began to realise that they had something more than a political crisis on their hands – something more like a revolution. On 17 April 1789, Madame de Laage wrote: 'the comte d'Artois has had a long conversation with the Queen; he did all that he could to make her feel the extent to which she was being calumnied and towards how great a precipice they were all advancing. He used the strongest language; he indicated the most dangerous people.'

It is not improbable that the name of Mirabeau figured high on Artois' list of dangerous men. He often appeared so, but Mirabeau was at heart a royalist, albeit a royalist who favoured a constitutional rather than an absolute monarchy. 'The destiny of France is decided,' he asserted; 'the words *liberty* and *taxation consented by the people* have sounded throughout all the land. The only way forward is a government more or less on the lines of that of England.'

Above all, Mirabeau wanted the Court party to take the initiative and to put themselves in the forefront of the Revolution. 'The moment the ministers of the Crown consent to reason with me,' he affirmed, 'they will find me devoted to the royalist cause and to the salvation of the monarchy.'

By the end of September 1789 the comte de La Marck was becoming uneasy about the effect of his relationship with Mirabeau on his standing at Court. 'I begged Madame d'Ossun', he wrote, 'to inform the Queen on my behalf that my connection with Mirabeau, which was beginning to be noticed, should not inspire any lack of confidence in my devotion to the royal cause; that in my *rapprochement* with Mirabeau I had two objectives in view: the first, to moderate as much as possible his revolutionary flights of fancy; the second, to prepare him for being useful to the King when his ministers found themselves obliged to connive with him, which I foresaw would inevitably be the case.'

The Queen, however, without doubting the probity of his motives, told him that he could never succeed in his aims. 'I do not think we shall ever be so unfortunate', she said, 'as to be reduced to the painful extreme of having recourse to Mirabeau.'

Neither Marie-Antoinette, nor most of the members of the Court party, seemed to have had any conception, at that time, of the dangers which they faced. 'What do they think they are doing?' asked Mirabeau of La Marck at the end of September; 'cannot they see the abyss which is opening under their feet?' On one occasion even, goaded into a state of exasperation more violent than usual, Mirabeau exclaimed: 'all is lost! The King and Queen will perish and, you will see, the populace will mutilate their bodies.'

'He noticed the horror which that expression made me feel,' continues La Marck; '"Yes! Yes!" repeated Mirabeau, "they will mutilate their bodies; you do not sufficiently understand the dangers of their position; it must be made clear to them."'

It was not made clear to them. At the beginning of October an event took place which may have been in itself innocent enough, but which, in the hands of the *factieux*, was manipulated to provide the spark which detonated the next great explosion of the Revolution.

'On 1 October,' writes Madame de La Rochejaquelein, 'the Gardes du Corps invited the Gardes Nationales and certain other soldiers to the dinner which was to become so famous.' It took place in the new Opera House which had been constructed for the wedding of Marie-Antoinette:

> The whole Court was seated in the boxes to witness the banquet. At every moment soldiers were coming in from the regiment of Flanders, from the Garde Nationale, from the Gardes Suisses; they were invited to drink to the health of the King. There was a very moving cordiality about this whole reunion. The King and Queen had been invited to attend this *fête*; they accepted. The Queen appeared holding in her arms her son, the new Dauphin. As soon as they were seen in the grand tier all joined in an ovation and the orchestra struck up the air [from Grétry's fashionable opera *Richard Coeur de Lion*]: 'O Richard! O mon Roi!' The King was then persuaded to

> come down onto the stage and make a tour of the tables; the Queen followed him. She spoke to everyone with that charming grace which she knew well how to use to captivate all hearts when she chose to. After half an hour she and the King retired. All were intoxicated by their enthusiasm; they were moved to tears . . . there were cries of 'Vive le Roi! Vive la Reine! Nous les défendrons jusqu'à la mort!'

The marquise de La Tour du Pin was also present. She states positively that she heard cries of 'Vive le Roi!' and no others. 'We went, my sister-in-law and I, towards the end of the dinner to watch the scene, which was magnificent. Toasts were being drunk and my husband, who had come to meet us and to take us to one of the stage boxes, had time to say to us, in a low voice, that feelings were running high and that rash words had been spoken.'

When the royal family entered, the Dauphin, who was not yet five, was taken by a Swiss officer and placed on the table which he managed to pick his way round 'very boldly, smiling and not at all frightened by all the noise that was going on round him'. Marie-Antoinette, however, was obviously relieved to have him once more in her arms.

This too great enthusiasm for the royalist cause was doubly dangerous; it gave a false sense of security and it provoked opposition. Madame de La Rochejaquelein, however, is quite explicit: 'I never heard expressed any insult to the National Assembly, nor to any other popular party.'

The papers, needless to say, published grossly exaggerated accounts of the occasion which was described as an 'orgy' in the course of which the tricolour cockade had been trampled underfoot and white, royalist cockades distributed to all at table. 'This imaginary crime of *lèse-nation*', wrote the comte de Saint-Priest, 'reverberated through all the street corners of Paris to summon the citizens to vengeance.' Madame de La Tour du Pin asserted 'this thoughtless piece of nonsense was no more than one bow of white ribbon which Madame de Maillé, an irresponsible young woman of nineteen, detached from her hat.'

On 5 October a hungry, angry crowd, led largely by women, began to march on Versailles. Some of them genuinely wanted bread, some of them were determined to avenge the alleged insult to the tricolor cockade. They compelled La Fayette to accompany them. By two o'clock they were at the gates of the palace.

Marie-Antoinette had passed the afternoon at Trianon. Despite the ominous clouds she had ventured into the gardens; it was the last time she was ever to see them. Louis was out shooting at Meudon. Her children were in the Palace with the marquise de Tourzel, and she was alone. Artois, the Polignacs, Vaudreuil, Besenval – all had fled on hearing the news of the taking of the Bastille. The little coterie of Trianon had broken up. She was by herself, Madame Campan informs us, 'livrée à de douloureuses reflexions'. The events of the last months had been so terrible, so unexpected. There were so many stories about her, so many lies. The Deputies had come here to Trianon expecting to find evidence of a fantastic extravagance, rooms with golden pillars encrusted with diamonds. They would not believe that this was just a stage setting for the *Dormeur Eveillé*; they would not believe the simplicity in all that they saw.

There was one place in the gardens which corresponded with her mood. There was a wood up behind the Belvédère where a heap of moss-grown boulders overhung a little ravine down which a cascade brought its tumbling waters. Here had been contrived the Grotto. 'This grotto', wrote the comte d'Hézècques, 'was so dark that the eyes, dazzled before, needed a certain time to be able to discern objects clearly.' It was carpeted with moss and cooled by a little stream which flowed through it. It was a place designed for solitude, and by means of a little crevice, it overlooked the meadow before it and 'enabled one to detect from afar anybody who *might* have wished to approach this mysterious retreat.'

It was here that the messenger, sent by the comte de Saint-Priest, found the Queen and brought the news that the mob from Paris was marching on the palace. For years she had played at make-believe in these lovely gardens, pretending to be 'an ordinary individual'. Now the game was up. There were carriages in readiness which could have taken her to safety, but she refused them proudly. 'Since there is danger,' she said, 'my place is by the King's side.'

She found the palace upon tip-toe of expectation. The courtiers, 'in the grip of mortal fear', were thronging the state apartments, each trying to keep as closely as possible in touch with the course of events. Across the courtyards the iron grilles, some of which 'had not turned upon their hinges since the days of Louis XIV', were closed and locked and the National Guard, whose loyalty was doubtful, was drawn up in front of the main gates. Beyond was a sea of discontented humanity, calling for bread but looking as if it was thirsting for blood. Through the windows came that most terrifying of all sounds, the sullen murmur of an angry mob. At three o'clock the King returned from Meudon at a gallop, omitting, in his haste, to acknowledge the salute of the Regiment of Flanders. He went straight into his apartment and stayed there in an agony of indecision – now agreeing with Saint-Priest and La Tour du Pin to retreat to Rambouillet – now cancelling the order – always repeating: 'I do not want to compromise anyone.'

In the Grande Galerie, which had witnessed so many brilliant occasions of the Court, a tense and anxious silence now prevailed. 'They were pacing up and down,' wrote Madame de La Tour du Pin, 'without exchanging a word.' As for herself, she admitted, 'I was in such a state of agitation that I could not stay one moment in the same place. Again and again I went to the Oeil de Boeuf where I could observe those who came and went from the presence of the King, in the hopes of either seeing my husband or my father-in-law and of hearing from him the latest news. The suspense of waiting was unendurable.'

Only the Queen's apartment, where a number of her *entourage* was gathered in the Grand Cabinet, afforded a scene of calm and self control. Madame de Tourzel was perforce a witness: 'Marie-Antoinette', she wrote, 'showed on this day that great spirit and great courage which have always characterised her. Her expression was noble, her countenance serene . . . no-one could have read in it the slightest sign of alarm. She ressured everyone, thought of everything.'

Madame de Tourzel's account is corroborated by Antoine de Rivarol, who devoted his not inconsiderable literary skill to the service of the royalist cause. 'On the evening of 5 October', he writes, 'we saw her receiving a large crowd in her Grand Cabinet; she was speaking forcefully and with dignity to all who approached her and communicated her own calm to those who could not conceal from her their fears. "I know", she said, "that they are coming from Paris to demand my head; but I was taught by my mother to have no fear of death and I shall await it without flinching."' It was for this reason that she gave instructions to Madame de Tourzel that, in the event of an alert, she was to take the Dauphin not to her room but to that of the King. 'I would rather expose myself', she said, 'to any danger that there may be, and so to draw them away from the King's person and from my children.'

The marquise de Tourzel is one of the many who described the events of that night. It is not to be expected that, in the panic and confusion which ensued, the different accounts would be synoptic. The human mind, subjected to such violent emotion, is seldom an infallible recorder. Nevertheless it is possible to follow the course of events through the eyes of those who were very close to them if not actually spectators: the marquise de La Tour du Pin, whose husband was in charge of the militia; Madame Campan, whose sister, Madame Augier, was in waiting on the Queen; the comte de Saint-Priest and the comte d'Hézècques, who were both in attendance on the King – all tell what is substantially the same story.

Between eleven and twelve o'clock La Fayette arrived in the last stages of exhaustion, and was immediately admitted to the King's presence. In half an hour he had convinced Louis that there was no immediate danger. A detachment of the Gardes du Corps, which had been drawn up beneath the windows of the Queen's apartment, was sent to Rambouillet; most of the King's attendants were dismissed. At two o'clock the Queen went to bed, insisting that her two ladies-in-waiting did the same. They decided, however, to keep watch. The Ushers in the Grande Galerie announced that the Queen had retired and everyone departed. 'The doors were closed, the candles were extinguished,' wrote Madame de La Tour du Pin; 'le calme le plus absolu régnait dans Versailles.'

It was not, however, to last very long. 'It was a sight worthy to be seen,' wrote Rivarol, 'the profound sense of security of the royal family, sleeping defenceless in the middle of a horde of assassins reinforced by twenty thousand soldiers – and all on the word of a general who himself admits that he only led, or rather followed his army from fear of being hanged in the Place de Grève! It is perhaps the first time that so great a fear inspired so great a confidence.'

At the end of the Aisle des Princes, in the apartment of the princesse d'Hénin, Madame de La Tour du Pin retired to rest. Her husband, vigilant as ever, made his round of the sentry posts. Everything was in order. 'Not the slightest sound was to be heard, either in the precincts of the palace or in the surrounding streets.' Nevertheless he could not, or would not, sleep. He took up his position in an open window in the Aisle des Ministres, the first building on the left as one enters the first courtyard of Versailles. From here, Monsieur de La Tour du Pin overlooked the narrow courtyard called the Cour des Princes, between the main block and the Aisle des Princes. The entrance to this court was barred by a wrought iron grille and gateway. Once within the court, however, one could pass behind the pillars of the colonnade at the end of the wing and enter the Cour Royale. This passage was guarded by a single sentry. On this fateful night, 'by a negligence which would have been unpardonable if it were not actually culpable', the gateway to the court was left unlocked.

At about the break of day, Monsieur de La Tour du Pin, still at his open window, heard sounds of footsteps approaching in large numbers from the direction of the Orangerie. To his horror he saw that the gate which he had presumed to be locked was open and an ugly looking mob was pouring into the Cour des Princes. Conspicuous among them was a hirsute savage armed with an enormous axe. His name was Nicolas Jourdan, but they called him *coupe-tête*.

At the same time, Madame de La Tour du Pin was suddenly awakened by the sound of the tumult in the street below. Above the hubbub she could hear voices crying, '*À mort*! *À mort*! Kill the body guards!' Scarcely had she recoiled from the window when her faithful maid Marguerite, panting and pale as death, burst into the room and collapsed into an armchair gasping: 'O my God! We are all going to be massacred!' She had decided at daybreak to rejoin her mistress and had walked straight into the mob just in time to see the unfortunate Deshuttes, the sentinel in the Cour des Princes, dragged before Jourdan and brutally beheaded. More sinister, she had witnessed the arrival of a man whom she was convinced she recognised as the duc d'Orléans.

In the Queen's apartment the two ladies-in-waiting, Madame Augier and Madame Thibaut, were keeping their vigil in the Salon next to the Queen's bedroom. At about six they heard the sounds of the mob as it rushed up the Escalier de la Reine. Only two rooms separated the Salon from the head of the staircase, the anteroom and the Salle des Gardes.

Madame Thibaut ran into the anteroom, where she found one of the guards, Miomandre de Sainte-Marie, trying to barricade the door with his musket. He turned, his face streaming with blood: 'Sauvez la Reine!' he shouted; 'on vient pour l'assassiner!' Madame Thibaut ran back, bolting the door behind her, and burst into the Queen's room. 'Sortez du lit, Madame!' she screamed; 'ne vous habillez pas! Sauvez-vous chez le Roi!' Hurriedly throwing a skirt over her nightdress, Marie-Antoinette fled by means of a concealed door in the corner of the room, through her Petits Cabinets, to the Oeil de Boeuf. The door of the Oeil de Boeuf was bolted on the other side.

The King at this moment, awakened by the uproar, was hastening by means of a secret passageway contrived in an *entresol* which afforded a private communication between his bedroom and that of his wife.

In the Oeil de Boeuf, Marquant, one of the *valets de la garderobe*, was aroused by a frantic knocking at the door. 'He ran to open it and was astonished to see his Queen, half-dressed, flying from the blows of the assassins.'

Meanwhile, in the rooms beneath, Madame de Tourzel had been alerted. 'I leapt out of bed,' she recounts, 'and immediately carried the Dauphin to the King's room.' She found Marie-Antoinette there in complete possession of herself. 'The danger to which she had been exposed had in no way affected her courage. Her countenance was sad but calm.'

Marie-Antoinette was called upon, during that day, to show a supreme degree of courage. La Fayette insisted on her showing herself to the crowd; it was necessary, he told her, if order was to be restored. Taking her children by the hand she advanced onto the balcony which overlooks the Cour de Marbre from the King's bedroom. There were muskets levelled in the crowd. She was greeted with a yell of 'No children!' Motioning her children back into the room she stood for a while alone upon the balcony. The muskets were lowered. For a moment the situation was saved, but the insistent clamour of 'The King to Paris!' could not be ignored. Finally the order was given for the royal family to return to the capital which it had virtually forsaken since the early years of Louis XIV.

Just before their departure, Madame Campan found Marie-Antoinette alone in her Petits Cabinets. The pent-up emotion of the last twenty-four hours had finally overtaken her. 'She could hardly speak; her face was streaming with tears.' In her heart she probably knew that she was leaving Versailles for ever.

As the royal family was getting into the berlin that was to

take them to Paris, Louis turned to the marquis de La Tour du Pin. 'You remain in charge here,' he said; 'try and save me my poor Versailles.'

The next day, 7 October, began at Versailles the saddest spectacle that a building can witness; the courts rang to the sound of the voices and footsteps of the carriers, of furniture being piled into carts never to return, of windows and shutters being closed never to be reopened, of carriages rolling out of the golden gates, never to re-enter.

It was the end. Madame de La Tour du Pin went back to her lodgings in the Aisle des Ministres. 'A great emptiness already reigned in Versailles.'

The Tuileries

While the royal family were preparing for their departure from Versailles, a courier had been dispatched at the gallop to warn the marquis de la Suze, grand maréchal du Logis of the Tuileries, that the King and Queen intended to take up residence that evening. The prospect of such an invasion must have been appalling. Only six years previously a report had been addressed to the King stating that 'the royal apartments no longer really exist; they have been partitioned off; unless something is done about it they will not be able to offer His Majesty's family even a month's shelter.' Nothing had been done.

The Tuileries had not been used as a royal palace since 1722 when the young Louis XV moved into Versailles. Marie-Antoinette had a *pied à terre* here which she used on her visits to Paris. Otherwise the building was chiefly known to Parisians as a theatre. It was commonly called the Salle des Machines on account of the elaborate scenic effects made possible by its equipment, and was in constant use. The scenery, in accordance with the topography of the palace, was marked 'côté cour' or 'côté jardin'. Long after the Opera left the palace the words 'cour' and 'jardin' continued to mean right and left in the language of the stage. Apart from its theatrical function, the palace was mostly used to provide lodgings for a miscellaneous crowd of retired officials and pensioned-off artists.

With the sudden arrival of the royal family and the Court on 6 October the Tuileries became once more the residence of the King. Not only did all these pensioners have to be evicted at a moment's notice, but furniture, fuel, food and other bare necessities of life had to be found for no fewer than 677 persons. According to the comtesse de La Rochejaquelein, some 2 000 vehicles arrived at the Tuileries in the course of that day. It had to be furnished at the expense of Versailles. 'For several days', wrote Roussel d'Épinal, 'there was one long convoy of vehicles loaded with an immense amount of furniture which had been collected in the palace during the course of three reigns.'

It was not until ten o'clock that night that the royal family reached the palace, or rather, as d'Hézècques insisted, 'this prison disguised under the name of palace.' 'It is all very ugly here,' the Dauphin compained to his mother. 'My son,' she replied, 'Louis XIV lived here and found it to his liking. We should not be more difficult than he was.' But they did not now find 'even those little commodities which the meanest bourgeois would have expected in his house.' The courtiers spent the first night as best they could, sleeping on sofas, on tables or the benches that lined the anterooms.

On the following day, Wednesday 7 October one of Marie-Antoinette's first thoughts was to write to Mercy. She wrote again on the Saturday.

> I hope you received my letter of Wednesday, which will have given you some reassurance; I am quite well and in spite of all the malicious things that they continue to do to me, I hope nevertheless to win back the more sane and honest of the bourgeoisie and the people . . . with gentleness and a persistent patience one must hope that at least we may succeed in destroying this terrible distrust which is in everyone's mind and which continually drags us down into the abyss where we are . . . It is unbelievable what has taken place in the last twenty-four hours. You would do well not to come here for some time . . . it would cause more anxieties. For the rest I cannot receive anyone in my private apartments, I have only my little room upstairs, my daughter sleeps in my cabinet next to me and my son in my big bedroom; although that is inconvenient I prefer to have them close to me.

Marie-Antoinette was putting a brave face on it. An English diplomat, Lord Robert Fitzgerald, was at the Tuileries on 8

October. 'The King was much dejected,' he observed, 'and said little. Her Majesty's voice faltered and the tears ran fast down her cheeks as she spoke and all her attendants seemed impressed with the deepest melancholy and concern.'

By 13 October, Count Fernan Nuñez, the Spanish Ambassador, could report: 'the King is already occupying his apartment which, although both vast and beautiful, has been more or less abandoned for more than a century. Once it has been fitted up it will be magnificent, and the King, who has already made it known to the National Assembly that he will fix here his regular residence, will have an agreeable abode for the winter and will be able, during the rest of the year, to go to Versailles and the other royal *châteaux* to take advantage of the fresher air.'

In a surprisingly short time the old way of the life of the Court was more or less re-established. So deeply was the ceremonial of Versailles ingrained in the minds of the courtiers that it was found easiest to transfer the nomenclature of the rooms. Thus the first antechamber of the Tuileries became the Salon de l'Oeil de Boeuf although it possessed no oval window by virtue of which it might merit the name.

Life at the Tuileries was becoming daily more like life at Versailles. 'The royal family receive the Corps Diplomatique on Sundays and Thursdays,' wrote Fernan Nuñez; 'there are gaming tables on those days and on Tuesdays. On Sunday there will be a *grand couvert* at dinner as it used to be at Fontainebleau.' Another nobleman who described the new life of the Court was the comte de Paroy. 'The King', he wrote, 'had his times of reception at his *lever* and at his *coucher* for those who had the honour of being presented; the public could see him when he went with the royal family to mass. The Queen had resumed her ordinary routine and concerned herself a lot with the education of the Dauphin and Madame Royale . . . She occupies her time with the use of her needle and has undertaken a great piece of tapestry of which she has given portions to her ladies to work.'

There were, however, certain changes. The Court of the

Tuileries was open to a wider section of the public than the Court of Versailles. Institutions such as the Corps des Marchands were received. Deputies no longer attended in ceremonial dress, not even Bishops, and the commune of Paris no longer knelt when received by the King. As the comte de Damas observed: 'I could with difficulty accustom myself to finding the royal family guarded by a *garde bourgeoise* with no *gardes du corps*, without that imposing paraphernalia which distinguished the Court of Versailles from the rest of Europe; to see the apartments of the King and the Queen filled with the kind of people who would not have been admitted under the old system.'

Early in 1790, when the Assembly was debating the Civil List, Le Brun, the future second Consul, said: 'you desire your King to be the most magnificent of Kings, as you are the greatest of nations. You do not want to destroy a splendour which distinguishes the French Court.'

Louis was voted a civil list of 25 000 000 livres a year as well as the revenues of the Crown Domain. But in September 1790 the royal hunt was abolished and Louis was deprived not only of his greatest pleasure, but of a form of exercise which was, possibly, necessary to his health.

In spite of the fact that Louis and Marie-Antoinette had apparently accommodated themselves to life in the capital they were constantly being advised to leave it as soon as possible. They were advised to drive to Chambord with an ever increasing military escort; they were advised to set up their Court at Metz, but of all the schemes perhaps only two need to be taken seriously.

On 7 October Jacques Matthieu Augeard, the Queen's secretary, who had been to the country to see his daughter, returned to Paris and was immediately summoned to the palace. 'I had scarcely entered and closed the door', he writes, 'than the Queen went herself to see if we were not overheard.

'"We are not safe here; let us go somewhere else."

'The same attentiveness at the door of this room.

'"We are not safe here."

'She took me to another room where we found her daughter. "Leave us, my child, I have work to do with Monsieur Augeard. Just look", she said to me, "how she has slept." An ottoman had, in fact, served her for a bed.

'She recounted to me all the horrors of 5 and 6 October and in the greatest detail.'

That experience had been a nightmare. 'The day', wrote Rivarol, 'was sombre, cold and wet; the infamous militia splashing through the mud; these harpies, these monsters with human faces and those two heads carried aloft.' Madame de Chastenay adds the ghoulish detail: 'the heads of the *gardes du corps*, borne in triumph, to which, with a refinement of horror, were given at Sèvres a hair curl, all blood-stained as they were.' The marquis de Ferrières describes the women, 'covered with tricolor cockades, carrying branches of poplar; other women sitting astride the cannons, preceded and followed the King's coach. All the guns were decorated with oak leaves in token of victory, a running salvo of musketry, cries of "we are bringing the baker, the baker's wife and the baker's boy," were followed by gross insults to the Queen and menaces against the priests and nobles; such was the *cortège*, insolent and barbarous, in the middle of which the King, the Queen and the royal family, after a journey of more than six hours, arrived at the Hôtel de Ville.' No doubt Marie-Antoinette could have elaborated the theme.

> 'The Queen does me the honour to relate to me all these atrocities in order to ask my advice?'
>
> 'Yes, for sure.'
>
> 'Your Majesty is a prisoner.'
>
> 'My God, what are you saying?'
>
> 'Madame, it is all too true. From the moment that Your Majesty no longer has her guard of honour, she is a prisoner.'
>
> 'Those fellows there are, I dare to say it, more attentive than our guards.'
>
> 'The attentiveness of gaolers.'
>
> 'What, then can be done?'
>
> 'Your position is infinitely critical, and it would be a crime even to disguise from you that the country is suffering from a

very serious disease, and one which will do nothing but worsen from month to month.'

'But there must, in the end, be some remedy. You do not regard the situation as being devoid of hope?'

'I do not think so'.

Augeard then entered into a careful assessment of the situation in Austria. The King should send to Vienna a trusted and faithful person in whom he had the fullest confidence.

'That is exactly our intention.'

'I only know one person in the world capable of fulfilling this mission.'

'And who is that?'.

'It is Your Majesty.'

'What! and leave the King alone?'

Augeard then proceeded to outline a plan of escape for her. She was to travel not as Queen, not as a princess, but as an ordinary individual, taking with her Madame Royale and the Dauphin dressed as a little girl. Augeard's own daughter would come to Paris to escort them. They would descend the little staircase into the Cour des Princes. There they would find 'a very simple two-horse carriage' which would take them to Augeard's house. They would then depart for the frontier with Marie-Antoinette in the role of governess.

'I would not hesitate for a moment,' replied the Queen, 'if it were not for the King; but I could not bring myself to leave him alone; I would be afraid for his life.'

On the same day, 7 October, a much more important person than Augeard was also considering the necessity of an escape from Paris – Mirabeau. Early in the morning he paid a call on the comte de La Marck: 'if you have any means of making yourself understood by the King and the Queen,' he said, 'try to persuade them that it will be the end of them and of France if the royal family does not leave Paris. I am working on a plan for getting them out of it: would you be in a position to assure them that they can count on me?'

On 25 October Mirabeau produced a *mémoire* which he sent to the comte de Provence. He insisted on retreat from Paris, but where was the royal family to go to? To retreat to Metz or any other border town would be to declare war on the nation and to abdicate from the throne. 'A King who is the only safeguard to his people does not run away from his people.' That was not a possible option. Nor would it be advisable to retreat to somewhere like Chambord and appeal for the support of the nobility. The nation had come, rightly or wrongly, to regard the aristocracy as its most implacable enemy; for the King to identify himself with the nobility would be even worse than to cast himself upon a foreign army.

Finally Mirabeau arrived at a solution that was possible though not without danger. Secrecy would be of the utmost importance. No-one must have the slightest knowledge of the plan except for those directly involved in it, and these should not be informed until the last possible moment. If every precaution was taken, thought Mirabeau, the King could leave the Tuileries in broad daylight. His destination should be Rouen. 'It has to be Rouen,' wrote Mirabeau, 'because such a choice announces that there is no question of an escape and that it is just a move nearer to the provinces; because Normandy is thickly populated and its inhabitants have more tenacity than other Frenchmen; finally that it would be easy to affect a coalition with Brittany and Anjou which would constitute already an irresistible force.' This was all put before the comte de Provence. He told La Marck that he approved the scheme in principle but that he was certain in advance that the King would not agree to it. 'I invited Monsieur to speak of it to the Queen,' said La Marck, 'who, once persuaded, would perhaps obtain the consent of the King. "You are wrong", he told me, "in thinking that it is in the power of the Queen to make up the King's mind on so weighty an issue."'

At the beginning of April 1790, Mercy approached La Marck with a request to meet Mirabeau in conditions of the utmost secrecy. La Marck lived at that time in the Hôtel Charost. Its courtyard opened onto the faubourg Saint-

Honoré. Its garden gave access to the Champs-Elysées. It was decided that Mirabeau should enter this side and was to mount directly to La Marck's bedroom, while Mercy was to arrive, as always, by coach to the front door.

Once again Mirabeau urged the absolute necessity of the King's leaving Paris but not France. At least this conference established a mutual respect between Mercy and Mirabeau. The latter in particular found Mercy 'far superior to what I had been led to believe'. This opinion was endorsed by the comte de Ségur, who told Gouverneur Morris that Mercy was 'one of the ablest statesmen in Europe'.

The next step was for La Marck to confer with the Queen. The audience was fixed for the next day. He was instructed to go to the rooms of Madame Thibault, 'une bonne vieille femme' whose simplicity and good nature made a very favourable impression on him.

When La Marck was admitted into the Queen's presence he found that she had already agreed with the King that it was time to approach Mirabeau. She asked, however, what part, if any, he had taken in the provoking of the events of 5 and 6 October. La Marck was personally in a position to establish Mirabeau's alibi and to affirm his innocence and ignorance in the whole affair. 'You give me great pleasure,' the Queen replied; 'I had great need of reassurance on that point, for, according to certain rumours which were circulating at the time, I have to admit, I have felt towards the comte de Mirabeau a feeling of horror.'

At this moment the King entered. 'Without any preamble and with his usual abrupt manner he said to me: "the Queen will already have told you that I wish to employ the comte de Mirabeau if you think that he is willing and able to be of use to me. What do you think about that?"' La Marck could only answer by referring to the 'extrême maladresse' of Louis' ministers. The King replied that anything done by Mirabeau must remain a total secret from the ministers.

La Marck was absolutely dumbfounded by this reply. 'I could not imagine how the King could dream of employing, without his ministers knowing, a man such as Mirabeau. Indeed the counsels and the actions of the latter could not fail to be in direct opposition to those of the ministers, and what use could there be in such a contradiction?'

La Marck, nevertheless, offered to try to negotiate with Mirabeau. 'See him then,' agreed Louis; 'and you will give an account of what is decided either to the Queen or to myself.' 'Sire, would you not rather that I tell the comte de Mirabeau, on behalf of Your Majesty, to put down in writing his ideas in this connection?' 'Yes; better still,' concluded Louis; 'you will deliver to me what he has written by the hand of the Queen.'

Louis then left the room. Marie-Antoinette gave La Marck permission to come and see her as often as he desired, but advised him to choose those times on which Madame Thibault was in service. 'She was not exactly complaining about Madame Campan, the second *femme de chambre*, but this lady had certain connections which were displeasing to the Queen.'

La Marck now had to return to Mirabeau, who was appalled to think that anyone could have regarded him as responsible for the horrors of 5 and 6 October. But he was clearly flattered by what he was told. 'The effect which my opening remarks produced on his self-esteem', claimed La Marck, 'did not escape me. I saw this man, who considered himself, and not without reason, so highly placed above the others, subject none the less to that sort of magic which royal personages can exercise when they know how to appear benevolent.' La Marck put much emphasis on this royal magnetism and bemoaned the lack of it in the current situation. 'I am convinced that the majority of those who made the most audacious harangues [in the National Assembly] would have become ardent royalists if the King and his ministers had had the ability to attract them.'

By 'ardent royalists' La Marck did not mean to imply any return to the absolutist position. 'It was not this antique monarchy which Mirabeau was minded to defend. His dream was to modify, to regenerate and to arrive finally at a form of government similar to that which had raised England to the apogee of her power and glory.' But Mirabeau's position was somewhat that of *l'Apprenti Sorcier*: he had given momentum to the Revolution and now he wanted to halt it.

When La Marck reported back to Marie-Antoinette his first concern was to stress the importance of relieving Mirabeau of his crippling debts. Once this had been agreed the Queen began to talk about the old days:

> The hope which she derived from the services which Mirabeau would render seemed to have blinded her to the dangers which surrounded her on all sides . . . the purpose of my visit seemed to have been lost to sight; she was trying to push it aside. Once I started talking about the Revolution she became both serious and sad, but once the conversation turned on other matters I found her at once more lovable and gracious. And this tendency says more about her character than anything else I could say. In fact Marie-Antoinette, who has been so often accused of wanting to become involved in public affairs, had no taste for them. With a soul at once noble and elevated she combined a quickness and decision and an energy of will of which she had already given proof on more than one occasion. It was precisely this strength of determination in which Louis XVI was lacking. The enemies of royalty were aware of this at an early date and directed all their attacks against the Queen because they were afraid of her influence. Thus it can be seen that from the first days of the Revolution they spoke only of the virtues of the King and kept silence on the subject of the Queen.

What began as a mere silence rapidly developed into a campaign of calumny from which Marie-Antoinette was never to escape. The Emperor Joseph, writing to his brother Leopold on 8 October said: 'I have been as much afflicted as you by all the horrors they spread about the Queen of France, but what can be done with insolent madmen? They cannot get away from the idea that my sister has secretly sent me millions, whilst I do not know why or how I should have received them or how she could have got them to me; I have never seen a *sou* from France.'

On 29 May 1790, Marie-Antoinette wrote to her brother

Leopold: 'I believe that they will allow us to take advantage of the fine weather by passing several days at Saint-Cloud, which is at the gates of Paris. It is absolutely necessary for our health that we should breathe a purer and a fresher air.'

It was not until 4 June, the anniversary of the Dauphin's death, that they finally got to Saint-Cloud. With them came the King's two aunts, Mesdames Adelaïde and Victoire, the comte and comtesse de Provence, the marquise de Tourzel and her daughter Pauline, who was allowed – contrary to all etiquette, for she had not yet been presented – to eat at the royal table, and the King's sister Madame Elizabeth, who made the significant comment on the famous view from the terrace: 'Paris is beautiful *when seen from a distance.*'

It was here that Mirabeau finally met the King and Queen. On 3 July he went to stay with his niece at Auteuil, in order to be able to approach the palace undetected. 'From there he went,' writes La Marck, 'at the agreed time, to the Queen's apartment, where he also found the King.'

It is not known what was said in the course of the interview, but La Marck recounts how, the first time that he saw the Queen after the meeting, she assured him that both she and the King had become convinced of the sincere devotion of Mirabeau to the cause of the monarchy. 'As for Mirabeau, he spoke only of the pleasure of this interview. He had left Saint-Cloud enraptured. The dignity of the Queen, the grace which permeated her whole person, everything about her had charmed him more than he could possibly say.'

Mirabeau was also impressed by Louis. 'He was no less touched by the calm resignation of the King and by the moderation of his views on the re-establishment of the royal authority. He told me again on this occasion that, if Louis had had ministers of greater ability it would have been easy . . . to avert the evils occasioned by the Revolution.'

The visit of Mirabeau did not long remain a secret. Shortly afterwards, and for several days, the newsmongers of Paris were crying 'La grande trahison de Monsieur de Mirabeau!' 'Sorry times', commented La Marck, 'when a member of the

National Assembly could be accused of treason for having been to see his sovereign.'

On 14 July 1790, France decided to celebrate the anniversary of the fall of the Bastille with what was called the 'Fête de la Fédération'. One of the people closely concerned was Madame de la Tour du Pin, whose husband was in charge of most of the arrangements.

The Champ de Mars, almost the only possible site for such a concourse, was a huge area in front of the École Militaire. It was recast into a vast amphitheatre by volunteers from Paris. There were some 200 000 of them – men and women, old and young and of every condition of life. 'A more extraordinary spectacle', wrote the marquise, 'will never be seen again; thousands of wheelbarrows, pushed by people of every walk of life . . . women of the streets, easily recognised by their clothing, harnessed together with Capuchin monks to little tip-carts with shafts; beside them were washerwomen together with knights of Saint-Louis, and in this coming together of all classes of society, not the least disorder, not the smallest dispute. Each one was moved by the same, single thought of confraternity.'

The scene as described by Madame de La Tour du Pin is reminiscent of that upsurge of faith evoked by the rebuilding of Chartres Cathedral after the disastrous fire. It had been the high moment of the twelfth century renaissance. Perhaps the restructuring of the Champ de Mars was the high moment of the French Revolution. It was described by Madame de Tourzel as 'le dernier beau jour de la Reine'. The comte de Saint-Priest, however, took a different view; his wife's carriage had been stopped by a group of these workers, who had subjected her to the grossest insults for being an aristocrat. 'All honest people in Paris', he stated, 'felt a great relief when they saw the end of that abominable undertaking.'

Although the Fête de la Fédération celebrated the destruction of the symbol of tyranny, it was not in itself anti-monarchical. The little Dauphin was dressed in the uniform of a *garde nationale*. There was a group of officers of that corps waiting to receive the royal family. 'He has as yet no *bonnet*,' said the Queen. 'No, Madame,' came the answer, 'but there are many at his service.'

The Fête de la Fédération was a quasi-religious occasion. Talleyrand, the Bishop of Autun and, according to Madame de La Tour du Pin, 'the least estimable of French priests', celebrated the mass. He was served by his brother Archambauld wearing Court dress – 'en habit brodé, l'épée à côté'. The ritual was punctuated by torrential rain, on which occasions the crowd 'opened thousands of umbrellas of every imaginable colour; it afforded the most astonishing spectacle that could possibly be seen.'

Saint-Priest was not alone in his distaste for the occasion; as the royal family departed, Madame de La Tour du Pin found herself face to face with the Queen: 'accustomed as I had been for a long time to the expressions of her face, I could see that she did great violence to her feelings to conceal her ill-humour, without, however, succeeding sufficiently for her own benefit or for that of the King.'

La Fayette made the same point about Marie-Antoinette in a conversation with the marquis de Bouillé. 'She has all that is needed to win the hearts of the people of Paris, but she has a deep-seated pride and a moodiness which she does not know how to conceal and which, most often, alienates them.'

There were, however, forces at work which no modesty or good humour on the part of Marie-Antoinette could have overcome. In the autumn, Madame La Motte, who had long since escaped from prison, returned openly to Paris, having published her so-called 'mémoires' in which she actually claimed to have had a lesbian relationship with Marie-Antoinette which she described in some detail. Other pamphlets printed an 'admission' by Louis that he was not the father of the Queen's children.

'They say for certain', wrote the Baron de Staël-Holstein on 10 November 1790, 'that Madame La Motte is to demand a revision of her trial and that she often sees Madame de Sillery [as Madame de Genlis had now become] who is

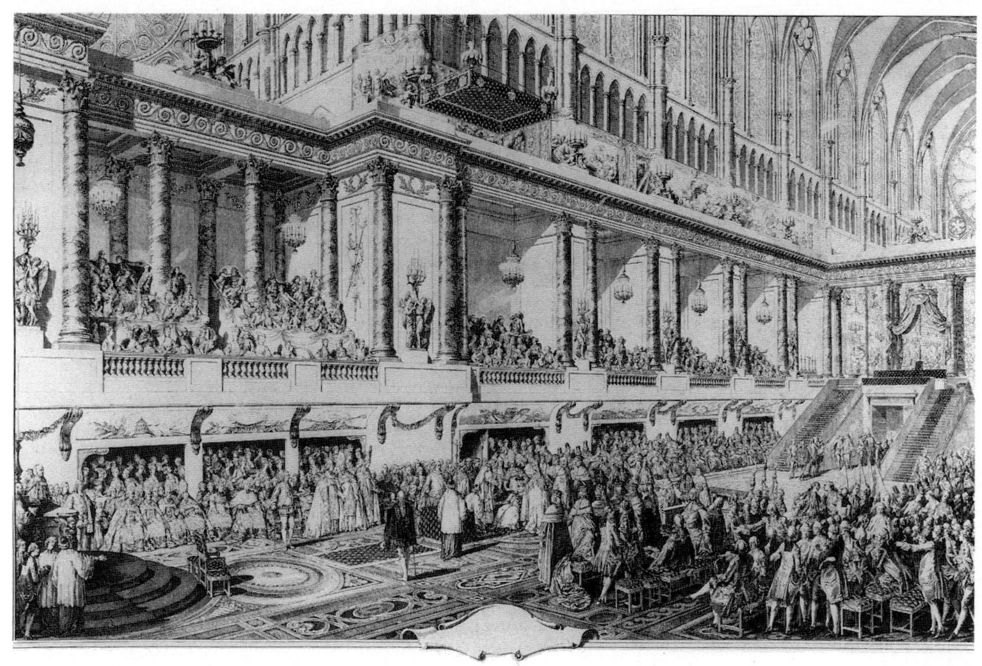

12. The Coronation of Louis XVI: drawing by Moreau le Jeune.

13. Marie-Antoinette announces to Madame de Bellegarde her husband's pardon, 1777: engraving by Duclos.

14. Marie-Antoinette: painting by Perin-Salbreux.

15. Marie-Antoinette: painting by Kucharski.

16. Count Axel Fersen: painting by Dreuillon.

17. The Château de Choisy-le-Roi: engraving by Rigaud.

18. The Château de Meudon: engraving by Rigaud.

19. Marie-Antoinette: bust by Le Comte.

20. Louis XVI: bust by Houdon

21. Louis XVI and the duc d'Orléans: wax profiles by Curtius.

22. Mass in the Tuileries: painting by Hubert Robert.

23. The royal family arriving at the Temple: engraving by Berhault.

24. The Dauphin Louis-Charles: painting by Kucharski.

25. The execution of Marie-Antoinette: engraving by Monnet.

governess to the children of the duc d'Orléans. Dark and terrible things are being plotted against the Queen. She is the one whom the *enragés* fear and wish to destroy, because they regard her as their implacable enemy and the only person in a position to rally a party around her.' The aristocrats, he suggests, were no longer prepared to suffer in patience the legislation against them but were ready to resort openly to the use of force. 'This could lead to the explosion which one has so often thought was about to be detonated.'

Mirabeau, who was furious to learn of Madame La Motte's manoeuvre, states in his memoir of 12 November: 'it is not merely to amuse public malignity that the revision of Madame La Motte's trial will be brought about. It is the Queen at whom it is directly aimed.' Mirabeau supported Staël-Holstein in his judgement: 'the Queen, whose character they know, as also her clearness of perception and her strength of character, would be the primary object of their attack, both as the first and firmest rampart of the throne and as the sentinel watching most closely over the safety of the monarch.'

It was no easy task. Louis' position was rapidly becoming untenable. One of the logical consequences of the departure of the King from Versailles was that the Assemblée Nationale should follow him to Paris. This brought that body under the influence, and later under the control, of the city. It underwent, in the words of the comte Roederer, Procureur Syndic (Attorney General) to the Commune, 'a complete metamorphosis'. It is described by the English statesman Edmund Burke. 'The republic', he wrote, 'is to have a first functionary, under the name of king or not, as they think fit. This officer, when such an officer is permitted, is however, neither in fact nor in name to be considered a sovereign, nor the people his subjects. The very use of these appellations is offensive to their ears.' On another occasion he takes up the same theme: 'If the French King has, in his own person and in that of his Queen, really deserved these unavowed, but unavenged murderous attempts and those frequent indignities more cruel than murder, such a person would ill deserve even that subordinate, executory trust which I understand is to be placed in him.'

In a prophetic passage written in January 1791, Edmund Burke proclaimed: 'they will assassinate the King when his name will no longer be necessary for their designs, but not a moment sooner. They will probably first assassinate the Queen, whenever the renewed menace of such an assassination loses its effect upon the anxious mind of an affectionate husband. At present the advantage which they derive from the daily threats against her life is her only security for preserving it . . . They choose to make monarchy contemptible by exposing it to ridicule in the person of the most benevolent of kings.'

As the Revolution gathered momentum there began to emerge another theme which was to bring matters to a head. It was the deep dislike and distrust of the clergy. On 10 October 1789, Charles-Maurice de Talleyrand, a prince of the house of Périgord and, although widely reputed not to believe in God, Bishop of Autun, proposed in the Assembly that the vast wealth of the clergy should be placed at the disposition of the nation. On 2 November this was agreed with the condition that the State made itself responsible for the payment of the clergy and the upkeep of religious buildings. That was the thin end of the wedge. On 24 August 1790, the 'civil constitution' of the clergy was approved by Louis. It was a dangerous step in the direction of state control, but worse was to come. On 27 November the Assembly introduced a measure that required all clergy to take an oath accepting the civil constitution, on pain of losing their jobs. 'That was the fatal stroke', wrote the abbé Gosselin, 'which was to deal the death blow to the Church in France.

'For any man with any knowledge of the discipline of the Church, which was manifestly overthrown by the Civil Constitution,' continues Gosselin, 'not the slightest doubt could arise as to the obligation to refuse the oath.' Pope Pius had stated, as the marquis de Férrières puts it, 'that if His

Majesty approved the decrees concerning the clergy, he would be leading a whole nation into error, he would precipitate the country into schism and perhaps into a cruel war of religion.'

On 26 December, nevertheless, Louis gave his assent to the measure. It created an immediate schism between the clergy *sermenté*, who had taken the oath, and the clergy *non-assermenté* who had not. Soon the term *non-assermenté* gave place to the word *réfractaire* – recalcitrant, rebellious and therefore enemies of the Revolution.

Once more Louis wrote to the Pope – or rather the Archbishop of Aix wrote on his behalf – asking for papal ratification of the new diocesan boundaries imposed by the Assembly and papal consent to the canonical institution of the new bishops. It was of vital importance, he urged: 'the silence or the refusal of your Holiness will determine the schism.'

On 1 January 1791, 'le jour fatal', the clergy in the Assembly had to decide whether to take the oath or to refuse. At the moment when they were called, relates Férrières, cries could be heard from outside: 'Burn all those who refuse!' Under these conditions, the clergy gave their response. One after another the bishops and priests of the Catholic Church refused the oath. The Revolutionaries could not restrain their anger. Attempts were made to facilitate acceptance, but to no avail. Finally the Assembly, instead of calling them one by one, invited all those who were prepared to swear to come to the desk. Only a very few came.

It was a moral victory for the Church. Bishops were emboldened to stand up to the Assembly. Most dioceses declared that any sacrament celebrated by priests who had taken the oath was invalid; they were forbidden to hear confession or to pronounce absolution. Anyone receiving communion at their hands would be excommunicated. The Revolutionaries replied with a campaign of calumny in the form of the most obscene caricatures. The Church may have won, but it was to pay a heavy price for its victory.

Meanwhile Mirabeau kept up his correspondence with

Marie-Antoinette and the King, writing memorandum after memorandum on the ever worsening state of affairs and the possible means of turning the tide. The National Assembly must be discredited and made to dissolve itself; the new Assembly must meet anywhere but in Paris. 'No deliberating body, and I do not except the National Assembly, is free today alongside the formidable influence which they have given to the people.' The King and Queen must regain their popularity; they must show themselves more in public, appear in the Assembly, visit hospitals and larger workshops. He waxes eloquent over the condition of the kingdom. 'Unhappy nation! See how a handful of men have put intrigue in place of talent and have been led by emotions in place of concepts. Good but feeble King! Ill-fated Queen! Behold the terrible abyss to which vacillation between a confidence too blind and a mistrust too exaggerated has brought you! One more effort can be made, but only one.'

Those words were written on 23 December 1790. A month later the comte de La Marck wrote to Mercy almost in despair. The King was meditating day after day on the life of Charles I, whose portrait hung in his room, but it was more in order to learn how to suffer and how to die than to learn how to resist. The Queen, more active and energetic, saw her energy paralysed by her husband's inaction.

It is clear that Marie-Antoinette was the more active of the two and it is quite possible, as Girault de Coursac maintains, that she not infrequently acted without Louis' knowledge. A woman who is a wife and a mother has a divided loyalty. If the crown could not be saved for her husband, perhaps it could be saved for her son. But she was not really qualified to take the reins of government. Her old faults continued to dog her. 'One has to admit', wrote La Marck, 'that, neither in matters of moment nor even in conversation, does she bring to bear that degree of attention and consistency which is indispensible if one is to get to the root of the matter.' In another passage, La Marck continues the same line of thought: 'the Queen certainly had a character that was active and decisive, but, if she had the courage of Maria Theresa, she did not combine, to the same degree, the high ideals and breadth of vision of that Princess. She hated being involved in politics. She saw clearly the dangers which threatened her, but the mere hope of having avoided them was enough to turn aside her fears, and the slightest lightening of the most sombre horizon made her forget the storm.'

She was, however, more competent than Louis to face the storm. On 8 April 1791, Gouverneur Morris had a conversation with the Foreign Secretary, the comte de Montmorin. 'Speaking of the Court, he tells me that the King is absolutely good for nothing; that at present he always asks, when he is at work with the King, that the Queen be present.'

It is doubtful whether Mirabeau's proposals could have succeeded even if there had been some person with the necessary qualities to make them work. Mirabeau himself was not that person. Even his greatest friend, La Marck, admitted in a letter to Mercy that 'he wanted to reconcile an apparent willingness to serve with inactivity, to push others forwards but to hold back himself.' But Mirabeau did not live to see the success or failure of his plans, for on 2 April 1791 he died.

On 2 April Gouverneur Morris recorded the death of Mirabeau. 'I have seen this man, in the short space of two years, hissed at, honoured, hated, mourned. Enthusiasm has just now presented him as gigantic; time and reflection will shrink that stature.'

One of Mirabeau's last actions in the Assembly had been to protect the passage of Mesdames, Louis' aunts, on their journey to Rome. Their departure had been accomplished openly and officially. They obtained passports and left the Château de Bellevue on the night of 19 February. With them went the comte de Narbonne, Chevalier d'Honneur to Madame Adelaïde.

They travelled without much difficulty into Burgundy until they came to Arnay-le-Duc. Rather unfortunately their arrival here had been preceded by a demand that the roads should be improved by 'travaux extraordinaires' to facilitate the passage of the princesses. By the time that Mesdames arrived – about 2 pm on Tuesday 22 – hostile feeling had been generated. The comte de Narbonne presented the passports, which were found to be in order, but a considerable crowd had collected under the leadership of a *garde nationale* named Fondard, who demanded that the passports should be checked by 'the people' – that is to say by his own supporters. The municipal authorities meekly agreed to send to Paris for a confirmation by the National Assembly of its authorisation for the departure of the princesses, who were obliged to stay at the Auberge de la Croix Blanche where they were surrounded by a guard mounted, ostensibly, 'for their security and tranquility'.

Narbonne promptly returned to Paris and demanded the authorisation of the National Assembly to respect the validity of its passports. Thanks largely to the eloquence of Mirabeau he obtained his request and returned with the authorisation to Dijon, whence it was transmitted to Arnay-le-Duc.

The leaders of the local Jacobin Club, however, passed a resolution on 25 February that 'the decree of the Assembly should not be respected'. A second deputation was dispatched from Arnay-le-Duc to Paris and this time the comte de Narbonne was detained in custody. The envoys were met by the Ministre de l'Intérieur, de Lessart, who firmly told them that the municipality of Arnay-le-Duc would be exposed to severe measures of discipline if it continued in its culpable resistance to the decree of the Assembly and the orders of the King.

On 4 March Mesdames left Arnay-le-Duc and continued their journey. One of the preconditions for the escape of the royal family had been removed.

The Flight to Varennes

During their stay at Saint-Cloud in the summer of 1790 the royal family's position outside the confines of the capital offered a real opportunity for escape. On one occasion Louis was out riding with the duc de Brissac and the comte d'Esterhazy. The Queen and the rest of the royal family were known to have gone out in a barouche. The King prolonged his ride much farther than was his wont – as far, in fact, as Maisons. Brissac and d'Esterhazy were beginning to entertain hopes that his intention was to cross the Seine and make for Chantilly. They little knew their man. Louis dispelled all their dreams by ordering relay horses for the Pont du Pecq and returning to Saint-Cloud. Madame Campan describes the same occasion: 'one evening in the month of June, at nine o'clock, the personnel of the Château, seeing that the King had not returned, were walking about uneasily in the courtyard. I believed that they might have departed and I could hardly breathe in my anxiety, when I heard the sound of the carriages.'

'The more I thought of it,' wrote d'Esterhazy, 'the more I came to believe that such an end would be easily achieved. We could have reached Chantilly before anyone became aware of our flight.' Back at Saint-Cloud he made his ideas known to Marie-Antoinette. 'She told me that she thought the same, but that she despaired of ever obtaining the King's assent; that, so far as she was concerned, she was determined never to be separated from him and to accept the lot which destiny was preparing for them.'

In April 1791 the royal family tried again to spend a few

days at Saint-Cloud. This time they were prevented. The marquis de Bouillé suspected that it was the departure of Mesdames which put the seditious groups on their guard and saw in the royal family's leaving for Saint-Cloud another attempt at escape.

'The King', wrote Madame de Tourzel, 'was making ready to spend Holy Week and Easter at Saint-Cloud. He decided to leave on Monday of Holy Week . . . the King and Queen got into their coach after mass, together with the Dauphin, Madame [Royale] and Madame Elizabeth. I was with the Princess in the front of the vehicle and was a witness of the horrible scene which took place on that cruel day. The grenadiers of the Garde Nationale . . . seeing the horses ready to depart, held their heads and declared that they would not allow the King to leave. Bailly and La Fayette tried without success to overcome their resistance . . . the King, putting his head out of the window, said: "it is astonishing that, having given liberty to the nation, I should not be free myself."'

'The extraordinary events of this week', wrote Lord Gower, 'have given manifest proofs of the absolute anarchy under which the country labours. An endeavour to compel the King to attend mass celebrated by priests who have taken the oath has caused the constitutional laws of the country to be violated by those who were specially armed for the defence of them; for it was the national guard, not the mob, which prevented Louis from going to Saint-Cloud.'

La Fayette, no doubt annoyed at his inability to assert his authority, offered to use force. 'It is up to you', said the King with some vivacity, 'to see to what you should do to make the Constitution work.' 'Although the King claimed on his behalf the simple rights of man,' wrote Bouillé, 'he was forced back into his prison after a resistance that lasted two hours, during which the Queen and her children were threatened and some of their suite, among others the young marquis de Duras, were ill treated.' The King made the same statement in his Declaration, which is written in the third person and ends with the words: 'His Majesty was constrained to yield and to go back into his prison; for after that there was no other name for his palace.' Count Fernan Nuñez states that he was informed by an eye-witness that 'a grenadier had said in a loud voice, that could have been heard by the monarch: "if there is a single shot fired, the second will be for this fat pig in the coach and he will be torn to pieces."'

Two days later Louis entrusted to Fersen a letter to the Emperor stating that he had, as the result of that incident, determined on escaping from Paris. In the Declaration which Louis sent to the Assembly on 21 June he states: 'the immediate causes of my departure are the outrages and threats which were made on 18 April to my family.'

But if the decision was made at this point, the plans had been maturing for a long time. The first actual move was the ordering of the coach. There was living in Paris at that time a Russian lady of the title baronne de Korff. She was a good friend of Fersen and well received at the Tuileries. It was decided that the royal family should leave Paris with a passport in her name and in a coach ordered by her.

Much of the evidence from which the story of the flight to Varennes may be reconstructed comes from the depositions made later by some fifty persons involved, or thought to be involved. Among these was Jean Louis, coachmaker. He stated that on 2 December 1790, 'Madame la baronne de Korff sent for him and told him that she wished to order a *berline de voyage*, mounted on springs and commodious enough to contain six persons . . . in order to go to Russia.' Two days later a man representing the baronne, whom the witness later recognised as Fersen, concluded the deal. On 3 February Marie-Antoinette wrote to Mercy to say that Madame de Tourzel and either the duc de Brissac or the duc de Villequier would accompany the royal family in their berlin.

The coach was described in some detail by Roussel d'Épinal. It was immense – 'a little house on wheels'. It was equipped with 'a sort of a larder; and there you will see a cooker for reheating meat or soup; raise this double floor: it offers you a dining-table. On removing the cushion from this seat, you will find a commode; all that it lacks is a bed. Nothing more ingenious could be imagined than this vehicle.' The final cost was 5 940 livres. On 18 June the berlin was delivered to Fersen's residence in the faubourg Saint-Honoré. By this time the plans for the flight had been completed.

There were three phases in the escape, each of which posed its own peculiar problems: getting out of the Tuileries, getting out of Paris and arriving safely at their destination. Of these the first was by far the most difficult.

Although the Château des Tuileries retained the aspect of a royal residence, the transition from palace to prison had already been largely affected, even if the bars were still gilded. The *gardes du corps*, whose first loyalty was to the King, had been disbanded and replaced by some *gardes nationales*, whose first loyalty was to the nation. They were constantly in attendance on the royal family and although the outward forms of a Court were still observed, the step was short which separated service from surveillance.

One of the captains of the guard, Philippe Dubois, described his vigilant attendance on Madame Elizabeth. There were no less than eight soldiers guarding her. She was accompanied by Dubois to and from her meals and at night 'one of the *garçons de la chambre*, having locked her door from the inside, went to sleep in a little room immediately to the right of her apartment, while one of the *chasseurs de la garde*, having placed his mattress across the door in such a way that it was impossible to go out of the said door without stepping over the body of the *chasseur* asleep on the said mattress, spent the whole night there.' The first and most formidable of the problems of an escape was for the members of the royal family to get out of their own rooms.

The problem was solved largely by the creation of secret doors. Captain Dubois and Private Mercier, two of the *grenadiers* who guarded the apartment of Madame Elizabeth, gave detailed descriptions. 'The two doors which were locked by the jointed keys', said Dubois, 'are hermetically sealed within the thickness of the walls and the panelling corresponds so exactly with the doors, which are themselves covered with tapestry, that it is impossible, without the most minute inspection, to detect them.' To this Mercier adds the detail that this door was in the library of the Princess and opened onto the foot of a little staircase which led to an *entresol* which separated the apartment of Madame Elizabeth from that of the Queen. The door had been made, he said, some six months previously – that is to say some time in February.

In April, further means of eluding the guards was undertaken. Étienne Trompette, cabinet maker to the King, was instructed to make a wardrobe of mahogany inlaid with oak, about eight feet high; within the wardrobe were to be two sliding doors concealed behind shelves. 'It would be possible', admitted Trompette, 'by removing the shelves . . . and after having opened the sliding door in the middle and the sliding door at the back, to pass through the wardrobe as one passes through a door.' Another witness, Marie-Pierrette Dutour, was told by Trompette's apprentice that several such wardrobes were placed in the Tuileries so as to mask the door behind them; 'one can go out of the door itself against which stands the wardrobe.'

Finally, the royal family needed to be dressed in clothes which did not give away their status. It was hardly disguise; the King wore a brown frocked coat and waistcoat, a brown wig and a round hat. The Queen wore a black hat with a veil. For Madame Royale a very simple linen dress of 'goose-turd green' sprigged with blue and white was ordered. Madame de Tourzel's daughter, Pauline, had made 'a little dress of linen with a bonnet to dress Monseigneur le Dauphin. We made use of it', added the marquise, 'with success.' This is confirmed in the account given in the Auckland Manuscripts. William Eden, later Lord Auckland, was undoubtedly in touch with Fersen, a circumstance which lends particular authority to his version.

Fersen was the most active agent in planning the escape and

all the arrangements for the departure from Paris were made under his supervision. Once clear of Paris he was to leave the royal party and ride to Valenciennes. From that point, all the arrangements were made by the marquis de Bouillé who commanded the troops in the area known as 'les Trois Evêchés' – Metz, Toul and Verdun. Under his command was the duc de Choiseul-Stainville, a nephew of Louis XV's famous minister.

Choiseul, who was closer to the Court, has more to say about the background:

> The King had no desire to leave his kingdom; consequently none of the plans which had been suggested to him for this undertaking, to go to Belgium or to England, was acceptable to him. It was therefore necessary for him to choose a place in which he could enjoy full security against any sort of insurrection; where he would be surrounded by a faithful armed force and where it would be possible, in peace and quiet, as I have often heard him say, for him to make himself the arbiter between all parties, the regulator of all claims and to make them all submit to the yoke of reason and of the public good . . . He was resolved, once the just rights of the royal authority had been re-established and the Constitution, freely debated, had been sanctioned by him, to go to Compiègne. He would stay there for quite a long time and enforce the fundamental laws of the State, far from the pressures of Paris and its mob, and remain there until the Constitution was in full working order.

Louis' destination was, however, no longer a question of geography. Mirabeau had suggested Rouen because, in October 1789, Normandy was particularly loyal to the King. But now the Revolution had its army. Louis must be protected by military force. Choiseul is insistent: the King's desire to be surrounded by the most loyal troops was for his protection only. There was but one man whose devotion was beyond all doubt and whose control over his troops was equal to the occasion, and that was the marquis de Bouillé. 'The confidence that his soldiers had in him,' wrote Choiseul, 'the brilliance of his courage, the good luck that always seemed to accompany him, made him almost by necessity the man for the job.' But the same necessity dictated Montmédy, the central stronghold of the area which he commanded, as the only possible place for the King to go to. Louis himself said: 'it is absolutely necessary that I go to the area of the only general who has remained at his post and has not abandoned me.' Montmédy, therefore was to be the destination, and the road to Montmédy passes through Varennes.

According to the comte Louis de Bouillé it was in October 1790 that the planning began. The Bishop of Pamiers, Monseigneur d'Agoult, proposed the idea. The project was put before Louis who gave the answer: 'the King has not yet considered any plan for retreat or for flight, but he approves the idea which has been offered to him and he counts upon the favourable dispositions both of the Emperor and of Spain.'

On 26 October d'Agoult arrived in Metz to confer with Bouillé. It was necessary to assure him that the King's ultimate aim was to set up the Constitution, for as Bouillé's son said, 'it was no part of his principles to serve despotism which he detested as much as he detested anarchy.' Once satisfied as to the purity of Louis' intentions, Bouillé was ready to stake all for his cause.

The young Bouillé, who was barely twenty-one at the time, was his father's emissary and agent, and on Christmas day 1790 he came to Paris to establish liaison with d'Agoult and Fersen. Fersen alone maintained contact with the King and Queen.

Bouillé and Fersen established a code which they were confident could never be deciphered. All the main personalities mentioned were given two names, which were used alternately; the King was Arnoult or Barbier; La Fayette was Ervé or Fourreau, Mirabeau was Erissel or Fayel. The alphabet was mostly numerical. In the course of six months' correspondence this code was never cracked.

The first action was for the King to ask the Emperor to make hostile demonstrations on the frontier a fortnight before the date of the departure of the royal family from

Paris. This would enable the marquis de Bouillé to make a redisposition of his troops, without incurring suspicion, so that the most loyal units could be concentrated in the vicinity of Montmédy and disposed along the route which the royal family was to follow. Mercy insisted on the necessity of this escort; 'one shudders to think of the horrors which would ensue if you were betrayed or arrested.' Fersen was not of the same mind. On 29 May he wrote to Bouillé: 'there are no precautions to be taken from here to Chalons, the best of all precautions is to take none; everything depends upon speed and secrecy.' He suggested having no troops before Varennes, 'so as not to excite any attention in the countryside. The King would simply pass through.'

On 15 June Louis gave his orders: 'my intention being to go to Montmédy on 20 June, the Sieur de Bouillé . . . is commanded to place troops as he judges necessary for the security of myself and my family.' He disposed them as follows. At Pont de Somme-Vesle, the next posting station after Chalons, the first detachment of forty hussars was to await the King. At Sainte-Menehould would be forty more; at Clermont 140. At Varennes would be another forty and a relay of horses ready as it was not a posting station. At Dun another detachment of 100 was to join the escort and at Stenay 300. The royal berlin was to arrive at Montmédy surrounded by a small army of 730 troops. The official, but plausible pretext for this escort was to safeguard the passage of bullion for the payment of the troops.

The duc de Choiseul was to leave Paris twelve hours in advance of the royal party and to take command of the first detachment at Pont de Somme-Vesle. Here he was to seek the instructions of the King on the question of his incognito. If Louis was to preserve this, the troops were to pay no attention to the berlin, but to follow it half an hour later. If Louis was to travel as King, they were to escort him. In either case a small rear-guard was to be left to intercept any messengers from Paris.

It was decided that the royal party should leave on Sunday

19 June at midnight. The Emperor had at last agreed that on the 15 June an army of 15 000 would make a hostile demonstration on the frontier. The plan was ready to be put into action, but on the evening of 15 June a letter from the King announced a delay of twenty-four hours. Madame de Rochereuil, one of the *femmes de chambre* to the Dauphin, was still in service and her attachment to La Fayette rendered her suspect. The departure was fixed for Monday, 20 June, at midnight.

Three women and three men were to accompany the royal family – the marquise de Tourzel, Gouvernante des Enfants de France; Madame de Neuville, Première Femme de Chambre to the Dauphin; Madame Brunier, Première Femme de Chambre to Madame Royale. All three were unshakeable in their loyalty. The men were all drawn from the faithful of the former *gardes du corps* – Jean-François Maldent, François-Melchior Dumoustier and François-Florent Valory. These were to be the outriders. None of them knew of the project until it was almost time to depart.

The day passed exactly as it would have done normally. Only Madame Royale seems to have detected any difference in her parents. Marie-Thérèse was thirteen at the time; she described her experience a few years later:

> During the whole of the day my father and my mother seemed to me to be much agitated and occupied, without my knowing the reasons. After dinner [which was at half past one] they sent my brother and myself off into a room and shut themselves up with my aunt. I have learned since that it was at that moment that they informed my aunt of the plans they had for escaping. At five o'clock my mother took my brother and myself out for a walk at Tivoli, Monsieur Boutin's, at the end of the chausée d'Antin.
>
> During the walk my mother took me aside and told me not to worry about all that I saw, and that we would never be separated for long; that we would all be together again soon. I was dumbfounded, and I did not understand a word of all that: she kissed me and said that if my ladies asked why I was so agitated I was to say that she had scolded me but that we had made it up again. We returned at seven o'clock; I went back to

> my rooms feeling very sad, not understanding anything of what my mother had said.

The royal apartments in the Château des Tuileries were in the part of the building between the central Pavillon de l'Horloge and the Seine. Nearest the river, at the southern extremity of the façade, was the Pavillon de Flore in which were the rooms of Madame Elizabeth. The next two blocks contained the rooms of the Queen on the ground floor and of the King on the first floor, their windows overlooking the gardens. Behind the King's rooms and overlooking the entrance courts was the Galerie de Diane.

Louis' bedroom was approximately in the centre of the suite, with the Dauphin's room immediately to the south and that of Madame Royale beyond it. Marie-Antoinette's bedroom was beneath that of the Dauphin and communicated with it by means of a small staircase. Behind the Queen's rooms was a long corridor. At the northern end of the corridor was a door opening into the now empty apartment of the duc de Villequier. From the north end of this apartment a door opened into a courtyard.

The forecourt was divided by two low walls into three separate courtyards. In the centre, the Cour Royale opened towards the Louvre into the Place du Carrousel. This was the main entrance to the palace. To the south of the Cour Royale was the Cour des Princes. It was into this court that the duc de Villequier's apartment opened. Answering this court on the north side of the Cour Royale was the Cour des Suisses, much encumbered by buildings. Beyond this, and outside the confines of the Tuileries proper, was a square named the Petit Carrousel which connected by means of the rue de l'Échelle with the rue Saint-Honoré. It was a common sight to see standing here the carriages of visitors to the duchesse de La Vallière, whose house had no courtyard.

According to Lord Auckland:

> In the evening of 20 June Fersen went to receive the King's final orders. His Majesty observed to him that some suspicions

> were certainly entertained . . . and that the guards and sentinels had been doubled. Fersen observed that his departure might still be put off without any risk of discovery. The King said, perhaps without any risk to himself, but he saw danger for others. Fersen assured him there was none; and that de Bouillé would in the present circumstances find, if called upon, something plausible to say for having sent the detachment towards Chalons. The King thought for a minute and then said: 'No. Were I to perish at the gates of the Château I would still go. I would have given to all Europe an unequivocal proof of my sentiments.' He then spoke with cheerfulness, and added that, having finally taken his determination, he felt at ease.

As usual the comte and comtesse de Provence joined the royal family for supper. The comte de Provence, when he was Louis XVIII, wrote his own account of the events. He and his wife were also to emigrate that evening and successfully reached Brussels, thanks to the brilliant management of the young marquis d'Avaray, said Choiseul, 'who gloriously justified the choice for such an honour'.

'I went down to the Queen's rooms,' wrote Provence; 'I had to wait for her for some time as she was closeted with the three *gardes du corps* . . . At last she appeared; I ran to embrace her: "be careful not to cause me too much emotion," she said; "I don't want anyone to see that I have been crying." We had supper and we remained together, the five of us, until nearly eleven o'clock.' The King and his brother then went upstairs for the ceremony of the *coucher*.

In the meanwhile, the royal children had gone to bed at their accustomed hour of nine o'clock. Madame Brunier, whose duty it was to sleep in Madame Royale's room, had not yet passed into her own room to undress when Marie-Thérèse said that someone was knocking on the door. It was only when she heard the voice of the Queen, said Madame Brunier in her deposition, that she opened it. The Queen had come in and ordered her to get Madame up, to dress her at once and to come with her to the Dauphin's room; at the same time she was told that she and Madame de Neuville were to depart also. All she knew was that they were going to Claye where she would be given further instructions. No packing of any sort was possible; 'Madame est partie avec son mouchoir dans sa poche.'

She thought the time was about eleven o'clock when she went with Madame to the Dauphin's room; she found there Madame de Neuville and Madame de Tourzel. Madame Royale describes the meeting: 'my brother had also been woken by my mother and Madame de Tourzel conducted him to my mother's *entresol*. I went down with him. We found there one of the *gardes du corps* named Monsieur Maldent who was to take us out; my mother came several times to see us. My brother was dressed as a little girl; he looked sweet. As he was heavy with sleep he did not know what was going on. I asked him what he thought we were going to do. He said he thought we were going to act a play because we were dressed up.'

From there they went to an *entresol* which Madame Brunier had never known of before and from there they came down 'the little staircase which gives into the Cour des Princes and all the doors were open as usual'.

Madame de Neuville tells the same story from her own point of view. Some time between ten and half past ten, she had had her supper and was sitting reading a book when the marquise de Tourzel entered and gave her the order: 'get Monseigneur le Dauphin up, we have to leave!' When they got to the *entresol* they found the Queen, Madame Royale, Madame de Tourzel and Madame Brunier. Only Madame de Tourzel made mention of the state of emotion which must have been shared by all. When asked if Mesdames Neuville and Brunier had gone to the *entresol* or to the Queen's apartment she could only answer that 'in the state of agitation that she was in', she had not noticed.

At about a quarter past eleven Madame de Tourzel and the two children left the Cabinet de la Reine. The Queen conducted them along a corridor, which Madame de Tourzel had never seen before and which led to the door of the former apartment of the duc de Villequier. A man, whom Madame de Tourzel did not recognise, joined them and took the Dauphin by the hand. Madame de Tourzel took Madame Royale by the hand. Once again, being 'in a great state of agitation at this moment' she could give no details of the costume of this man. In the Cour des Princes a fiacre was waiting.

According to Quintin Crawfurd, a Scotsman who was a close neighbour and friend of Fersen, 'it was at half past ten that Fersen, disguised as a coachman, brought a vehicle which resembled a hired carriage into the Cour des Princes. Madame de Tourzel came out soon afterwards with the Dauphin and Madame Royale. Monsieur de Fersen, who came down from his seat to help them into the vehicle, told me that Madame Royale was in floods of tears.'

Madame Royale herself adds: 'to put people off the scent we drove about Paris for a little. At last we returned to the Petit Carrousel, which is very near the Tuileries. My brother was lying on the floor of the carriage beneath the skirts of Madame de Tourzel. We saw Monsieur de La Fayette drive past, who had been at the *coucher* of my father. We remained waiting there for one long hour without knowing what was happening. Never has time seemed to pass so slowly.' Presently Madame Elizabeth joined them.

Meanwhile the King had made no attempt to hasten the ceremony of the *coucher*. Pierre Hubert, *garçon du Château*, was precise about the timing: at twenty past eleven he had seen the King in his bed. He then went himself to sleep in the Salle du Billard, next but one to the Queen's bedroom. He stated that he had heard nothing that night which might have suggested a departure.

Louis, having got up almost immediately and dressed, left the Tuileries by the main door, according to Madame de Tourzel, 'avec une grande tranquillité'. He had taken the precaution of having the chevalier de Coigny, a man of a similar build and stature, go out of the same door at the same time in the same clothes for the last fortnight, with the result that no-one took any notice of him. He joined his children in the carriage. While they waited for the Queen, La Fayette drove past once more. 'On seeing him', said Lord Auckland, 'the King showed some emotion, but not of fear, and said, loud enough for Fersen to hear him, "the scoundrel!"'

The Queen was the last to leave. 'They waited for her a full quarter of an hour,' continues Auckland; 'she had been detained by unexpectedly finding a sentinel at the top of the stair she was to descend by. He was walking negligently backwards and forwards and singing. The Queen at last observed that as he went forward from the stair the pier of the arch must prevent him from seeing her. She took that opportunity quickly to descend without noise.'

Louis had found this waiting for his wife almost unbearable. 'The extreme attachment that he felt for her', says Madame de Tourzel, 'showed itself clearly in these circumstances by the way he expressed his uneasiness. As soon as she got into the vehicle he took her in his arms and kissed her with the words: "que je suis content de vous voir arriver!" They all embraced each other; all the royal family honoured me in the same way, and, convinced that we had cleared the obstacle which was the most difficult to overcome, we began to hope that Heaven looked with favour on our journey.' At about midnight they started off from the Petit Carrousel and drove to the Barrière Saint-Martin.

The last stage of the departure from Paris is described by Baltazar Sapel, Fersen's coachman. During the evening of Monday 20 June, four English horses were harnessed to the berlin. He had orders to drive the coach so as to arrive at exactly midnight at the 'new barrier of the faubourg Saint-Martin'. Sapel drew attention to the fact that one of the reins was broken, but the departure was not delayed. He stated that he had waited at the barrier for one and a half or two hours. At about half past two, 'when the day was beginning to break', he saw a carriage arriving at full speed, which drew up door to door with the berlin; a number of people got out of the one vehicle and into the next; Fersen mounted next to Sapel and gave the command 'now for it! Drive fast!' All the way along the road to Bondy Fersen was cracking his whip and saying. 'Come on, Baltazar, your horses are not in good fettle, drive faster!' Thus they arrived at Bondy in less than half an hour. They were, nevertheless, considerably behind schedule. Madame Brunier and Madame Neuville, who had left Paris in a separate vehicle, had to wait at Clayes for one and a quarter hours. Madame Neuville stated that she was 'greatly relieved by the ease with which they had passed the Barrière Saint-Martin.'

At Bondy, Fersen took leave of the King and Queen and rode off for Valenciennes. He only went on the absolute insistence of Louis. His departure left the royal family with no-one in charge – except for Louis himself: the duc de Choiseul was very uneasy that 'not one of the personnel was an experienced traveller.'

Choiseul was in Paris on the Monday. It had been agreed that he should leave at eleven that night and that he should take with him the Queen's coiffeur, Léonard. It was not until their carriage was beyond Claye and well on the way towards Meaux that Choiseul told the bewildered and indignant Léonard that the purpose of the journey was to collect a most important letter which he, Léonard, was to convey to the Queen. He ordered his courier to stop at Montmirail where they were to have supper and spend the night.

The next morning they passed through Chalons; 'all was very peaceful.' They arrived at Pont de Somme-Vesle at eleven. It was only a little before their arrival here that Choiseul told Léonard the real truth: in two hours' time the King, the Queen, the Dauphin, Madame Royale and Madame Elizabeth would arrive. Léonard was so overcome with emotion that he burst into tears.

On arrival at the posting station of Pont de Somme-Vesle, they found Monsieur Aubriot, who had just been promoted to Aide-de-Camp. On the pretext of seeing to the horses, Choiseul took Aubriot to the back of the stables and told him that their real business here was to protect the royal family on their way to Montmédy. Such was the intensity of Aubriot's devotion to the royal cause that he was almost overcome with emotion. 'I felt a tremor all over my body; it was as if sparks of fire coursed along my veins; in fact this confidence threw me into such confusion that I was unable to reply to the duc, who was in a state of agitation equal to my own.' With eager anticipation the two officers awaited the appearance of their sovereign.

The King was himself in a state of ever increasing euphoria. Once past the Barrière Saint-Martin, according to Madame de Tourzel, 'he began to be optimistic about his voyage. "Here I am out of that city of Paris where I have drunk so deeply of the cup of bitterness. You can be sure that once I feel my arse on the saddle I shall be a different man from what you have seen of me recently." At eight o'clock he took out his watch and observed: "At this moment La Fayette is personally much embarassed."'

'The more we advanced along our route,' continues Madame de Tourzel, 'the more we allowed ourselves to hope.' But on two occasions, she says, the horses fell and on one occasion all the traces were broken. 'we lost more than an hour repairing this disaster.' By the time that they reached Chalons they were something like three hours behind schedule. It does not seem to have worried them. One of the three former *gardes du corps* who accompanied the royal party, François-Florent Valory, has left his own account. 'Already the Queen and Madame Elizabeth showed signs of satisfaction and even of a little gaiety.' At the last relay before Chalons Marie-Antoinette said to him: 'François, it looks as if all is going well. If we were going to be stopped we should have been by now.' 'There is no longer anything to fear,' answered Valory; 'I have seen no signs of movement or suspicion anywhere. Courage, Madame! *Tout va bien.*' The King clearly thought the same. 'Once we are through Chalons, we will have nothing to fear. We will meet at Pont de Somme-Vesle the first detachment of troops and our journey is assured.'

All went smoothly at Chalons. 'After that', wrote Madame

de Tourzel, 'we were in a state of the utmost tranquility. But on arriving at Pont de Somme-Vesle what agony and anxiety we felt when the couriers reported that they could find no trace of the troops nor anyone who could give us any information; that they did not dare to make any enquiries for fear of arousing suspicions and that we must just hope that at Orbeval, which was the next post, we might be more lucky. But our luck had come to an end.'

During that afternoon the duc de Choiseul had been waiting with his hussars at Pont de Somme-Vesle. In a letter written on 10 June, Fersen had assured Bouillé that the berlin would arrive here 'by half past two at the latest'. Choiseul confirms that 'according to our calculations and agreements, the courier was to have preceded the vehicle by at least an hour. We expected to see him arrive at about two in the afternoon and the vehicle at three. At three o'clock, no courier, no vehicle. We walked along the roadway and one of us was always in advance on some raised ground from which one could see further. I cannot describe what I suffered from the need to restrain my feelings, to disguise the thoughts which were disturbing me, to maintain an appearance of unconcern when I was the prey to the deepest misgivings.'

The presence of the hussars was causing considerable unrest at Pont de Somme-Vesle. By one of those chances which it is easy to attribute to fate, there had been a local dispute over certain dues and rights between the duchesse d'Elbeuf and her tenants and the latter had been threatened with armed force. 'When they saw the hussars arrive,' wrote Choiseul, 'they thought that it was in order to take action against them.' Hostile crowds began to gather round Choiseul's deatchment. They said openly in front of the troops that the hussars were fine enough but that they outnumbered them. Already there were rumours that it was the Queen for whom they were waiting.

> Four o'clock struck. No courier, no news; and around us the gatherings and grumblings of the populace were increasing every minute; I persisted in remaining, I only took the action

> of sending my cabriolet as far as Stenay. In it went Léonard with a message for Monsieur D'Andoins at Sainte-Menehould in which I spoke of my fears occasioned by such an extraordinary delay, and of the obligation which I might face of removing my detachment . . . Might it not be a blunder on our part of the first order ourselves to create dangers for the King and not to put an end to the fermentation of the people if our removal of ourselves could have contributed to this? My whole duty was expressed in the words '*so act that the vehicle continues on its route without impediment.*'
>
> We heard five o'clock sound in the midst of the most lively and cruel anxieties, and our position became more and more fatal to the execution of the project . . . By persisting in remaining we could be the cause of a movement which would have resulted in the arrest of the King. It was about half past five; it was therefore four hours since the courier was due.

At this point Choiseul enquired of the post-master if there was no news of a convoy of money going to Metz. He was told that one had passed in the morning. Using this as a pretext, Choiseul ordered the withdrawal of his troops, saying: 'that is doubtless the convoy which we were expecting . . . our mission is of no further use, it only remains for us to depart.' They took a cross-country route to Varennes.

Not long after the hussars left Pont de Somme-Vesle the berlin entered. According to Choiseul this must have been after a quarter past six, when he himself departed. It is extremely difficult to establish even an approximate time scale. Witnesses often vary by as much as an hour, but there is more agreement between those at Sainte-Menehould than elsewhere. The post-master put the arrival at a quarter past seven, the Municipality, in a letter to the Assembly, at half past seven. The distance from Sainte-Menehould to Pont de Somme-Vesle is twenty-five kilometres. The average speed, as worked out by Girault de Coursac, was about ten kilometres per hour. This would place the arrival of the berlin at Pont de Somme-Vesle at about five o'clock. It would be difficult to place it much later than half past five. This later time would fit better with the statement by the Municipality of Chalons, and corroborated by Madame Royale, that the berlin had passed through there at about four o'clock. From Chalons to Pont de Somme-Vesle is a distance of seventeen kilometres. It seems as if Choiseul has somewhat exaggerated the time of his waiting, but he is hardly less accurate in his timings than anyone else.

The royal party, however, passed through the village without mishap, but deeply distressed at finding no troops. 'At Orbeval', continues Madame de Tourzel, 'we were no more fortunate. The same silence, the same uneasiness. We arrived at Sainte-Menehould in a state of violent agitation; it was made even worse when Monsieur d'Andoins, a captain in Choiseul's regiment, came for a moment to the vehicle and said: "the arrangements have been made badly; I must distance myself from you so as not to arouse suspicion." These few words pierced us to the heart, but there was nothing to do but to continue our journey.'

Captain d'Andoins makes no reference to this episode in his letter to the President of the Assembly. He states that at about seven in the evening he gave his troops the order to retire. About half an hour later (according to the report of the Municipality) d'Andoins noted that 'a large vehicle drove through which created no little sensation. After it had passed little groups began to form; they began to whisper; they were becoming excited. The call to arms sounded. There were cries of "arrêtez! Arrêtez!" Suddenly the street filled with armed men . . . the *garde nationale* came up to me and said that the King had been recognised and that we had been accused of having come to protect his passage. I went to the Hôtel de la Commune, which was already full of citizens of every class, each more excitable than the last.' D'Andoin's firmness restored order, but already the tocsin was sounding. From steeple to tower and from tower to steeple the call to action spread through the countryside. From Arger and Verrières, from Chaudefontaine and La Neuville-au-Pont, people came thronging to see what was happening at Sainte-Menehould.

What was happening was described in a letter written by the members of the Municipality early the next morning to the President of the National Assembly.

> Between half past seven and eight o'clock this afternoon there passed through this town two vehicles, crossing it from west to east; they were preceded by a courier and followed by another, both of them were dressed in the colour of chamois leather, and they went out, after having changed horses, without anyone having any suspicions about the persons who were being driven in them.
>
> Hardly had the vehicles been lost to sight, when the Sieur Drouet, post-master, having suspected some mystery, felt obliged to warn the Municipality. We assembled forthwith and all the inhabitants took up arms . . . At the same time we were confirmed in our fears by a despatch which was sent to us by the Directoir du Département de la Marne. We had already charged the Sieur Drouet, post-master, together with another of our inhabitants, to ride after the vehicles and to make them stop if they could catch up with them.

At Clermont, the next posting station, the comte de Damas was in charge of the troops. He had taken up his position earlier in the day and had informed himself of the dispositions between Clermont and Montmédy and especially about Varennes. General Goguelat, who was acting as courier, had reassured him: 'this little town was in no position to offer the slightest obstacle to the progress of the King.' Bouillé's younger son and Monsieur de Raigecourt were in charge of the sixty hussars there.

At half past seven a cabriolet arrived containing Léonard, who handed Damas a letter from Choiseul which stated: 'there is no likelihood that the treasure will pass today; I am leaving to rejoin Monsieur de Bouillé; you will receive further orders tomorrow.' It sounded plausible enough; the King had already postponed his journey several times. Damas, however, decided to remain at Clermont as long as was possible. Two hours later, at about half past nine, he ordered his troops to their quarters. It had the desired effect. The crowds dispersed; the inhabitants returned to their homes. Damas was left to his thoughts. 'Darkness had almost come and all was tranquility in the town, and although I had lost all hope I could not turn my attention nor my eyes from the road to Paris, when suddenly I heard the noise of carriages; I caught sight of a courier and the royal family arrived.'

The courier was Valory, who was riding with the vehicles instead of an hour in advance of them. Damas urged him to get on as quickly as possible to Varennes. It only took ten minutes to change the horses. Damas had a brief exchange of words with the occupants of the coach: the Queen especially managed to convey her sense of satisfaction at seeing him. He did his best to appear detached, 'but what would be impossible for me to describe was the joy that I felt when I saw the postilions mounted . . . and leaving the town . . . As they left one of the couriers called to the postilions to take the road to Varennes . . . Once they arrived at this post I regarded them as being secure. There were only three leagues [twelve kilometres] to Varennes and a superb roadway.'

He reckoned without Drouet.

Jean-Baptiste Drouet, post-master at Sainte-Menehould and formerly a dragoon in the Regiment de Condé, has left his own account. When the berlin arrived his curiosity was aroused. 'I thought I recognised the Queen, whom I had seen once before,' he wrote. 'Noticing opposite her a rather large man, I was struck by the resemblance to the image of the King that was printed on the fifty livre assignats.' The animated way in which this man conversed in a low voice with his courier, the arrival of dragoons, supposedly to escort the passage of bullion, the haste with which the horses were harnessed, all contributed to confirm his suspicions, but still he hesitated to raise what might be a false alarm. 'I let the vehicle pass,' he records, 'but seeing the dragoons getting ready to mount their horses I ran to the guard room; I sounded the call-to-arms; the *garde nationale* opposed the departure of the dragoons, and, feeling sufficiently convinced, I went with Guillaume in pursuit of the King.'

Drouet, who naturally presumed that the destination of the royal family was Metz, took the road for Clermont; had he reached it, Damas would have arrested him. But somewhere just short of Clermont he met his postilions returning. They had overheard the King's courier ordering the new postilions to turn left for Varennes, as Damas had noted. Drouet and Guillaume turned off the highway and took to the woodland by-roads in order to head off the berlin before it reached Varennes.

Somewhere in this same Forêt de l'Argonne, Choiseul and his hussars, after their retreat from Pont de Somme-Vesle, were stumbling through the darkness. 'The route through this wood', wrote Choiseul, 'is extremely difficult and dangerous; its ups and downs were precipitous. Night overtook us, so that we were often obliged to proceed on foot in order to explore the ground and to avoid falling into deep pits. One hussar did fall into one; his comrades would not abandon him; we had to look for him, pick him up and wait for him to recover consciousness, and this accident lost us some three quarters of an hour.'

For Drouet and Guillaume it was a race against time. Once the King was through Varennes it might be impossible to prevent him from reaching Montmédy. All that Drouet recorded of that ride was that the night was very dark.

Down on the main road the berlin passed without being noticed through the little village of Neuvilly. There were only eight kilometres to go. 'We continued our route,' writes Madame Royale. It was now nearly twenty-four hours since they had left the Tuileries; physically and psychologically they were exhausted; 'the night had fallen and in spite of the agitation and uneasiness that was felt, everyone was asleep in the vehicle. We were awakened by a terrible jolt and at the same time we were told that no-one knew where the courier was who rode in front of the coach. You can imagine the fear that we felt; we thought he had been recognised and taken.'

The courier, the comte de Valory, had been the first to

arrive at Varennes. He had, he claimed, 'a secret presentiment that he would not find in the agreed place the relay horses, which were the responsibility of the younger son of Monsieur de Bouillé.' According to Bouillé it had been agreed that General Goguelat was to position relay horses at Varennes for the King 'so that he would find them at the entrance to the town'.

Valory inspected the outskirts of the forest, he penetrated into the woods; he tried to make his voice heard; he came back out of the wood . . . he called again, without result; no-one answered. Convinced that the relay horses were not here, he had no alternative than to enter the town in order to get information as quickly as possible from an inn as to whether a coachman, a postilion and four horses were not awaiting a carriage . . . It was nearly eleven o'clock at night; the town was quiet . . . In the silence of the night he heard the King's carriage coming down the hill and then stopping . . . he decided to go back to the vehicle to see if by any chance the horses were being changed.

It was at this moment that Drouet and Guillaume arrived at Varennes. Drouet's account is:

> It was eleven at night, it was very dark, everyone in Varennes was in bed; the carriages were drawn up alongside the houses and there was a dispute going on between the postilions and the drivers of the vehicles; the post-master at Clermont had forbidden the postilions to continue beyond Varennes without first refreshing their horses. The King, fearing that he might be pursued, was trying to hasten their departure and would not hear of any time for refreshment; so that while they were disputing we ran quickly into the town and left our horses at an inn [Le Bras d'Or] which we found open. I spoke to the inn-keeper [Monsieur Le Blanc]; I took him aside, because there were a lot of people there and I did not want to be overheard. I said: 'are you a good patriot?' 'Yes, you may depend upon it,' came the answer. 'Good, my friend, run quickly and alert all whom you know to be honest men, tell them that the King is at the top of the town and that he is going to come down and that we must stop him.'

They then went and overturned a furniture cart across the entrance to the bridge.

Meanwhile Valory was leading the berlin down the hill into the town. They had to pass beneath an archway which attached to the Church of Saint-Gengoult and spanned the road. 'As we came out the other side of the archway,' said Valory, 'about six men, each one armed with a gun with bayonet fixed, took aim at him and called on him to stop or they would open fire . . . at this moment the tocsin began to ring, the call to arms was sounded and people began to throng the streets. Madame Neuville and Madame Brunier were forced out of their carriage and taken to the house of the district attorney, Monsieur Sauce. They were asked to produce their passport. They were both absolutely terrified – 'saisies de frayeur' – they said that the passport was in the next vehicle. Unfortunately the passport stated that 'Madame de Korff' was travelling to Frankfurt. The road to Frankfurt was by way of Verdun and Metz. No one travelling to Frankfurt would have turned off for Varennes.

Monsieur Sauce was in a difficult position. The passport, as such, was in order. The suspicion that the berlin contained the royal family was only a suspicion. Seldom can a *petit fonctionnaire* in an utterly unimportant little township have been called upon to make so momentous a decision. He took the only action which was safe in the circumstances: he played for time. He insisted on the travellers getting out of their coach and coming into his house. He would deal with the matter at daybreak.

Louis was also in a difficult position. He was still officially posing as the man-servant of the baronne de Korff. He could not assume the rights of royalty and act as King without admitting the falsity of his passport. The matter was decided by Sauce. There lived at Varennes a judge, a Monsieur Detez, who was in a position to recognise the King. Detez was summoned and confirmed that it was indeed the royal family.

There was nothing Louis could do but admit the fact. '"Oui, je suis votre Roi!" he cried, and by an outpouring of his soul, tender and paternal, he embraced those who surrounded him.' Deep in the heart of every Frenchman was an almost hereditary love of his sovereign, but more recently and more vividly this had been overlaid by a love for his country. For many, King and country were still inseparable in thought, but Drouet had implied that the King was deserting his country. 'The scene was deeply moving,' continues the *procès-verbal* of the Municipality, 'but it did not shake the commune in its desire to keep its King . . . He, however, persisted that he should depart for Montmédy, adding on his word of honour as King, that he would not leave the country and inviting the *garde nationale* to accompany him.'

By this time Choiseul had arrived with his hussars and was offering to force a way through the crowd and extricate the royal family before it was too late, but, as Bouillé later observed, 'he had to resign himself to that *cruel goodness* of Louis XVI, which was perhaps as disastrous for France as it was for him, and which led him on this occasion, as on so many others, to oppose any measure which might shed blood on his behalf.'

Choiseul found the royal family in two wretched rooms on the first floor; 'I went up a spiral staircase which led to them,' he wrote; 'in the middle of the room was a table on which there was some bread and a few glasses; on one bed, overcome with fatigue, slept Monsieur le Dauphin; Madame de Tourzel was seated by this bed with her head in her hands, with Mesdames Brunier and Neuville beside her; next to the window were Madame Elizabeth and Madame Royale. The King and Queen were standing and talking to Monsieur Sauce and some members of the municipality.'

At about half past twelve the comte de Damas arrived also and saw the same scene. 'The King seemed full of confidence in the promise of the municipality. His bearing was firm but calm. At daybreak I went downstairs to see what state of mind prevailed. I went to the Hôtel de Ville; the Commune was assembled. It was utter chaos. The Mayor, who appeared to have the best intentions, could not make himself heard. Some were shouting that the King must be taken to Paris, others, to Verdun.' Damas extricated himself with some difficulty and returned to the house of Monsieur Sauce. Outside there were shouts of 'Vive le Roi! Vive la Reine!' There were shouts of 'À Paris! À Verdun!' The confusion, continues Damas, 'became ever greater, the obstacles increased each minute'.

In the middle of all this pandemonium, Monsieur Sauce's grandmother heard that the royal family was at his house. She came to pay her homage. 'It is a picture which I shall not omit,' wrote Choiseul. 'On Monsieur Sauce's bed could be seen the two angelic forms of the young Prince and Madame Royale sunk in the deepest sleep.' Madame Sauce, who had already passed her eightieth year, 'struck by the beauty of the two children, by the majestic air of the Queen and by the calm courage of the King, fell on her knees, burst into tears and begged permission to kiss the hands of these children . . . she prayed beside them, blessed them and departed in tears.'

Their fate was soon to be sealed. At about five o'clock, according to Choiseul, a Deputy from the National Assembly, Monsieur Romeuf, arrived at Varennes. He had been joined at Chalons by an officer of the *garde nationale* of Paris, named Baillon. It was he who first entered into the presence of the King, his hair in disorder, his clothes in disarray and his voice trembling with emotion. 'Sire . . . they are all cutting each other's throats in Paris . . . our wives, our children may all be massacred . . . you will not go any further . . . Sire, the welfare of the State . . . Yes, Sire, our wives, our children!' 'Am I not a mother also?' asked Marie-Antoinette, indicating her two children. 'What is it you really want?' asked Louis. 'Sire, the decree of the Assembly.' Louis was handed a note which was in effect the warrant for his arrest. He passed it on to the Queen with the words: 'There is no longer a King in France.'

The Constitution

The return journey from Varennes is described by Madame de Tourzel. She was a person wholly devoted to the principle of absolute monarchy in general and to the royal family of France in particular. She constantly applies the adjective 'auguste' to them. She was every inch a courtier and was equally outraged to see a man with his hat on in the presence of the King as by the 'insolent familiarity' with which Their Majesties were so often addressed.

'One cannot imagine the sufferings of the royal family on this luckless journey; their suffering was both physical and moral, nothing was spared them.' The weather was insufferably hot and the land was dry and the clouds of dust put up by those who accompanied the coach added to their discomfort. They were not allowed to lower the blinds to shade themselves from the pitiless glare of the sun. The people must be allowed to see them clearly and to gloat. The air was filled with their clamour; cries of 'Vive la Nation! Et l'Assemblée Nationale!' resounded in the ears of the royal party and was redoubled at every village and township through which they passed. Ugly incidents occurred.

'As the King was going along the high road between Clermont and Sainte-Menehould,' continues Madame de Tourzel, 'we heard shots and saw a crowd of national guards running into a field. The King asked what was going on. "Nothing," came the reply; "it's a madman and they're killing him." We learnt a little later that it was Monsieur de Dampierre, a gentleman of Clermont and brother of the Bishop, and that his eagerness in seeking to approach His

Majesty's carriage rendered him suspect in the eyes of the national guard.' This was a great shock to the royal family and their own suffering was increased by the thought of the danger to which those who showed any attachment to them were exposed.

Wherever they halted for a meal or to change horses they were greeted by the jeering of the populace and often by official insults from district presidents or mayors who rebuked Louis for trying to desert his country and to deliver it into the hands of its enemies – for such was the official interpretation put on the attempt to reach Montmédy.

There were, however, certain moments of respite – interludes which offered relative peace and the consolation of being treated with kindness and even respect. 'The town of Chalons', asserts Madame de Tourzel, 'was far from sharing the opinions of those others through which the King had passed.' The sympathy of the inhabitants for the sufferings of the royal family could be read on almost every face, which clearly showed those sentiments which they dared not express.

The royal visitors were lodged in the Hôtel de l'Intendance, the same house in which Marie-Antoinette had stayed on 11 May 1770 on her first arrival into France, when the fireworks had flashed and sparkled in the night and all the public fountains flowed with wine.

Meanwhile, the National Assembly had appointed Latour-Maubourg, Barnave and Pétion to go and meet the royal family and to accompany them on the last stage of their return journey. It is to Pétion that we owe the account of the mission of the three Deputies.

'Off we went, on a very fine day,' he wrote; 'the postilions, who knew the object of our journey, drove us at a great speed. In the villages, the market towns and cities everywhere along our route we were greeted with expressions of joy, friendship and respect.

'At about a league and a half before Épernay we caught sight of a great cloud of dust and we could hear a great noise.

People came up to our carriage and said: "Voilà le Roi!"' The Deputies stopped and waited for him.

They were greeted by the Queen and Madame Elizabeth with some enthusiasm. Their presence was welcomed as a safeguard against any maltreatment of their *gardes du corps* or of themselves. Marie-Antoinette hastened to inform the Deputies: 'the King had no intention of leaving the country.' Louis also assured them: 'I was not going out; I have declared as much; that is true.' It was clearly not regarded as true by Petion and his companions.

They told the King that it was understood that they should travel in his coach, but it already contained six persons. Louis would not consent to any of these being separated from him and begged the Deputies to seat themselves. 'The King, the Queen and the Prince Royal (for such was the new style of the Dauphin) were facing forwards. The Queen took the Prince on her knees, Barnave placed himself between the King and the Queen. Madame de Tourzel took Madame on her knees and I took my place between Madame de Tourzel and Madame Elizabeth.'

Once they were settled, Pétion began to adjust to the experience of finding himself at very close quarters to the royal family. 'I became aware of an atmosphere of simplicity and a sense of family, which pleased me; there was no royal ceremoniousness but a feeling of ease and of happy family; the Queen called Madame Elizabeth *ma petite soeur*; Madame Elizabeth replied in the same way. Madame Elizabeth called the King *mon frère*; the Queen dandled the Prince on her knees; the King looked on at all this with an air of satisfaction, though with little emotion or sensibility.'

As the disorderly procession approached Dormans and the light was beginning to fade, Pétion turned his attention to Barnave and observed that his bearing towards the Queen seemed honest and reserved and that their conversation had 'nothing mysterious' about it.

The next day, Friday 24 June, Pétion sat between the King and the Queen. 'We were very uncomfortable. The young

Prince sat on my knee and played with me; he was full of gaiety and very restless.'

Louis attempted to make conversation with Pétion – about England and the commercial genius of that country – 'but after a few phrases he became confused, noticed the fact and blushed. This difficulty in expressing himself I noticed several times. Those who do not know him might be tempted to take this shyness for stupidity; but they would be wrong. It is very rare for him to let slip anything ill-judged and I have never heard him say anything foolish.'

Thus the journey continued past Château-Thierry towards La Ferté-sous-Jouarre and Meaux. 'The windows were always down,' states Pétion; 'we were baked by the sun and suffocated by the dust; but with the people from the countryside and the national guard following us in procession it was impossible to do otherwise because they wanted to see the King.'

La Ferté-sous-Jouarre provided another pleasant interlude; they stopped to dine at the house of the Mayor, 'beautifully situated on the banks of the Marne'. The Mayor, the Sieur Renard, writes Madame de Tourzel, 'had provided in advance everything that could have alleviated the situation of the royal family during the short time that they passed under his roof. They found the rooms cool, refreshments and a simple but properly served dinner and an excellent staff. Madame Renard, having the delicacy not to wish to eat with the royal family, dressed herself as a cook and served them with as much attention as respect.' Renard himself admitted to Louis 'that he dared not give outward expression of the sentiments which he felt . . . but that his heart was wholly devoted to the King.' If the giving of a cup of water to a thirsty man earns the giver a place in the Kingdom of Heaven, the Renards qualified for theirs on this day.

After dinner, Pétion took on Madame Elizabeth in a *tête à tête*. 'I described to her how the King was surrounded by the wrong people, counselled by the wrong people. I spoke to her of all the intrigues, all the manoeuvring of the Court, with the dignity of a free man and the disdain of a wise man.'

Meanwhile Barnave was talking quietly to the Queen, 'but so far as I could see', noted Pétion, 'in a fairly indifferent manner.'

It was a more relaxed party that took the road again for Meaux. Marie-Antoinette was in a more communicative mood. 'The King is often blamed,' she argued, 'but people do not fully realise the position that he is in. He is given accounts of events which contradict each other; he does not know what to believe. He is given a succession of counsels which cross and cancel each other out; he does not know what to do . . . his position is untenable . . . it is this which determined him to leave the capital.'

The final stage of the return from Varennes is described by Lord Gower in his dispatch of 25 June. 'The King and royal family arrived this evening at seven o'clock. The order and regularity with which the whole of their entry was conducted was astonishing. They were carried round the outside of the walls of the town till they came to the Grille of Chaillot and from thence proceeded in a direct line through the Champs Elysées and the Place Louis XV to the gardens of the Tuileries.'

The marquis de Ferrières also describes the reception given by Paris to its recaptured King. In contrast with the yelling and shouting which had for so long accompanied the royal family, they were now greeted with sullen and ominous silence. 'The people', he wrote, 'observed the most profound silence; they saw Louis XVI go past without experiencing the slightest feelings of compassion. The national guards shouted: "keep your hats firmly on! He will appear before his judges." Louis XVI, however, was subjected to no personal abuse. Placards had been put up that morning in the faubourg Saint-Antoine: "anyone who applauds the King will be beaten with rods; anyone who insults him will be hanged."'

Among the spectators was the Spanish Ambassador, Count Fernan Nuñez. 'The procession came to a standstill', he wrote, 'at the pedestal of the statue of Louis XV in that same square which the sovereigns had crossed, in the days of their splendour, amid the most enthusiastic acclamations of this same people, who seemed to need to show their adoration for them at the time of their marriage and after the birth of the Dauphin. To what reflections must they not have given themselves up in so cruel a situation? I was a witness to this atrocious spectacle; my hair stood on end and tears started involuntarily in my eyes. At last, at seven o'clock, they crossed the bridge [the Pont Tournant at the entry to the Tuileries gardens] and arrived before the palace which they had had as much joy as difficulty in leaving four days previously.'

Ferrières appears to have been present there also. 'On arrival at the palace,' he wrote, 'the Queen was at the extremity of weakness. The vicomte de Noailles and the baron de Menou helped her out of the coach and conducted her to her apartment, accompanied by a numerous guard. The King went to his own rooms. The Dauphin was put into a separate room.' Fernan Nuñez fills in the details: 'The King behaved in his usual manner, and as soon as he found himself in his own apartment he asked to see his ministers . . . The Queen was in a more emotional state than the King, but without losing her outward dignity, although the effort which she had to make to maintain it betrayed the just anger which was devouring her soul.' Fernan Nuñez knew Marie-Antoinette extremely well and he could read her features. 'The innocent, unhappy Dauphin was laughing and skipping as if he had no idea what was happening; his sister, who is of an age to have feelings but not to hide them, showed without any reserve the state of her heart.'

On 18 July Gower made the observation: 'though the rage of republicanism may be overcome, it will be difficult to conquer the disgust the King's behaviour has inspired.' It was, of course, not so much Louis' conduct as the interpretation put upon it by his enemies which created the disgust. Madame Roland – a bitter opponent of kingship – wrote in her memoirs: 'Varennes was my greatest argument.'

The news of the return from Varennes brought Gouverneur Morris back to Paris from London. 'The intention of the Assembly is, I find, to cover up the King's flight and cause it to be forgotten.' For the moderates in the Assembly the urgent need was to demonstrate the solidarity between the King and the Government, for the time was fast approaching when their project for a Constitution which incorporated a hereditary monarchy had to be agreed by both the Assembly and the King. The leader of the moderates was Barnave.

During the return journey from Varennes, and unnoticed by Pétion, Barnave had been successfully striking up a relationship with the Queen. While Pétion was flattering himself that his masculine charms had so attracted Madame Elizabeth that 'had we been alone she would have fallen into my arms and yielded to the dictates of nature', Marie-Antoinette was making a real conquest of Barnave.

Antoine Barnave, a young lawyer from Grenoble, had appeared in the early days of the Revolution as an enemy of monarchy, but by now he was a moderate and a firm believer in constitutional monarchy. Being, as he was, thrown together with Marie-Antoinette was an opportunity not to be missed.

The Queen, however, did not make nice distinctions between different grades of Revolutionaries. To her they were all enemies of the Crown. She had no real common ground with Barnave. 'I felt', she wrote to Jarjayes, the husband of one of her *femmes de chambre*, 'that there was nothing for it but to reach and establish a sort of correspondence with him, but holding back, as the first condition, from always saying how I really thought.'

Barnave particularly wanted her to persuade her brother, the Emperor, of the necessity of the Constitution for the regeneration of the monarchy. He wanted Leopold to acknowledge the new government and to 'express in no uncertain terms his friendly and pacific intentions towards the French nation'. Barnave really hoped that the Revolution could be regarded as having achieved its object. 'Everyone must feel that it is the common interest that the Revolution should come to a halt.'

Marie-Antoinette wrote to the Emperor as requested, but she sent a note to Mercy at the same time saying: 'I felt obliged to yield to the decrees of the leaders of the party here. It is extremely important for me that for some time still they believe that I am wholly in their way of thinking.'

She was nothing of the sort. Her real intentions are made clear in her correspondence during all this time with Fersen.

On 30 June, soon after the return from Varennes, Marie-Antoinette wrote to Fersen: 'I still exist . . . How anxious I have been about you and how I feel for you in all that you suffer from having no news!' On the same day Fersen had written to her: 'I leave tomorrow for Brussels and from thence to Vienna in order to negotiate and try to get all the Powers together.' Fersen enclosed a letter from Gustavus to Louis: 'I pray Your Majesty to have no doubts about the sympathetic attitude which we all take to your misfortune. Your friends will not abandon you. Endure with firmness your present position, as you have endured the dangers which have surrounded you; above all do not suffer anyone to debase your royal dignity and kings will come to your rescue'.

On 4 July Fersen received a letter written in the Queen's cipher. It was not in her handwriting and it was not signed, but it is difficult to see from whom it might have come if not from her. It is a mixture of instructions about methods of communication and professions of love and devotion. 'Je peux vous dire que je vous aime,' she wrote. 'Goodbye, most loved and loving of all men. I embrace you with all my heart.'

Four days later, on 8 July, the Queen wrote again to Fersen. Her letter purports to be a passing on of the thoughts of Louis. Four of the paragraphs begin with 'The King thinks . . .' She summarises herself: Louis 'desires that the captivity of the King should be known and established by the foreign powers; he desires that the good will of his relations, friends and allies, and the other sovereigns who would be willing to join forces, should manifest itself in the form of a congress in which the method of negotiation would be followed, it being understood that there will be an imposing force to back them up, but always well in the background to avoid provoking crimes and massacres.'

After the King had accepted the constitution, Marie-Antoinette wrote: 'to refuse would have been more noble but it was impossible in the circumstances in which we are.' Fersen replied, asking if she was really in sympathy with the Revolution; if she needed help; if she had a plan. 'Forgive all these questions,' he concluded; 'I flatter myself that you will see them only as the desire to be of service to you and as a proof of an attachment and a devotion which knows no bounds.'

Fersen now steps into the position of the director of Marie-Antoinette's action and behaviour. He tells her to whom she must write, and how to write; he advises when it should be for the King to write in person; he reminds her to thank those who have obliged her; above all he is perfectly frank in indicating where the most obvious dangers lie.

The exact nature of Marie-Antoinette's relationship with Fersen has intrigued her biographers. He was utterly devoted to the royal family. He was an ardent royalist and desired passionately to save the crown of France. The death of Louis XVI appalled him; so did the death of his son. On Saturday 27 June 1795, he wrote in his journal: 'the post arrived and brought me the fatal news of the death of the young King Louis XVII. This event caused me the keenest sorrow. It was the last and only interest which remained to me in France.'

Within the royal family, of course, Fersen had a very special devotion to Marie-Antoinette. It could be called a tender affection; but was she ever his mistress?

For evidence one would naturally look at the voluminous correspondence between them and see if either gave anything away. Much of this correspondence was in the archives of Stafsund, belonging to the descendants of Axel's sister Hedda. In 1878 the Baron R. M. Klinckowstrom published twenty-two letters and portions of Fersen's *Journal Intime*. But there were many erasures. These were blotted out in the original letters and represented by a series of dots in the printed version. The family believed that these erasures had been made by Fersen himself. When the Baron Axel Klinckowstrom inherited the archives he found the appropriate envelope empty and concluded that his father had burnt the letters.

The reason for these erasures and for the burning of the original letters must be a matter for conjecture. The letters from Fersen to Eleanore Sullivan, his mistress, were also burnt and it looks as if Klinckowstrom was interested in protecting Fersen's name from scandal. It has also been suggested that the passages erased might have contained information about codes or the means whereby letters were conveyed. The times were perilous and there were many matters which it might have been prudent to expunge.

The only identifiable occasion on which Fersen might be thought to have slept with Marie-Antoinette was the night of Monday 13 February 1792, when he made a secret visit to Paris on behalf of Gustavus III. His *Journal Intime* has survived and Alma Soderhjelm reproduced the relevant page in her book, *Fersen et Marie-Antoinette*.

He has, he says, arrived safely in Paris at half past five in the afternoon. He had, or thought he had, a *rendez-vous* with Goguelat, now the Queen's private secretary, at six o'clock, which seems to have been the usual hour for private or secret meetings with the King or Queen. Goguelat finally turned up at seven. Fersen's letter to him had only arrived at midday and it had not been possible to contact him.

Now comes the important passage (I have inserted accents and punctuation): 'allé chez *elle*; passé par mon chemin ordinaire; peur des gards: nat:; son logement à merveille; pas vu le Roi.' There follows a smudged erasure which covers the space of about eight letters.

If 'allé chez *elle*' does not mean the Queen it must almost certainly mean Eleanore Sullivan, with whom Fersen usually stayed in Paris. Usually when Fersen mentions the Queen he writes 'Elle' – with a capital E; usually when he mentions Eleanore he writes El. If *elle* means the Queen that implies that Fersen went to the Tuileries that evening. It is suggested by Alma Soderhjelm that the smudge conceals the words *resté là* which Fersen often uses to remind himself that he slept with the lady in question. What interpretation is put on these facts is a matter of conjecture.

Meanwhile the plans for establishing the Constitution were going ahead. On 5 August Lord Gower was able to enclose a copy of the projected Constitution to which Louis had to agree. 'The great difficulty', he wrote, 'seems to be how this is to be done; if in his present state of confinement it will be a mere mockery; if he is previously allowed his liberty it is uncertain what use he may make of it; so far, however, from that being the case at present, the guard at the Tuileries has been increased within these two days. It is generally believed that the King will go to Rambouillet or Fontainebleau, where he will accept the Constitution.'

In spite of the show of enthusiasm for the Constitution it was soon apparent that it could never work. On 30 September Morris wrote to George Washington: 'it is a general and almost universal conviction that the Constitution is inexecutable.' The flight to Varennes had shown Louis that he was wrong in hoping that the provinces would rise in his support. There seemed to be no hope of restoring order from within France; could there be any help expected from outside?

A letter from Burke's son Richard, dated from Brussels on 6 August, gives his father's opinion on the situation: 'in the present state of things, you have nothing to hope *from the interior of your dominions*, nothing, nothing *for a long time to come* . . . It is only from abroad that relief can come.' A fortnight later Edmund Burke himself wrote to Marie-Antoinette: 'If the King accepts the Constitution you are both of you lost. It is not adroitness, it is firmness alone that can save you.'

On 26 August Marie-Antoinette wrote to Mercy: 'we have

no other resource than that of the foreign powers. At all costs they must come to our rescue, but it is for the Emperor to place himself at the head and arrange everything. It is essential that, as a first condition, he should stipulate that the King's brothers and the French [*émigrés*], but particularly the former, should keep back and not show themselves.'

On 27 August Leopold met with Frederick William of Prussia at Schloss Pillnitz in Saxony. They declared their intention to enlist the support of the Powers of Europe 'in order to place the King of France in a position to consolidate the bases of monarchic government, equally expedient for the rights of sovereigns and for the welfare of the French nation'.

On Wednesday 14 September Gower sent to Whitehall a copy of Louis' letter to the National Assembly accepting the Constitution. 'He came in a state coach attended by the ministers, and having said that, in order to add to the solemnity of his acceptation, he thought it should take place in the Assembly, he repeated the oath prescribed by the Constitution and returned to the palace of the Tuileries through the gardens, on foot, attended by the members of the Assembly. The King upon his passage was very much applauded by the people. The Queen was present at the ceremony.'

On Friday 23 September Gower reported again. 'The King has of late omitted no opportunity of gaining popularity and of convincing the people that his acceptation was free and voluntary. On Sunday the Tuileries were magnificently illuminated and the King and Queen went in their carriages to the Champs Elysées to see the fireworks and illuminations which the municipality had ordered in that place.'

'On Tuesday they were at the opera, for the first time since the Revolution.' Morris was there too. 'At five, go to opera, *Castor and Pollux*. The King and Queen are here; they are received with great applause.' The marquis de Férrières was also present and adds a significant detail: 'when the actor pronounced the verses in *Castor and Pollux*: "régnez sur un peuple fidèle", the aristocrats and those who were paid to applaud made the house resound to the clapping of hands.' *Castor and Pollux* was followed by the ballet *Psyche*. Another observer, Madame de Staël, recorded that at the moment when the Furies danced to the light of their flambeaux 'she saw the faces of the King and Queen in the pale glow of this imitation of Hell and was gripped by baleful forebodings about the future.'

The Queen's 'apparent marks of confidence', wrote Madame Campan, 'were very far removed from the state of agitation in her heart. "These people have no desire for sovereigns," she said; "we will succumb to their perfidious but unwavering tactics; they are demolishing the monarchy stone by stone."'

Marie-Antoinette's use of the word 'sovereign' is significant. It was fast becoming the doctrine of the Revolution that 'sovereignty' lay with 'the People' and that the only place for a king in such a constitution was that of the highest functionary of the State.

It is perhaps difficult today to understand the passionate intensity with which the supporters of the *ancien régime* believed in the divine right of kingship. The King of Spain, Charles IV, on hearing of the situation in France as early as 4 February 1790, could not retain his indignation. 'My cousin', he exclaimed, 'has already forgotten that he is King'.

Later, on 26 November 1791, it was to the King of Spain that Louis sought to justify his position. 'When I accepted the Constitution I was aware of all its defects and of the impossibility of making it work, but I felt it my duty to subscribe to it in order not to be the cause of even greater troubles, and thus to regain the confidence of the majority of the nation which had only been led astray by the sedition-mongers.'

'I desired at the same time', continues Louis, 'the concentration of all the powers. I have observed with pleasure that this idea has also entered into the wise outlook of Your Majesty. This Congress, presenting behind it an imposing armed force, is the only true manner of arriving at a state of affairs which is more to be desired; on the one hand, by moderating the ardour of the *émigrés*, who should never be the principal party and whose impatience could cause a lot of harm, and on the other by intimidating the sedition mongers and by giving encouragement to the friends of order and of monarchy.'

The problem of the *émigrés* was of long standing. It dates back to the days immediately after the fall of the Bastille. Among the first to leave the country were the comte d'Artois and the prince de Condé. Within a week or two of leaving France Condé published a manifesto. It was a sort of aristocratic equivalent to 'Workers of the World Unite!', for it put loyalty to a social order higher than loyalty to a nation. 'La noblesse est une,' it stated; 'it is the cause of all the princes, of these gentlemen whom I defend . . . I will go at the head of the nobility of all the nations and I will attempt to deliver this unfortunate monarch!'

Marie-Antoinette, according to Goguelat, had reacted with great joy to the manifesto but Fersen judged it both impetuous and premature. D'Esterhazy agreed with Fersen. 'I fear', he said, 'that Monsieur le prince de Condé has not the skill of William Tell and that he will strike the head without demolishing the apple.'

Condé and Artois made Koblenz their headquarters and gathered around them an army that was in danger of consisting entirely of officers. But they had taken with them the old factions and rivalries of Versailles. On 12 August 1792, Lord Gower reported: 'the divisions which are known to subsist among the emigrants render the preparations on the other side of the Rhine less formidable than they would otherwise be; it is known that they are divided into two parties, that of the prince of Condé and Monsieur de Calonne and that of the baron de Breteuil and Monsieur Bouillé. The Queen is as adverse to the former as she is partial to the latter; this occasions another division in the party of the princes and accounts for the coolness which subsists between the comte d'Artois and the prince de Condé.'

Earlier in 1791, before the flight to Varennes, Augeard was in Brussels. 'I found a group of the *grande noblesse française* established in this capital. Nearly all these great houses complain bitterly of the behaviour of the Queen . . . I am bold to say, in the most indecent manner.'

Augeard was astonished to find that there was a marquis de La Queuille in Brussels who called himself 'Ministre du comte d'Artois'. These *émigrés* seemed to forget that they still had a legitimate King. Louis' brothers were more interested in preserving the crown of France – which both were to inherit in turn – than in protecting or rescuing Louis and his family.

The *émigrés* were, in fact, a source of real danger to the royal family. It was known that they were intending an armed invasion of France. It was easy for the Revolutionaries to put about rumours of reprisals, of wholesale massacres and hundreds of 'good patriots' to be broken on the wheel. The *émigrés* clearly had numerous supporters who had not left France and who might be ready to rise in support of such an invasion. Among them, of course, was a large number of *non-assermenté* clergy.

In October 1791 the Assembly devoted much of its time, according to Gower, to the 'manoeuvres and anti-constitutional machinations of clergy *non-assermenté*'. In November he agreed 'it is true that they are creating disturbances in every part of the kingdom; that of Caen is the most serious, where they are in a state of civil war and blood has been shed on both sides.'

On 2 December Lord Gower made the ominous remark: 'a universal expectation of an approaching crisis prevails. Everybody acknowledges that France cannot long continue in its present state, but what the dénouement of this tragi-comedy will be remains to be known.'

It was the issue of the *non-assermenté* priests which was to bring matters to a head. On 5 May François de Neufchâteau claimed that there were 'fifteen to twenty thousand priests telling simple men that . . . to pay their taxes was to incur damnation.' He moved that all such priests should be deported.

The measures proposed that if twenty 'citoyens actifs' demanded the deportation of an ecclesiastic, that should suffice to condemn him. Only if the authorities of the Department disagreed with this was any verification of the charge to be allowed. One Deputy, named Thuriot, complained that any such verification would prevent the Assembly from realising its end. All that needed verification was the authenticity of the signatures.

The debate lasted eleven days. On one side Monsieur Dalmas stated that it would be 'atrocious despotism' to condemn one man on the mere accusation of twenty – who might have been his personal enemies, or *factieux*, or even criminals. On the other side Lacroix maintained that the mere fact that twenty citizens were agreed to denounce a priest rendered him 'suspect' and that was enough.

The Revolution had reached the stage when to be accused was to be condemned and to be suspect was in itself an offence. It had not yet reached the point at which being 'suspected of being a suspect' was sufficient.

The measure was adopted on 27 May. Roland was the minister responsible. On 12 June the King dismissed Roland together with Servan, another minister forced upon him by the Jacobins, and he imposed his veto. He must have known what the response to this action would be.

Monday 20 June was the day fixed for the demonstration. Ostensibly it was in order to plant a 'tree of liberty' in the Tuileries gardens opposite the meeting place of the National Assembly and to present petititions to the Assembly and to the King.

By an agreement of 11 February that year, the number of those permitted to accompany a petition was limited to twenty and it was stipulated that they should not carry arms. At about ten o'clock on the Monday the area surrounding the Assembly hall was invaded by a crowd estimated at 20 000, many of whom did carry arms. The Deputies were harangued by the orator Gonchon, who introduced his supporters as 'ready to use extreme measures to avenge the outraged majesty of the people'.

The marquise de Tourzel was an eye-witness to all that happened in the Tuileries. 'By ten o'clock the Carrousel was already filled with an immense crowd, and the *gendarmerie nationale* lined the entrances to the Château. It was commanded by Monsieur de Rulhières, an honest man and attached to the King but whose zeal was paralysed by the municipality which he was obliged to obey . . . The interiors of the courts and gardens were guarded by the *garde nationale* with their cannons.'

Outside the precincts of the palace 'an armed multitude which, without enquiring what they were going to ask the King, without knowing anything, without desiring anything, mindless, furious and at the same time light-hearted; threatening, excited, singing, saying the most terrible things about the royal family, made its way towards the Assembly.

'The account brought to the Tuileries caused the most lively alarm. The King, the Queen and all the royal family gathered in the King's rooms, as being the safest, and awaited with great anxiety the outcome of this fateful day.'

A little after three o'clock, according to Madame de Tourzel, a municipal officer opened the gate of the Terrace des Feuillants and the mob poured into the Tuileries gardens. When they had reached the main entrance to the palace, again the doors were opened for them. Soon the rooms and galleries were overflowing with armed men who even dragged a cannon up into the Salle des Cent Suisses.

'The King, the Queen and the royal family were in His Majesty's private bedroom, surrounded by a few servants whom he had permitted to remain close to his person. The King, seeing that the doors were going to be broken in, decided to anticipate the sedition-mongers and to overawe them by his presence . . . He demanded that the Queen and his children should be taken elsewhere, wishing to expose himself alone to the danger. This Princess, parting from the

King with tears in her eyes, addressed, with a tone full of feeling and of confidence, these touching words to those who surrounded her: "Frenchmen, my friends, grenadiers – save the King."'

Louis passed into the Salon de l'Oeil de Boeuf just as the mob burst in at the other end. Some of the men threatened him with their weapons and the *grenadiers* would have drawn their sabres, but Acloque, who commanded the battalion, prudently prevented them, crying: 'no arms! You will have the King assassinated!' He pulled Louis into a window embrasure where he and the old maréchal de Mouchy stood to either side of him.

Madame Elizabeth, who had kept close to her brother by holding onto his coat tails, managed to get into the adjacent embrasure. She was immediately taken for the Queen. There were cries of 'l'Autrichienne! Où est-elle? Sa tête! Sa tête!' 'Do not undeceive them,' ordered the Princess; 'if they mistake me for the Queen there will be time to save her.'

Madame de Tourzel assures us:

> [Marie-Antoinette] was absolutely determined to return to the King and to share his dangers. We had great difficulty in persuading her that, at such a critical moment, her place was beside her children and that she ought in any case to conform with the wishes of the King . . . We had to drag her more or less by force to the Dauphin's rooms, but the mob broke into the first room of this apartment and the Queen and her children were forced to regain the King's bedroom . . . The Queen was still in the King's bedroom when a *valet de chambre* of the Dauphin burst in, beside himself, and warned this Princess that the room was taken, the guard disarmed, the doors of the apartment forced or broken in and they were upon his heels. It was decided to take the Queen into the Salle du Conseil, through which Santerre was making his troops file out . . . She confronted these sedition-makers between her two children with that courage and great-heartedness which she had shown on 5 and 6 October.

Louis' postscript to the day, was recorded in the Logograph – the official minutes of the proceedings of the Assembly – on

21 June. 'The King only opposed the threats and other insults of the sedition-mongers with his conscience and his love for the public welfare. The King does not know just how far they are prepared to go; but he has need to say to the French nation that violence, to whatever excess it may be carried, will never extort from him his consent to anything which he believes contrary to the public interest.'

This was published the next day in the form of a *livre blanc* to the whole country. The *livre blanc* put out by the Jacobins puts a predictably different complexion on the account. 'It avers', writes Girault de Coursac, 'that these inoffensive "petitioners", filled with "joy and gaiety" at the idea of "offering their homage to the King" had been led by the King into an ambush from which they had only escaped thanks to the vigilance of Monsieur Pétion's emissaries.' Sinister allusions were made to 'a great quantity of men dressed in black', who were 'doubtless plotting a massacre of St Bartholomew' of patriots.

In early August 1792, Dr John Moore accompanied the Earl of Lauderdale to Paris. He had previously spent some two years here and had been much impressed; 'the affability, the ease and peculiar gaiety of the French nation left a very pleasing impression on my mind, and I often regretted that a people so formed for enjoying and communicating happiness should labour under the oppression of an arbitrary government and unequal laws. I often said how supremely happy would a people of such dispositions be, were they able to obtain a system of government as free and impartial as that which Great Britain has enjoyed since the [Glorious] Revolution.'

And now, three years after the desired Revolution in France had taken place, John Moore could see for himself these people liberated from their oppression. He was appalled. He spent much time in the National Assembly and observed at once that the pressure exerted by the rabble in the public galleries made nonsense of the whole system. 'How can men be thought to deliberate and vote with freedom, who are pursued, insulted and menaced by a mob for the opinions and votes they give?' Moore even recorded a voice from the gallery shouting: 'the National Assembly ought rather to obey our dictates, since they are only the representatives of the people, whereas we *are* the people ourselves.'

The marquis de Vaublanc openly complained that he had been 'sought after and pursued by assassins . . . and had not ventured to sleep in his own house'. As for the debates themselves, the conditions were impossible. 'The noise and disorder', continues Moore, 'were excessive: fifty members were vociferating at once. I never was witness to a scene so tumultuous: the bell, as well as the voice of the president, was drowned in a storm compared to which the most boisterous night I ever was witness to in the House of Commons was calm.'

Gouverneur Morris, who was later to become Minister Plenipotentiary to the Court of France, made much the same observations as Dr Moore. 'It is impossible to imagine a more disorderly Assembly. They neither reason, examine nor discuss. They clap those whom they approve and hiss those whom they disapprove. But if I attempted a description I should never have done . . . So much for that licentious spirit which they dignify with the name of "Love of Liberty".'

Meanwhile events were moving fast beyond the Rhine. The Duke of Brunswick, in charge of the Prussian army, was advancing towards the frontier. On 30 June Fersen wrote to Marie-Antoinette begging her not to accept any of the offers which were being made to take her to safety. 'Do not try to leave Paris, then it will be easy to get to you and that is the plan of the Duke of Brunswick. He will have his entry preceded by a very strong manifesto in the name of the allied powers which will make the whole of France, and Paris in particular, responsible for the persons of the royal family.'

Marie-Antoinette grasped eagerly at this last straw. 'All is lost if the *factieux* are not checked by fear of imminent punishment.'

On 3 August the manifesto was proclaimed in Paris. It offered to protect all villages and towns which submitted to the King of France, but any who fired on the Prussian troops 'will be punished with all the rigour of the rules of war'. If any violence was shown to the royal family, 'their Imperial and Royal Majesties will take an exemplary and never-to-be-forgotten vengeance by giving up the town of Paris to military execution . . . and the guilty rebels to the death which they deserve.'

It was a serious psychological error. It antagonised the population of France without intimidating the Revolutionaries. It provided them with a slogan for rallying the people by an appeal to patriotism, and with a fresh pretext for attacking the monarchy.

On Friday 10 August the Tuileries was sacked and three days later the King was 'suspended from his functions' and imprisoned in the Temple.

The week had begun badly. On Sunday, Madame Campan relates, the Chapel choir, by secret arrangement, 'trebled the force of their voices in a terrifying manner when they repeated the words in the Magnificat, '*deposuit potentes de sede*' ('He hath put down the mighty from their seat'). The royal family gave up using the Chapel and services were said in the Gallery. By Thursday 9 it was clear that a major uprising was to be expected. Two interesting accounts of the events of the next twenty-four hours come from Roussel d'Épinal and François de La Rochefoucauld, both of them eye witnesses.

That evening, for the first time ever, the ceremony of the *coucher* was cancelled. The loyal supporters of the King took what rest they could on the chairs, on the tables and even on the floor, in spite of the insistence on the part of some of the officers of the Royal Household that it was contrary to etiquette to be seated in the King's room.

François de La Rochefoucauld was extremely tired; he had been arrested and interrogated twice that week already, but now a new strength was given him: 'at such a time zeal makes good whatever is lacking.' Charged with this reserve of energy, the whole palace was in a state of tense and anxious expectation.

Meanwhile, in the room beyond the King's bedroom the little Dauphin slept. 'His calm and peaceful slumber', wrote the marquise de Tourzel, 'formed the most striking contrast with the agitation which reigned in every heart.' No-one else in the Tuileries went to bed that night; 'everyone remained in the royal apartments and awaited fearfully the issue of a day which was ushered in with such baleful auspices.' At about three in the morning the tocsin started. The great bourdon of the Cordeliers began to toll; it was soon answered by another and then another. In tower after tower the bells took up the strong, pulsating rhythm – the quickened heartbeat of an over-excited city. Bells that were meant to summon men to prayer now intoxicated them for slaughter.

The Queen, Roussel d'Épinal records, had had a special bullet-proof waistcoat made of nine layers of white satin interlined with horsehair. She urged the King to don this and to put himself at the head of his devoted subjects. 'If you are to die,' she exhorted him, 'let it be with your sword in your hand and defending the crown, of which you are only the trustee. Be like Henri IV! Arm yourself and fight!'

She must have known that Louis would never have fought against his own subjects, nor was he capable of inspiring others. At about six in the morning Louis went out to 'review' the Guards. La Rochefoucauld went with him. 'Although I was very close to his person', he wrote, 'I never heard him say a single word to the troops.' General Vioménil, who was in charge of the defence of the Tuileries, admitted to Madame Campan, 'our means of defence are nil. They could only exist in the vigorous action of the King – and that is the only virtue which he lacks.'

At about half past eight the comte Roederer, the Procureur Syndic (Attorney General), persuaded the royal family to take refuge in the hall of the National Assembly. The mob, however, had already invaded the Tuileries gardens. At the foot of the terrace the King encountered a furious crowd, hurling insults at him and threatening him with their pikes. 'I feared at each moment', wrote La Rochefoucauld, 'to see him massacred before my eyes and in the middle of his family.'

Before leaving the Tuileries, Louis had said to his faithful supporters: 'I beg you retire and give up this useless defence; there is nothing to be done here, neither for me nor for you.' The inmates of the Tuileries were left to their fate. The result was a massacre in which the chief victims were the faithful Swiss Guards. Needless to say Louis was blamed for the casualties on the other side. John Moore comes to his defence. 'As to the question of who fired first, it appears of little or no importance; for although it were proved that it was the Swiss, still it would appear that the people were the aggressors. Did they not show a determination to break into the palace? What were the Swiss placed there for? Was it to act as gentlemen ushers to an armed multitude? No; they certainly did their duty as soldiers in firing upon those who came for no other purpose than to force their post.' But there is an old French saying: 'cet animal est très méchant; quand on l'attaque, il se défend!'

François Hue survived the massacre but found his lodgings on the Place du Carrousel in flames. He wandered about all night until six in the morning when he learnt that the royal family were sleeping in the convent of les Feuillants, next to the meeting place of the National Assembly, and managed to gain access to the room where the King lay sleeping. Hue wrote:

> He was still in bed, with his head covered by a coarse linen cloth. His eyes, filled with emotion, sought mine; he summoned me and, clasping my hand, asked me with the keenest interest about the details of what had happened at the Château after his departure. Overcome by my agony and by my tears I was scarcely able to express myself. I informed the King of the death of several persons whom he had in affection – among others the chevalier d'Allonville, who was assistant Governor to the Dauphin. 'At least I have the consolation', said the King to me, 'of seeing you safe from this massacre.'
>
> The King and his family occupied, in a corridor which was

> formerly the dormitory of the nuns, the lodging of the architect of the hall used by the National Assembly. That night the King said to his *entourage*: 'there have been expressions of regret that I did not oppose the rebels before they attacked the Arsenal; but, the terms of the Constitution apart, the National Guard would have refused to be the aggressors – what would have been the outcome of such an attack? The dispositions had been made too well for our party to have been victorious, even if we had not left the Château.'

They were interrupted by cries from outside the window demanding the head of the Queen. 'What has she done to them?' asked the King indignantly.

The royal family had brought nothing with them when they left the Tuileries. One of the surviving Suisses, named Pascal, who was about the same size as Louis, sent certain articles of clothing. The duchesse de Gramont did the same for Marie-Antoinette. The wife of the British Ambassador, the Countess of Sutherland, who had a son the same age as the Dauphin, sent to the young prince *des vêtements de première necessité*. The Earl Gower's wife was Countess of Sutherland in her own right.

There could be no question of the royal family returning to the Tuileries. The Assembly decided on the Temple. It was held to offer the best security. 'The Queen shuddered when she heard the Temple proposed,' wrote Madame de Tourzel, 'and said to me under her breath: "they will put us in the tower, you will see, and they will make it a real prison for us. I have always had an absolute horror of that tower which I have asked Monsieur le comte d'Artois a thousand times to pull down."'

The Temple, as its name suggests, had been the headquarters of the Knights Templars in Paris until their savage suppression by Philippe le Bel in 1307. It had since been occupied by the Knights of Malta and it was as Grand Prieur of that Order that the comte d'Artois made the Prior's Lodging his town house.

It was to this building, the 'Palais', that the royal family was escorted on 14 August. They were served with supper in the state apartments. 'In the belief', wrote Hue, 'that henceforth the Palais du Temple was to be his residence, the King wanted to see all the rooms and took pleasure in allocating the various apartments in advance, while the municipal officers took a cruel pleasure in his misapprehension.' Those in attendance on the King, however, had been informed that the royal family would sleep elsewhere. At eleven o'clock Hue and his fellow servants were told to follow one of the commissioners:

> A municipal carrying a lantern preceded me. In the faint light which it gave I tried to make out the place which was destined for the royal family. We stopped at the foot of a block of buildings which the darkness of the night made me think was considerable . . . The upper parts of the roof appeared to be surmounted by spires, which I took to be belfries, and they were crowned with battlements on which, from space to space, were burning lanterns. In spite of the light which these shed at intervals I could not make out what this building could be.
>
> At this moment one of the municipals broke the mournful silence which he maintained up till now. 'Your Master', he said to me, 'has been accustomed to gilded panelling. Very well; now he will see how we house those who assassinate the people; follow me.'
>
> I went up several steps; a low and narrow doorway led to a spiral staircase . . . I realised that I was in a tower. I entered a room lit, during the day, by a single window, lacking for the most part even the most necessary furniture and having only a poor bed and three or four chairs. 'That is where your Master will sleep,' said the municipal. Chamilly had joined me. We looked at each other without saying a word; they chucked us, as if it were a favour, a couple of sheets.
>
> An alcove with neither hangings nor curtains contained a couch of which the wicker-work mattress proclaimed that it was full of insects. We set to work to make the room and the bed as clean as possible. The King entered. He showed no signs of surprise or of ill-humour. Some engravings, most of them rather indecent, decorated the walls. He removed them himself. 'I do not wish to leave such objects before my daughter's eyes,' he said.
>
> His Majesty lay down and slept peacefully. Chamilly and I

remained all the night seated by his bed. We contemplated with great respect the irreproachable calm of a man fighting against misfortune and mastering it with his own courage. How was it, we asked ourselves, that one who was able to exercise such control over himself was not made to command others?

Imprisonment in the Temple

On 12 August the news of the sack of the Tuileries had not yet reached Fersen in Brussels, but his letter to his sister Sophie was full of forebodings. 'My fears for the life of the King and Queen are always in my mind; the *factieux* no longer make any secret of their intentions and the Château is in constant danger. Their Majesties can no longer go out of doors or even sleep at the same time. They take their rest alternately and there is always one on guard expecting to see their apartment broken into by these cannibals; it is really horrifying and the situation is heart-rending. It is on the 15th that the Prussians are to enter France: that moment will be critical.'

By the 15th Fersen had learned of the events of 10 August. He wrote to his friend the Baron Taube in Stockholm: 'Silversparre will send you the details of this execrable day of the 10th; you will find them horrific. The royal family exists, but how?'

Some of the best accounts of the existence of the royal family after the King had been 'suspended from his functions' come from three eye-witnesses: Madame Royale and the two valets Hue and Cléry, who were in the service of the King and the Dauphin.

'The King, my father', writes Madame Royale, 'arrived at the Temple on 13 August 1792 at seven in the evening with his family . . . nothing had been prepared. My aunt slept in the kitchen.' With them came the princesse de Lamballe, the marquise de Tourzel and her daughter Pauline, the two valets Hue and Chamilly to look after the King and four other ladies to look after the Queen and the princesses. On the 20th the order came from the commune that all those who were not royal family were to be removed to the prison of La Force. In spite of the Queen's objection that the princesse de Lamballe most certainly counted as royal family, she was taken too. Their parting was a very difficult moment for Marie-Antoinette; 'ma mère ne pouvait s'arracher des bras de Madame la princesse de Lamballe.' They were informed on the next day that their companions would not be coming back, but at nine o'clock they were surprised and delighted to see Hue return. The others Pétion replaced by a couple named Tison, 'pour faire le gros ouvrage'.

Somewhat surprisingly, Pétion appointed Cléry, who had been a valet to the Dauphin since 1782. The Temple was also penetrated by certain loyal supporters. One was named Turgy, formerly a *garçon servant de la bouche du Roi*, who managed to be taken on as a member of the kitchen staff; with him came Marchand and Chrétien, two of his former colleagues. This ensured that the royal family was well fed and increased its contact with the world outside. Turgy has left his own account.

There were always four municipal officers in attendance with orders never to let the King out of their sight and to prevent any surreptitious conversation. When any meal was being prepared, wrote Turgy, it had to be cooked and tasted in front of them; the carafes and coffee pots had to be filled before their eyes; the table was shown to them top-side and under-side before it was laid, the napkins were unfolded and the bread cut in half so that it could be sounded with a fork, or even with the fingers. One officer, noted Cléry, insisted on peaches being cut in half and their stones opened to see if they did not contain illicit correspondence.

The constant scrutiny of the municipal officers was potentially irksome, but some of them had feelings of decency and compassion and some were won over to respect for the royal captives and even became devoted to them. François-Adrien Toulan was one of the latter. Turgy tells how 'his behaviour and the way he talked during his first day at the Temple were both exaggerated and made us dread the return of his day's service. However, the sight of the misfortunes of Louis XVI, the princesses and the august children, their magnanimity, their kindness, had made from the start an impression that was as strong as it was unexpected on the keen and sensitive soul of this young man, so that he resolved to employ every means of alleviating the lot of the royal family.'

Cléry took up residence in the Temple on 26 August. 'It would be difficult', he wrote, 'to describe the impression made on me by this august but unfortunate family.' He did, however, describe it in vivid and often heart-rending detail. The extent of their misfortune became evident all too soon. The response of the Revolutionary Party to the invasion of France by Prussia was to massacre all the royalists already in prison.

On 2 September the area of the Temple was in a state of fermentation and the municipals were clearly uneasy. The royal family had gone out for their daily walk in the garden but were ordered back indoors again. One of the municipal officers, a *ci-devant* friar named Mathieu, told the King the news: the country was in the greatest danger; the enemy had entered Champagne and the King of Prussia was advancing on Chalons. 'We know that we and our wives and children will perish,' said Mathieu, 'but the people will have its revenge; you will die before we do.' He then arrested Hue, who did not, this time, return.

On the next day at about one o'clock the royal family asked to walk in the garden as usual. They were refused permission. The same state of fermentation still reigned outside; drums could be heard and the clamour of a mob. After the royal family had had their dinner Cléry went down to have his with Tison and his wife. They had hardly sat down when a head on the end of a pike appeared at the window. 'Madame Tison uttered a loud cry; the assassins thought that they recognised the voice of the Queen and we could hear their gloating laughter. Believing that the Queen was still at table, they had so placed their victim that it could not have escaped her vision. It was the head of Madame de Lamballe; although bleeding it was in no way disfigured; her blonde hair, still in curls, floated round the pike.

'I ran immediately to the King's room. Terror had so altered my countenance that the Queen noticed it; it was important to conceal from her the cause of it. "Why do you not go to dinner?" the Queen asked me. "Madame," I replied, "I am not feeling well."'

At this moment two municipal officers entered. The King asked if his family was safe. They said that the word had gone round that they were no longer in the Tower; 'they are demanding that you should appear at the window, but we will not endure that; the people should have more confidence in its magistrates.' The cries from the street were growing louder; another municipal officer entered with four men deputed by the mob to satisfy themselves that the royal family was still in the Tower. They insisted that the prisoners should show themselves at the window. The municipals continued to oppose them. Then one of the Deputies, 'in the grossest way possible', said to the Queen: 'they want to hide from you the head of la Lamballe which has been brought to you to show you how the people takes its revenge against its tyrants; I would advise you to show yourselves if you don't want the people to come up here.'

'At this threat the Queen fainted. Madame Elizabeth and Cléry helped her to an armchair. "We are ready for anything", said Louis, "but you might have spared the Queen this frightful horror."' The mob departed; its object had been achieved.

The head of the princesse de Lamballe was taken straight to Marie Grosholz, later Madame Tussaud, so that a death mask could be made and added to her uncle's celebrated Salon de Cir as one of the 'Famous Criminals'. Marie, while she was employed at Versailles, had seen the princesse a thousand times and to hold her severed head upon her lap and smooth it out before applying the wax was a bizarre experience. 'The features, beautiful even in death', she wrote, 'and the auburn tresses, though smeared with blood, shone with all their natural brilliance and lustre.'

It was clear that the mob outside the Temple was eager to add another royal head to Marie's collection. Cléry could hear one of the municipal officers haranguing the crowd. 'The head of Antoinette does not belong to you; the Departments have their rights also. France has entrusted its great offenders to the City of Paris; it is your business to help us guard them until the justice of the nation avenges its people.' It was a whole hour, however, before he could disperse the crowd. 'At eight in the evening', writes Cléry, 'all was calm in the neighbourhood of the Temple.' The royal family settled down once more into its monotonous and humiliating routine.

It is useful, in order to picture the life of the royal family, to have some idea of the topography of the Petite Tour in which they were lodged. It was a building which adjoined the Grosse Tour without having any internal communication with it. In ground plan it formed an oblong with turrets at its two corners. One turret contained the staircase; the other a circular cabinet on each floor.

The building was of four storeys. On the ground floor were kitchens which were not in use. The first floor consisted of an anteroom, a dining-room and a cabinet in the turret which contained a library – for the Petite Tour had housed the archives of the Knights of Malta. The second storey was divided in the same manner. The largest room served for a bedroom for the Queen and the Dauphin, the second was occupied by Madame Royale and Madame Elizabeth. One had to pass through their room to reach the cabinet in the turret, and this cabinet, which served as a privy, was shared by the royal family, the officers of the municipality and the soldiers.

The King lived on the third floor and slept in the big room. The cabinet in the turret was his reading room. Next to this was a kitchen separated from the bedroom by a little dark room which had been occupied by Chamilly and Hue. The fourth floor was closed.

By the greatest good fortune, the library of the Order of Malta had remained in place and Louis had the choice of some 1500 books. By the time of his death, according to Cléry, he had read 250 of them. One day he was with Hue in the library and indicated to him the works of Voltaire and Rousseau. 'These two men', he said in a low voice, 'have been the ruin of France.' Louis spent much of his time reading the Latin authors, partly for pleasure and partly to help him to teach his son.

The family breakfasted together at nine, after which the Dauphin had his lessons until eleven. Louis taught him to recite passages from Corneille and Racine; he gave him exercises in drawing maps, a skill in which he himself had excelled as a boy. 'The precocious intelligence of the young Prince', noted Cléry, 'responded perfectly to the attentions of his father. The Queen, for her part, concerned herself with the education of her daughter . . . The rest of the morning was spent in sewing, knitting or doing work on a tapestry.'

But even these harmless activities were liable to arouse suspicion. Cléry, in order to help the Dauphin with his arithmetic, had drawn up a multiplication table. One of the municipal officers immediately objected that the boy was being taught to use a code – so his arithmetic had to be abandoned. The Queen also was deprived of her tapestry – a work which helped to while away the time – on the grounds that she might be using hieroglyphics.

The gaolers lost no opportunity to insult or humiliate their prisoners. One of them, named Rocher, 'd'une figure horrible', noted Cléry, 'avec des longues moustaches', stood in the doorway when the family went out into the garden. 'He took up his position by the last door, a long pipe in his mouth and blew a puff of tobacco smoke into the face of each of them, especially the princesses.' Some of the *gardes nationales*, continues Cléry, 'who were amused by such insolence, gathered round him and shouted with laughter at each puff of smoke.'

In spite of the vigilance of the municipal officers, little bits of news and little acts of kindness brought moments of alleviation to the royal family, but usually only to be reversed by some new excess, some new atrocity.

Turgy was allowed to go out two or three times a week to do the catering, and this gave him the opportunity to discover the latest news. It was both difficult and dangerous, however, to communicate this news to the King and Queen. Suspicion was easily aroused. 'To take precautions against such inconveniences,' Turgy records, 'the Queen and Madame Elizabeth had the idea of corresponding directly with me by means of signs.'

A few examples will suffice to suggest the system. If the news were of the English, Turgy would raise his right thumb to his right eye. If they were landing in the region of Nantes, he put his thumb to his right ear; if it was in the region of Calais he put it to his left ear. The longer a finger or thumb was held in place, the more important was the combat referred to. Thus the royal family were kept roughly informed of the progress of the armies and the proceedings of the Convention.

Not long after the September massacres, Cléry was able to bring the news that Madame de Tourzel and her daughter were still alive and living on one of their properties; also that the princesse de Tarente and the marquis de la Roche-Aimon had survived the attack on the Tuileries.

The marquise de Tourzel tells the story of her own deliverance. She and her daughter were helped to escape from La Force in the middle of the massacre by an unknown man who might have been the original of the Scarlet Pimpernel.

On 2 September, the marquise wrote in her memoirs, 'we had scarcely gone to sleep when we heard someone drawing the bolts of our door and we saw a man come in, well dressed and of mild aspect, who went up to Pauline's bed and said: "Mademoiselle de Tourzel, get ready quickly and come with me" . . . I was in such a state of emotional disorder and distress on seeing my daughter thus taken from me that I remained frozen without the power to move . . . My poor

Pauline then came to my bed and took my hand, but the man, seeing that she was dressed, took hold of her arm and dragged her towards the door. I heard the bolts fastened again; I cried after her: "God help you and protect you, my dear Pauline!"'

The next day the massacres began. 'It was impossible to conceal from oneself the danger to which we were all exposed, but the danger in which I imagined Pauline to stand excluded all other thoughts from my mind. Then I caught a glimpse of the man who had so harshly bereft me of my daughter: the sight of him made me shudder and I was trying to avoid him when, passing close by me, he said in a low voice: "your daughter is safe," and moved away immediately.'

The knowledge of Pauline's safety gave her mother a new courage and new presence of mind with which to face her interrogation. 'During all this time my liberator, Monsieur Hardy [for she had discovered his name] did not forget me and was busily carrying out his promise to Pauline that he would use every possible means to save me.' At one moment she was surrounded by 'men of the most frightful aspect who did not conceal from me the fate which was in store for me. Monsieur Hardy, who sensed that I would be lost if I came before the tribunal, had the idea of getting them drunk. In this he succeeded.' She did, however, come before the tribunal and, after ten minutes' questioning, the President put the question which was to decide her death or release. 'A cry of "Vive la Nation!" (which I knew to be that of salvation) informed me that I was saved.'

At last her escort managed to get her into a fiacre. 'I had myself taken to the house of that good marquise de Lède, who received me with a truly maternal kindness.' The next day she was united with her daughter.

The news of the rescue of Madame de Tourzel and her daughter brought a moment of consolation to the prisoners in the Temple, but almost immediately afterwards came the news that those in custody at Orléans, among whom was the duc de Brissac, had been transferred to Paris, but the mob had intercepted the convoy as it passed through Versailles and all were massacred. 'The King was prostrated with grief', wrote Cléry, 'at the unhappy end of the duc de Brissac, who had never left him for a single day since the beginning of the Revolution.'

On 21 September, at four in the afternoon, a municipal officer named Lubin, with a mounted escort and a considerable crowd around him, made a proclamation in front of the Tour du Temple. He had the voice of a stentor and could be heard clearly by those inside. He announced the abolition of the Monarchy and the inauguration of the Republic. Hébert – notorious for his writings under the name of 'le Père Duchesne' – happened to be the municipal officer on duty observing the royal family and gave the King a gloating leer. Louis continued his reading unperturbed.

Early in October the rooms of the royal family were searched in order to deprive them of paper, ink, pens and pencils. The Queen and Madame Royale managed to hide their pencils, but the King and his sister gave up theirs. It did not save Madame Elizabeth, later on, from being accused of the somewhat difficult offence of forging *assignats*.

It was on the day of this search Louis was told that he was to be relodged in the Grosse Tour and separated from his family. 'At this frightful news', wrote Madame Royale, 'my mother lost her usual courage and firmness. We left him with many tears, hoping nevertheless to see him again.' He had no choice but to take leave of his family. 'This separation', observed Cléry, 'which already heralded so many other misfortunes, was one of the most cruel moments that Their Majesties had yet passed in the Temple.'

He followed the King into his new prison. Louis made a request for some books which he had left in the Queen's rooms which was accepted, and it was Cléry who had to accomplish the transfer since the municipal officer was unable to read. 'I found the Queen in her room, surrounded by her children and Madame Elizabeth; they were all in tears and their pain was increased by my appearance. They asked me a thousand questions about the King to which I could only reply with a certain reserve.' The next day, however, the municipal officers allowed the family to eat together, 'while forbidding us to speak in low voices or in foreign languages, but aloud and *en bon français*'. One of the municipal officers told Marie-Antoinette that Pétion did not desire the death of her husband, but rather that he and the Dauphin should be imprisoned for life in the Château de Chambord.

On Tuesday 11 December, the call to arms was sounded throughout Paris and the grounds of the Temple began to be filled with cavalry and artillery. At about eleven o'clock Louis was taken away from his family, but it was not until three hours later that Pétion, the Mayor of Paris, accompanied by Chaumette, Procureur de la Commune and Santerre, the commander of the Garde Nationale, entered his room and read the decree that: 'Louis Capet should be brought to the bar of the National Convention.' Louis merely commented that his name was not Capet. It was rather like calling Queen Elizabeth II 'Plantagenet'.

It was not until the 20 December that Fersen, who had left Brussels for Düsseldorf, learned of the decision to put the King on trial. Fersen was every inch a royalist and was deeply shocked: 'quelle indignité!' he exclaimed, but he was impressed by the way in which Louis stood up to his interrogation: 'il a répondu à merveille.'

During the period of the trial Louis was permitted no contact with Marie-Antoinette or Madame Elizabeth. It was decreed that he could only see his children on condition that they were separated from their mother and aunt until the trial was over. 'You see the cruel alternatives with which they have faced me,' said Louis to Cléry; 'I cannot decide to have my children with me: for my daughter that is impossible and for my son I feel all the suffering that it would cause the Queen. I shall therefore have to consent to this latest sacrifice.'

About this time Cléry and Turgy managed to devise a means of communication between the King and his family.

Louis had the use of pen and paper for preparing his defence and could therefore write to them. Cléry wrapped the letter in a ball of string which he left in the cupboard where the plates were kept. Turgy collected it and conveyed it to Madame Elizabeth and concealed the answer in a ball of wool which he threw under Cléry's bed as he passed by. 'His Majesty saw with great pleasure that his means of obtaining news of his family had succeeded.'

Once the King's trial was announced he was permitted to choose his own counsel for the defence. His first choice, Target, declined the brief, but Louis' old Ministre de la Maison du Roi, Lamoignon de Malesherbes, offered, at great personal risk, to defend his former master. Malesherbes received the highest praise possible from Lord Shelburne. It was recorded by Mademoiselle de l'Éspinasse: 'he went to see Monsieur de Malesherbes; he came back enchanted. He said to me: "I have seen, for the first time in my life, something which I did not believe could exist. It is a man whose soul is absolutely free from fear or ambition, but who is, nevertheless, full of life and fire. Nothing in creation can trouble his peace; nothing is indispensible to him and he takes a passionate interest in all that is good. In a word," he added, "I have travelled much and I have never come away with so profound an impression. If I accomplish anything that is good in the time that remains for me to live, I am certain that it will be the memory of Monsieur de Malesherbes that will have inspired my soul."'

Cléry, whose wife brought him regular news, was optimistic. 'Public opinion', he claimed, 'always appeared to be favourable to the King. The question was bound to arise, should not the fate of the King be decided by the wishes of the people? On this matter Saint-Just made the telling remark: 'on a parlé d'un appel au peuple; n'est-ce pas rappeler la monarchie?'

Dr John Moore has much to say on the subject. 'As far as I can perceive, however, the real citizens or bourgeoisie of Paris by no means desire the death of the King; and if by "the people" is understood the profligate, idle rabble of the suburbs and the wretches who are hired to clamour in public places, what probability is there that they will ever cool or be satisfied with any decision except what those who hire them, or their own savage dispositions, suggest?'

Looking at the country as a whole, he observed: 'it is evident that, although the Departments in France are, in theory, allowed to have an equal share in the government, yet in fact the single Department of Paris has the whole power of government.' But the government of Paris was largely in the hands of those who occupied the galleries in the Assembly. 'All the Departments of France . . . are obliged to submit to the clamorous tyranny of a set of hired ruffians in the tribunes who usurp the name and functions of Le Peuple Souverain . . . No nation was ever more indulgent to the caprices of its tyrant than France is at present to that most capricious and bloody of all tyrants – Le Peuple Souverain.' The words of the Deputy Pastoret, spoken against the *ancien régime*, apply with equal force to the Revolutionary government: 'la force des tyrans est dans la patience des peuples.'

On Christmas day 1792, Louis wrote his last will and testament. It is a noble profession of faith by a devout and obedient Catholic, but one who, at such a time, could be thinking of those of his former subjects who were not in communion with his Church: 'je ne les aime pas moins tous en Jésus Christ.' He writes as a Christian, as a King, as a husband, as a father. On the two latter counts his words are deeply moving: 'I pray God in particular to cast his merciful eyes on my wife, my children and my sister, who have shared for a long time in my sufferings, that He will sustain them with His grace should I be taken from them.

'I commend my children to my wife; I have never doubted her maternal tenderness towards them . . . I beg my wife to forgive me all the ills that she has suffered for my sake and for any grief that I may have caused her in the course of our union, as she may be certain that I hold nothing against her . . . I recommend to my son, if he should be so unfortunate as to become king, to bear in mind that he must dedicate his whole self to the happiness of his fellow citizens.'

Wednesday 16 January was the day of judgement, but it was not until the following day that Louis learned of it. Malesherbes arrived at the Temple at nine o'clock and said to Cléry: 'all is lost; the King is condemned.' When Louis heard the news he said to Malesherbes: 'you see now that from the first moment I was not deceived and that my condemnation had been pronounced before I had been heard.' To Cléry that evening he found an opportunity to say: 'I have no grounds for hope, but I am deeply distressed that the duc d'Orléans, a relation of mine, should have voted for my death.'

The duc d'Orléans, who was to end on the scaffold himself, had taken the name of Philippe Egalité. Mirabeau had been scathing about him. 'He is held in contempt by the provinces; they know of his incapacity, his fickleness; Paris knows of his immorality. What is there to fear from such a man?' Dr Moore was even more scornful. 'It has been said that a weak or wrong-headed man of very high rank . . . is like a man on the top of a steeple, from whence all the world seems *little* to him and where he seems little in the eyes of the world.'

Madame Royale records a conversation between the King and Malesherbes, who was cherishing a last hope: 'every honest man will come to save your Majesty or perish at your feet.' 'Monsieur de Malesherbes,' said my father, 'that would compromise a lot of people and start a civil war in Paris; I would rather die. I beg you to give orders in my name that there must be no movement to save me.'

Cléry also tried to revive hopes of a popular uprising in Louis' favour. 'I would be very annoyed if there were one,' answered the King; 'there would only be more victims. I am not afraid of death,' he added, 'but I cannot envisage without horror the cruel lot that I leave behind me for my family, for the Queen, for our luckless children.' When on Sunday 20 January, Garat, Ministre de la Justice, informed Louis that he was to die on the following day, he assured him also that 'la

Nation, toujours grande et toujours juste', would take care of his family.

Louis asked for a deferment of three days in which to prepare for death. His request was refused. He asked for the services of a Catholic priest, the abbé Edgeworth de Firmont. Somewhat surprisingly, this request was granted.

Marie-Antoinette only learnt of the sentence from the pedlars who cried the news beneath her windows. It was not until seven o'clock that Sunday that Louis was allowed to see his family. 'At seven in the evening', wrote Madame Royale, 'a decree of the Convention allowed us to go down to his room; we ran there and found him much changed. He shed many tears for us, but not from fear of death; he told my mother about the trial, making excuses for the scoundrels who were the cause of his death. My mother ardently desired that we should spend the night with my father; he declined to do so, suggesting to her that he had need of tranquility.'

The pathos of this occasion inspired the artist J.-J. Hauer to reconstruct the scene. But Hauer had not been present and was not familiar with his subjects. The one person who might have captured both the pathos and the likenesses was Madame Vigée-Lebrun. At first she longed to do so. 'Above all,' she wrote, 'I was haunted by the memory of Louis XVI and Marie-Antoinette, to the point that one of my most lively desires was to do a picture which represented them in one of those solemn and moving moments which must have preceded their deaths. I knew that Cléry had found refuge in Vienna. I wrote to him and informed him of my desire, begging him to help me in its execution.'

Cléry, who had himself been a witness to the last meeting of the royal family, replied to Madame Vigée-Lebrun and attempted to describe the scene in full pictorial detail. First he outlined the main features of the room. It was about fifteen feet square, the walls covered with a paper representing freestone, 'which gives a good idea of the interior of a prison'. On the right, near the door, was a large window; the walls were some nine feet thick so that the window was set back about eight feet in its embrasure. Through it could be seen heavy iron bars. In the wall opposite were double doors, one of which was open, allowing the eye to penetrate into the bedroom; to the left a glazed door led to the small room which served as a dining-room.

'Louis, dressed in a brown coat, a white waistcoat of *piqué de Marseilles*, breeches of grey kerseymere and grey silk stockings, has just come out of the dining-room and is advancing towards the entrance door. The King is holding with his right hand the Queen who is hardly able to stand; she is leaning on his right shoulder; the Dauphin, on the same side, is enclasped by the Queen's right arm; he holds in his little hands the King's right hand and the Queen's left, which he kisses and waters with his tears. Madame Elizabeth is on the King's left, clinging with both her hands to his arm and raising her eyes to Heaven. Madame Royale is in front, holding the King's left hand and filling the room with the most heart-rending cries. The King, always calm and always august, did not shed a tear, but could be seen to be cruelly affected by the distressing state of his family.'

At this point Cléry passes from description to narrative. 'He said to them in the softest tone of voice, but full of the most touching expressions: "I am not saying *adieu*; rest assured that that I will see you again tomorrow morning at seven o'clock."

"Do you promise that?" asked the Queen.

"Yes, I promise you," said the King; "*adieu*."

'The sobs and sighs redoubled their intensity; Madame Royale fell almost unconscious at her father's feet. The King made a painful effort to control his emotion; he tore himself from their arms and passed into his bedroom.'

'This letter', wrote Madame Vigée-Lebrun, 'made such a cruel impression upon me that I realised the impossibility of undertaking a work in which every touch of the paintbrush would have reduced me to tears.' The picture was never painted except in the words of Cléry.

The sequel to this meeting is related by Madame Royale:

'When we had gone he told the guards not to allow us down again, as our presence would be too painful for him.' That evening was the last time Marie-Antoinette saw Louis.

It is recorded in the funeral oration preached by John Milner on 12 April 1793 to the French refugee clergy in St Peter's chapel, Winchester, that at this point the Dauphin tried to get out of the Temple. 'Whilst the rest of the royal prisoners were agonizing at the feet of the King, when they were permitted to bid him a final adieu, the young Louis, having eluded the vigilance of his jailors, was found running through the court of the temple leading to the street by the sentinel there on guard, who interrogating him whither he was going: "I am going", replied hastily the amiable child, "to speak to the people and to entreat them not to kill my dear Papa. For heaven's sake do not prevent me from speaking to the people."'

It rained hard that night and Monday 21 January dawned cold and wet. 'On the morning of that terrible day', explains Madame Royale, 'we arose at six o'clock. That night my mother had scarcely had the strength to undress my brother and put him to bed; she flung herself fully dressed upon her bed and all night long we could hear her trembling with cold and with anguish. At a quarter past six someone came to find a prayer book for mass for my father; we thought we might be going down to his room, and we continued in this hope until the roar of applause of a people in delirium announced that the crime had been committed.' Later Cléry returned with Louis' marriage ring and the lockets of his family's hair which he had always cherished.

Cléry tells the same story from his own experience. 'At seven o'clock the King came out of his cabinet, called for me and, taking me into the window embrasure, said to me: "give this signet ring to my son."' In a later footnote Cléry, now in exile, records that on the second anniversary of Louis' death he had been to Blankembourg to offer the manuscript of his journal to Monsieur, now Louis XVIII. 'When the new King reached the passage about the ring he went to his desk and, showing me with some signs of emotion a signet ring, he said: "Cléry, do you recognise this?" "Ah! Sire, it is the same!" "If you have any doubt, read this note." I took it with a trembling hand . . . I recognised the writing of the Queen and the note was signed by the Dauphin, then Louis XVII, by Madame Royale and by Madame Elizabeth. You may imagine the strong emotion which I experienced.' The note and the ring had been delivered to Louis XVIII by the chevalier de Jarjayes, Marie-Antoinette's former secretary.

If the manuscript of Cléry's journal was in a condition to be offered to the new King in January 1795 it must have been written very soon after the events which it records. On the first page, Cléry claims that he was able to make certain notes on the principal events at the time. There are therefore no grounds for doubting the accuracy of his memory. He was, of course, totally devoted to Louis and his family and this no doubt coloured his account. Not many people today understand the devotion of servant to master or mistress nor realise how often this was mutual.

The parting, therefore, between Louis and Cléry was almost as painful as the parting between Louis and his family. 'I was behind the King, near the fireplace, and I held his coat for him. "I will not need that," he said to me, "just give me my hat." I passed it to him. His hand encountered mine, which he clasped for the last time.' Louis asked that Cléry should be allowed to continue serving the Dauphin, 'then, turning to Santerre, he said: "let us go." . . . I remained alone in the room, overwhelmed with grief and almost unconscious. The drums and trumpets announced that His Majesty had left the Temple . . . An hour later the salvos of artillery and the cries of "Vive la Nation!" could be heard. The best of kings was no more.'

Dr Moore wrote his epitaph: 'I am persuaded that none of his ancestors had so just a claim to the epithets which the public . . . have affixed to their names as the unfortunate Louis XVI has to that of *Louis le Trop Bon*.'

One of the municipal officers who had been converted by

his personal experience of contact with the royal family, Charles Goret, records his encounter with them on the evening after the execution. 'I noticed', he writes, 'how much it had affected the whole family; the Queen above all, who had declined into a state of considerable emaciation, could no longer be recognised. Madame Elizabeth, like her, maintained a mournful silence; the children seemed dumbfounded.'

All four were seated round a table; at the appearance of Goret they all relapsed into tears. '"Madame," I said to the Queen with a trembling voice, "you must conserve your strength for the sake of your family." It was all I could say; she only interrupted her sobbing to pronounce these words; "we are aware of the tragedy that has befallen us; we heard this morning all the preparations, the movements of men and horses; our tragedy is certain and we wish to go into mourning." Not being able to hide my feelings, I uttered only a few broken words: "hélas! Madame, hélas! Madame." I took my leave giving my assurances to the Queen that I would see to the mourning for which she had asked. "The simplest possible," she added.' Marie-Antoinette then specified the name and address of the person whom she wished to make the clothes.

The news of the execution, writes Beauchesne, caused horror and dismay in London. The Theatre Royal was closed and the French Ambassador, the marquis de Chauvelin, was given his passports. He left on 30 January, the day on which the Church of England celebrated the martyrdom of Charles I. In the United States, continues Beauchesne, 'which owed so much to Louis XVI, the funeral knell resounded in every parish from the rising to the setting of the sun.'

It has to be remembered that in those days the slowness of communications greatly increased the agonies of suspense. On Thursday 24 January, three days after the execution, Fersen, who had moved to Düsseldorf, had still not heard the news. To his sister Sophie he poured out his heart. 'It is not until tomorrow that we shall learn the final results [of the trial] but my fears are beyond imagining. Poor, unfortunate family; poor Queen, if only I could save her at the price of my own blood it would be the greatest happiness for me, the sweetest consolation to my soul . . . judge from that if I am not unhappy and if my situation is not appalling. Yes, my dear Sophie, it is almost insupportable.'

To Taube he wrote on the same day: 'we still have not heard anything; our courier has not yet returned.' When the news did come it was wrong. On Saturday 26 January at nine in the evening Fersen was told by the Directeur des Postes Impériales that a courier had brought the news that the King had been decapitated and the whole family massacred.

Believing that the Queen was dead, Fersen wrote another passionate letter to Sophie. 'Would that I had died at her side for her and for them on 20 June . . . never will her adored image be effaced from my memory.' He was, of course, misinformed. Marie-Antoinette had not yet been put out of her sufferings. On 15 February Fersen, who knew the truth by now, allowed himself to entertain a glimmer of hope for the Queen and her children, but he was still haunted by the horror of the act of regicide: 'the image of Louis XVI mounting the scaffold never leaves me.'

Madame de Tourzel and Pauline, now retired to the Château d'Abondant near Dreux, were also overcome with sorrow and anxiety; 'the cruel death of our good, unhappy King, was the final blow.' What made it worse was the difficulty in obtaining accurate information. A fortnight after the event, however, one of Madame de Tourzel's women, a Mademoiselle Pion, was asked to prepare the clothes for Madame Royale to go into mourning. She was the person named by Marie-Antoinette in her conversation with Goret. It took her two days and she was able to bring back assurances that the royal family were all in good health.

'I cannot tell you', she continued, 'all that I felt on seeing that my poor little person could bring a ray of light and consolation to the faces of this august family. Their looks said more to me than their words could have done; and Monseigneur le Dauphin, whose age excuses his monkey tricks, took the opportunity to put to me, in the form of a game, all the questions which the royal family would have desired to ask. He ran now to me, now to the Queen, to the two princesses and even to the municipal officer. Each time he came to me he did not fail to ask me some question about people in whom the royal family were interested. He charged me to give a kiss to you, as well as to Mademoiselle Pauline, did not forget any of those whom he loved and played his part so well that one could hardly suspect that he had spoken to me at all.'

The good health of the royal family, of which Mademoiselle Pion had spoken, was not to last. First, Madame Royale had a pain in one leg which threatened to become serious. 'Brunyer, the children's doctor, was sent for who found that she wanted for even the most necessary objects as, for instance, linen with which to dress her leg, and he was obliged to bring some of his own.' He, too, could report to Madame de Tourzel on the sweetness of the young Princess in the midst of her profound grief, and the patience with which she bore her suffering.

At the beginning of May Louis-Charles became ill. Marie-Antoinette petitioned the Conseil Général to send Dr Brunyer, 'médecin ordinaire de mes enfants'. On Friday 10 May the council decreed that 'the ordinary prison doctor would go and look after the little Capet, it being understood that it would be an offence against equality – *blesser l'égalité* – to send any other.'

Fortunately the 'ordinary prison doctor', Thierry by name, had been doctor to the old maréchal de Mouchy and was *persona grata* with Madame de Tourzel. This enabled her to obtain from him more first-hand news of the royal family. He also took the trouble to seek out Brunyer and to discover the temperament of the child and continued to keep in touch with him. The young Prince had damaged one of his testicles while riding hobby-horse. On Tuesday 11 June the Conseil du Temple notified the Conseil Général de la Commune that the boy had a hernia and that the doctor who visited him recommended the attentions of the *citoyen* Piple (or Pipelet) 'bandageist des prisons', who was instructed to visit the Temple without delay.

On 22 May Fersen mentioned another physician who had penetrated the Temple – La Caze, as he spells it. 'He found the Queen little changed but Elizabeth was so altered that he only recognised her when the Queen addressed her as "my sister" ... The little Madame had her whole body covered in ulcers which threatened a dissolution of the blood ... It is reported from Paris that the young King had been ill and the commune had refused the doctor whom the Queen had asked for on the pretext that he was an aristocrat.'

Quintin Crawfurd, writing to Lord Auckland from Brussels on 23 May, confirms Fersen's information. 'There are accounts directly from the Temple as late as the eighth of this month. They come from La Case, an eminent surgeon who formerly attended the royal family. He was permitted to see them on account of the indisposition of the Princess Royal, whom he found in a very dangerous way; her brother was then well, but it is said has lately had a fever. The Queen did not appear to him to be so much altered: he says "her countenance announced a profound melancholy, but her conversation and behaviour [announced] that composure and magnanimity she has constantly shown since the beginning of her misfortunes."'

In June, Fersen was beginning to take a more optimistic line. There had been talk in the convention of deporting the royal family. On 9 June he wrote to Sophie: 'the news is good on all sides; may it continue the same; that which concerns the august prisoners is very reassuring and so far there are neither motions nor commotions against them; that gives me a little hope to see them one day delivered from their long captivity.'

The greatest threat to the royal family was the constant fear on the part of the authorities that there might be some conspiracy to rescue them. Their fears were only too well founded. In March the baron de Batz aided by the municipal officers Michonis and Toulan, who had conveyed Louis XVI's last mementos to Marie-Antoinette, her former secretary the chevalier de Jarjayes and others devised a plot for getting the royal family out of the Temple. It had every chance of success, but it had to be restricted to the escape of the Queen alone and she refused. 'We have had a beautiful dream,' she wrote to Jarjayes; 'that is all. But we have gained much in finding on this occasion a fresh proof of your total devotion to me. My confidence in you has no limits. You will always find in me a strength of character and courage, but the interest of my son is the only one which guides me. Whatever happiness I should have felt from being out of here, I cannot consent to being separated from him.'

Her son was now her only *raison d'être*. His education had been his father's chief concern and delight; it was now to be hers. She could have had no more engaging a pupil. Hue records an occasion when the boy's schooling had been interrupted by political events and his tutor, the abbé Davaux was able to resume his work. 'Your last lesson', he said, 'if I remember rightly, was on the subject of the three degrees of comparison – the positive, the comparative and the superlative. But you have forgotten it all.' 'You are wrong,' replied the Dauphin; 'listen to me and I'll prove it. The positive is when I say "my abbé is a good abbé;" the comparative, when I say "my abbé is better than any other abbé;" the superlative, he continued looking towards the Queen, is when I say: "Mama is the most loving and best of all mothers!" The Queen took Monsieur le Dauphin in her arms and held him to her heart; she could not restrain her tears.'

Louis-Charles seems to have been all that a mother's heart could have desired. 'To his sensitivity', wrote Cléry, 'the young Prince added considerable charm and all the loveableness of his age [he was eight on 27 March 1793]. Often, by his naivety, the playfulness of his character, his little monkey-tricks, he caused his august parents to forget their unhappy situation.' Even Hébert fell under his charm. 'I have seen the little child of the Tower,' he told Pache; 'he is as beautiful as the day and as interesting as is possible.' But it was Hébert who was preparing the final blow from which Marie-Antoinette was never to recover and was plotting the destruction of her son.

On 3 July the blow fell. According to the official minutes, 'at half past nine in the evening, we, the Commissioners on duty, entered the apartment of the widow Capet whom we notified of the decree of the Comité de Salut Public de la Convention National and invited her to comply with it. After certain representations (instances) the widow Capet at last made up her mind to hand over to us her son, who was conducted into the apartment designated by the decree of the Council of today's date and placed in the hands of the citizen Simon, who took charge of him. We make the further observation that the separation was accomplished with all the sensitiveness which one could expect in circumstances in which the magistrates of the people showed all the respect compatible with the severity of their function.'

That was how bureaucracy recorded the event. The Princess Royal recounts the same occasion in rather more human terms, from the point of view of the Queen and of the Dauphin. 'As soon as he heard it,' wrote Marie-Thérèse, 'he threw himself into my mother's arms crying out aloud not to be separated from her. My mother, for her part, was prostrated by this cruel order; she refused to hand over my brother and defended against the municipals the bed on which she had placed him. These, determined to have him, threatened to employ violence and to call up the guard. My mother said that it was only over her dead body that they would have her child; an hour passed thus in resistance on her part, in abuse and threats on the part of the municipals, in tears and defences from all of us. Finally they threatened so positively to kill him as well as myself that she had to yield for love of us . . . this poor little boy kissed us all tenderly and went out with the municipals crying his heart out.'

The marquise de Tourzel who, as governess to the royal children had loved Louis-Charles as a mother her son, was prostrated by the news. 'It would be impossible to express what we suffered when we heard that the young King had been taken away from the Queen . . . I pictured to myself the profound grief into which the family was plunged and tears always rose to my eyes when I looked at the portrait of the dear little Prince.' Worst of all, he had been put in the custody of Simon, 'an atrocious man who had shown what he was made of in the Temple.' Simon had been one of the municipal officers on duty at the Temple and Marie-Antoinette knew his character. 'She had been overwhelmed by this separation,' wrote Marie-Thérèse; 'her devastation reached its utmost limits when she learnt that it was Simon . . . to whose care the unfortunate child had been committed.'

Antoine Simon, 'one of the most ardent members of the Club des Cordeliers', was proposed for the guardianship of Louis-Charles by Marat, seconded by Robespierre. He was required never to leave his prisoner and on no pretext whatever to leave the Tour du Temple. His brief was to make a good little citizen out of the little Louis Capet, to efface the stigma of royalty from his brow and replace the crown with the red bonnet of liberty. In other words, Simon set out to brutalise the boy.

Most of the horrific stories are recorded by Alcide de Beauchesne, who was an ardent royalist, but some are attested by Revolutionaries such as the Conventionel Harmand de la Meuse. He tells how Simon, 'without regard for his young age, for which sleep is so imperative a need, would call him several times in the night, crying: "Capet! Capet!' The Prince replied: "here I am, citizen." "Come here that I may see you!" . . . He then sent his victim sprawling with a kick, shouting: "Go and lie down, wolf cub!"' Harmand adds: 'this has already been written, but I record it because the commissaries [at the Temple] gave us an account of which the recollection makes one shudder.'

Beauchesne bases his account on oral evidence obtained in conversation with three women who were closely connected with Madame Simon. 'We repeat these scenes', he claims, 'just as they were recounted to us . . . certain that if the lips by which they were spoken may have involuntarily changed something, they have invented nothing nor altered the underlying truth.' It is not known at what date he had these conversations.

The general picture to emerge from Beauchesne's anecdotes is of a determined effort to break the boy's will and brainwash him into a condition in which he would say anything. For some time the boy resisted. On one occasion, soon after his transfer to Simon's tutelage, says Beauchesne, the young Prince was loudly protesting that no-one had shown the law by which he could be separated from his mother. Simon shouted at him: 'Silence, Capet! Or I'll show these citizens how I wallop you when you deserve it.'

Marie-Thérèse and Madame Elizabeth could often hear him singing with Simon Revolutionary songs such as the *Marseillaise* and the *Carmagnole*. 'He was made to sing out of the windows so that the guard could hear him,' continues Marie-Thérèse, 'and he was taught to use the most horrible swear-words against God, against his family, against the aristocrats. My mother, mercifully, could not hear all these horrors.'

The one solace now left to Marie-Antoinette was to walk behind the battlements of the Grosse Tour from which advantage point she could sometimes gain, through a narrow crack, a distant glimpse of her son. 'She would remain there for hours on end waiting for the moment when she could see her child; it was the only thing to which she looked forward and her only occupation.'

On 1 August this one solace was taken from her. The National Convention, inspired by a rhetorical tirade from Barère, decreed that 'la Veuve Capet' should be brought to judgement and consequently transferred from the Temple to the prison of the Conciergerie. In the early hours of 2 August Marie-Antoinette was awakened and informed of the decree. Taking what she must have known to be her last farewell of her daughter and her sister-in-law, she left the building in which she had lived for nearly a year. As she went out she struck her head on a low beam. One of the guards enquired if she had hurt herself. 'No,' she answered; 'nothing can hurt me now.'

The Conciergerie

The prison of the Conciergerie was part of a larger ensemble which had once been the Parisian palace of the kings of France. The earliest depiction of it which exists, the exquisite miniature in the *Très Riches Heures du Duc de Berry*, shows the Palais de la Cité as it was after the important additions and reconstructions of Philippe le Bel. The scene is idyllic – the juxtaposition of a proud and princely architecture with the simple rustic charm of the island before it. In the background is the palace, an exciting medley of high-pitched roofs with correspondingly acute-angled gables and towers capped with pointed pepper-boxes. In the foreground is a meadow; the peasants are scything the hay while their women rake it into little stooks beside the pollarded willows which line the stream. It is a halcyon day and it only needs a kingfisher to complete the picture.

High above the crowded roofscape soars the upper storey of the Sainte-Chapelle, built by Saint-Louis to house the Crown of Thorns. The Sainte-Chapelle is one of the great achievements of the Gothic style. As late as 1890, Sauveur-Jérome Morand was generous in his praise: 'the piety of Saint-Louis has been most happily complemented in the industry of his architects . . . it seems as if some more than human hand was at work in this superb monument.'

On 22 February 1358, the palace was the scene of a revolt, led by Étienne Marcel. Robert de Clermont and Jean de Conflans were murdered in the presence of the Dauphin, later to rule as Charles V. When Charles came to the throne he abandoned the scene of this outrage and took up residence at the Hôtel de Saint-Pol near the Bastille. Made over to the use of the Parlement de Paris, the vast agglomeration of the Palais de la Cité was placed in the care of its *concierge*. In due course it became known as the Conciergerie. Its main designation was to house the Palais de Justice, but it also contained a prison. 'You who have not passed a night here in the midst of that assemblage of horrors,' wrote the comte Beugnot after his own imprisonment, 'you have endured nothing; you have never suffered in this world.'

In 1793 the concierge of this prison was one Toussaint Richard, a painstaking and hard-working man. It was his wife, Marie-Anne, however, who seems to have been the real centre of authority. 'I never saw my mistress at a loss,' wrote her *femme de chambre*, Rosalie Lamorlière; 'she answered everyone with few words; she gave her orders without any confusion; she hardly slept more than a few instants and nothing happened either inside or outside without her being promptly informed.'

Rosalie Lamorlière, of whom the Court painter Joseph Boze, himself a prisoner in the Conciergerie, has written the testimonial, was twenty-four at the time. 'This excellent girl', wrote Boze, 'was cook to the *concierge* and in this capacity prepared the meals for the unfortunate Queen Marie-Antoinette and made her bed. Rosalie, in spite of the times, which were so evil, had retained an honest heart and the most correct opinions. The respect which she showed for the august prisoner every time that she came to her cell, and the consternation which she showed on her face when the Queen was condemned and when that unfortunate Princess left for the scaffold, were noticed by the turnkeys, with the result that the coarser sort of person no longer called her Rosalie but *Mamzelle Capet*.'

By a strange chance the last human being to be closely associated with Marie-Antoinette was a simple serving girl. Two people between whom birth could not have placed a wider gulf – one the daughter of an Empress and widow of a King, the other the daughter of a peasant from Picardy, had found the only equality that matters, the equality of common humanity.

Rosalie Lamorlière has left an account of Marie-Antoinette's last days which is certainly 'eye-witness', and told with a direct simplicity which encourages confidence.

> On 1 August 1793, just after dinner, Madame Richard said to me in a low voice: 'Rosalie, tonight we will not be going to bed; you will sleep on a chair; the Queen is to be transferred from the Temple to this prison.' She gave orders that General Custines should be removed from the *Chambre du Conseil* in order that the Princess should be lodged there. A turnkey was dispatched to the *tapissier* of the prison. He was asked for a trestle bed, two mattresses, a bolster, a coverlet and a wash basin.
>
> These small furnishings were brought to the damp chamber vacated by Monsieur de Custines; to it was added a common table and two prison chairs.
>
> Towards three in the morning, I was drowsing in an armchair; Madame Richard, tugging me by the arm, woke me up hurriedly and said these words: 'Rosalie, come, come, we must wake up; take this flambeau, here they come.'

It has to be remembered that, for a simple girl like Rosalie, a Queen was still a figure infinitely remote and august. The reverence to royalty, which until so recently had come so naturally to a French subject, was not extinct; neither was it eclipsed by the compassion which was evoked by Marie-Antoinette's condition. 'I went downstairs trembling,' continued Rosalie, 'and accompanied Madame Richard to the cell of Monsieur de Custines, situated at the end of a long, dark corridor.'

A detailed description of Marie-Antoinette's cell was written in 1797 by the historian Montjoye:

> This closet was divided into two equal halves by a wooden partition which left a gap in the middle which Richard closed with a wretched screen. The door gave access to the left-hand compartment; opposite the door was a window provided with iron bars which looked onto the yard known as the Cour des Femmes . . . In this left-hand part were stationed two gendarmes . . . who put up a camp-bed during the night.

> The Queen occupied the right-hand compartment; her bed was placed at the end opposite the window . . . The wall was lined throughout its length and height with a panel of wood. They had, however, nailed onto this panel a cloth to which was stuck some paper painted with fleurs de lys.

The room measured four and a half by two and a half metres. The Queen was signed in there and then, and the escort retired, leaving Marie-Antoinette alone with Madame Richard and Rosalie. 'It was hot,' she wrote; 'I noticed beads of sweat which ran down the Princess' face. She wiped them off two or three times with her handkerchief. Her eyes gazed with astonishment at the horrible nakedness of the walls of this chamber; they were also turned with some attention on the wife of the *concierge* and myself.'

Although it was by now already daylight, Marie-Antoinette needed to go to bed. She hung her watch on a nail on the wall and began to undress. 'I approached respectfully,' wrote Rosalie, 'and offered my services to the Queen. "I thank you, my dear," she replied, without any pride or moodiness, "but since I no longer have anyone I do it for myself."'

For a month or so Rosalie had no particular function with the Queen. She helped the Richards to serve the meals – breakfast at nine o'clock and dinner usually at two or half past two. 'Madame Richard laid the table and I stood respectfully by the door. But Her Majesty deigned to notice me and did me the honour of saying to me: "come on in, Rosalie; don't be afraid."'

Rosalie gives a number of interesting details on the regime of the Conciergerie. In the first place Marie-Antoinette was reasonably well fed. 'Her Majesty ate with a good enough appetite; she cut her chicken in two, that is to say, to last her two days. She separated the meat from the bone with an unbelievable ease and dexterity. She left little of the vegetables which constituted the second course.' Marie-Antoinette never drank anything but water, except at breakfast, and the water from the Ville d'Avray was the only water that she could drink. Hue managed to establish a line of communication between the Conciergerie and the Temple and Madame Richard, known under the pseudonym of 'Sensible', was allowed to go each day to the Temple and obtain two bottles of this water.

The Queen had arrived with no spare clothes and no clean linen. Madame Richard dared not either lend her any or procure any for her. Michonis, one of the municipal officers at the Temple, finally brought over a packet which the Queen opened promptly. 'In it were beautiful chemises of cambric, pocket handkerchiefs, fichus, stockings of silk or floss silk, a white morning *déshabille*, a few nightcaps and several lengths of ribbon of different widths. Marie-Antoinette was deeply moved as she went through this linen, and, turning to Madame Richard and myself, said: "by the loving care with which this has been done I recognise the hand and the attention of my poor sister Elizabeth."'

The inventory drawn up after the death of the Queen reveals a fairly ample wardrobe. There was one difficulty, however; she had nowhere to put it all. She asked for a box in which to keep her clothes, but once again Madame Richard did not dare ask the administrators for such a privilege, 'but she authorised me to lend the Princess a cardboard box,' said Rosalie, 'which she accepted with as much satisfaction as if one had assigned her the most beautiful piece of furniture in the world.'

Four or five days after Marie-Antoinette's admission to the Conciergerie the administrators took her watch from her. She had brought it from Austria when she had first come to France and it had great sentimental value. 'I was not with her', writes Rosalie, 'when they caused her this distress, but Madame Richard talked of it in our room and said that she had wept much at handing over her gold watch. By good luck the commissioners did not know that she carried an oval medallion of great price hung round her neck with a black cord. The medallion contained some locks of hair and a portrait of the young King. It was in a little yellow leather glove which had once been worn by Monsieur le Dauphin.'

One day Madame Richard unintentionally upset Marie-Antoinette by bringing her youngest son, known as 'Fanfan', with her to the cell. Fanfan was a distinguished-looking child with fair hair and lovely blue eyes. 'The Queen started visibly on seeing this beautiful little boy; she took him in her arms, covered him with caresses and kisses and began to weep, talking to us of Monsieur le Dauphin who was of the same age. She thought about him day and night. The incident caused her grievous pain. Madame Richard, as soon as we were back upstairs, told me that she would take care never to bring her son again to the cell.'

Apart from the incident of the gold watch, Marie-Antoinette does not appear to have suffered so much in the way of petty persecutions as she did in the Temple, until an ill-starred attempt was made to effect her escape. It became known as 'l'affaire de l'oeillet'.

On Wednesday 28 August Jean-Baptiste Michonis, administrator of prisons, entered the Queen's cell. He was followed by another man at the sight of whom Marie-Antoinette showed strong signs of emotion. She recognised him as one of those who had stood by the royal family in defence of the Tuileries on 20 June and 10 August. He was known as the chevalier de Rougeville, but his real name was Alexandre Gousse; he was a chevalier de Saint-Louis. He let drop a bunch of carnations in which was concealed a letter. In a hurried conversation, Rougeville told Marie-Antoinette that he had both money and arms at his disposal and urged her to take courage. After his departure she read the letter and tore it into a thousand little pieces. She later admitted at an inquest to having received the letter and claimed that it only contained 'vague phrases: "What do you mean to do? What do you intend to do? I have been in prison; I got out by a miracle; I will come on Friday."' She also admitted to having pricked out with a pin on a piece of paper: 'Je suis gardée à vue, je ne parle ni écris.'

She entrusted this reply to Jean Gilbert, one of the two *gendarmes* who guarded her night and day. On the day before the intended escape, the night of 2 September, one of the *gendarmes*, although already bribed, gave the plot away. The next day Gilbert denounced the conspiracy. Rougeville escaped; Michonis was arrested and much later guillotined for an offence of which he was entirely innocent; the two Richards were sent to prison. Rosalie qualifies the occasion as 'a great misfortune which did much harm to the Queen'.

On 23 September a Miss Chowne, who later married a diplomat from Saxony, the Count von Brühl, wrote to Lord Auckland:

> before I close my letter, I must just mention an affecting description of the Queen of France which I have received from an English gentleman who saw her a short time before the decree [of September 7] came out against all the English . . . He was admitted to see the Conciergerie, and, upon expressing a wish to see the unfortunate Queen, was told it would be readily granted if he showed no signs of compassion, but that if he did he must not think of ever coming out of the place again; the conditions being agreed to, he was led into a room in which the poor Queen was sitting, on an old worn out chair made of straw, which scarcely supported her weight. Dressed in a gown which had once been white, her attitude bespoke the immensity of her grief, which appeared to have created a kind of stupor, that fortunately rendered her less sensible to the injuries and reproaches, which a number of inhuman wretches were continually vomiting forth against her.

After the imprisonment of the Richards, a new *concierge* was appointed named Bault; Rosalie consistently calls him Lebeau. 'He seemed a rough and severe man at first sight,' she observed, 'but at heart he was not a bad man.' He was, however, a frightened man. He was to answer with his head for the security of the Queen. Henceforth he and he alone held the key to her cell.

The windows of the cell were placed low in the wall space and it was possible for those outside to see into it. It was also possible for Marie-Antoinette to see into some of the cells opposite. One day, records Rosalie, 'she noticed, opposite her windows, through the iron bars of a cell, a female prisoner who joined her hands and raised her eyes to heaven as she said her prayers. "Rosalie," said this great and good Princess, "look up there at that poor nun, with what fervour she prays to the good Lord."'

Not much can be said with confidence about Marie-Antoinette's religious convictions, but she certainly did not have her mother's robust faith. With the experience of adversity, but above all as the result of her close association with the saintly Madame Elizabeth, it is not improbable that she began to find a deeper consolation in religious practice. Her daughter noticed it in the Temple.

The Church also had been affected by the times. During the *ancien régime* there was much to criticise; the system was badly corrupt and clergy often deservedly unpopular. During the Revolution some of the clergy – and many more monks – joined the ranks of the *enragés* and become some of the most dangerous Jacobins. Others, forced to choose between taking the oath and disobedience to the Pope, suffered persecution and death. Some, however, managed to avoid taking the oath and continued to minister, at great personal risk, to Catholics who had remained loyal. Many of them contrived to minister to those in the prisons and, by stationing themselves at strategic points along the route to the guillotine, even to those in their last minutes before death. Among many names worthy of respect, that of the abbé Emery has been authenticated by the abbé Gosselin.

Gosselin assures us that Emery, himself a prisoner in the Conciergerie, was able on at least one occasion to pronounce the words of absolution to the Queen. 'He has himself asserted several times', writes Gosselin, 'that being lodged above the Queen, and having had the ability to correspond with her by means of certain other prisoners, he sent her a note one day which read: "prepare to receive absolution; today at midnight I will be outside your door and will pronounce the priestly words."' Whether anyone could have heard anything through that door is hard to imagine. A painting, engraved as early as 1796, shows a priest, not outside the door but thrusting his hands through the bars of the cell. It must have been a tradition dating from very soon after the event.

The abbé Magnin, who under the restoration became *curé* at the royal parish of Saint-Germain l'Auxerrois, also claimed that he had had 'the good fortune on two occasions to confess the Queen of France and to bring her the blessed sacrament when Richard was still *concierge*.'

It was through the good offices of Mademoiselle Fouché that Magnin was put in touch with Marie-Antoinette. He explained that all the articles needed for a celebration were available – a very small chalice which could be dismantled; a missal printed in 18°, an altar stone just larger than the foot of the chalice, all could be put in a little work bag and concealed in a pocket.

According to Mademoiselle Fouché the *concierge* Bault let them in at some date 'during the first days of October'. Mademoiselle Fouché and two of the *gendarmes* expressed a desire to receive communion also. 'Without losing an instant we prepared, on the little table, all that was necessary,' wrote Magnin; 'I celebrated the sacrifice of our altars and I gave communion to the Queen who, nourished with the eucharistic bread, received from God the courage to endure, without complaining, all the anguish which awaited her.'

There are certain difficulties in accepting these stories. There exists a document sometimes called the 'testament' of Marie-Antoinette which is in the form of a letter to Madame Elizabeth. It contains the words: 'having had no spiritual consolation, not knowing if there still exist any priests of this religion, and also the place where I am would expose them too much if they entered.' It was possible, we know, to see into the Queen's cell.

There are, however, serious doubts as to the authenticity of this document; some are based on differences in the handwriting, some on the near impossibility of her having achieved it in the time available. Rosalie knows nothing of it. But the abbé Magnin, who clearly accepted the authenticity of the 'testament' explains the matter thus: 'prudence and the desire not to give away the priests who had assisted her as well as those persons who had exerted themselves to introduce them, were enough to suggest this reflection.'

Magnin was taken ill shortly after giving communion to the Queen, but Mademoiselle Fouché was able to bring another priest, the abbé Cholet, to celebrate mass on the night of 12 October.

On 13 October the drama moved into its last act; the Queen was to stand trial the next day, but the preparations for this move had been in hand for some time.

On 3 October it was decreed that the Revolutionary tribunal should proceed 'without delay or interruption' to the judgement of the 'Veuve Capet'. Two days later, Fouquier-Tinville complained that he had not received any documentation for the prosecution. He did not receive any before 12 and 13 October. It was only this day that any counsel for the defence was appointed – Claude Chauveau-Lagarde and Guillaume Tronçon-Ducoudray. Chauveau-Lagarde proceeded at once to the Conciergerie and was conducted to the Queen's cell. 'After passing through two wicket gates, one finds oneself in a dark corridor, on entering which one can only proceed by the glimmer of a lamp which is always lit.

'Her Majesty was dressed in white and with the most extreme simplicity. Nobody, imagining himself to be in such a place and putting himself in my position, could possibly feel what I experienced on seeing here the wife of one of the most worthy successors of Saint-Louis, the august daughter of the Emperors of Germany, a Queen who by her grace and goodness had been the centre of attraction in the most brilliant Court in Europe and the idol of the French nation.'

It must be remembered that Chauveau-Lagarde was a devoted royalist and that he published his memoirs in 1816, just when Louis XVIII was beginning to conduct a propaganda campaign to whitewash Marie-Antoinette and thus to blacken her persecutors. The contrast between Marie-

Antoinette enthroned at Versailles and Marie-Antoinette imprisoned in the Conciergerie was none the less extreme.

'I made my first notes for the defence,' continues Chauveau-Lagarde; 'I went up to the office of the clerk of the court to examine what they called the documents of the case; I found a heap of them so confused and so voluminous that it would have taken weeks on end to examine them. I went back down into the prison and it seems that I am still present [so vividly could he remember it] at the interview which I had, on this occasion, the honour of having with Her Majesty.'

Chauveau-Lagarde suggested that the Queen might ask for a respite so that he coud examine the papers. 'To whom', asked the Queen, 'should one apply for it?' 'I was afraid of answering and I pronounced in a low voice the name of the Convention Nationale. "No," replied the Queen, turning her head away; "no, never!"' For some time Chauveau-Lagarde argued in vain; finally he played his trump card. 'I added that we had to defend, in the person of Her Majesty, not only the Queen of France but also the widow of Louis XVI, the mother of the King's children and the sister-in-law of our Princes, all referred to in the accusation.' This appeal succeeded. 'At the words *sister*, *wife* and *mother*, nature prevailed against sovereignty; the Queen, not without heaving a sigh, took the pen and wrote to the Assembly.' The letter was ignored. The trial began on the next day.

Meanwhile activities of a different sort were being set in motion by Hébert. Much of the evidence comes from a source which records an extraordinary success by English spies on the continent. 'Perhaps the most remarkable documents describing affairs in France', states the introduction to the Dropmore papers, 'will be found to be a series of "Bulletins" in French which reach Grenville [the Foreign Secretary] by way of Genoa through Francis Drake, our resident there.' At a time when the British government had no representative in Paris and information was difficult to obtain, it is particularly precious to have first hand accounts of the sittings of the Committee of Nine (the Committee of

Public Safety). 'Your Lordship may rely on the authenticity of it,' insists Drake, 'as it was drawn up by a person who is employed as secretary of that committee and who conceals his real principles under the cloak of the most extravagant Jacobinism. Lord Mulgrave will explain to your Lordship the route by which his communications are transmitted to me.'

The first Bulletin describes the session of 2 September, 1793. The Committee of Public Safety, composed entirely of extremists such as Robespierre, Hérault de Séchelles and Barère, was the true centre of power in the Convention. It was here that the fate of Marie-Antoinette was sealed – 'on y resolut la mort de la Reine.'

Cambon tried to suggest that her value as a hostage ought not to be overlooked, but the proposition met with a torrent of abuse. The new King, Louis XVII, it was pointed out, provided as good a bargaining point. Hébert would listen to no argument. 'I have promised the head of Antoinette,' he thundered; 'and I will cut it off myself unless it is given to me without delay. I have promised it on your behalf to the *sans culottes* who demand it and without whom you would cease to exist . . . You must give satisfaction to the *sans culottes*; they will kill all your enemies, but they must be kept at full heat and you can only do that by the death of Antoinette.'

If the committee really wanted to use Louis XVII as a hostage, they would have been well advised to have treated him better. The bulletins forwarded by Drake give details of his degradation. It seems that responsibility for the young King was shared between Simon and Hébert and that some of the excesses of Hébert may have been attributed to Simon:

> He admits, however, that he had given him the habit of taking strong drink and that he was receiving no sort of education; that Hébert and the soldiers by whom he is surrounded teach him nothing but blasphemies and obscenities . . . Simon has no doubts that the King is infected with venereal disease, although, since the death of the Queen, no more prostitutes have been introduced; but he believes that what was done at

> that time was in order to make him give evidence against his mother and to prove, by his state of health, the truth of his depositions, which was enough to corrupt and pollute him. He [Simon] claims therefore in no uncertain terms that he is ill and nothing has been done to cure him.

It is clear that the boy's health was deteriorating from day to day and that he suffered from almost continual diarrhoea. Hébert, according to Simon, often threatened to guillotine him; this threat caused him such horrible fright that he was seen to faint. The two members of the national guard gave similar details.

On 6 October Hébert and Chaumette with Pache and four other officials went to the Temple and, together with Simon, confronted the boy with an admission that his mother and Madame Elizabeth had instructed him in the practice of self abuse and that he had had intercourse with his mother. Louis-Charles signed this. The next day he was made to repeat his admission in front of his sister and his aunt, which he did.

Vincent Cronin, who interprets these admissions by Louis-Charles as proof that he had been brainwashed, has sketched in the background to the fanatical hatred felt for Marie-Antoinette and for the readiness, if not the eagerness, to believe the most revolting allegations against her. Pamphlets, among the most potent influences upon public opinion, became more and more explicit. To the *Soirées Amoureuses du général Mottier et de la belle Antoinette* of 1790, succeeded *Fureurs utérines de Marie-Antoinette, femme de Louis XVI* in 1791, only to be overtaken by *Tentation d'Antoinette et de son cochon dans la Tour du Temple* in 1792. 'Some of the pamphlets', writes Cronin, 'have illustrations of great obscenity.' The theatre, always able to provide a vivid visual aid to propaganda, did not lag behind. The production in August 1792 of *La Journée Amoureuse, ou les Derniers Plaisirs de M . . . Ant . . .* marked an all time low. 'The Queen came to be seen as a loathsome, unnatural creature, sapping the strength of an impotent King and prepared to indulge her sexual voracity at no matter what cost to the people.'

It was a short step from the depravities enacted in *La Journée Amoureuse* to the accusation of the sexual abuse of her son, but here it was given a political significance. 'There is reason to believe', claimed Hébert, 'that this criminal intercourse was dictated, not by pleasure, but by the calculated hope of enervating this child, whom they still liked to think of as destined to occupy a throne and whom they wished to be sure of dominating morally.' Hébert knew what he was talking about; he and Simon had achieved this moral domination in their own interests. But, for once, this calumny went too far.

When the accusation came up in the trial the Queen took no notice of it. The President Herman did not make use of it, but one of the jury – he was, perhaps significantly, not mentioned by name – brought the attention of the court back to this accusation. 'Citizen President', he said; 'I invite you to have the goodness to remind the accused that she has not replied to the occurrence of which the citizen Hébert spoke concerning what took place between herself and her son.' This gave Marie-Antoinette the chance that she needed. Hitherto she had mostly confined herself to simple denials of each charge; now she rose from her seat. 'If I did not reply,' she said, 'it is because nature refuses to reply to such an accusation made to a mother. I appeal to all those who may be present here.'

No attempt was made to drive home the charges. Herman, in his summing up, prudently made no mention of them. Even Robespierre, according to Joachim Vilate, deplored the scurrilous device. At supper that night with Barère and Saint-Juste, he became so angry on hearing of it that he broke his plate and cursed 'cet imbécile d'Hébert' for having given the Queen 'ce triomphe d'intérêt public'.

If Marie-Antoinette scored a 'triumph', it availed her nothing. Her condemnation was determined on before the trial began. She was condemned.

It would be difficult to imagine a more incompetent piece of legal procedure than the trial of Marie-Antoinette. Endless questions, many of them leading questions, were put and usually met with a simple denial. Witnesses referred to documents which they claimed to have seen but could not produce in court. There are even vague demands for individual opinions. The Administrateur de Police, Dange, for instance was asked: 'what is your opinion of the Accused?' He answered prudently: 'if she is guilty she ought to be sentenced.'

One of the earliest English records of the trial, by John Adolphus, was not far wrong in stating that 'this composition was a mass of absurd allegations supported by abusive epithets and outrageous calumnies.' As the comte de La Marck put it: 'It is enough to read the proceedings of the Queen's trial to see that after three years of a raving Revolution, they could not gather a single count of an indictment that would have stood up before an impartial jury.'

What is strange is that it was thought to be necessary to go on with this farce for so long. On the first day it lasted from nine in the morning to three in the afternoon and then from five till eleven; on the second day the first session again lasted from nine till three and then from five till four on Wednesday 16 October. Merely to have sat it out must have been a considerable ordeal for anyone in Marie-Antoinette's condition. It was a bad time in the month for her and, as Rosalie informs us, she was subject to severe haemorrhages.

One rather touching detail is recorded by Ventre de la Touloubre, known more familiarly as Montjoye. Lieutenant de Busne of the *gendarmerie* complained that he was accused by a colleague of the heinous offence 'of having given a glass of water to the accused,' and of having held his hat in his hand, 'because of the heat and for my comfort', he insisted; 'not out of respect for a woman who stood, in my opinion, condemned'. He later offered her his arm to descend the interior staircase of the Conciergerie. She was so tired that she could scarcely see to walk. The news did did not take long to reach the Conciergerie. 'At a little past four in the morning of 16 October', wrote Rosalie, 'we were told that the Queen of

France was condemned. I felt as if a sword had pierced my heart and went and wept in my room.' She continued,

> The *concierge* heard of the condemnation with pain, but he was more accustomed to such things than I was . . . At about seven in the morning he told me to go down to the Queen and to ask if she wanted any sustenance. On entering the cell, where two lights were burning, I perceived an officer of the *gendarmerie* seated in the corner on the left, and, having come nearer to Madame, I saw her, dressed all in black, stretched out on her bed, her face turned towards the window and her head supported on her hand. 'Madame,' I said to her with a trembling voice, 'you took nothing yesterday evening and practically nothing during the day. What would you like to take this morning?' The Queen shed copious tears; she replied: 'My dear, I have no longer any need of anything; it is all over with me.' I took the liberty to add: 'Madame, I have kept on my stove a soup and some vermicelli; you need something to give you strength; allow me to bring you something.' The tears welled up again in the Queen's eyes and she said to me: 'Rosalie, bring me some soup.' I went off and fetched it; she sat up, but could only manage to swallow a few spoonfuls.

A priest who had taken the oath was sent by the government and offered to hear her confession, but she declined his ministry. He accompanied her, nevertheless, to the scaffold.

At daybreak Rosalie came to help the Queen to dress. There was a *gendarme* present and Marie-Antoinette made signs to Rosalie to stand between them while she changed her linen.

> The officer immediately approached and stood by the bolster of the bed and watched her undress. Her Majesty immediately put her fichu round her shoulders and with great gentleness said to the young man: 'in the name of decency, sir, allow me to change my linen without being observed.' 'I cannot consent,' said the officer bluntly; 'my orders state that I am to keep an eye on all your movements.' The Queen sighed and put on her chemise for the last time with all the precautions and modesty possible and chose as her garment not the long, black widow's skirt that she had worn before her judges, but the white *déshabillé* which she wore in the mornings.

The parting was too much for Rosalie. 'I left her without saying good bye . . . and went off to cry in my room and to pray to God for her.'

Perhaps the most dispassionate account of the last days of Marie-Antoinette comes from the pages of the Moniteur:

> During her interrogation, Marie-Antoinette nearly always preserved a bearing which was calm and assured. During the first hours of her interrogation she could be seen to run her hands along the bar with the appearance of abstraction as if she were playing a *forte-piano*. On hearing her sentence she did not show any signs of faltering and she left the Court without saying a word to the judges or to the public.
>
> It was half past four in the morning of 16 October; she was conducted back to the condemned cell in the prison of the Conciergerie.
>
> At five o'clock the call to arms was sounded in all the sections; at seven the armed force was on parade; cannons were placed at the ends of the bridges and at the squares and crossroads from the Palais to the Place de la Révolution; at ten o'clock along all the way a large number of patrols were circulating in the streets.
>
> At eleven o'clock Marie-Antoinette, 'Veuve Capet', in an informal dress of white *piqué*, was driven to her execution in the same manner as other criminals, accompanied by a constitutional priest dressed as a layman, and escorted by a large number of detachments of *gendarmerie*, both mounted and on foot.
>
> Antoinette, all the way along, appeared to look with indifference on this armed force which, numbering 30 000 men, lined the streets two deep on the route along which she passed. One could detect in her countenance neither dejection nor pride and she did not appear to hear the cries of *Vive la République*, *à bas la tyrannie*! which she heard unceasingly along the way. She spoke but little to her confessor.
>
> On arrival at the Place de la Révolution she looked in the direction of the Jardin National [the Tuileries]; one could see on her countenance the signs of deep emotion [did she remember her first delirious reception here by the populace of Paris?]; she mounted the scaffold with firm courage. At a quarter past twelve her head fell and the executioner exhibited it to the people amidst the long repeated cries of *Vive la République*!

Madame de Tourzel nearly broke down when she heard the news. 'I cannot put into words all that went on in my heart; the pain of her loss, the anxiety about the rest of the royal family caused me a despair so violent that I thought I was losing my sanity.'

In England, the Duchess of Devonshire wrote to her mother: 'the impression of the Queen's death is constantly before my eyes. Besides the admiration that is universally felt for her and the horror at the barbarians, her answers, her cleverness, her composure, greatness of mind blaze forth in double splendour and the horror of making the child depose against her is what one should have hop'd that the mind of man was incapable of.'

On Monday 21 October Fersen wrote to Sophie: 'I can think only of my loss. It is dreadful not to have any positive details. That she should have been alone in her last moments, without anyone to speak to, to hear her last wishes. That is the horror.'

Bibliography

Any single title is cited once only, even if it was referred to again for subsequent chapters.

Du Côté de Versailles

Campan, Madame: *Mémoires de Madame Campan* (1823), 1979.
Chesterfield, Lord: *Letters to his Son*, 1753.
Dunlop, I.: *Versailles*, 1970.
Franklin, B.: *Papers*, 1757.
Flammermont, J.: *Rapport . . . sur les Correspondances des Agents Diplomatiques Étrangers*, 1896.
Gaxotte, P.: *Siècle de Louis XV*, 1974.
Grouchy, vicomte de: *Journal Inédit du duc de Croÿ*, 1906.
La Rochefoucauld, duc de: *Voyage en France, 1781–1783*, 1938.
Lemontey: *Nouveaux Mémoires de Dangeau*, 1818.
Leroy, C.-G.: *Louis XV et Madame de Pompadour Peints et Jugés par le Lieutenant des Chasses du Parc de Versailles* (1802), 1876.
Luynes, duc de: *Mémoires du duc de Luynes sur la Cour de Louis XV*, 1865.
Nolhac, P. de: *Marie-Antoinette Dauphine*, 1898.
Nolhac, P. de: *Versailles au Dixhuitième siècle*, 1926.
Northumberland, Duchess of: *The Diaries of a Duchess*, 1926.
Reau, L.: *L'Art Français sur le Rhin au 18e siècle*, 1922.
Saint-Priest, comte de: *Mémoires*, 1929.
Ségur, marquis de: *Au Couchant de la Monarchie. Louis XVI et Turgot*, 1909.
Wraxall, N.: *A Tour Through the Western, Southern and Interior Provinces of France*, 1784.

Du Côté de Schönbrunn

Goldsmith, M.: *Maria Theresa of Austria*, 1936.
Gooch, G. P.: *Maria Theresa and other studies*, 1951.

Kuhnel, H.: *Die Hofburg, Wien*, 1971.
Kugler, G.: *Schönbrunn*, 1986.
L. Lehmann and Bassett, R.: *Vienna, A Traveller's Companion*, 1988.
Ostry, V. L.: *The Presidential Chancellery*, 1978.
Raschauer, O.: *Schönbrunn*, 1960.

The Archduchess

Amiguet, P.: *Lettres de Louis XV à l'Infant de Parme*, 1938.
Anon: *Description de la Fête donnée le 17 avril 1770 au Palais du Belvédère*, Hausarchiv, Familienakten 50.
Anon: *Reception de l'Archiduchesse Marie-Antoinette à Strasbourg*, 1770.
Von Arneth, A: *Maria-Theresia und Marie-Antoinette, mit Briefen des Abbé de Vermond an den Grafen Mercy*, 1865.
Barthélemy, E.: *Marie-Antoinette à Chalons 1770*, 1861.
Chalon, J. (Ed): *Mémoires de Madame Campan*, 1979.
Christoph, P.: *Maria Theresia*, 1980.
Croÿ, duc de: *see* Grouchy.
Girault de Coursac, P. and P.: *Louis XVI et Marie-Antoinette*, 1990.
Von Goethe, J. W.: *Memoirs*, English translation, 1824.
Grouchy, vicomte de: *Journal inédit du duc de Croÿ, 1906.*
Ludman, J. D.: *Le Palais Rohan de Strasbourg*, 1979.
Moreau, J. N.: *Mes Souvenirs*, 1898.
Moulin, J.-M.: *Le Château de Compiègne*, 1987.
Müller, E.: *L'Archiduchesse Marie-Antoinette à Strasbourg*, 1862.
Nolhac, P. de: *Marie-Antoinette Dauphine*, 1898.
Oberkirch, baronne d': *Mémoires*, 1883.
Pöllnitz, Baron: *Memoirs*, translated by S. Whately, 1745.
Vuaflert, A. and Bourin, H.: *Les Portraits de Marie-Antoinette*, 1910.
Weber, J.: *Mémoires concernant Marie-Antoinette*, 1822.

Louis-Auguste

Bouet de Martange, M. A.: *Correspondance de Xavier de Saxe*, 1898.
Craufurd, Q.: *Mélanges d'Histoire, de Littérature etc*, 1809.
Duffo, F.: *Le Dauphin, Père de Louis XVI*, 1936.
Girault de Coursac, P.: *L'Éducation d'un Roi, Louis XVI*, 1972.
Martange: *see* Bouet.

Sénac de Meilhan, G.: *Du Gouvernement, des Moeurs et des Conditions en France avant la Révolution*, 1795.
Stryenski, C.: *La Mère des Trois Derniers Bourbon*, 1902.
Thevenot, A.: *Correspondance inédite du Prince Xavier de Saxe*, 1874.
Vauguyon, duc de la: *Portrait de feu Monseigneur le Dauphin*, 1766.
Véri, abbé de (Ed: Witte, Baron J. de): *Journal*, 1928.

The Wedding

Boysse, E.: *Journal de Papillon de la Ferté*, 1887.
Feray, J.: *Opéra de Versailles*, in *Monuments Historiques de la France*, 1957.
Girard, G.: *Correspondance entre Marie-Antoinette et sa Mère*, 1933.
Nolhac P. de: *Versailles au Dixhuitième Siècle*, 1926.
Northumberland, Duchess of: *The Diaries of a Duchess*, 1926.
Starhemberg, Prince: quoted from Girault de Coursac, *op. cit.*
Stern, J.: *François-Joseph Belanger*, 1930.
Vigée-Lebrun, Madame: *Souvenirs*, 1835.
Welvert, E.: *L'Éminence Grise de Marie-Antoinette* (abbé de Vermond) In *Revue de l'Histoire de Versailles*, 1922.

The Marriage

Arnaud-Bouteloup, J. *Marie-Antoinette et l'Art de son Temps*, 1924.
Cooper, M.: *Gluck*, 1935.
Dunlop, I.: *Royal Palaces of France*, 1985.
Frénilly, baron de: *Souvenirs*, 1908.
Hézècques, comte d': *Souvenirs d'un page de la Cour de France*, 1895.
Lescure, M. de: *Correspondance secrète inédite sur Louis XVI, Marie-Antoinette, la Cour et la Ville de 1777–1789*, 1886.
Toynbee, P.: *Lettres de la marquise du Deffand à Horace Walpole*, 1912.

The Coronation

Bertin, R.: *Mémoires de Mademoiselle Bertin*, 1824.
Dunlop, I.: *The Cathedrals' Crusade*, 1982.
Geoffroy, A.: *Gustave III et la Cour de France*, 1867.
Goy, J.: *Le Sacre des Rois de France*, s.d.
Hardy, S. P.: *Journal*, 1912.
Ljublinski, V.: *La Guerre des Farines*, 1979.

Morellet, abbé, A.: *Lettres à Lord Shelburne*, 1898.
Pichon, T. J.: *Journal Historique de Sacre et Couronnement de Louis XVI*, 1775.
Ségur, marquis de: *Au couchant de la Monarchie*, 1921.
Stormont, Lord: *Despatches*, P.R.O. SP: 293–296.
Viri, comte de: in J. Flammermont: *Rapport . . . sur les Correspondances des Agents Diplomatiques Étrangers*, 1896.

The King

Beaune, H.: *Mémoires du marquis de Séguret*. In *Université Catholique*, 1877.
Boigne, comtesse de: *Mémoires de la comtesse de Boigne*, 1971.
Chateaubriand, vicomte de: *Mémoires d'outre-tombe*, 1848.
Creutz, Count: In *Correspondance Diplomatique du baron de Staël-Holstein*, 1881.
Cronin, V.: *Louis and Antoinette*, 1974.
Magnieu, E. de and Pratt, H.: *Correspondance inédite de la comtesse de Sabran et du chevalier de Boufflers*, 1875.
Moleville, B. de: *Histoire de la Révolution de France*, 1801.
Tilly, comte de: *Mémoires du comte Alexandre de Tilly*, 1929.

The Queen

Bachaumont, L.: *Journal* ou *Mémoires secrets pour servir l'Histoire de la République des lettres depuis 1762*, 1777–1789.
Bacourt, M. de: *Correspondance entre le comte de Mirabeau et le comte de La Marck*, 1851.
Bertin, G.: *La Princesse de Lamballe*, 1908.
Besenval, baron de: *Mémoires de Monsieur le baron de Besenval*, 1805.
Bessborough, Earl of: *Georgiana: Extracts from the Correspondence of Georgiana, Duchess of Devonshire*, 1955.
Bombelles, marquis de: *Journal*, 1977.
Browning, O.: *Despatches from Paris, 1784–1790*, 1909.
Dorset, Duke of: *see* Browning.
Esterhazy: *Mémoires du comte Valentin Esterhazy*, 1905.
Hailes, D.: *see* Browning.
Lévis, duc de: *Souvenirs et Portraits*, 1882.
Ligne, prince de: *Pensées et Lettres*, 1890.
Ségur, comte de: *Mémoires ou Souvenirs et Anecdotes*, 1824.
Schönfeld, Baron von: *see* Flammermont, *Rapport*.
Söderhjelm, A.: *Fersen et Marie-Antoinette*, 1930.

Tour du Pin, marquise de La: *Journal d'une Femme de Cinquante Ans, 1778–1815*, 1954.
Young, A.: *Travels during the Years 1787, 1788 & 1789*, 1792.

The Queen a Mother

Fleury, comte: *Angélique de Mackau, marquise de Bombelles et la Cour de Madame Elizabeth*, 1905.
Stedingk, comte de: *Mémoires posthumes du feld-maréchal comte de Stedingk*, 1841.

The Court of Louis XVI

Beaufort, H. de: in Liedekerke-Beaufort, comte de: *Souvenirs d'un page du comte de Provence, Revue de Paris*, 1952.
Chateaubriand, vicomte de: *Mémoires d'outre-tombe*, 1848.
Lameth, T. de: *Mémoires*, 1913.
Mansel, P.: *The Court of France 1789–1830*, 1988.
Mercier, L. S.: *Le Tableau de Paris*, 1781.
Montbarrey, A. de Saint-Mauris, Prince de: *Mémoires*, 1826.
Solnon, J. F.: *La Cour de France*, 1987.
Ventre, A.: *Les Transformations successives du Palais Royal*, in *Monuments Historiques de France*, 1936.

The Petit Trianon

Beugnot, comte de: *Mémoires du comte Beugnot, 1783–1815*, 1866.
Blaikie, T.: *The Diary of a Scotch Gardener at the French Court at the end of the Eighteenth century*, 1931.
Cognel, F.: *La Vie Parisienne sous Louis XVI*, 1882.
Desjardins, G.: *Petit Trianon*, 1885.
Morris, G.: *The Diary and Letters of Gouverneur Morris*, 1889.
Nolhac, P. de: *Les Consignes de Marie-Antoinette au Petit Trianon*, in *Revue de l'Histoire de Versailles*, 1899.
Nolhac, P. de: *Le Trianon de Marie-Antoinette*, 1924.
Vaublanc, V. N. de Viennot, comte de: *Mémoires*, 1857.

The Diamond Necklace

Arneth, A. d' and Flammermont, J.: *Correspondance secrète du comte de Mercy-Argenteau avec l'Empereur Joseph II et le Prince de Kaunitz*, 1889.

Browne, R.: *The Diamond Necklace Affair revisited*, in *Renaissance and modern studies*, 1989.
Castries, duc de: *Papiers de Famille. Journal du maréchal de Castries*, 1977.
Campardon, E.: *Marie-Antoinette et le procès du collier d'après la procédure instruite devant le Parlement de Paris*, 1863.
Georgel, abbé J. F.: *Mémoires*, 1817.
Hastier, L.: *La Vérite sur l'Affaire du Collier*, 1970.
Mossiker, F.: *The Queen's Necklace*, 1961.
Oliva, Mademoiselle le Guay d': Interrogation of on 19 January 1786. Archives Nationales, X2B. 1417.

The Sunset of the *Ancien Régime*

Augeard, J. M.: *Mémoires secrètes de J. M. Augeard, Secrétaire des Commandements de la Reine*, 1866.
Aussonne, M. Lafont d': *Mémoires secrètes et universelles des Malheurs et de la Mort de la Reine de France*, 1836.
Baudeau, abbé: *Chronique secrète de Paris sous le Règne de Louis XVI*, in *Revue Retrospective*, vol. 3. 1833–1838.
Boullé: *Lettres de Boullé*, in *Revue de la Révolution*, 1888.
Castries, duc de: *L'abbé de Véri et son Journal*, in *Revue de Paris*, November 1953.
Chamchine, B.: *Le Château de Choisy*, 1910.
Chevalier, P.: *Journal de l'Assemblée des Notables de 1787*, 1960.
Dunlop, I. *op. cit.* for Fontainebleau, Saint-Cloud and Meudon.
Ferrières, marquis de: *Mémoires du marquis de Ferrières*, 1822.
Fleury, comte M. de: *Le Palais de Saint-Cloud*, 1907.
Gaudillot, J. M.: *Voyage de Louis XVI en Normandie*, 1967.
Laage de Volude, marquise de: *Souvenirs d'Émigration*, 1869.
Rochejaquelein, marquise de la: *Mémoires*, 1889.

Revolution

Babeuf, F. N.: *Pages Choisies*, 1935.
Berville, M.: *Mémoires de Rivarol*, 1824.
Chastenay de Lanty, comtesse de: *Mémoires*, 1896.
Cheverny, J. Dufort, comte de: *Mémoires sur les règnes de Louis XV et Louis XVI et sur la Révolution*, 1886.
Deflue, L.: *Relation de la redition de la Bastille*, in Godechot.
Godechot, J.: *La Prise de la Bastille*, 1965.
Le Fèbvre, G.: *La Grande Peur*, 1932.

Maleissye, A. de Tardieu, général marquis de: *Mémoires d'un officier aux Gardes Françaises*, 1897.
Paroy, Le Gentil, comte de: *Mémoires*, 1895.
Rigby, E.: *Letters from France*, 1880.
Saint-Priest, comte de: *Mémoires: La Révolution et L'Emigration*, 1929.
Tourzel, duchesse de: *Mémoires de la duchesse de Tourzel*, 1969.

The Tuileries

Anon: *Arrestation de Mesdames de France à Arnay-le-Duc*, in *Société Eduenne*, 1910.
Burke, E.: *A Letter from Mr Burke to a Member of the National Assembly* 1791.
Damas, R. comte de: *Mémoires 1787–1806*, 1907.
Dard, E.: *Le comte de Narbonne*, 1943.
Dunlop, I. *op. cit.* for Tuileries.
Gosselin, abbé: *Vie de M. Emery*, 1861.
Leveson-Gower, Lord Granville: *Private Correspondence*, 1916.
Mousset, A. *Un Témoin ignoré de la Révolution; le comte Fernan Nuñez, Ambassadeur d'Espagne à Paris*, 1924.
Roederer, comte: *Oeuvres*, 1853.
Roussel d'Epinal, P.: *Le Château des Tuileries*, 1802.

The Flight to Varennes

Berville & Barrière: *Mémoires sur l'Affaire de Varennes*, 1823. Contains memoirs of Bouillé, Damas, Deslon, Goguelat, Raigecourt and Valory.
Berville & Barrière: Duc de Choiseul: *Relation du Départ de Louis XVI le 20 juin 1791*, 1822. Contains memoirs of Drouet, Rémy, Aubriot, Brisack and Deslon.
Bimbenet, E.: *Fuite de Louis XVI à Varennes*, 1868.
Browning, O.: *The Flight to Varennes*, 1892.
Burgess, Sir James: *Selection from the Letters & Correspondence of Sir James Bland Burgess Bt. sometime Under-Secretary of State for Foreign Affairs*, 1855.
Dard, E.: *Un Rival de Fersen*, 1947.
Fournel, V.: *L'Évènement de Varennes*, 1890.
Girault de Coursac, P. & P.: *Sur la Route de Varennes*, 1984.
Lenotre, G.: *Le Drame de Varennes*, 1921.
France, Marie-Thérèse de: *Relation du Voyage de Varennes*, 1852.

The Constitution

Browning, O.: *Despatches of Earl Gower, English Ambassador at Paris from 1790 to August 1792*, 1885.
Chabaud, A.: *Le Retour de Varennes*, 1930.
Girault de Coursac, P. and P.: *Enquête sur le Procès du Roi Louis XVI*, 1982.
Girault de Coursac, P. and P.: *Louis XVI et la Question religieuse pendant la Révolution*, 1988.
Goguelat, F.: *Mémoires de Tous*, 1835.
Hue, baron: *Souvenirs du baron Hue*, 1903.
Moore, J.: *A Journal during a Residence in France from the beginning of August to the middle of December 1792*, 1793.
Pétion, J. *Le Retour de Varennes*, in M. Mortimer-Ternaux: *Histoire de la Terreur*, 1862.
Rochefoucauld, F. de La: *Souvenirs du 10 août*, 1929.
Staël, baronne de: *Considérations sur les principaux évènements et les conditions en France avant la Révolution*, 1862.

Imprisonment in the Temple

Beauchesne, M. de: *Louis XVII: Sa vie, son agonie, sa mort*, 1853.
Beaucourt, marquis de: *Captivité et derniers moments de Louis XVI*. Récits originaux et documents officiels. 1892. Contains memoirs of Hue, Cléry, Turgy, Goret, Verdier, Moëlle and Lepitre.
Cléry, J.: *Journal de ce qui s'est passé à la Tour du Temple pendant la captivité de Louis XVI, Roi de France*, 1798.
Eckard, M.: *Mémoires historiques sur Louis XVII*, 1817.
L'Espinasse: Shelburne on Malesherbes, in Morellet.
Harmand de la Meuse, J.: *Anecdotes*, 1814.
Hue, F.: *Dernières Années du Règne et de la Vie de Louis XVI*, 1860.
Morellet, abbé: *Mémoires de l'abbé Morellet sur le Dixhuitième Siècle et sur la Révolution*, 1821.
Tussaud, Madame (M. Grosholz): *Mémoires*, 1838.

The Conciergerie

Adolphus, J.: *Memoirs of the French Revolution*,, 1799.
Boze, J.: In Chauveau-Lagarde.
Campardon, E.: *Marie-Antoinette à la Conciergerie*, 1863.
Chauveau-Lagarde, M.: *Note Historique sur le Procès de Marie-Antoinette d'Autriche, Reine de France*, 1816.

Dropmore Papers, Historical MSS Commission: *Manuscript of J. B. Fortescue preserved at Dropmore*, 1894.
Lafont d'Aussonne, G.: *Mémoires sur les Malheurs de la Reine de France*, 1824.
Lamorlière, R. in Lafont d'Aussonne (*op. cit.*) and Campardon (*op. cit.*)
Lenotre, G.: *Le Roi Louis XVII et l'Enigme du Temple*, 1921.
Macé de Lépinay, F. and Charles, J.: *Marie-Antoinette du Temple à la Conciergerie*, 1989.
Montjoye: *see* Ventre de la Touloubre.
Ventre de l Touloubre, C. (known as Montjoye): *Histoire de Marie-Antoinette-Joséphe-Jeanne, Archiduchesse d'Autriche, Reine de France*, 1797.

General

Arneth, A. d' and Geoffroy, M.: *Correspondance secrète entre Marie-Thérèse et le comte de Mercy-Argenteau, avec des lettres de Marie-Thérèse et de Marie-Antoinette*, 1874.
Arneth, A. d' and Flammermont, J.: *Correspondance secrète du comte de Mercy-Argenteau avec Joseph II et le Prince de Kaunitz*, 1887–1891.
Cronin, V.: *Louis and Antoinette*, 1974.
Lever, E.: *Marie-Antoinette*, 1991.
de la Rocheterie, M.: *Histoire de Marie-Antoinette*, 1905.
de la Rocheterie, M. and Beaucourt, marquis de: *Lettres de Marie-Antoinette*, 1895.
Webster, N.: *Louis XVI and Marie-Antoinette*, 1937.

Index